ALEXANDER

THE

GREAT

ALEXANDER THE GREAT

LEWIS V.
CUMMINGS

GROVE PRESS
New York

Printed in the United States of America
Published simultaneously in Canada

Reprinted by special arrangement with Houghton Mifflin Company

Library of Congress Cataloging-in-Publication Data

Cummings, Lewis Vance.
    Alexander the Great / Lewis V. Cummings.
       p. cm.
    Originally published: Boston : Houghton Mifflin Company, 1940.
    Includes bibliographical references and index.
    ISBN 0-8021-4149-8
       1. Alexander, the Great, 356–323 B.C. 2. Generals—Greece—Biography. 3. Greece—History—Macedonian Expansion, 359–323 B.C. 4. Greece—Kings and rulers—Biography. I. Title.

DF234.C75 2004
938'.07'092—dc22
[B]   2003064147

Grove Press
841 Broadway
New York, NY 10003

04 05 06 07 08   10 9 8 7 6 5 4 3 2 1

PREFACE

I<small>T IS</small> a task of considerable magnitude to write a new version, acceptable in the light of modern knowledge and thought, of the history of Alexander III of Macedonia, also known as Alexander the Great. For as the student masses his data it becomes clear that his sources vary greatly, not only in details but in the attitude of the writer to the conqueror. Many of the later commentators, among them a churchly bishop, regarded him as perfect in all things; most of the earlier regarded him as an egoistic madman whose inordinate self-love and boundless lust for power were the greatest factors in the destruction of the independence and old *laissez-faire* of the Greek city-states as constituted at that time.

Neither viewpoint is wholly correct, though both have some reason behind them. Alexander was far from perfect, either as a king or as an army commander. Many of his faults in both capacities are so glaringly obvious that the careful student can only attribute his series of amazing successes to his utter and sublime confidence in the protection of the gods and the ascendancy of his star, and the incompetency of his enemies. Nor can he be accused of the destruction of the Greek political system. That system had begun to crack decades earlier, and Philip destroyed it by craft and dealt it the final crushing blow at Chaeronea. Had Philip not intervened, the recovery of the cities can be accepted as a foregone conclusion; for though political systems decline and change, yet as long as people live as a political unit, their retention of that type of unit can be accepted. Political systems rarely change save as a result of unbearable pressure from the outside.

The older works on the history of Alexander often leave us wholly ignorant of the routes he followed and the places, even areas, visited by him. Frequently the ancient Greek accounts, even to the names of the towns, were used, simply because definite knowledge of these places was not possessed by Europeans. Today all that is changed. In recent years Europeans have explored these routes, mapping many, and made their reports in detail. The author himself has personally explored some of the lesser-known regions involved and made a serious study of many of them. He is therefore able to correct definitely certain errors universally made in earlier histories.

The list of authorities, reports, and other sources consulted and drawn upon to complete this work is too long to detail, but where probably debatable data are given, the source is generally cited in footnotes.

Lewis V. Cummings

Brooklyn, New York
July 2, 1939

CONTENTS

MAPS

I

PHILIP OF MACEDON

WHEN the twenty-three-year-old Philip, third son of King Amyntas II, ascended the throne of Macedonia in the year 359 B.C., the throne was a thorny seat indeed. The country was beset by enemies both without and within, with such success that both his kingship and his country, as a political entity, could almost be said to exist more in theory than in fact. But Philip had no intention of letting such a condition continue. The homeland of the Macedonians was a goodly heritage of fat and fruitful lowland, a place worth fighting for.

According to tradition the Macedonians were a mixed people; one element of the nation being the original inhabitants of the region, the other, or at least the dominant and ruling clan, the Argeads, were accepted [1] as early as the fifth century as being Hellenes, the descendants of a noble family of Argos, in the eastern Peloponnesus. Traditionally, they had fled the city

[1] Strabo, 279–330; Plutarch, *Thess.*, 16; Herodotus, I, 56.

centuries earlier as a result of some historically unrecorded political or other upheaval in the Peloponnesus. They passed northward along the shores of the Thermaic Gulf, crossed the great Haliacmon (Gr. Vistritza; Tur. Kara Su) River, and drove determinedly into the wide fertile plain of Emathia. Here they met and vanquished the earlier occupants of the rich lowlands, a people known today to us under the title of 'Pelasgians,' [1] seemingly a designation meaning only 'the old people.' These were either killed or driven out. Possibly the men were slain and their women and children captured and absorbed [2] into the organization of the newcomers. It may have been that they needed them, for they may have been a purely military group, with a minimum of dependents. At least they were a strong body of fighting men; they must needs be to force their way into the land of fighters such as the Pelasgians were. These, a people of the same stock as their more northern congeners, were an Aryan type, tall, blond, and blue-eyed, and it is probable that intermixture with them was the major reason that even as late as the fourth century the Macedonians were fairer of skin, taller, and heavier of body than the Greeks. Thus they had entered the region with their leader, whoever he was, and he 'conquered lands for his subjects and became their king.' [3] They cleared the riverine lands of the Haliacmon of its owners, drove on across the plain to the smaller Lydias (or Ludias) River, and followed it up to the foothills where lay the ancient 'Illyrian' capital city of Edessa. The newcomers captured Edessa; then, taking cognizance of its site upon a high plateau overlooking and dominating the Emathian plain below, they made it their own capital. They changed its name to Aegae, occupied it for several centuries, and buried their kings there.[4]

---

[1] Justin, VII, 1.

[2] Demosthenes, *Philippics*, I, 10; *Olynthiacs*, III, 24. The orator taunts Philip with being a half-breed, slurring the Macedonians as barbarians — that is, not pure Greek. His viewpoint was that of most Greeks of that day, convinced that all non-Greeks were inferior to the Hellenes.

[3] Thucydides, II, 99.

[4] We know relatively little of Macedonia proper at this period; much of our know-

West and south of Aegae lay the sweeping curve of the Haliacmon Valley, beyond which lived the tribe known as the Orestians. North of them were the mountains of the Lyncestians; still farther north were the Elimiotians and the Pelagonians. West of them were the loosely affiliated group known as the Illyrians, and beyond them, along the border of modern Albania, were the tribes of Epirus. North of Emathia and along the upper course of the Axius (Vardar) River was the rough mountain home of the hard-fighting Paeonians. Between the lower Axius and the Strymon (Struma) River to the eastward were the Mygdonians, a Thracian tribe. Beyond the Strymon, which was the eastern border of Macedonia, were the numerous and savage fighting tribes of Thrace.

Southward of Emathia lay the rich alluvial plain, anciently called Pieria and Bottiaea, stretching along the Thermaic Gulf, and bearing the coastal towns of Pydna, Methone, and ancient Therma, the latter guarding the mountain-pass road leading eastward into Thrace. Beyond Therma lay the trident-shaped peninsula of the Chalcidice. Beyond it stretched the shores of Thrace (now European Turkey), the Thracian Chersonese (Gallipoli Peninsula), the Propontus (Sea of Marmora), and the shores of the Euxine (Black) Sea, already strung with a narrow selvage of Hellenic cities and colonies. These were mostly founded by Athens and Corinth, and in general, at this time, were still under the suzerainty of the mother cities. As these were soon to play a not inconsiderable part in the expansion of Macedonia, it might be well to give a brief account of the nearer areas.

The three peninsulas forming the Chalcidice seem to have been designed by nature to be the maritime appendage of the provinces lying behind it, and its natural advantages were so numerous that it is not to be wondered that, sooner or later, the attentions of the acquisitive Macedonian kings turned toward it with lust

ledge and information being gleaned from the early Greek writings of and about the times. When, if ever, archeologists find and unearth the tombs of the old kings in or near modern Vodena, we may expect to find material of value, perhaps filling some of the woeful gaps in our existing histories.

for possession. Its highly mineralized mountains were covered with hardwood forests, its shores studded with flourishing colonies, a kingly prize worthy of empire. The easternmost peninsula, Akte, is over forty miles long, with an average width of four miles, and terminates in the six-thousand-foot limestone cone of Mount Athos. The central (Sithone) and the western (Pallene) peninsulas were less rough and far more populous. At the neck of land connecting Pallene to the mainland lay the dominating and well-to-do Corinthian city of Potidaea. On the west coast of Sithone, Torônê was the largest and most influential place, first founded by Euboeans from Chalcis, who had given their name to the Chalcidice. At the head of the long, narrow gulf of Torônê lay the most important Chalcidian city, Olynthus. Along the shores of the peninsulas were many small places and several large and important cities, of which the most important yet unnamed were Amphipolis, Acanthus, Sanê, and Stagira. Amphipolis, second in size and importance, sat securely in a bend of the Strymon River, guarding the river passage of the road between Macedonia and Thrace. A day's march distant reared the lofty Mount Pangeus with its gold and silver mines, already worked since the memory of man began and still yielding their valuable metals. South of the inner edge of the Emathian plain that was Macedonia, and past the narrow foreshore where Mount Olympus shouldered down to the sea, was the wild land of the Thessalians, famous for their fine horses and mounted fighters, the luxury of their ruling houses, the debasement of their coinage, legendarily for their traditional magicians and sorcerers; a hard and self-sufficient people, Greeks, but inimical to Greeks and Macedonians alike.

The record of the first two hundred years of the existence of the Macedonians as a nation is lost in the mists of antiquity, though we are told a pretty fable [1] about it. Fables, however, need not concern us except to bear in mind that fables, in those days, were often accepted as fact, and it is axiomatic that fable is less important than truth, if the untruth is believed truth.

[1] Herodotus, VIII, 137.

4

Fable said that the kings of Macedonia were justified in their claim to descent from Argos and the legendary founder of that city, the demigod Heracles, benefactor of all mankind and son of Zeus, and in this case fable accepted as truth triumphed over truth. The few glimpses we get of the Macedonian kings between the years 700 and 500 B.C. enlighten us little. From them we can only infer an almost unbroken series of wars with neighboring tribesmen in which the aggressors are sometimes the Macedonians, bent on conquest and enlarging their narrow territories, sometimes the tribesmen, retaliating with greater or lesser success against them. The lowland men were more successful than their opponents and victims, and their holdings gradually grew larger, a career of conquest hardly halted by even the Persian hordes in their successive invasions of Greece. Thus it was that Alexander I (498–454) bowed to the might of the gigantic Asiatic military machine and pretended to accept his Persian overlord's plans to make Macedonia the center of a great vassal state. The vassalage seems to have been more theoretical than actual, and in some way, perhaps as a result of high-handed treatment by the Persians, he suddenly appears greatly desirous of being accepted by the Greeks as one of them. The story is told [1] that in 496 he appeared at the Olympic games in Elis and submitted his name as a competitor. The committee denied him the right to compete, holding that he was a 'barbarian' and that only full-blooded Greeks were eligible to participate. Alexander immediately produced proof of such character that he was accepted and officially recognized as an Argead, descended of the stock from Argos and the demigod Heracles, who had himself founded the games. He was an outstanding competitor, for we hear later that the famous Theban lyric poet, Pindar, wrote a poem eulogizing the Macedonian and his victories there.

Greece at that time was awaiting the return of the slow-moving colossus that was the Persian army, and it may have been subtle diplomacy on the part of the Greeks thus to grant the

[1] Herodotus, V, 22.

costless boon that gave such pleasure to Alexander. If he could be won to the Greek side of the invasion and war they saw inevitable, the hard-fighting tribesmen of the north would be welcome and valuable allies. What Alexander thought about it we have no way of knowing, but he shortly moved his capital from Aegae down to the little town of Pydna (Kitros), under the great shoulder of Mount Olympus along the strait foreshore of the Thermaic Gulf. The inference is that he had tired of the provincial Aegae and wanted to be on the main road between Thrace and Greece, probably for the purpose of reaping rich payments to permit passage over it both ways; perhaps to facilitate communication and passage for himself to the Greek cities of the south. Be that as it may, four years later, in 492, another Persian invasion rolled into Thrace and Macedonia, through Pydna and on into Thessaly and Greece. In the interim Alexander's sister, Gygae, had somehow met and married a Persian nobleman of high rank, and no doubt had much to tell and say which affected Alexander's attitude. Also Greece had once more become disorganized. The petty internecine quarrels and jealousies of the city-states made them into hostile groups of whom some, willing to submit to the show of force, joined alliance with the invader to the detriment of the others. Alexander, considering the impossibility of fighting the Asiatic horde with any hope of success when discord ruled the Greeks, dissembled his real feelings and submitted to the Persian general Mardonius, remaining faithful to his pledged word even after the death of Darius (Darayavaüsh) seven years later, and to his successor Xerxes (Khshayārsha). When the Persians again poured into Hellas in 480, Alexander went south with them. The defeated Spartans left Thermopylae, where the Persians avenged themselves for Marathon. They marched on into Attica. Then the doubtful battle of Artemisium was followed by the brilliant victory of Salamis and the land battle at Plataea. Alexander had, seemingly, a change of heart, for in the evening before the battle he rode down to the Athenian pickets, publicly proclaimed himself a friend of Greece, and betrayed to them the

6

Persian plans for the coming action. For this he was later given the title 'Philhellene' (Friend of the Hellenes).

Revolt broke out in Babylon against Xerxes, and he returned precipitately to the Asia Minor capital of Sardis. The Asiatic tide receded into Asia once more, and Alexander sat in his little capital to think over the political situation. A few miles to the north lay Methônê, an independent Greek city, but allied with Athens, while the whole coast and the Chalcidic peninsula opposite were covered with Greek colonies with no sympathy for the Macedonians. Especially since the last Persian invasion they realized that their natural ally and guardian was Athens, the maritime power to the south. And every so often Athens decided to enlarge her holdings! Alexander thoughtfully considered the possibility of being one of those whose holdings Athens might find desirable. In that case, Pydna was entirely too easy of access by water. He concluded the problem unsolvable at present; besides, the tribes were again growing restless and it were better he be back at the center of his kingdom. His kingdom had expanded faster than it could be consolidated. He resigned himself to being only the petty king of the Macedonians, and forthwith moved his capital back to Aegae.

Perdiccas II succeeded Alexander, reigning from 454 until 413, during which time we only know he intrigued with several alliances [1] to keep himself free of the fratricidal Peloponnesian War that had begun in Hellas in 432. Outside of that he did little. His illegitimate son, Archelaus (413–399), climbed to the throne by a method hallowed by long usage in Macedonia. He murdered his uncle, cousin, and brother, a not uncommon method of attaining succession in those, or later, days. It seems almost that it was worth while, for Thucydides [2] is fulsome with his praise and insists that Archelaus, in his fourteen years' reign, did more to benefit Macedonia than all his eight predecessors. Not that he had an easy time, for both now and much later the great feudatory tribes continued to war against the ever-increasing domination of the lowlanders. At the outset he transferred

[1] Thucydides, II, 100, 101.   [2] Thucydides, II, 100.

the capital elsewhere, this time to the little city of Pella, placing it farther down the Lydias River, on an elevation above the deep, clear-water Lake Borborus (now only a noisome swamp near which the site of Pella is plowland, identified only by an occasional stone or carved fragment), below which the Lydias was navigable to the sea. The site was in the middle of the low-land plain, more centrally located, less accessible to attack, and far easier to defend than the hill-girt Aegae. From the new capital presently radiated a network of roads, to Thessaly and Greece, to the wild hills in the north and west, and a great highway through Thermê to Amphipolis and the Chalcidice. He built a new city of Dion [1] (Dium) and dedicated it to the Macedonian Zeus, setting it aside as holy and sacred to the celebration of festivals and thanksgivings to the god. He remodeled and reorganized his army (though we are not told specifically how) and sent several expeditions into the moun-tains to beat the tribesmen into a semblance of quietude. He then settled down to enjoy a little leisure in the arts of the Greeks.

In Hellas during this time the Peloponnesian War raged murderously. Athens and Sparta, two opposing political sys-tems, iron-fisted oligarchy and Attic democracy, were pitted against each other, with most of the rest of Greece allied to one or the other. Archelaus took advantage of the turmoil there to invite many of the most brilliant Greeks of the day. Many accepted, no doubt glad to exchange the nerve-racking strain of the constant hostilities for the quiet and security of a court where they were honored guests. Among them were Zeuxis, one of the greatest painters of the period, a man who placed such a high price on his art that he would give it away rather than accept a payment less than he deemed proper; the epic poet Choerilus, a dandified elegant; Timotheus, poet and musician, favorite of the Athenians; Agathon, tragic poet and companion of Plato and Socrates; Euripides, then an embittered old man,

[1] Arrian, I, 11. See also Holm (*Griechische Geschichte*, III, 14, p. 230) for analysis, etc.

soured by the unfaithfulness of his two consecutive wives, and cynically preaching justification of almost anything. One of his most widely publicized sayings, 'It is worth while committing injustice for the sake of empire; in other things it is proper to be just,' [1] and another, 'My tongue took an oath, but my mind remained unsworn,' [2] and doubtless others of the same type, seem to have been some of the guiding tenets of Archelaus and later Macedonian kings, for they certainly lived up to the uttermost interpretations which could be placed upon these casuistries.

Down in Hellas, about 412, the Persian king again began to take part and sides in the war. Sparta in desperation accepted the Great King's gold. With it she built the fleet which was to be the means of ending the war by carrying her forces to the Chersonese, where, on the little Thracian river of Aegospotamus, was fought a bitter battle which was the real end of the war, though it continued nominally a little longer. But so great was the anger of most Greeks against Persian interference that we hear, probably in 408, the famous Gorgias deliver his famous speech at the Olympic games. He exhorted the Greeks to cease their fratricidal fighting, city against city, and unite in a common cause, to make a *revanche* against Persia, to destroy the Persian power in Asia Minor and free the Greek cities there from the detestable yoke of the Persians. A small thing at that time, but a preaching destined to bear marvelous fruit in later years.

It would seem, however, in Macedonia that many others than the king listened to the embittered old Euripides and his cynical philosophy, for Archelaus was murdered in 399 and wild turmoil ensued. The discordant units of the kingdom reverted to hostile and warring factions. Ten years later, in 389, Amyntas, nephew of the dead Perdiccas, himself murdered the reigning king, seized power, and soon assumed the kingship. He seems to have been able, but circumstances and fate were against him. The mountaineers of the west again swarmed out of their stony fast-

---

[1] Euripides, *Phoenissae*, 534.   [2] Euripides, *Hippolytus*, 508.

nesses to raid and loot the rich plain. Amyntas promptly drove them back again, pursuing his red way as far as the lands of the Lyncestians. Here he made peace with the Lyncestian king, Irras, and accepted his daughter Eurydice [1] as earnest of peace. He married her and returned home. She bore him three sons, and one daughter whose name we are not told. We have little positive data of the next few years, but from them we glean that Amyntas had a thoroughly interesting and active, if unhappy, career. Several of the clan chiefs in the lowlands seem to have meditated rebellion or precipitated active revolt. The Lyncestians, unmollified by the marriage alliance, and other tribes continued to pour raiders into the kingdom, and he was often hard pressed by them. On the other side of the country, the Olynthians, having cajoled or coerced most of the cities of the Chalcidice into confederation with them, raised an army and moved along the Pierian plain to capture Methônê and Pydna. Seemingly, then they turned northward and drove Amyntas from Pella itself.[2] Next we hear, in the year 383, that several envoys from the Chalcidian cities of Acanthus and Apollonia have arrived in Sparta and are pleading with them for assistance. They appeared before the assembly and begged to be relieved of the fear of Olynthus. The latter, they said, had invited them to join the Chalcidic federation, threatening compulsion for failure to accept voluntarily. The envoys carefully played upon the fears of the Spartans, already warily conning the political scene for an attempted restoration of Athenian power, crushed in the long Peloponnesian War, by stressing that the Olynthians had already begun negotiations with Thebes and Athens for an alliance. Regarding Macedonia, they said,[3] 'King Amyntas had already all but fallen out of his kingdom.' The Spartans were convinced at last. They sent a small expedition, which was unable to make any headway against the city's army. A second and larger force was dispatched. Together they beat Olynthus to her knees and broke her hold over the Chalcidic

[1] Strabo, 236.
[2] Xenophon, *Hellenica*, V, 2, 13.   [3] *Ibid.*

league. They then compelled the league members to become allies of Sparta.

The real winner of this abortive attempt at conquest, and the Spartan interference with it, was Amyntas. The actual winner gained little but the opprobrium and reprobation of the rest of Greece. But the Spartans had removed the league's threat from the Macedonian king, leaving him only the tribesmen with whom to deal. It is interesting to conjecture that, had not the Spartans interfered, and had the Olynthians maintained their hold on Amyntus' territories, it is probable that Macedonia, cut off from the sea and the Greek shore road, would have remained the small and relatively weak country she was then. But Sparta did commit her political blunder, and when the time came, as it soon did, that Macedonia was in the hands of a king able enough and unscrupulous enough to take advantage of every possible opportunity to strengthen and increase his kingdom, it is probable that many Spartans could look back and see exactly where her actions and policy were the factors making that expansion possible. But now Amyntas was once more lord of his own territories,[1] free of the threat of the domination of Olynthus. However, there was still a possibility that the Olynthians would find some way to influence Sparta toward the subjection of Macedonia, if for no other reason than to keep him from an alliance and understanding with Athens and her friends. That turned Amyntas' mind toward the latter city. The Persians, in their latest foray into the country, had taken Amphipolis from Athenian control and turned it over to the Macedonians, whose acceptance of it was an act alienating the sympathies of the great republic; and the Spartans, under the impression Amyntas would never surrender the city to its old masters, considered no such possibility. But the Spartans, now feeling they had friends and allies in the Chalcidic league, grew so high-handedly arrogant that they brought a revulsion (378) against themselves by the Athenians and Thebans. In 375 the Athenian admiral

---

[1] Xenophon (*Hellenica*, V, 2, 13) says the Olynthians actually drove him from Pella and occupied the city. Nothing is said for their withdrawal, or the reason for it.

Chabrius sailed, with the whole power of the Athenian fleet, to the Chalcidice, and forced the Olynthians to renounce their alliance with the Spartans in favor of one with Athens. Matters came to a head three years later at the little Boeotian town of Leuctra. The Spartan and Theban forces met. The Theban phalanx, reportedly fifty men deep, scythed its way through the lighter Spartan lines, breaking Sparta's army and sending the survivors scurrying back to the Peloponnesus. The everlasting bickerings and jockeying for political advantage continued in the Greek world.

While the three great powers were thus at daggers drawn with each other, their attentions were too closely centered upon one another to pay attention to other spheres. In the north, in Thessaly, other adventurers awaited just such an opportunity. And it was there the next threat to Amyntas' security was to originate. A certain Jason, a man of much ability, activity, and great ambitions, made himself *tagos* or military overlord of Pherae in 374. Jason made no secret of his intention of subduing the rest of Thessaly, then extending his rule over Greece and Macedonia. With these unified under his control he would next move on to his ultimate objective, which was nothing less than the humbling of the Persian king himself, a matter he professed to believe would be less difficult than bringing the Greeks together.[1] He hired mercenary soldiers and began his preparations against the other Thessalians, while Amyntas, having much reason to foresee his success and realizing he was the next potential victim of the Pherean's ambitions, cast about for a way to forestall him. He had been but recently restored to his throne by the providential intervention of the Spartans, and was still militarily too weak to hope to cope with a new attempt upon his kingdom. He therefore sent his envoys to the regular meeting of the Attic Naval League at Athens, and at an assembly there in 371, he formally renounced claim to Amphipolis and recognized the Athenians' rights to the town. The reaction of

[1] For the Greek view of Jason and his policy, see in Xenophon's *Hellenica*, 6, 1, his report of a speech made by Polydamas of Pharsalus at Sparta in 374.

the Athenian public to his announcement was pleasingly grati-
fying to the Macedonian king, no doubt shivering in his boots
at the prospect of an invasion by the wild horsemen of Thessaly.
Luckily for him, however, he had no reason to put the presumed
friendship of Athens to the test. Jason was murdered shortly
afterward, and the menace of his ambitions removed. Two
brothers succeeded Jason; one soon murdered the other and was
in turn murdered by a third, who became a brutal and ruthless
tyrant. Numbers of the wealthier and noble Thessalians fled to
Macedonia for safety.

Amyntas also died that year, 371 B.C., poisoned [1] by his wife
and queen, the Lyncestian Eurydice. Their daughter had, some
time previously, married one Ptolemy, a native of Alorus.
Eurydice herself fell violently in love with her own son-in-law,
and, it seems, considered that her husband stood in the way of
consummation of her incestuous desires — a condition she did
not permit to last long. History is silent thereafter regarding
her daughter, and it is interesting to conjecture on her fate,
probably the same as that of Amyntas.

Amyntas' oldest son, Alexander II, succeeded his father for a
trouble-filled and uneasy reign of two years. The fugitives from
Thessaly appealed to him for aid against their oppressor, and
Alexander committed the error of accepting the appeal. He
enlisted [2] a number of the fugitives in his cavalry, invaded
Thessaly, and captured the cities of Larissa and Crannon. This
political blunder is difficult to understand. Thebes was then at
the height of her power, and traditionally Thebes had deemed
the rich plain of Thessaly as her own inalienable sphere of
influence. The Theban general Pelopidas marched into Thessaly
and, as Alexander retired sullenly ahead of him, occupied Larissa.
The Macedonian considered it unwise to debate the matter with
the power of Thebes, and gloomily withdrew to Pella.

A year later Ptolemy of Alorus and his mistress-queen-mother-
in-law treacherously murdered [3] Alexander at an entertainment

---

[1] Justin, VII, 4.
[2] See Anaximenes, in *Fragmenta Historicorum Graecorum*, frag. 7.   [3] Justin, VII, 4.

they had prepared for him, and Pelopidas marched into Macedonia to forestall anarchy. Pelopidas forced the Macedonians to accept Ptolemy and Eurydice as regents to the second son, Perdiccas. At this time, however, a pretender to the throne, one Pausanias, who had obtained backing from the tribes of Thracians east of the Strymon River, swept into the eastern provinces. The Athenian general Iphacrates, adopted son of the dead king Amyntas, suddenly arrived [1] and drove Pausanias out and back to Thrace. Pelopidas remained some time at or around Pella, and when he left he took with him some thirty hostages in the form of young nobles of the region, including the third son of Amyntas, the young prince Philip.

Perdiccas, the second son, was then a minor; Ptolemy and Eurydice, the regents, holding the real power. Of Perdiccas we know little, but he must have been gifted with the ability to see clearly yet hold his own counsel, for we can hardly credit the murderous queen with permitting anyone, son or no, to attain power unless she could remain the invisible control, the power behind the throne. However, in 364 Perdiccas attained his majority and formally ascended the throne. His first official act was to order the execution of Ptolemy. Eurydice, enraged at her lover's death and what she must have considered her betrayal by her own son, went storming back to her mountain kinsmen to stir them up for revenge. The Lyncestians immediately made an alliance with their neighbors the Illyrians and began to raise an army. Perdiccas took cognizance of the gathering storm on his western frontier and also the fact that his eastern frontier was decidedly vulnerable. He forthwith dispatched a considerable force eastward, which seized Amphipolis as a fortress against another threatened incursion by Pausanias at the head of a strong force of Thracians. Then Perdiccas gathered the rest of his army and met the Lyncestians and their allies as they descended into the plain of Macedonia. The opposing forces clashed, and Perdiccas and four thousand of his

---

[1] See Schafer, *Demosthenes*, II, 6, for arguments on the relationship between Macedonia and Athens, as of this period.

followers were slain in the battle, the king leaving only an infant son, Amyntas, as his heir. The allied army of tribesmen swept through the land, killing and burning. From the north the Paeonians left their homes and they too stormed down into the lowlands with fire and sword. In the east Pausanias hastily gathered his forces and advanced toward the Strymon. The outlook for Macedonia was black indeed, and the vacant throne was crying for a man to fill it. It was then that Philip took over the kingship of the country.

Philip had been brought up at Pella, perhaps born there in the troublous times of 383 when his father was virtually a fugitive from the encroaching Olynthians, ruler only over the Emathian [1] plain, and very insecure there. The people of the country, the Macedonians proper (that is, the inhabitants of the Emathian plain), were of hardy peasant stock. Even at this late date, when the king and court had become quite Graecized, they were still largely sheep-grazers of the hills [2] or small farmers, retaining much of the fundamentally primitive tribal government forms and organizations. The state itself at this time consisted only of a loosely bound voluntary hegemony of clans and tribes not yet divided into social orders or classes. The people were fighters, it being recorded [3] to us that a man who had not yet slain a foe was forced to wear a cord about his body; clan still fought against clan; district against district; the people of the highlands against the people of the lowlands. The king was, as we have seen, acknowledged ruler of the lowland clans, but overlord only to the more numerous hill tribes, restless and rebellious under the yoke, slight as it was, and chafing continually for their ancient freedom. The Macedonian kings, one after another, had fought them savagely for centuries, and it was only after more savage warfare under Philip and his son, Alexander III, that they were finally subdued and incorpo-

[1] Thucydides, II, 99.

[2] See Arrian, VII, 9, in which Alexander at Opis taunts his Macedonian soldiery with their primitive condition when his father Philip came to the throne.

[3] Plutarch, *Alexander*, 51; Aristotle, *Politics*, VII, 2, 6 (1324b).

15

rated into the body politic of Macedonia as citizens. The king, even to these, seems to have retained much of his old-time patriarchal monarchical attitude, which is to say that, though he was patriarchal, he was still, 'in his single person, lord of all things, both open and secret, at once General and Lord Absolute and Treasurer.' [1] The Greek humanitarian conception that the king existed primarily for the benefit of the people failed to penetrate north of Hellas. None of his subjects, as individuals, had any rights before the king; they had privileges only,[2] to be granted or withdrawn at will. They were, however, proverbially free of speech [3] and lacked the servility exacted by other kings, but they 'must follow whenever and wherever the king might lead, and leave farm or market to fight his battles.' [4] But they had one right, in the assembly of the army, which had definite class privileges. It had the duty of electing the king, or at any rate of confirming him in power by acclamation, without which he was not nor ever would be king. Thus, though the king incumbent could appoint his successor, the appointment lacked validity without the approval of the army. Another right possessed by the army in assembly was that of trying and judging all persons accused of high treason against the king or country, and if the accused were found guilty, of passing sentence and carrying out its execution.[5] In lesser charges the king alone could judge.[6]

The army, comprising as it did, in time of war at any rate, the majority of the able-bodied men, was really the nation. The Macedonians had no subject peoples under their domination; the original inhabitants from whom they took the Emathian plain seem never to have been enslaved, and their only slaves, then relatively few in number, were apparently captured or purchased prisoners of war. Military rank was based partly

---

[1] Demosthenes, *On the Crown*, 235.   [2] Polybius, V, 27, 6.   [3] *Ibid.*
[4] Demosthenes, *Olynthiacs*, II, 15, in which he tells us the Macedonians were weary of Philip's many wars, but helpless to protest against their continuation.
[5] Curtius, VI, 8, 32; Arrian, III, 26, 27; also IV, 14.
[6] Plutarch, *Alexander*, 42.

on social position and partly on wealth, both of which, as can be easily imagined, in turn were based on the favor of the king, and on his whims or desires. This seems, in the case of Philip at any rate, to have been exercised with wisdom, but one can imagine also the chaos which would have ensued had it been otherwise. In civil matters the king was supreme, and as representative into whose hands the scales of justice were given, his subjects not infrequently brought their tangled affairs to him in person.[1] His judgment, in the small lowland kingdom, was likely to be governed by a personal knowledge of the condition or affair to be adjudicated, and given accordingly. All men were obligated to military service,[2] the nobility and richer landholders to serve the king on horseback, in the cavalry forming the body known as *hetairoi* or 'companions.' It is typical of the attitude of all, however, that the king wore no emblem to mark his rank, and his dress was rarely distinguished from that of the *hetairoi*; the purple *chlamys* (mantle or cloak) and the wide-brimmed *causia* (hat) of the king were worn without jealousy or heart-burning by the nobility also. About the fourth century the footsoldiers, free farmers and peasants and other poor men who had formerly assisted in war as an ill-organized, ill-directed rabble, were organized (probably by Archelaus) into regular infantry, well armed, trained, and drilled. Thereafter they too received a title of honor, being called the *pezhetairoi* or 'foot companions,' who became, under Philip, the most efficient and deadly body of fighting men in Greece.

Physically the Macedonians were sturdy and hard-muscled, capable of great endurance, their physiques built up, not like the Athenians' or Romans', by physical exercises in the gymnasium, but by the chase in the hunting-field or by hard military service. They were stolid, fatalistic men, a type which, under the right commander, makes much better fighting men than the quick-witted Athenian, swift to recognize peril, or the highly trained Spartan, to whom fighting had become reduced to mechanics. The Athenians called them barbarians, claiming

---

[1] Plutarch, *Alexander*, 42.   [2] Arrian, I, 24; VII, 12.

they ate too much meat and drank to excess. The charge was, by Athenian standards, certainly true. The Macedonians were heavy eaters when opportunity permitted, and heavy drinkers at all times. There was certainly a vast difference between the intellectuality displayed in an Attic symposium and the drunken riots in which Macedonian feasts were wont to terminate. The contempt of the cultured Greek for the rude Macedonian was heartily reciprocated, at first because the former was looked upon as effete, and later, when the Macedonians had grown into a masterful and cohesive people, because their intense and narrow nationalism biased their attitude toward the *poleis* of the democratic Greeks. This fact, borne in mind, will do much to clarify the psychological reasons for many historical occurrences.

It cannot be too strongly stressed that the Macedonian ruling clan, the Argeads, were accepted by the Greeks, as well as the Macedonians, as being descendants of Heracles of Argos, who, traditionally, had been sired by Zeus upon a mortal mother. The Argeads therefore looked upon themselves as Greeks; the court of Macedonia aped the ways and manners of the Greeks and habitually used the Attic speech. Plutarch tells us that Alexander himself always affected the language of Athens, except that under stress of unusual excitement he would unconsciously revert to the hard Macedonian *patois*. Dionysus (Bacchus) was another real man, and another son of Zeus by a mortal woman who, after greatly benefiting mankind, was also admitted to the inner circle of the gods. He, the god of ecstasy who had conferred upon mankind the boon of the grape, was the god of the people of Macedonia. He was also the god of illusion, deity of the cult of Bacchi and Bacchae,[1] his male and female followers who identified themselves with the god, and whose extravagant devotions to him have given us the word 'bacchanalian,' synonym of the most unbridled and orgiastic passions. This concept had enormous influence upon the women

[1] For the most detailed modern work, see J. E. Harrison, *Prolegomena to the Study of Greek Religion*, chapters 8 ff. Also Strabo, 10; Herodotus, 11, 51.

of northern Greece, Macedonia, and Thrace, and notably upon Olympias, the Bacchiad Epirian who was to become the mother of Alexander III, later known as 'the Great.'

This, then, was the situation the half-caste Macedonian-Lyncestian Philip found upon his accession to the throne of Macedonia. The kingdom was not only in danger of defeat; with determined enemies invading it from three directions at once, it was in danger of complete annihilation. But the task found him not unready.

Philip had been a boy of thirteen when he was taken as a hostage to Thebes. He had been well treated, and placed in charge of Epaminondas, perhaps the greatest Greek of that day. The Theban was a man of culture, an orator of the first caliber, a politician of consummate shrewdness and ability, a strategist and general with the driving power of a Spartan. By sheer force of domineering will power he had won from the people of Thebes their blind obedience and made himself supreme in the city. He had tried, fruitlessly, largely by diplomatic chicane, even to the extent of intriguing with the Persian king and even sending Pelopidas to dance attendance upon the foreign monarch, to force Theban ascendancy in matters pertaining to the policies of all Greece. It was later said that Epaminondas' intentions were the same as those of Jason, ultimately to use his ascendancy to force unity of Greece for the purpose of attacking the Persian Empire. But he had run into the stone wall of insular hatred that kept all Greeks in constant bitter turmoil. The Greek city-states, jealous of their individual prerogatives and governed by frequently changed personalities, would never agree to genuine co-operation, or, having agreed, would break any agreement to gain an advantage or upon the slightest fancied insult. They had become politically incapable of forming a lasting confederation for mutual defense or betterment, and were individually too weak to defend themselves in the face of any logical combination or alliance. Epaminondas had failed in his dream, but the scope of his vision, mental resources, military prowess, and diplomatic cleverness had fired young Philip's imagination. Pelopidas too, the ruder soldier of Thebes, is better known to us than is his master, a more human figure, though one of the ancient biographers [1] says of him, '*Magis historicus quam vulgo notus*'; he too was beloved of the crude Thebans. Both men must have impressed the young Philip indelibly, for when he comes to power in his own right, we find in him much that reminds us strongly of the weaknesses and the strengths of each. And from it we get a picture of him, but one that unfolds only as history unfolds. But he had learned his lessons well, so well that in a few short years he rose superior to his teachers, a more subtle diplomat than Epaminondas, a more effective soldier than even Pelopidas. Especially did he then study the Theban military organization and tactics. Hitherto Greek armies had looked upon war and battle in the light of a competition, a deadly one, to be sure, but a competition nevertheless. The armies had fought according to custom and unwritten rules, and the chief function of their commanders seems to have been the making of inspiring speeches just before the opening of conflict. The battle itself usually consisted of a frontal attack by two armies facing each other in parallel lines, and the issue was usually decided in a few minutes, the side losing the most retiring from the field and admitting defeat by sueing for the return of the bodies of their dead, while the victors raised a memorial of triumph on the field. In the negotiations that followed, the victors not infrequently lost the very point for which the battle had been fought. The Spartans had developed this style of fighting and by it had won their reputation. Epaminondas had changed all that. He divided his own front into two parts, one an unusually deep and heavy offensive wing of his best heavily armed troops, the other and lighter wing being reserved for defense. His offensive wing was to move forward and break the enemy line in a concentrated attack, while the defensive wing moved slowly up to engage at the proper moment and bring about a decision. The Theban had gone even further: he had placed his cavalry on both flanks, to protect

[1] Nepos, *Pelopidas*, 1. See also Nepos, *Epaminondas*.

them during the battle; afterward the cavalry pursued and cut down the broken and flying fugitives as long as possible. With these tactics Epaminondas had crushed the power of Sparta at Leuctra in 371, to take her place in the leadership of Greece, a thing the Spartans never forgave. They had indeed made an attempt to recover their lost ground several years later, but again at Mantinea, in 362, Epaminondas had read her a terrible lesson, though he lost his own life in the battle. But after the first great victory, the Thebans had become so harshly insolent [1] that they earned the hatred and reprobation of the other Hellenes. So plain was this that, young though Philip was, it seems credible in view of later happenings, even then he must have realized that as soon as Epaminondas should die, Theban supremacy would die with him.

Philip, then, upon his accession to his throne had had several years in which to digest his lessons in military strategy and, what was more important, strategic statesmanship. If, as there is every reason to believe, Philip had had personal instruction from Epaminondas and Pelopidas, it helps explain why Philip, from the very beginning, so plainly shows he knew exactly what he wanted done, and knew how to do it, and immediately set about doing it. At once the most dependable fighting men, probably those who had most to lose from his possible failure, rallied about him. The child prince Amyntas was made his ward and promptly put aside. Philip had three half-brothers, as always, in that time, a threat to be removed. One he put to death, but the other two fled, to appear next at Olynthus two years later. To remove Athenian help [2] from Pausanias he withdrew his garrison from Amphipolis, recognized the Athenians' right to the city, and sent Pausanias' chief Thracian supporter a large bribe to keep peace on the eastern frontier. The Paeonians were bought off with a heavy cash indemnity. Then he turned swiftly, with all his army, upon another contender for the throne, one Argaeus, who had seized the ancient city of Aegae as his headquarters. He captured Argaeus and put both

[1] Demosthenes, *On the Crown*, 18.   [2] Justin, VII, 4.

him and his Macedonian followers to death, but the rest of the pretender's forces, mostly tribesmen from Orestes and Aeordea, were released and permitted to return home with no punishment at all, a political gesture which assured in the future, if not their active alliance, at least benevolent neutrality on their part. The 'Illyrians,'[1] however, were fighting for the honor, as they conceived it, of a woman, the spitfire Eurydice, and could not be bought off. But the news of Philip's sudden offensive gave them pause, and as winter was coming on, they withdrew to gather additional strength, and he gained a few months' time to push his preparations.

Philip returned to Pella, took cognizance of the state of the treasury, and probably ordered extra taxes or other income. He hired mercenary[2] soldiers from southern Italy and Greece and put them to training the Macedonians for war. His discipline was harsh, his punishments for its infraction brutal. The hours of drill were long, and he forced his men to route marches of thirty-five miles (two hundred and fifty Attic stadia) a day with full equipment and flour for a month, to harden them physically and toughen them morally for that great test of war to which he intended to put them. It is told[3] that one of his officers, a Tarentine drillmaster, was so unfortunate as to be reported to Philip for taking a warm bath that winter. The erring officer was instantly dismissed, Philip telling him harshly that Macedonian women washed with cold water even in childbed. Two other officers were dismissed as summarily for bringing a prostitute into camp.

[1] Our Greek sources often use this term, when it cannot, obviously, be correctly applied to the peoples or tribe mentioned. For the real Illyrians to reach Macedonia, it would be necessary for them first to cross the lands of the Lyncestians, then those of the Aeordeans, and of course Philip would find it necessary to reverse the procedure. It may be that the Lyncestians joined alliance with the Illyrians, but it is very doubtful that the Aeordeans would likewise join in, for this tribe had been vassals to the Macedonians for centuries. This was also true of the Orestians to the south of the Haliacmon Valley, and we know of no historical account of either of them warring with Macedonia. It must be considered that the Greek sources use the term 'Illyrian' because they recognized no distinction between them.

[2] Demosthenes, *Olynthiacs*, II, 17; Diodorus, XVI.

[3] Frontinus, IV, 1, 6; Polyaenus, IV, 2.

By spring he had hammered together an army of ten thousand infantry and six hundred cavalry, the nucleus of the most famous and effective body of cavalry the world had ever known, which, under his son, was to be the heralded *hetairoi*, the famous Macedonian 'companions.' They had trained long and arduously; the time to test the value of his theories had arrived. With intent to eliminate forever the recurring threats of the mountain tribes on his frontiers, and to push back those frontiers to include them, he turned first against the northern Paeonians and subdued them in a single battle. The 'Illyrians,' under their chief Bardylis, were of sterner stuff, and the battle was long and fierce. The Macedonians won at last; the tribesmen fled the field, then sent back an embassy asking permission to bury their dead, the recognized formula acknowledging defeat. Philip granted the request and withdrew until the enemy were disorganized. He then ruthlessly fell upon them again [1] and killed seven thousand of them, driving the panic-stricken survivors in wild confusion back into their hills.[2] Eurydice disappears from our history from now on.

Philip turned back southward, crossed the Emathian plain, marched through the hill-pass back of Thermê, and descended upon the unsuspecting city of Amphipolis. When he had returned the city to Athenian control the year before, after a three-year occupation by Macedonian troops, he had greatly gratified both Athens and Amphipolis: from the former he had removed doubts that he had designs upon the city for himself; the latter because he had relieved them of a burdensome garrison of the hated 'barbarians.' But now, as the astonished and worried inhabitants became aware of the approach of the grim array, they dispatched a hurried embassy to Athens with urgent appeals for immediate assistance. Athens in 358 was almost at the height of her power as a result of her naval confederation, and she had also but recently obtained control of the Thracian Chersonese, and, what was equally important, had finally

[1] Diodorus, XVI, 4; Polyaenus, IV, 2, 5.

[2] Diodorus (XVI, 8) says he pushed his punitive expedition as far as the borders of Epirus.

wrested the long island of Euboea, on her east coast, from the last vestiges of Theban control. But right at that moment she was faced by the beginning of the 'Social War' of 357–355. Four of Athens' most important subject allies, the islands of Cos, Chios, Rhodes, and the Propontic city of Byzantium, as well as several smaller ones, had revolted from what they deemed unjust treatment, and were prepared to fight. Simultaneously another embassy arrived from Philip bearing assurances that though he was indeed besieging the city he would turn it over to them after punishing it. The Athenians thought the matter over, and realizing it would be highly impolitic to make a dangerous enemy of a possible valuable ally at the outset of what promised to be a long struggle with their revolted colonies, they dismissed the Amphipolitan suppliants with contumely. Philip threw his army about the walls of the city and pressed the siege vigorously, at the same time intriguing with his partisans within. The city fell at last. Philip promptly expelled all Athenians [1] and their sympathizers and garrisoned it heavily. He knew only too well its value to him and firmly resolved to hold both it and the adjacent coast, though for some time he carried on a subtle diplomatic war with Athens over it. He next seized the neighboring mining village of Crenides, fortified and garrisoned it to protect the famous mines of near-by Mount Pangeus, and named it Philippi. The year before a number of Thasian miners had immigrated into Crenides, apparently as *bona-fide* colonists, but there is reason to believe — for Philip gives us many instances of his long-range planning — at his invitation.[2] Thus the needed and experienced miners were immediately at hand. They were put to work on such a scale that the mines at once brought in a revenue of a thousand talents [3] a year. He then began to strike the Macedonian staters,[4] that most common and widely disseminated of all gold coins of antiquity.[5]

[1] Demosthenes, *Olynthiacs*, I, 8.   [2] Diodorus, XVI, 3.
[3] See Chapter V.   [4] Strabo, 331.
[5] J. Evans, *Coins of Ancient Britons*; also Charles Seltman, *Greek Coins*.

It was about this time, 357, that Philip visited the island of Samothrace, some sixty miles distant by boat, there to be initiated into the mysteries of the Cabiri and the Orphic and Dionysiac rites.[1] Here he met Olympias, daughter of Neoptolemus, king of Epirus, who traced his lineage back to Neoptolemus, son of Achilles.[2] The wild freedom of the girl, who had also come to partake of the rites, struck Philip forcibly. He fell in love with her, and as she was an orphan, after obtaining the consent of her brother he married her, probably the only time in his life Philip ever let his heart rule his head. The marriage was, however, not wholly devoid of political implications and advantage, for by his alliance with the royal house of Epirus he secured the safety of the frontier between the now subject Illyrians and their western neighbor.

Back in Pella once more, he proceeded to reorganize the army, creating something new in that world of citizen soldiers who took up their weapons as needed, served until the crisis of the moment had passed, then resumed civil life. Philip started building the first *national* standing army, of men who were soldiers as their regular life's trade, to whom were given high pay and the spoils of war, whether in *valuta* or captives, as the reward of service. He achieved thereby a double result, obtaining an army with a length of service and sufficient experience to acquire the *esprit de corps* that only perfect discipline can give, creating a military psychology designed to make military service the goal of each young man's life. The clan and tribal units were, for the present, left under command of their own chiefs, and the mixing of these units brought contacts of hostile elements whose hostility disappeared in association as brothers in arms. The ancient feuds and hatreds melted under the new order, and slowly but surely a consciousness of national unity began to replace the narrow old clan spirit. The pride of being a Macedonian supplanted the pride of being a tribesman. Our ancient biographers tell us that at the end of Philip's labors he

[1] See footnote, p. 18.

[2] Plutarch, *Alexander*, 3; cf. Pausanias, I, 9, 8.

had an army always armed and fully equipped,[1] ready to march at any time,[2] the striking unit, the phalanx, having its full complement of auxiliaries of all arms, light infantry, light and heavy cavalry, archers and slingers, light and heavy artillery, and siege trains. He thus occupies the unique place in military annals of being the first commander to combine all arms, and co-ordinate them in a single tactical unit working together to achieve a common end. Morale, as Napoleon was to say two thousand years later, is to material force as three to one, and though Philip was probably not aware of even a word equivalent to or denoting morale, that was the objective toward which he was working. War was, then even more than today, a matter of morale; it counts more than battalions, second only to leader-ship. And in creating this intangible but enormous military factor, Philip, and after him Alexander, were pre-eminent. Philip also realized that to build up the desired military psycho-logy, soldiers must be caught young. He therefore created what was to be the first cadet school; the sons of the nobility and larger landholders were taken to court to serve as pages to the king in time of war, as gentlemen of the chamber and equerries in times of peace, and always to study the duties and actions of the officers, whose places they would some day take. By this means Philip intentionally built an officers' corps whose lives were wholly bound up with the army and whose only pride lay therein. That he succeeded is attested by the fact that their nationalistic and military pride, in Persia, barred even Alex-ander's attempt to remodel the army into units combining Mace-donians and elements of other races. At Susa he abolished the allies' regiments with no difficulty, but when he sought to expand the sadly decimated Macedonian units by incorporating with them the dissolved units, he provoked open mutiny. Thus Philip, at his death, left Alexander in command of an army about fifty to sixty thousand strong, with a military spirit so strong and so well established that when, upon Philip's death,

[1] Demosthenes, *On the Crown*, 235.
[2] Diodorus, XVI, 8, and 74; also Arrian, I, 6.

Demosthenes in Athens exultingly proclaimed the imminent break-up of the Macedonian kingdom, the wise old general [1] Phocion warned the Athenians, on the contrary, that the dagger which took the king's life had but reduced the Macedonian army by a single man.

Philip had recognized early during his apprenticeship under Epaminondas that only under one head, ruling supreme as king and general, could a national policy be formulated and maintained, both in internal and foreign relationships. To the south, Athens was a glaring example of the result of the fundamental policy of the Greek *poleis*, the political democracy of the day. In the democracies, questions of national and international import were decided only after much time had been wasted by oratorical demagogues of rival factions of opposed viewpoints with different ends to serve, which the monarch decided swiftly, for good or evil, but decisively. Now that Philip's army was in an advanced state of perfection, he cannily surveyed the political situation of the Hellenic states, and decided the time was ripe for his long-planned campaign of territorial aggrandizement. His own situation was excellent. He had already secured several of his primary objectives, and circumstances worked in his behalf to prosecute his intentions still further. He had secured the political integrity of his northern and northwestern frontiers by conquering the Paeonians and the Lyncestians, and his campaign against the Illyrians was going well; he had obtained a port, a bit of seacoast, and an assured revenue by the seizure of Amphipolis and the mines; and had assured himself of the enthusiastic support of the lowland Macedonians in all he desired.

The situation in Greece was all that Philip could have desired. Sparta, the oligarchic erstwhile power in the Peloponnesus, was still crushed from the Theban victories at Leuctra and Mantinea. Thebes had found no one to replace Epaminondas, either as governor or diplomat. Athens, whose empire Philip was about to attack, was fighting the costly and losing Social War

[1] Plutarch, *Phocion*, 16.

around the Propontus and the Aegean Islands. Her territories and colonies, strung in a narrow selvage along the coasts of Thrace and the Thracian Chersonese, were Philip's aim. He had planned carefully; he executed the plan cautiously. First, agents with ample funds were dispatched to Thrace to estrange a powerful Thracian chieftain who had made alliance with Athens, and to the Chersonese to corrupt the tribes and cities there who were under Athenian influence. We have also Demosthenes' [1] word for it that Philip had placed his agents in Athens itself as early as 356. Other agents were sent to the Athenian allies, the cities of Pydna and Potidaea, and, after their leading citizens were corrupted, these cities opened their gates to him. Philip, partly for army training, partly first to arouse and later to quiet the fears of the city of Olynthus, first marched to Pydna, then around to Potidaea to accept the city. Olynthus in alarm sent messengers to inquire the cause of the invasion. Philip casually handed the two cities, together with neighboring Anthemus, over to the reconstituted Chalcidic confederation headed by Olynthus,[2] and withdrew to Pella once more, knowing Olynthus would be made the butt of Athenian animus for estranging their cities and in effect receiving stolen goods. Philip knew also he could repossess them, together with the whole confederation, whenever he should desire. Plutarch tells us that when Philip was under the walls of Potidaea, messengers arrived with three items of good news: his expeditionary force against the 'Illyrians' had won a great victory; his team had won at the Olympic games; and his wife, Olympias, had borne him a son, Alexander,[3] destined to be the third of that name to be king of Macedonia.

[1] Demosthenes, On the Crown, 19.

[2] For a contemporary viewpoint on the nature of the federation, see Xenophon, Hellenica, 5, 211 ff.

[3] H. Nissen, with data drawn from many sources, published the view that this year of 356 the Olympic games began on or about September 27. His scholarly work has been accepted as substantially correct by most inquirers. (See also B. Niese, Geschichte, p. 51.) We need have, therefore, no qualms about also accepting it. The date of Alexander's birth, then, can be considered, for reasons much too long to cite here, as having occurred in the first five or six days of the month of October, 356 B.C. Rheinisches Museum, XL, 350.

Philip in this expedition found several things lacking in his governmental methods and organization. He spent the next two years correcting them and was not ready to move again until the spring of 353. By that time he had become convinced that Athens was genuinely financially and militarily exhausted. The Social War had deprived her of most of her former allies, her fighting forces of hired mercenaries were dissolved for lack of money to pay them, and her state revenues reduced almost to the vanishing point. She was wholly incapable of waging war. Philip did not want war with Athens, and he reasoned her political and economic condition would prevent her declaring for hostilities. He had spent great sums on paid propaganda in Athens, and he must have known very well indeed the political situation there. The Thracian allies of the Athenians had accepted not a little of his gold,[1] and there matters seemed propitious for his next move against the Athenian Empire. Philip marched eastward and prepared to attack the Athenian [2] colonies of Abdera and Maronea, but the Thracians, not yet wholly won from the influence of Athens, took fright and sent for help. The Athenian admiral, the notorious *condottiere* Chares, arrived with the fleet, but Philip evaded it, and marched angrily around the Thermaic Gulf of Methônê, the only city on the near-by seaboard of any importance yet to remain under Attic control. The Macedonians found the gates closed against them. Philip ordered the scaling ladders put up; then, when his army had climbed to the top of the wall, he took the ladders down [3] to force the soldiers to continue the attack. Philip himself lost an eye, shot out by an arrow. Methônê was captured with little trouble after the final assault was begun. The citizens were driven forth in only the clothing they stood up in, and the town was looted and razed to the ground. This siege marked the beginning of genuine hostilities against the dependencies of Athens; though he had seized Amphipolis before,

[1] Cf. Diodorus, XVI, 34; Demosthenes, *Aristocrates*, 183.
[2] Demosthenes, *Olynthiacs*, III, 4; Polyaenus, IV, 2, 22.
[3] Polyaenus, IV, 2, 15.

Philip excused the act by the sophistry that the city had not been *de facto* a genuine dependency. Though he had taken Pydna, Potidaea, and the lesser Anthemus, he had not retained them for himself, but had turned them over to Olynthus, nominally an Athenian ally. It is worth noting that Philip always, and Alexander after him, avoided open conflict with Athens on the soil of Attica proper, though he whittled down both her power and her holdings elsewhere, reducing her at last to a condition of innocuity save in Hellas itself. When Athenians were captured during his warlike operations he always released them without payment of ransom, save once, nor did he ever permit a single soldier to violate or invade Attica or violate Athenian rights there. But his aggressions elsewhere caused the Athenians many nervous moments; and this, the capture of Methônê, was the last straw. She declared war at last, a war, however, which was to change the status of affairs very little indeed. The Athenians never pressed active hostilities against Philip; he in turn almost ignored them and still refrained from active hostilities in Hellas against the city.

Circumstances then played right into his hands. Southward of Macedonia, Thessaly, since the death of the tyrant Jason, had been plunged into internal strife and dissensions. One of the great houses of Thessalian Larissa asked alliance with him to crush the new tyrant of Pherae, Lycophron. Philip cheerfully mustered his army and marched south. His confidence was misplaced, however, for the Pherean had hired seven thousand mercenaries from the Phocian despoilers of Delphi, and Philip, outnumbered, fought two engagements, but could make no headway against them. Disgruntled, he withdrew to Pella in the autumn, and in the winter following he demanded more substantial assistance from the Larissians. Returning in the spring, his allies enabled him to take the field with twenty thousand infantry and three thousand cavalry. Down in Athens the orator Hypereides and others vainly tried to get the Athenians awakened to the implications of Philip's continued expansion, raise an army, and go to the assistance of the Phereans. It was of no use; they would not force the war they had declared. Philip, aware of what was going on in Attica, delayed going into action in Thessaly until he was sure the Athenians would not intervene, haggling long over terms with his allies. Convinced at last that he had nothing to fear from the Athenians, he met the enemy on the plain of Volo and won a decisive victory, killing the Phocian general and destroying his army. An Athenian fleet standing offshore rescued most of his flying enemies, but he managed to capture and crucify three thousand of the Phocians as sacrilegious men beyond the pale of human rights. The Pherean army had lost so heavily and decisively that the tyrant precipitately left the city and fled south through the defiles of Thermopylae. Philip moved into position before the port of Pagasae and besieged it. The people appealed to Athens for help, but though the Athenians ordered the fleet to their assistance, it arrived too late. The district of Magnesia and its magnificent port and splendid bay, from whose anchorages his privateers could constitute a menace to Euboea and the south, had already fallen into Philip's hands.

Philip then seems to have got the idea that it would be well to appear before the eyes of the Greeks as the champion of the Delphic Apollo. The second Sacred War, between the Phocians, sacrilegiously financed by robbing the treasures of the sanctuary of Apollo at Delphi, and the Boeotians and Thebans had been raging intermittently for ten years. Athens had definitely sided with the Phocians. Now Philip was appealed to by the Thebans for assistance against the desecrators of the sanctuary. He marched south toward Thermopylae, preparing to seize the pass, the southern gateway to Thessaly. But Chares, the Athenian admiral, was hanging offshore; he got news of the Macedonian's intention, and hastily dispatched a report to Athens. By the time Philip was ready to move, the Athenians, startled at last out of their lethargy by the prospect of having an invading army larger than any since the time of Xerxes at the pass and threatening Hellas, swiftly raised an army of defense and sent it to bar Philip's passage. Philip, despite the open defiance and fully aware that his battle-hardened men could trample the tiny force underfoot with ease, still desired no active hostilities with Athens, and philosophically turned his energies back to Thessaly. During the next two years, by bribery, fraud, and chicane,[1] he played the dissident factors against each other until at last the whole territory slipped peacefully into his hands, though there must have been some objectors, for we hear of the general Parmenio reducing the town of Halys as late as 346. In the meantime, in order to secure Thessaly, Philip's agents, gold, and diplomacy reached across into Euboea, where hitherto Athenian influence had been supreme, and soon strong Macedonian parties in Chalcis and Eritrea were diligently attempting to foment discord and civil war. When Athens finally stirred at last in response to the frantic appeals of her own sympathizers and dispatched her general Phocion with an army of assistance, he was to find all the leaders of his presumed Euboean allies already corrupted by Macedonian gold. Athens never again ruled supreme in the island.

For the next three years we know little of Philip's actions. The little we do see of him in our incomplete history of him, is, however, illuminating; an amazing picture of a man of ruthless energy and determination. For we find him once more beating the northern marches, suppressing the more distant Paeonians and Illyrians; we see him driving the tribesmen before him on Lake Ochrida; then again turning eastward into Thrace to visit condign punishment upon those tribes which were so obtuse as to prefer their own freedom to Macedonian oppression. We also know that toward the last the Athenians were highly vocal in their outraged claim that he had suppressed the freedom of at least thirty-two [2] Hellenic cities and colonies, from the Chalcidic peninsula to the Thracian Chersonese. His imperialistic intentions were now plain to the dullest, and we hear in 351 (some place the date as early as 349) Demosthenes deliver the first of his recorded attacks upon Philip in his bitter *First Philippic*,

[1] Polyaenus, IV, 2, 19.

[2] Callisthenes, *Fragmenta Historicorum Graecorum*, 42.

urging the Athenians to press more energetically the war they had declared three years before, unless they wished to see all their cities of the Thracian seaboard in Macedonian hands.

In 349 Philip decided the time was ripe and the occasion auspicious to break the hold of Athens upon neighboring areas he coveted. Dragging a long siege train, the first ever seen in Greece, he moved south into the three-pronged peninsula of the Chalcidice. Olynthus, then ruled by an iron-handed oligarchy of aristocrats, had risen to power after the fall of the first Athenian Empire, and now, after the downfall of Sparta, it again headed the Chalcidic federation of cities she had alienated from Athenian influence. After years of opposition, the Olynthians had not only no real claim to the friendship of the Attic city, but even deserved opprobrium for actions inimical to her interests. Therefore, when we later find Demosthenes and other Athenians demanding punishment of Philip for his seizure of Olynthus,[1] we are constrained to believe the sudden furor is raised only as the rallying-cry of certain political interests. In the peninsula Philip ruthlessly broke into the confederate cities one after another, and, in reply to anxious queries by the Olynthians, assured them he was not at war with themselves, but merely chastening fractious and unruly members of their confederation. Afterward, he said, he would hand the cities back to her, even as he had the cities of Potidaea, Anthemus, and Pydna, seven years before. Olynthus believed him, and made no preparations against possible attack. Philip moved slowly from city to city, until he had forced his will upon them all. Then, unexpectedly, the long spears of the Macedonian array gleamed before the gates of Olynthus, and a Macedonian herald proclaimed to the shocked and frightened inhabitants that the city was sheltering behind its walls two of Philip's half-brothers, sentenced to death long before. There was no demand for surrender, only Philip's appalling ultimatum that the world itself was not wide enough for Philip and Olynthus both.[2] The amazed city shut its gates and cast desperately

---

[1] See also Demosthenes, *Third Philippic*, II.

[2] Demosthenes, *Olynthiac*, III, 11.

about for help. Envoys were sent post-haste to Athens, already nominally at war with Philip, and though the appeal was received with little genuine enthusiasm, the notorious Chares was sent with thirty ships and two thousand men to the assistance of the Chalcidic city. How this force under the semi-pirate behaved on the peninsula can be read in Demosthenes' second Olynthiac oration. At any rate, they did Philip no harm, and as they received no pay, they were back home in October. In response to a second appeal from Olynthus, the Athenians sent the still more notorious *condottiere* and pirate, Charidemus, with four thousand light infantry and a small body of cavalry in eighteen ships. They harried the seaboard south of Pella, then appeared in the Chalcidice and looted some small Greek towns, to their profit, but neither injured Philip's cause nor helped that of Olynthus. In fact, their behavior was so bad that it led to complaints to Athens by Olynthus, and a third expedition, as futile as the first two, was dispatched. It soon returned after accomplishing precisely nothing. In the meantime the besieged Olynthians had tried two strong sorties and were repulsed only after severe fighting. Philip, however, preferred to gain his ends by other means than fighting. He sooner or later was going to have the city, and saw no reason to get his army killed off unnecessarily in the process. He called off the assaults in favor of intriguing, and at last his gold inside the city accomplished more than his army outside. Two of the ruling aristocrats sold out to the besiegers and opened the gates. Philip ruthlessly murdered his two half-brothers, sold the rest of the inhabitants into slavery, and razed the city to the ground. Then he returned to Dion (Dium) to thank the Macedonian Zeus with a great festival in honor of his victory and a united Macedonia.[1]

In the winter of 347–346 an Athenian herald arrived at Pella asking Philip to receive an embassy who wished to come to sue for peace, a heaven-sent opportunity for the guileful Macedonian. At the moment he had two projects in mind: one, to establish

[1] Diodorus, XVI, 55.

his supremacy south of Thermopylae; the other, to finish the subjection of Thrace and the few cities there remaining in Athenian hands. As a by-product of this last, he proposed to threaten Euboea, thereby keeping the Athenian navy anxiously alert in home waters and away from the Hellespont. The ten Athenian envoys, including the two orators, Demosthenes and Aeschines, arrived, were listened to, and entertained so well that they returned home quite overcome by Philip's hospitality, wit, and amiability. With them upon their return to Athens Philip sent his own herald agreeing to peace upon the basis of the *status quo*, and guaranteeing that he would not attack the cities of the Chersonese. The Athenians were glad of peace upon almost any terms and at almost any price, though those offered meant final resignation to the loss of Amphipolis and the valuable mines, whose output of a thousand talents a year would have been a very welcome augmentation to Athens' meager annual income of not over fifty [1] talents. A few days later, Philip's envoys, the generals Parmenio and Antipater, reached Athens and were accorded a great welcome by the city, but from then on peace discussions, though on a perfectly friendly basis, seemed to proceed with inexplicable slowness.

As soon as the Athenian envoys had departed, Philip ordered his newly gathered navy to sail from Amphipolis on Lake Cercinitis, while he with the army marched swiftly back to Thrace. There, while the peace conference in Athens was being suavely sabotaged by his envoys, he attacked and destroyed a tribe of Thracians friendly to the Athenians, and securely tightened his hold upon the cities, then returned to Pella. In May the Athenian envoys returned to Pella, after being deliberately delayed by refusal to grant them safe-conduct on the part of the previously instructed Thessalians. They finally ratified the peace terms agreed upon, to find themselves confronted by a condition which, though indeed the *status quo*, was nevertheless very different from the one they had envisioned when they agreed to Philip's terms a few months before. In fact, before they were

[1] Demosthenes, *On the Crown.*

finished with that master of duplicity, the Athenians had given the far-sighted Philip almost everything of value that they possessed, although they did not know it at the time. Never did Philip, master of deceit that he was, play more carefully and subtly, and never was the fact so carefully concealed. In the Vardar plain just outside the city lay the army, superior to any which any logical combination of Greeks could throw into the field against him; all any of the envoys needed for assurance of the fact was the sight of his own eyes. Yet despite the presence of the army, the court of Pella seems calculated to give rise to the firm belief that its master was a man who cared for nothing but drinking and carousing,[1] doubtless the very impression intended they should receive. But drink heavily though he did, there was one thing the diplomats failed to perceive, and that was that Philip, drunk or sober, was still their mental superior. Money Philip had in plenty, and was so generous with it that Theopompus the historian seems justified in this, his description of the court at Pella:

> When Philip became master of great wealth he did not merely spend it in haste. No, he flung it away and flung it into the street. He was the worst manager in the world, both he and his associates. In a word, not one of them had the least knowledge of right living or the prudent management of an estate. For this he himself was responsible, being insatiable and extravagant and doing everything offhand, whether he was getting or giving. He was always busy with his soldiering and had no time to reckon up income and expenditure. Moreover, his companions were men who had come pouring in from many places; some were from his home country, some from Thessaly, others from all the rest of Greece, and they were not selected on the grounds of merit. No! Pretty well every lecher and daredevil and buffoon in the Greek and barbarian world flocked to Macedonia and got the title of 'Philip's companion.' Even if a man was not a ruffian upon his arrival, he soon became one under the influence of the Macedonian life and habits. It was

[1] Athenaeus, quoting Xenophon, *Hellenica*, 70, says when Philip gave a banquet it was a veritable 'workshop of war,' referring to the riotousness and accompanying violence which reigned.

partly their wars and campaigns, partly their extravagances that turned them into daredevils, living not in orderly fashion, but prodigally, like highwaymen.

The news leaked out that Philip was going to march south, and the Greek world was agog with speculation as to his intentions. Of course, Parmenio was besieging Halys, and not making much headway with it; perhaps Philip was going to the assistance of the general — but perhaps he wasn't! The siege of a single small city was hardly likely to attract a man of his capabilities; then what? To him came nervous embassies from the Greek cities; representatives of the Amphictyonic Council; from Thebes, which asked his aid in punishing the impious Phocians; from the Phocians and the peoples of the Peloponnesus, all asking alliances and seeking favors. To each Philip talked, and discussed the many-sided phases of their own political situations, but committed himself to nothing, made not even half-promises. Suddenly he packed up the army and moved south with the still more nervous envoys intriguing murderously, but with diplomatic politeness, in his train. Philip stopped and went into camp at Larissa as if for a breathing-spell before going to assist Parmenio at the siege of Halys, and here at last, with his army threatening Thermopylae, he swore lasting peace with the Athenians, refusing their plea that he include the Phocians in his promises, and brought forth representatives from his cities (that were so recently Athenian cities) in Thrace to swear likewise. But before this, the Athenians were required to surrender all their ancient rights and claims to their islands of Rhodes, Cos, and Chios to Pixodorus, satrap of Caria in Asia Minor, with whom Philip had recently concluded an alliance. He had become the strongest power in the Greek world. We now get from our histories for the first time any hint of what Philip's real intentions were, for we are told now that it was Philip's desire 'to be designated Captain-General of Hellas, and to wage war against the Persians'; [1] for he has not only cleared himself

[1] Diodorus, XVI, 60.

a path to the Sea of Marmora, but has obviously started also to open his road in Asia Minor.

It was at this time, anyhow, that his anti-Persian aspirations were made public through all Hellas. Whether or not he was responsible for fathering the publication — as Philip was notably farsighted in his preparations for all actions, such may very well have been the case — of the letter of Isocrates in his *Philip* in 346, we have no way of knowing. We can be sure that even if Philip had not inspired it with his gold — for the paid propagandist was a great factor in both peace and war even in those days — it fell upon not unattentive ears.

Isocrates pointed out to Philip that for successful prosecution of a war against Persia the first requirement was to bring about *homonoia* (reconciliation) and accord with one another between the four leading states of Hellas, Athens, Sparta, Argos, and Thebes. These would enter into conference with one another through appointed ambassadors, and once agreement was reached, the small states would necessarily follow the examples of the larger. Philip was not only the most powerful ruler but was also a descendant of Heracles, venerated of all the Greeks, and as such the most natural leader of the proposed coalition. As for Persia, now was the best possible time to strike. The great empire was rent and weakened by internal revolts, and the Great King was busy putting them down. Philip need only enter Asia Minor to have the satraps rise at once of their own accord and greet him as their benefactor. Here Isocrates points out that Philip's great ancestor (much stress was laid upon this point), the demigod Heracles, had once overcome the city of Troy within a few days, and here Philip has the opportunity to show similar philanthropy and magnanimity to the Greeks. If the whole Persian Empire can be destroyed, well and good, but if not, the western coast of Asia Minor from Sinope to Cilicia should be taken, and Philip should there settle, as military colonists and to protect the outposts of Grecian culture, the homeless wanderers who were a terror and a menace to the country. In this way a chain of Greek cities would be reared across the immense peninsula that was Asia Minor, and would constitute a bulwark against renewed encroachments by the power of Persia. 'For in doing this, you will win the gratitude of all — the Greeks for the benefits you confer upon them; of the Macedonians that you rule them as king and not as tyrant; of other men that you have freed them from barbarian oppression and brought them under Greek care and protection.' [1]

If Philip was the real author of this letter it was his method of serving notice of his intentions, and giving the Greeks time to get accustomed to the idea of accepting it in all its implications from Philip's point of view. His ultimate intentions were to advance into Asia Minor and there attack the empire of the Great King. He had been working for over ten years building up the necessary political safeguards which alone would let him begin his eastward march; much had been accomplished, but much yet remained undone. He had by no means secured his much-desired hold upon Greece, nor yet obtained unquestioned control of the Propontus, though his alliance with the Carian satrap had gone far in that direction to give him protection from interference on the Asia Minor side. But it was necessary to have a far firmer hold upon both before he could give serious attention to the final details before launching his anti-Persian crusade. He had to have Greece by legal means, legal to prevent Attic sophistry from finding loopholes for evasion, peaceful, if possible, to avoid leaving in his rear rancor which might break out any time to the hurt or destruction of his plans.

The idea, as we have shown, of a *revanche* against the Persians was by no means new.[2] The destruction of their temples and cities had been a sore spot rankling in the breasts of the Hellenes ever since the last Persian invaders had departed from their shores. We have already seen Gorgias, about 408, preaching to the vast assembly the necessity of composing their quarrels and uniting against the Persians. In 388 Lysias was also earnestly

---

[1] See U. Wilcken, *Sitzungberichte*, Preuss. Ak., 313, 1929.

[2] Thucydides (I, 96, 1) gives the idea of a Persian *revanche* as the chief reason for forming the old Athenian-Delian League.

exhorting them at least to liberate the Greek cities of Asia Minor; Jason of Pherae had made no secret of his intent to humble the power of Persia, and there is excellent reason to believe that Epaminondas, the Theban, had the same dream and intent. It is also certain that the idea was by no means new to Philip; indeed his actions through the whole of his reign to date are such that into them can be read his obvious intention to accomplish wider aims than the mere consolidation of his own kingdom or even the unification of Greece under the aegis of Macedonia. It is even probable that his aims against the Persian Empire may date as far back as his association with Epaminondas in Thebes.[1] Now he was to enter at last into the peninsula of Greece itself, and push another step toward the completion of those plans to bring the whole under his domination.

The Athenian envoys, crestfallen at their diplomatic defeat, had hardly reached home before Philip marched south to Thermopylae, only to find it guarded by a strong force of mercenaries hired by Phocis, and a small body of Spartans. These latter hastily decamped, and Philip sent a communication to the mercenary general, asking permission to make a peaceful passage. The general's personal position was then in grave doubt; his men were on the verge of mutiny from lack of pay, he himself had but recently quarreled with the Phocian government, and the Macedonian force confronting him outnumbered him at least four or five to one. But perhaps Athens needed a good army, his own, to fight their battles for them! He asked and received time to consult Athens. He dispatched an urgent message to the city, and when the reply came he was informed that the Athenians were passing resolutions against Philip. Resolutions were absolutely useless to the mercenary; he could neither pay his men with them, eat them, nor use them as weapons. Philip paid his way through the pass. The mercenary marched away through the Peloponnesus and took ships to Crete.

Philip went storming through Phocis carrying death and de-

[1] Holm, *Griechische Geschichte* (III, chap. XVII, p. 278), coincides with this view.

40

struction. Twenty-three cities of the Phocians were captured and their walls dismantled, turning them into open towns where, by Philip's edict, not more than fifty families might live together. Three of the cities of Boeotia, Orchomenus, Coronea, and Corsiae, were placed under Theban control as recompense for siding against the Phocians, and to insure their continued friendship toward Philip. For that service the ancient Amphictyonic Council elected Philip to the empty seat vacated by Phocis, and also to the Pythian chair of presidency of the Olympic games that autumn.

Macedonian garrisons were placed at Thermopylae and in Phocis: in the former to guard the pass for Philip himself now that he had undisputed sway over Thessaly; in Phocis to keep his decrees in force and to have his own men, ready and willing to his orders, in Greece. He then marched to Thebes, and was received with great rejoicing as a benefactor of the city. After staying there a few days he marched back to Thessaly, halting only long enough to establish in authority in the four leading cities his own hand-picked Councils of Ten, to keep the four districts from a unity which might be dangerous to his supremacy, ordering them to remit [1] to him direct the revenues of the land and customs received in the port.

He then returned to Pella for the winter, to continue his plotting. He dispatched agents in all directions, paying particular attention to Greece. It seems he received impressions or information regarding the possibility of something untoward happening in Thebes, for he gave orders that his lieutenants should pay especial attention to that city. Others were sent to the Peloponnesus, where during the next two or three years they managed, by intrigues and threats of force, to break the ancient supremacy of Sparta in her own territory, forcing her to sign a peace treaty with Argos and surrender her rights to control of Arcadia and Messene.[2] In Elis the intriguing of his agents resulted in furious civil war and massacres.[3] In Euboea his 'golden

[1] Demosthenes, *Philippics*, II, 22; III, 26, 33.
[2] *Ibid.*, II, 13, 20, 26.   [3] *Ibid.*, III, 27; Pausanias, IV, 28, 4.

army' won over to the Macedonian viewpoint the leaders of every important city except Chalcis. In Athens Demosthenes, who was at least clear-sighted enough to discern Philip's intention, made a tour of the Peloponnesus in an attempt to stem the tide of disintegration setting against the old balance-of-power politics and alliances, only to find himself frustrated everywhere. He then returned to Athens and in his *Second Philippic* thundered invective against Philip as a 'sacker of cities' who cried for peace but made war, and suborned half the country to the subjection of the world.

Again, however, Philip showed his regard for the city he called the 'Theater of Glory' and recognized seat of culture. He dispatched frequent letters and envoys to soothe her fears that he had designs upon her, and testified time and time again to his lasting good will. He even sent a personal friend, Python, to plead for him, going at last so far as cautiously to propose amending those articles she deemed most obnoxious in the peace treaty he had forced upon her unwilling envoys. But just about this time he gave her new reason for fury against him. An island off the north coast of Euboea, Halonessus, which Athens had long considered her own, was being used as a pirate lair. A Macedonian admiral smoked out the pirates and occupied the island in Philip's name. The Athenians immediately protested against the seizure and demanded restoration of the almost worthless rock. Philip suavely replied that Athens had so long neglected to govern or even bother about the island that it could be rightfully considered that their interest in it had lapsed. However, in order to keep the peace about it he would be delighted to 'present' it to Athens. The Athenians, however, insisted that it be not 'presented,' for inasmuch as it was Athenian property it must be 'restored' — a bootless quarrel over two words, and one which accomplished nothing toward clarifying the tenseness of the citizens of the republic. While this argument was still going on in 343, the Athenians sent an envoy, one Hegesippus, to Pella to request action on the amendments to the peace of which Philip had written. Philip, unfortunately, had become irritated at the arguments over Halonessus, and sabotaged the attempts to reach an understanding with him. The negotiations broke up in mutual recriminations and quarrels, and led to the famous Demosthenic charge against his companion orator, Aeschines, that he had also been suborned by Philip.

Philip himself packed up, called his army, and set forth in the spring of 342 upon what he hoped would be the final campaign to break forever the resistance of the neighboring tribesmen to his rule. First we find him campaigning in the west, in Epirus and Ambracia. Then he departed for the north [1] to break the power of the Odrysian Thracians [2] (of Roumelia), the Triballians of the Danube River terrain, and the tribesmen referred to as 'Scythians' in the neighborhood of Dobrudscha. The following spring found him fighting the tribesmen of the upper Hebrus (Maritza), when news reached him that Diopithes, with the Athenian fleet, had attacked and captured his Chersonese city of Cardia and was raiding inland. Philip dispatched an immediate protest to Athens, and she publicly repudiated [3] the 'piracy' of their admiral. However, the Athenians had now awakened to the realization that Philip's intentions now included the seizure of their few remaining allied cities there, and that this, with his Carian ally across the narrow strait, would permit him to control the passage of essential grain ships [4] from the Euxine seaports, and hold the food supply of Greece subject only to his own will. This was an intolerable situation. The Athenians immediately sent an envoy to the Persian king, warning him of Philip's project and asking him to send assistance to the threatened Propontic cities. Demosthenes himself was dispatched to his old friend Leon, magistrate of Byzantium, to urge him to break off relationship with Philip and bar the city's gates to him. The Propontic cities had little love for Athens, but less for what

---

[1] Frontinus II, 8, 14; Strabo, p. 320.
[2] Demosthenes, *On the Chersonese*, Arg. 4.
[3] *Ibid.*, 28.
[4] For the importance of this grain supply, see Xenophon, *Hellenica*, 5, 1, 28; 4, 61, and Demosthenes, *On the Crown*, 87.

Philip had in store for them. Byzantium, Selymbria, and Perinthus determined to resist encroachments by the Macedonian. In the meantime Philip was busy founding three guard cities in northern Thrace to protect his newly conquered domain, one of which, Philipopolis, even yet retains the name he gave it. He then assembled another and even greater siege train than that he had employed at Olynthus, and marched south, in the spring of 340, with thirty thousand men following his standard.

Chares, the Athenian admiral, was again dispatched to the Chersonese with the fleet. In order to keep him out of the Hellespont, Philip marched into the Chersonese and seized the ports there,[1] then turned back and sat down around the walls of Perinthus (Erekli). Presently he was informed that a large number of Athenian ships were gathering near Byzantium and waiting for Chares to escort them safely through the Hellespont. Philip sent his own fleet hastily, and they seized two hundred and thirty fat and laden Athenian merchantmen. He confiscated their cargoes, seized their money, and tore up the ships to get timbers for his siege engines. Athens immediately declared war.

The siege of Perinthus marked two definite dates in world history. First, militarily epochal is the fact that here, for the first time in the ken of European historians, the planned and co-ordinated attack upon a walled city by simultaneous sap, bombardment, and assault occurred. Second, it was at this time that Philip's son, then a youth of sixteen,[2] enters our history and partakes of events in the making. Philip had sent for Alexander to join him at Perinthus, and the youngster there behaved himself so well that Philip sent him back to Macedonia with the imperial seal to act as regent. As it is obvious that Philip, before leaving Macedonia on his long-drawn-out conquest, had left the government in competent hands, Alexander found himself with little to do. He therefore initiated and carried out a short expedition against the Thracian Mardi, and after inflicting severe punishment upon them, founded in their territories a

[1] Justin, XI, 1.
[2] *Ibid.*, 1 C.

guard city and named it Alexandropolis,[1] the first of many cities named after himself he was to found in his short life.

It seems to have been during these few months of Alexander's regency that occurred the circumstances resulting in the often-told tale [2] of his reception of the Persian ambassadors at his father's court, probably sent as a result of the latter's recent treaty with the Great King. They had brought with them, considered as suitable gifts for a prince, a polo stick and ball, implements of the favorite game of Persian royalty. Alexander questioned the Persians closely on their country, its government, cities, roads, distances, topographical features, and political conditions, leaving the envoys not a little surprised at his swift intelligence and the grasp and scope of his general knowledge. Finally he picked up the presents they had brought him.

'This ball,' he said to the Persians, 'is the world, and I am the stick that will move it as it wishes.'

This attitude, surprising as it was to the Persians, was already an old story to Alexander, for Plutarch tells us that he had been prepared, through long association with Philip and his court, with purposeful knowledge of the intent some day to invade Persia, and he knew that he was destined to play a great part in that invasion. But it is doubtful if, in his wildest dreams then, he had the faintest inkling that he was to lead the army wholly, and conquer in his own right that kingdom which was so vast that no Greek had an idea of its immensity.

Meanwhile, things were going ill with Philip. The city of Perinthus was built upon a precipitous hill at the sea end of a long, narrow peninsula, and the lofty, huddled houses were built around the rock 'as in a theater.' [3] The Perinthians had constructed a strong wall across the neck of land, and Philip was perforce compelled to build and move up great towers and rams to beat it down. This was a long, slow task, and when it was accomplished the Perinthians retreated to a second wall they

---

[1] Plutarch, *Alexander*, 9. This place, somewhere in the upper Strymon Valley, has never been satisfactorily identified. Curtius (8, 1) tells the same story.

[2] Plutarch, *Alexander*, 5.   [3] Diodorus, XVI, 75.

had just completed, and the Macedonians moved up to batter it, behind a barrage of stones and arrows from their light artillery. The Perinthians stood firm, and beat off two direct assaults with heavy losses. Philip thereupon changed his tactics and divided his army into several sections, moving them up in reliefs and maintaining continuous attacks against the wall, keeping the defenders watchful and fighting day and night. Slowly, and despite the resistance of the desperate defenders, the siege engines beat down the second wall. At last a breach was made, and the Macedonians, enraged at the long futility of their assaults, rushed in, only to find the lowest tiers of houses converted into forts linked together by barricades, and there were as many barricades as there were streets. The siege had already lasted far into the summer, and the besieged were still being supplied with all the necessities of life by the ships of Byzantium from the sea side of the city. Philip was furious; he could not take the city without incurring crippling losses, and he was unable to find traitors inside whom his ever-ready gold could purchase. Also, the Athenian fleet under Chares had come up and was hanging off the Chersonese, and the satraps of Asia Minor were running guarded convoys of food, munitions, and armed men in to assist the beleaguered city.[1] Philip had foreseen this contingency long before, and had attempted to forestall it by forming a secret alliance with Hermias of Atarneus, across the Sea of Marmora, and in order to prevent any suspicion of an attempt upon Asia Minor he had also formed an open alliance with the Persian king. Unfortunately for his plans, several things had gone wrong. The defection of Hermias of Atarneus had been discovered by the Persians, and he was even then under arrest and being conveyed to Susa; his Carian ally, Pixodorus, had died and been replaced by a Persian satrap; the Great King had taken very seriously the Athenian warning of Philip's projected attack, and had issued stringent orders to the northern satraps to aid the foes of the Macedonian in every way possible.

Thinking to put an end to Byzantine assistance as the only

[1] Diodorus, XVI, 75.

way to end the resistance of the Perinthians, Philip drew off a heavy column of picked troops, moved up the coast, and assaulted Selymbria.[1] Our biographers tell us nothing beyond that, but we may assume the city fell, for immediately thereafter Philip's spears gleamed before the gates of Byzantium. The chief magistrate, Leon, who was later to be the historian of the siege, came out to parley, and asked the king what he wanted. The Macedonian, with grim jocularity, replied that he had quite fallen in love with the fair city and came to sue for her favors. The Byzantine's narrowed eyes rested upon the forbidding array of long spears behind Philip. 'But these are not lover's lutes!' he cried, and promptly re-entered the city. The place was far less strong than Perinthus, and Philip himself led the first storm, which was beaten off. The besiegers then started driving tunnels beneath the walls. The defenders built the walls stronger, and remained content to hold on and wait for help; they were not numerically strong enough to carry the fight into the open. The Macedonians decided upon a night attack, and the date was set. But as the troops were already beneath the walls one night early in the winter, a huge meteor [2] flaming through the skies showed the inhabitants the peril that was upon them. They rushed to man the walls and the storm troops retired. The Byzantines in commemoration of this event afterward raised a statue to Hecate, the Torch-Bearer, and placed upon their coinage her symbol, the crescent moon, from whence it was adopted, a thousand years later, by Islam. Again the Byzantines strengthened their walls and, like Athens of another day, even used stones from the tombs of the dead. Then the affairs of Philip came to an evil pass. The Athenian fleet broke through the blockade of Philip's vessels, entered the Sea of Marmora, and fortified a near-by island against the Macedonians, Chares being replaced in command by Phocion. The new satrap of Caria sailed into the Hellespont with all the ships of Rhodes, Cos, and Chios, and the news got around that they were there for the

---

[1] Demosthenes mentions this attack in his oration, *On the Crown.*

[2] Hesychius Milesius, 27.

purpose of transporting an army of Persians into Thrace; and all Greece was abuzz with talk of war. Philip realized he had taken on more than he could handle; he reluctantly gave up, lifted the siege, and retired inland.

The year before, a powerful chieftain in northern Thrace had appealed to Philip for assistance in beating off an army of raiding Scythians from north of the Danube, and Philip had dispatched a force to his assistance. However, the Scythians had drawn off, and when Philip's detachment arrived, the chief had not only refused to pay them, but had, on the plea of poverty, even refused to supply them with rations for their return trip. Philip now sent a messenger to the chief saying that he was coming north. The startled chief promptly asked why, and Philip replied that he had vowed to set up a statue of Heracles at the mouth of the Ister (Danube) River. 'Send it to me,' said the chief, 'and I will set it up.' 'But it must be guaranteed inviolate,' replied Philip, marching steadily nearer. 'If you set it up without my permission I will melt it into arrowheads and return it to you thus,' replied the chief. Philip maintained a running fire of sardonic messages until he reached the chief's country, fell upon it, and captured thousands of head of livestock and a great number of slaves. Satisfied with the result of the raid, and with his colossal vanity, badly injured at the Propontus, slightly soothed, he turned homeward. In the Haemus (Balkan) Mountains the Triballi in turn fell upon the Macedonians, captured all their spoil, and wounded Philip himself in the thigh so seriously that for a time his life was despaired of. The king returned to Pella to permit his wound to heal, and chew the cud of bitter reflection over the worst military setback he had ever received.

ALEXANDER
THE BOY

The mating of Philip and Olympias was unhappy for all concerned. It was later said (probably by fictioneers and romancers) that upon the night of the consummation of their union the skies were filled with portents and warnings; and on the stormy night in October when Alexander was born, the sanctuary of the great temple of Artemis (equated in the Hellenic mind with Diana) in Ephesus went up in flames. Though theirs was a love match at the outset, both Philip and Olympias had too many traits in common, and too many others widely at variance, to permit of continued happiness. Both were ambitious, aggressive, and energetic in attaining their own ends; both were headstrong, willful, and fiercely inimical to any outside control, but in different ways. Philip possessed tireless energy and iron will, but he was cool, craftily sagacious, capable of limitless dissemblance and patience when necessary, never in a hurry and never at a loss; completely the master of his emotions at all times, planning with farsighted calculation long in advance of expected results, then driving for them, circuitously if need be, but with indomitable tenacity keeping his goal always in view. The queen, on the other hand, was temperamental and impetuous, a woman of fire and brimstone, of barbaric and unbridled temper, superstitious to a degree, whose passionately ardent nature found its fullest expression in the wild ecstasies of the secret bacchanalia of the Orphic and Dionysiac rites to which she was addicted.

Alexander as a child grew up in the women's quarters, having little contact with the world of men, least of all with his warrior father, during the earlier years of his life. He was committed to the care of a nurse, Lanice (probably an affectionate diminutive of Hellanice), becoming the playmate of her young brother Clitus (called Melas, 'The Black'), his faithful friend who was to save his life at the battle of the Granicus, and whom, still later, he was to murder in a drunken rage. Another friend was Lanice's son, Proteas, with whom we see him consorting, years later, in Babylon. He was passionately fond of his mother, and was, both now and until the day of his death, a worn and paranoid ruler of half the earth at the age of thirty-two, a mother's boy, always exhibiting the greatest attachment for her. It was from her that he received that swift warmth of nature which attached him so strongly to whom he considered his friends; obscured his accuracy of judgment of the many who afterward betrayed him or his trust, though he treated them with generosity that almost ruined his empire's finances; and not infrequently manifested itself, as with Olympias, in the demoniac outbursts of temper we read about later. He seems to have far less of the canny shrewdness of his father than of the impulsive ebullience of his mother, and as he grows older, the little canniness he inherited is overlaid with other qualities. From Olympias, too, he received that deeply religious sentiment which we find later driving him in awe far beyond the bounds of mere form observance; once we even find him devastating a city for the privilege of worshiping at her shrine; again we find him utterly extirpating the inhabitants of another city for what he deemed a religious crime committed by their ancestors over eight-score years before.

Alexander's early life no doubt followed the pattern of that of the ordinary Greek boy of that age. For the first six years he had the run of the women's quarters, played with hoop and ball, and probably spent many of his winter evenings listening in childish wonder to the stories handed down by legend and tradition from an earlier age as history. At the beginning of his seventh year he was entrusted to the care of a man called a pedagogue, perhaps, as usual, an elderly and respectable male slave, not as a teacher, but more in the capacity of a monitor, to teach him manners and to keep him out of mischief. Alexander's pedagogue, one Lysimachus, was, by one reference we have to him, a mental mediocrity, yet we are surprised later to read an anecdote showing he was with Alexander on his Persian campaign, at least as far as Phoenicia. In Alexander's case more, of course, was done than was usual with the children of the common people. The services of a certain Leonidas, a man of the royal house of Epirus and a relative of his mother, were obtained as his tutor. Leonidas was no doubt an efficient teacher, but he was also a harsh and austere man and a stern disciplinarian. Under his tutelage Alexander received the best education obtainable in those days (Aeschines tells us that Alexander as a boy of ten recited from the *Iliad* to him and Demosthenes, at the time of the Athenian embassy to Pella), but it would seem a not inconsiderable part of his education stressed the physical side, for we are told that he was subjected to a Spartan regimen, and taught to endure hardship and privation and abhor luxury. Plutarch says:

> He was extremely temperate in eating and drinking, as is particularly illustrated by what he said to Ada — the one whom he dignified by the title of 'mother' and established as Queen of Caria. She, as a friendly attention, used, it seems, to send him daily not only meats and cakes, but went so far, finally, as to send him the cleverest cooks and bakers she could find. These, however, Alexander could find no use for. Better cooks he had already — those

his tutor Leonidas had given him; namely, as breakfast cook one named All-Night-Tramp, and as dinner cook one Lightweight Breakfast. 'Why!' said he, 'that man Leonidas would go and unlock my chests where I kept my blankets and clothes, and look in them to see that my mother had not given me anything I did not really need, or that conduced to luxury or indulgence.'

Leonidas thus instilled into him those precepts and attitudes eminently suited to a prince of the poverty-ridden mountainous kingdom of his native Epirus, or to the warlike young Macedonian prince who as king a few years later was to drag his invading and conquering army thousands of miles across mountains, plains, and deserts toward what he believed was the boundary of the world. The natural tendency of Alexander toward lavishness was checked, and Leonidas seems to have leaned to the petty side of being economical. In fact, the tutor laid himself open to the charge, made by later historical students, that he carried his spare severity too far, creating in the boy a like mental conditioning, making him harsh, willful, arbitrary, and imperious.

Sometime during Alexander's childhood — some believe the year after his own birth — Olympias bore another child, a girl named Cleopatra. She was destined to be an important *raison d'être*, the unhappy focus around whom were played important events, tragic and epochal for the kingdom of Macedonia.

When he was ten years old, in 346, the peace-seeking deputation from Athens, including Demosthenes and Aeschines, came to Pella to wait upon Philip, and it was here that Demosthenes' opinion of the boy was formed, an opinion which caused him, later, to sneer at the young king and call him a simpleton. Alexander, at the age of ten, may well have given that impression. Unhealthily dominated, physically by Leonidas, mentally and morally by his Bacchante mother, he lived a joyless and unreal life, his boy's perspective warped by his preceptors. We have seen what Leonidas did to him; his magic-loving mother made him accompany her to the sacrifices at the temples, there to study the art of augury and forecasting, the most common of which was the studious inspection of the entrails of the sacrificed victims, which, by their coloring and convolutions, were supposed to be as a written message betraying the wills of the gods. Demosthenes later said he spent all his time either at his studies or the gruesome practice of divination, probably continually under his mother's tutelage. Anything to keep him away from the society of the court, the courtiers, and his hard-drinking, hard-fighting warrior father, from whom Olympias had been long estranged. Thus Demosthenes can hardly be blamed for assuming that 'as the twig is bent so the tree is inclined,' for the boy must have impressed him at that age as a pious little prig.

There can be little doubt, too, that his jealous and violent mother must have not only told him, but firmly impressed upon his plastic mind, her own version of facts which were popular scandals at the court. Olympias, as an Epirian, was a devotee of the Zeus of Dodona in Epirus, and the Epirian Zeus was reputed — as I have said, we have no concern with the accuracy of a belief, but much with the fact that it was believed — to be another manifestation of the Egyptian god Ammon. Thus the two gods were, it might be said, interchangeable. She was also a fanatical devotee to the rites of the Cabiri, Orpheus and Dionysus, the rites of whom seem to have been largely based upon sexual indulgence. At any rate, the chastity of any woman devotee to the cults could be looked upon with well-grounded suspicion. Also, in the heroic past, it had been said to be not uncommon for the gods themselves to father, upon a mortal woman, usually a queen, a son and heir of knightly deeds. And one of the forms in which the god accustomedly appeared was in the form of a great snake, a habit to which Zeus-Ammon, the god of fecundity, was legendarily addicted. He was the god whose powers were manifested in thunderbolts, shooting stars, and whose voice was heard in the trees in a high wind. Afterward, they tell us, that on the night before her wedding Olympias dreamed that a thunderbolt shot from heaven and speared deep into her body, setting her on fire. Though a modern psychologist could easily explain the meaning of such a dream, to the young Bacchante, with her erratic brain filled with mysticism and religious fervor, it could mean only one thing: that the Zeus who was also Ammon was taking a direct and very personal interest in her. The night afterward, it is said, Philip had also a dream, in which he sealed up his wife's body with a seal whereon was the head of a lion. Olympias had no doubt told Philip of her dream and the combination of the two seemed, to Philip, to require an explanation. This was found in the court soothsayer, Aristander, who pointed out that one does not seal an empty receptacle, hence it was a warning that Olympias was pregnant and would be the mother of a lion-hearted son.

Legend further states that Philip once peered through a chink in his wife's door and to his horror saw her in bed with a large snake — in other words, mystically the god again.[1] 'Whether it was that he feared her as a witch,' says Plutarch, 'or believed her to be having relations with some god, and so deemed himself less acceptable, he grew less and less pleased with their intercourse.' Philip soon grew suspicious, not only of Olympias' chastity; but, with the naïve superstition of the day, he seems to have accepted as fact that the snake really was Ammon. His ardor cooled quickly and he soon began to stray into other fields, apparently taking other wives and mistresses by the dozen.[2] We have records of at least six other women who bore him children. This in turn angered Olympias, and as Philip continued flouting her, in after years her hatred of him became a devouring flame. And it seems she in turn taught Alexander to hate the roistering, quarrelsome, hard-drinking king.

When Alexander was about thirteen years old, Philip recognized the necessity of curbing certain undesirable tendencies in the lad. He was high-strung and emotional, prone to fits of ungovernable rage, a precocious genius, headstrong and willful as his parents, and equally inimical to any curb laid upon him

[1] Remember it was an article of faith with all that Olympias herself was a descendant of the *echis* (snake) born Achilles, whose mother was the sea-nymph Thetis.

[2] Athenaeus, XIII, 557.

by anybody. He would accept only guidance, but would rebel at authority. But though he was energetic and self-willed, it was a will indicative of precocious intelligence and inventiveness rather than simple stubbornness. He was a thoroughgoing aristocratic young snob, utterly and sublimely convinced of his superiority to all others, but he had the intelligent faculty of admitting error when it was pointed out to him. Illustrative of his general caliber is the accepted account of his acquisition of his famous horse Bucephalus. The context is such that he could scarcely have been over thirteen years old.

Philonicus of Thessaly had offered to sell his horse Bucephalus to Philip for thirteen talents. So they all went down to the plain to try the animal. He proved, however, to be balky and utterly useless. He would let no one mount him, and none of the attendants of Philip could make him hear to him, but he violently resisted them all. Philip, in his disgust, ordered the horse led away as utterly wild and untrained. Whereat Alexander, who was present, said: 'That is too good a horse for these men to spoil that way, simply because they haven't the skill or grit to handle him right.' At first Philip paid no attention to him, but as he kept insisting on being heard, and seemed greatly disturbed about the matter, Philip said to him: 'What do you mean by criticizing your elders, as if you were wiser than they, or knew so much more about handling a horse than they do?' 'Well, this horse, anyway, I would handle better than anyone else, if they would give me the chance.' 'In case you don't succeed,' rejoined his father, 'what penalty are you willing to pay for your forwardness?' 'I'll pay, by Zeus, the price of the horse.' Laughter greeted the answer, but after bantering with his father about the money arrangements, he went straight to the horse, took him by the bridle, and turned him toward the sun. This he did on the theory that the horse's fright was due to seeing his own shadow dancing up and down on the ground before him.⁶ He then ran along by his side awhile, patting and coaxing him, until, seeing he was full of fire and spirit and impatient to go, he quietly threw off his cloak, and swinging himself up, he sat securely astride of the horse. Then he guided him about for a while with the reins, without striking him or jerking at the bit. When he saw the horse was getting over his nervousness and was eager to gallop ahead, he let him go, driving him on with a sterner voice, and kicks of the foot. In the group of onlookers about Philip there prevailed from the first the silence of an intensely anxious concern. But when the boy turned the horse and came galloping up to them with pride and joy in his face, they all burst into cheers. His father, they say, in his excitement kissed him on the head, and cried: 'My son, seek thee a kingdom suited to thy powers; Macedonia is too strait for thee.' [1]

Bucephalus became the property of Alexander, and his inseparable companion. He was taken, it was said, on all his campaigns, and was usually the horse he rode in battle. It was also said the horse himself would allow no one else to mount him, all other riders being deemed unworthy. Arrian says he was a magnificent black charger, of a solid color save for a white spot on his forehead. Alexander was extremely fond of the animal. Once, while in the lands of the Uxii, a notoriously thievish tribe living in the mountains east of the Persian capital of Susa, the horse disappeared. The conqueror grimly had it proclaimed that if Bucephalus were not returned within a specified time he would massacre every man, woman, and child in the tribe. The horse was returned immediately, illustrating not only Alexander's regard for his mount, but also the Uxiian's dread of its owner. Bucephalus died many years later in central India, and a town was raised at that point and named after him.

When Alexander was about thirteen years old, Philip recognized the necessity of curbing or eradicating certain undesirable tendencies which had become manifest in the boy. He had already learned all that could be taught him by a simple teacher and instructor; that is, reading, writing, the more elementary mathematics, music. Now he needed a tutor who could pass Philip's strict requirements as a teacher of a future king, one who was to take over the empire he intended to create. Such a man was ready, and his services had already been bespoken. The man was Aristotle, prize pupil of the great Plato who had

[1] Plutarch, *Alexander.*

died only some five or six years before, and a boyhood friend of Philip himself. Aristotle was the son of Nicomachus, court physician to Amyntas II, Philip's father. The physician had died in 367, and the boy Aristotle was sent off to a school of philosophy in Athens about the same time the boy Philip was taken as a hostage to the city of Thebes. There seems to have been a curious friendship and regard of long standing between the two men, the brawling, drunken soldier and the quietly studious philosopher. They had maintained their friendship through the period of more than twenty-five years since they had last parted. Thus we have a letter purporting to be genuine, dating from 356 B.C., from Philip to Aristotle, handed down to us. It reads: [1]

'This is to let you know a son is born to me, for which I am thankful to the gods, not only at the birth of the child, but because he is born in your time; for I am hoping that he will ultimately be your pupil and that he will prove worthy of us and of succession to the throne.'

After Plato's death in 347, Aristotle had gone to live at the court of Hermias, lord of Atarneus and Assos, in the Troad, a district in northwestern Asia Minor. He had married the niece and adopted daughter of Hermias, and had probably been not a little responsible for the treaty of friendship Hermias and Philip had made shortly before the latter's attack upon the cities of the Propontus. Hermias had been somehow betrayed to the Persian authorities, captured, and taken to Susa, where he had been tortured to force from him a revelation of Philip's plans. Despite the torture, Hermias refused to confess, and was finally crucified by the exasperated Persians for his failure to betray his Macedonian ally.[2] Aristotle fled to Mitylene on the island of Lesbos, and it was there that Philip's letter found him. He was obviously the ideal preceptor to guide the thought-processes of the young prince. He was a deep thinker, who, however, as a

---

[1] The authenticity of this letter has been frequently questioned. Quoted by Aulus Gellius, *Noctes Atticae*, IX.

[2] See W. Jäeger, *Aristoteles, Grundlegung einer Geschichte seiner Entwicklung*, 1923, p. 113 ff.

friend of Philip, would be biased in favor of royalty; thus in teaching the boy he would instill into him the desirability of cultivating those faculties and habits of thought conducing him toward preparation to assuming the succession from his father, and to cause him unconsciously to pull away from the hovering maternalism and superstitious occultism of Olympias. That he failed in the latter course, as we see later, is no disparagement of the tutor, but testimony only that by that time Alexander's mind had been firmly molded in the fashion she had set. Aristotle was a man of the world, a lover of good food and wine, perfectly at ease in any social set, and a representative of the culture and intellectuality Philip so greatly admired in the Athenians. Withal he was only about forty years old, and had already begun to become known in the Greek world as a worthy successor to the famous Plato.

A school was prepared for Aristotle in the little village of Mieza, near the border of Thessaly, away from the noise and intrigues of the busy court. Plutarch tells us that in his time, five centuries later, the Grove of Nymphs and the great stone chair where Aristotle sat when he taught were still shown to visitors as the main attraction of the place. He stayed there eight years, then removed to Athens, and there, as Alexander had just mounted the throne of Macedonia and the tide of pro-Macedonianism was running high, he established his famous *peripatetic* (walking) school of the Lyceum, in the eastern suburbs of Athens. Alexander stayed at Mieza three, or possibly nearly four, years, for we have already seen him, at the age of sixteen, taking over the regency of Macedonia for several months then. That we have no documentary evidence of what Alexander was taught there is true, but from what we know Aristotle taught others, and wrote, we can draw a fairly exact parallel. He had a decided inclination toward theories of government [1] even then,

---

[1] If we analyze Aristotle's *Politics* closely, bearing in mind the innate inconsistencies and contradictions of the work, it seems to fall into two categories, first, Books II, III, VII, VIII, these covering his philosophy of the Ideal State; and Books I, IV, V, VI, covering what seems to be a more latterly formulated, empiric theory of constitutions. That there are sustainable objections to this arbitrary classification is true, among the

and had already formulated much of the material he later wrote into his *Politics* and other works. It can be safely assumed that he taught his pupils, especially Alexander, much of his own political philosophy, part of which [1] was a matter of faith with him: that united Greece could conquer the world, a theme often reverted to and reiterated in his writings. It would seem to be but natural that Aristotle, as master and tutor, strove to inculcate in his pupil not only what he as a teacher desired, but also what his generous patron Philip, aware of the growing estrangement sedulously fostered between him and his son by the boy's termagant mother, had perhaps insisted upon. Alexander had, from early childhood, fully intended some day to succeed his father in the kingship of Macedonia and Thrace, and to rule before that time as regent of the countries, when his father should carry the Macedonian arms across the Hellespont into Asia Minor, and perhaps even farther. Plato, teacher of Aristotle, had preached [2] that all barbarians (that is, non-Greeks) were enemies by nature, and that it was the moral right of all Greeks to wage war upon them, enslave them, or exterminate them. Aristotle, who had lived among the people of the southern Propontic coasts and the territories of Hermias, carried his hatred of them to the point of virulence,[3] and he so stated in his

most obvious being the complexity of Book III, and the inseparability of its contents with Book IV. There are others, too, but overingenious hair-splitting will serve no purpose here. It would seem, and others are in substantial agreement (Werner Jäeger, *Aristoteles*, etc.; and the English translation by Richard Robinson, Oxford, 1934; see also analysis of Professor Jäeger's work by E. Barker, *Classical Review*, XLV, 1931, and Kelsen, *Zeitschrift für öffentliches Recht*, XIII, 1923, p. 625 ff., that the former group were meditated upon, and very possibly written, at Assos and Mitylene in the period from 347 to 343. It has been suggested that Books III and IV had their genesis while Aristotle was in Macedonia and are the result of the undigested impact of the court of Pella upon their author. The second classification seems to be a product of his Athenian period. It is odd that the whole work was not retained by its author until completion, and thus have avoided the charge of inconsistency. For a contrary view to that expressed above, see von Arnim, *Zur Entstehungsgeschichte der aristotelischen Politik*, Sitzungberichte Wien, 1924.

[1] Aristotle, *Politics*, 1327b, p. 29 ff.

[2] Plato, *Republic*, V, 470C–471A.

[3] Ehrenburg, *Alexander and the Greeks*. Also Diehl, *Fragmenta Historicorum Graecorum*, frag. 3.

Politics,[1] repeating after Plato that they were natural slaves without any of the qualities entitling them to freedom. His ideal state envisioned a small body of aristocratic Greeks governing and exploiting a great body of non-citizens without civic rights,[2] beneath them, exactly the status under which Thebes, Athens, and, notoriously, Sparta, even in that illiberal period, existed. In Book III, dealing with the kingship, Aristotle described the king as one born to be a leader, pre-eminent in virtue above all others, 'for injustice will not be done to the superiors, if they are reckoned only as equal to those who are far inferior to them in *arete* [manly virtue] and in political capacity. Such a one may truly be deemed a god among men.' Elsewhere we find him speaking of such a king as 'governing as a god, and governed by none, not even by the Law.'

We have definite proof that Aristotle also infused into the mind of his pupil a keen interest and an inquiring attitude of mind regarding at least several of the sciences, and that great advances were made in human knowledge during his Asiatic adventures by the scientific and other specialists he took along with him to study their discoveries on the spot. During his expedition he used to send back reports on various subjects to his former teacher, notable among which was that explanation, sent from Egypt, regarding the strange periodicity of the Nile floods. Seemingly in response to a suggestion by Aristotle, Alexander placed a number of scientifically minded men throughout his conquered Asiatic territories to send the sage reports of their studies, and the sum of eight hundred talents was placed at his disposal for furthering the inquiries. This subsidy, and the data gathered by Alexander's men, resulted in the completion of Aristotle's monumental work on *Natural History*.

Two letters, presumably passed between them, are handed down to us. In one Alexander is protesting: 'You have not done

---

[1] Aristotle, *Politics*, 1, 8, 1256b, 1, 25. Also Plutarch, *Moralia*, 349B.

[2] W. W. Tarn, *Alexander and the Unity of Mankind*, British Academy, XIX, 1933. Aristotle was no doubt familiar with this system; he must have known it was the situation of the Pedieis at Priene; the Gergithes at Miletus; the Mariandyni at Heracleia; and the Phrygians at Zeleia, in Asia Minor.

well to publish your oral instructions in book form, for what is there now that we excel others in, if those matters in which we have been particularly instructed be laid open to all? For my part, I assure you, I would rather excel others in knowledge of what is transcendant than in the extent of my power and dominion.' The gist of another letter, this time from Aristotle to Alexander, is given us by Eratosthenes through Strabo: [1] 'He counseled him to be a hegemon to the Greeks and a despot to the barbarians; to look upon the former as friends and relatives, and to deal with the latter as with beasts or plants.' It was later said, however, that Alexander disregarded this advice, and made only the distinction between good and bad men regardless of race. The friendship between the two began to cool at last; whether, as some consider, as a result of Alexander's treatment of Aristotle's nephew Callisthenes (*q.v.*, chapter 11), or that the philosopher was gradually estranged by the reports sent back by and of Alexander in Asia, is immaterial, and grounds only for conjecture.

Alexander must have left his preceptor in the spring of 339 or before, for we have already seen him during that summer joining his father at the siege of Perinthus, then taking over the regency of Macedonia and starting a war of his own. About this time, or perhaps a bit earlier, we have a story of a clash between Philip and Alexander which illustrates the hypothesis that Philip and Olympias were estranged and at enmity toward each other, and is partial confirmation of the assumption that Olympias was striving to alienate father and son. That the two fiery parents had come to the separation point long before can be accepted as a foregone conclusion. Philip's notorious incontinence and amours cannot have failed to rouse the beautiful and passionate Olympias to fury many times, and ultimately to a complete break in conjugal relationship. Anyhow, Olympias now hates Philip, and is suspicious and revengeful.

It seems that Pixodorus, the Prince of Caria, with whom Philip had made alliance and who was privy to his plan to invade

[1] *Fragmenta Historicorum Graecorum*, 658.

Persia, desiring to further cement the alliance, proposed marriage between his daughter and Arrhidaeus, the son of Philip by Philinna, a Thessalian dancing-girl who had caught Philip's passing fancy. Naturally the proposal became known to Olympias, who saw in it a possible plot against Alexander's right to the succession, and suggested to him that the reason for the marriage was to provide another heir to Philip's throne. To forestall this, Alexander in his own right hurriedly sent a delegation to Pixodorus, proposing the girl marry himself rather than Arrhidaeus, whom he called a 'bastard and a fool,' the latter being also true, as Arrhidaeus is known to have been a half-wit. The overjoyed Carian, who had never dared aim so high as the heir apparent, naturally immediately notified Philip of the proposal. The king flew into a rage, ordered his son's messenger returned home in bonds, and banished five of Alexander's boy friends whom he believed to be privy to the scheme, if not actually active co-conspirators. These were recalled by Alexander immediately upon his accession to the throne: the club-footed Harpalus, later to be appointed treasurer of the empire at Babylon, and fated to betray his trust; the hook-nosed Ptolemy, son of Lagus,[1] who was to become one of Alexander's boon companions, commander, and later king of Egypt; Nearchus, boon companion, commander of cavalry, and admiral of the fleet from India to the Euphrates; Erigyius, who was given command of the auxiliary cavalry and is mentioned for the brilliance of his action at the battle of Arbela, and in far Aria; and his brother, Lacedemon (or Laodemon), who was made provost marshal of the prisoners taken in Asia. Philip then took Alexander aside and read him a harsh lesson in political statesmanship, reproving him, a prince of Macedonia, for even considering marrying into the family of a man who, powerful and wealthy though he might be, was nevertheless still only a vassal to a barbarian king. This incident must, of necessity,

---

[1] Arrian (J. Rooke's translation, p. xciv) makes the statement that Arsinoe, mother of Ptolemy, when with child by Philip, was married by him to Lagus; this, if true, makes Ptolemy half-brother to Alexander.

have occurred before the sieges of Perinthus and Byzantium, for Pixodorus had died before that, and was succeeded by Orontobates,[1] son-in-law of the powerful Persian nobleman who was to ascend the throne of Persia in the spring of 336 as Darius III. Philip forgave the indiscretion, but Olympias' influence remained paramount. It is possible that their disagreement dated back several years earlier, for Plutarch tells us that once when Philip, in one of his wars, captured a city, Alexander is reported to have exclaimed bitterly to one of his playmates, 'My father will have everything worth while, and I shall have nothing left to conquer with you that shall be worth anything.' Whether filial animus can be read into that statement probably rests with the reader. It might be construed simply as a remark to be expected from a hero-worshiping boy unduly influenced by stories of the heroic ages, or it may have been the result of a deliberate campaign on the part of Olympias to alienate father and son. Philip's final break with Olympias came in the year 337, when Philip became enamored of a young woman named Cleopatra. Arrian says she was sister to Attalus (Plutarch says his niece; Arrian is probably correct), one of his most trusted commanders, and son-in-law to the sixty-year-old general Parmenio. Apparently Philip was not to be permitted to treat her as he had many other girls, use her and move on to a new love; she must be married legally and recognized as the queen. Olympias was promptly put aside, and many of his friends at court began to have dark forebodings of Alexander's future; and, probably as a result of Olympias' suspicious watchfulness over his interests, Alexander, too, shared the feelings of his friends. At the wedding feast, Attalus became very drunk, so far that he forgot to be cautious, and arose proposing that the Macedonians pray to the gods for a legitimate heir, issue of Cleopatra, to succeed Philip. Alexander sprang up in a towering rage and hurled his cup into Attalus' face, shouting: 'Why, traitor, what am I? Do you take me for a bastard?' Philip rose to his feet in anger and drew his sword, but was too drunk to

---

[1] Sometimes written 'Othontopates.'

stand, and fell between the couches. Alexander, reading aright
his father's intent to do him violence, sneered to the assembled
Macedonians: 'Look! Here is the man that would go out of
Europe into Asia, yet stepping from one couch to another, you
see him laid flat on the floor!'

Olympias and Alexander, unable to tolerate longer the slight
put upon them by Philip, left for Epirus, which Alexander soon
left for Illyria. Here he remained until one of Philip's advisers,
Demeratus of Corinth (whom we next meet at the battle of the
Granicus), prevailed upon him to recall the boy and effect a
reconciliation. Olympias, however, remained implacable in her
bitter hatred of Philip, and endeavored to induce her brother,
Alexander the Molossian, now king of Epirus, to make war
against him.

Alexander was now grown to the swift maturity of a southern
climate and long accustomed to the forcing atmosphere of a busy
and intriguing court. He was of average height, but with the
physique of an Olympian athlete, and Plutarch, who saw the
Lysippean portraits and read works now lost to us, tells us that
he was famous in his day for the beauty of his face. His skin
was soft, white, and clear; his large blue eyes were what the
Greeks called 'moist,' his lips full, and his head crowned with
a mass of wavy blond hair. We are further told that he habitually carried his head slightly inclined toward the left shoulder,[1]
a trait copied by many of his emulators long after his death.
Not only, unfortunately, was he beautiful in face and figure,
but he was fully aware of, and vain,[2] about it, for he would
permit only Apelles the painter to portray him in color, and the
sculptor Lysippus in bronze. In the portrait busts we see of him
in the Louvre and the British Museum, we note especially the
eyes deep sunk under heavy brows, the full and ardent face, and
the curving sensuous lips. The effect upon the beholder is such

[1] According to Doctor A. Dechambre, *Review of Archeology*, ser. 1, IX, this habitual
pose was the result of torticollis, atrophy of the sterno-mastoid muscle of the right side.

[2] See C. L. Pierce. 'The Unconscious Motives Underlying the Actions of Alexander
the Great, etc. The Narcism of Alexander,' *Psychoanalytic Review*, X, 56–69.

as to create grave doubts either of the veracity or the accuracy of the knowledge of our ancient biographers who hold up Alexander to us as a model of sexual chastity in a day when such continence would have been regarded as a shocking deviation from normal behavior, and of a handsome young prince who could find desirable the impalpable arms of solitude.

His physique was, however, not deceptive. We are told that he was so swift of foot that Philip once asked him if he would care to participate in the races at the Olympic games. 'Yes,' replied Alexander, 'if I may have only the sons of kings as my antagonists,' meaning he would contest only with those he considered his equals. Utterly and sublimely convinced of his own superiority above all others of more common clay, it is surprising that he should realize the necessity of continuing his training to keep himself in physical perfection. But Plutarch tells us that if he was on a march which did not demand haste, he would exercise on the way, practicing archery, or leaping in and out of his chariot going at top speed, or on and off his galloping horse. It is also of interest to note that he held the purely professional athlete in disdain. When he was being shown the statues of the Olympian victors set up at Miletus, he inquired ironically, 'Where were all these famous physiques when the barbarians were besieging your city?'

His swift intellect recognized its own brilliance and his own genuine superiority, yet it is only after long years, during which he swept over the face of the earth like a destroying angel, that we find other than a boy who understands little of what he knows (for between knowing and understanding there is a great gulf), and that there is more than a glimmer of real and human understanding. And by then we find the hard brilliance of his intellect dulling and clouding under the long hardships and the many wounds he has suffered, and his participation in the orgies of Greece and the vices of the East.

III

PHILIP AND
ALEXANDER

THE winter of 339–338 passed while Philip nursed his wounded leg in Pella and kept his military staff laboring furiously to prepare the army to answer a call he received late in the autumn, perhaps even before his return, calling him forth again to war. The Amphictyonic Council had summoned him to chastise a refractory city in the bounds of Hellas, a call for which Philip had prepared long and carefully.

He knew, before he marched into Thrace, that it would not be long before that region, so necessary to the fulfillment of his plans, would be in his hands. He had, however, not reckoned upon the defeat he had sustained around the walls of the Pro-pontic cities. But, no doubt, as soon as his army had disappeared from those walls, his equally efficacious 'golden army' under command of his agents would bring him by peaceful means what he had attempted to secure by force. He had secured his hold upon Thrace. All that now remained was to obtain an equally firm footing within the boundaries of Hellas, and soon that too would be his own. But he must get that footing by legal means; forcible and unrequested armed invasion and an attempt to coerce Athens would probably mean the beginning of a Hellenic war; and he knew that if such a war occurred, his ally Thebes was too untrustworthy to depend upon. However, great men are those who are swift to grasp and utilize every advantage, and Philip possessed one valuable coign of vantage. He was president of the Amphictyonic Council, with all the prestige that exalted office carried; and he had active agents working for him in all the cities of Greece. It seems they finally found for him both a reason to be called into Greece and a way to bring about that call.

At the upper end of the bay of Crissa (Salona), on the northern shore of the Gulf of Corinth, lay the small fortified town of Cirrha, seaport of Crissa and landing-place of the numerous pilgrims who came by sea to visit the famous shrine of Apollo at near-by Delphi. The shrine had been famous for centuries, and the heavy pilgrim traffic made the little seaport wealthy, to the envy of less favored neighbors. Envy and jealousy, as usual, led to war as early as the sixth century. The result was that in order to remove from the vicinity such a fertile cause of strife, after the First Sacred War, the lands occupied by the people of Cirrha, clear back to the town of Crissa, had been cleared and dedicated to the Delphian god, the ancient consecration being pronounced that it should be 'forever unoccupied, untilled and uncultivated by man.' But man must eat, and even in those days Greece was a poor land and overpopulated. The portentous pronouncement had been permitted to lapse, and colonists from the neighboring town of Amphissa had rebuilt and reoccupied the city, the consecration being conveniently forgotten. During the Second Sacred War of 356–347 the people of Cirrha had allied themselves with the Thebans against the Phocian despoilers of Delphi and had suffered raids and oppressions from them. Naturally, therefore, as friends of Thebes they were hostile to Athens, which had maintained, if not friendship, at least tolerance of the Phocian sacrilege.

In Athens the *demos*, convinced that Philip was due to descend upon them next, feverishly prepared for war. They repealed an ancient and hampering law decreeing that all surplus state funds and income should be used for the Festival Fund and earmarked it for war. They hastily assembled a new fleet, armed and manned it, and piled up materials of war. So busy were they that they neglected to fathom fully the intent of the Amphictyonic Council, which was due to meet soon. It met in February, 339, at Delphi. Almost at once the Amphissian representative, covertly urged on by the Thebans, made a violent attack upon Athens for having rededicated at Delphi the shield trophies of Plataea before the temple was purified from contamination by the Phocian invaders, and declared the Athenians should be barred from the sacred precincts as punishment for the advocacy of the Phocian cause. Aeschines, one of the Athenian representatives present, immediately arose and in an impassioned speech pointed out that the Amphissian represented a city far more guilty of sacrilege, for it was her colonists who occupied even then the land long since consecrated to the god and his temple. Aeschines' speech must have been very good indeed, for indignation instantly ran high. The next day the Delphians trooped down to the sea and completely destroyed the little port city, but on their way home again the wrathful Amphissians fell upon and routed them.

This new complication called for further discussion, and an extraordinary meeting of the council was called to convene at Thermopylae.

When Aeschines returned to Athens and reported, the first reaction was one of elation that the tables had been so neatly turned upon the Amphissians, but shortly someone, with considerable political acumen and analytical ability, grew suspicious that danger lurked behind the meeting of the Amphictyonic Council. Both Athens and Thebes resolved not to attend the next. With these two cities absent from the council, the meeting was practically packed with Macedonian sympathizers. When the vote was taken, these saw to it that the Thessalian president *pro tem*, who was Philip's creature and acting in his name, was charged with the duty of seeing that the guilty Amphissians were punished. The members of the council raised a small army of mercenaries and sent them forth, but the Amphissians handled them rather roughly. The mercenaries failed to push the matter strongly, with the result that when the autumn meeting assembled little or nothing had been accomplished by them. Thus it was that someone proposed that, as proper diligence had not been shown in prosecuting the orders of the august council, Philip, the Macedonian, be called in to take over the duties the mercenaries had failed to perform. The proposal was carried and voted upon, and, as has been shown, the formal invitation went north asking Philip to enter the heart of Greece with his army. The sequel to the call was to be so important that many historians, taking into cognizance Philip's Machiavellian diplomatic cleverness and careful and unscrupulous planning, accuse him of being the prime mover, under cover, of the request. The setup of the council was such that it seems to this commentator a virtually inescapable conclusion. However, whether this is true or not, Philip eagerly seized upon it as the opportunity for which he had been waiting for, lo, these many years, a legal request and a legitimate reason for a military invasion of Hellas. Hence the activity in Macedonia that winter, assembling supplies and materials for the army and preparations for its movements in the spring.

Philip marched south through his province of Thessaly.

Here was the situation. The road from Macedonia, then as today, ran south from Lamia across the Sperchius (Hellada) River to Heracleia Tracheia. It divided there, one road branching east along the seacoast, passing through Nicaea and Thermopylae, thence over the ridge of Mount Callidromus and down into Phocis, the valley of the Cephissus (Mavropotamo) River, where the site of Elatea commanded the Paropotami Pass, at which point the ridge of Parnassus met the riverbank. Beyond the pass lay Boeotia, Thebes, the Copaic lake and plain, and still farther the Cithaeron Range and Athens. The second road from Heracleia Tracheia crossed the upper valley of the Cephissus (today the highroad follows the same route), ran through the gorge where Cytinium (modern Gravia) lay, and on to Amphissa, Delphi, and the Crissean bay. This road branched again in the Cephissus valley and the branch followed the valley down to the Paropotami, to rejoin the Thermopylae road there.

Had Philip planned only to obey the behest of the Amphictyonic Council, he would, and should, have gone straight to Amphissa from Heracleia Tracheia. Instead he turned eastward from there to Thermopylae. At Nicaea he replaced the Theban garrison with his own men and marched on to Elatea, which he himself had destroyed six years earlier in his punitive expeditions against the Phocians. He immediately put the army to rebuilding and refortifying the site as a base of operations dominating Phocis and the valley north of the pass. He seems to have waited several days, then sent an embassy to Thebes, asking them to abandon their alliance with the Amphissians and make common cause with himself against the impious desecrators of the holy ground of Apollo.

It is impossible to avoid the conclusion that this request was sheer hypocritical political opportunism. Philip's march to Elatea, instead of Amphissa, seems calculated to force Thebes and Athens to the conclusion that they, and not the Amphissians, were to be the target of his next move. Philip, of course, may have had information no longer available to us; namely, the intent of either city to declare for hostilities against him; but the possibility seems very remote. It would seem rather that he, having secured his boundaries everywhere, had now decided to force his unbreakable suzerainty over the rest of Greece before at last marching off to his projected Persian campaigns. And he intended to do this in such a manner as to make it seem that they — any possible objectors — would be the aggressors rather than himself. Otherwise there could have been no earthly reason for his own threatening actions at this time. He had planned and executed his moves very carefully, and the Athenians, with an astonishing gullibility for such a politically conscious people, rose to the deadly bait he dangled before them. They failed to recognize it for what it was.

In Athens the anti-Macedonian party partly correctly gauged the actions of the Macedonian army, and created consternation by spreading the news that Philip was fortifying the pass for the purpose of using it as a menace against the city. Even Demosthenes recognized this fact and presently backed up the thesis with his incomparable oratory. It would have been far better had his political sagacity seen further than the obvious, and realized also that it was for the purpose of causing them mortal offense, but in such a fashion that if they took umbrage it would seem that they, and not Philip, were the aggressors. Again Philip was demonstrating the fact, though they were not to realize it, that his cynically devious mentality was far superior to the wisdom of any of the Hellenes opposing his domination. It may have been that someone there did recognize the fact, but if so it was no one with the articulacy necessary to offset that of the party which immediately began to shout for war, which seems exactly what Philip desired. Besides, the anti-Macedonian ruling clique at Athens were facing political overthrow.

Athens had fallen far indeed from the days of her First Empire, and Pericles with his ideals which were almost too great for gods, let alone fallible human beings. Athens then was the center of the cultural world, a culture, however, based on levying heavy tributes on her colonial possessions for the purpose of spending it on her own citizens. Her free working class had been almost obliterated in state socialism based on slave [1] labor, and the citizen, cared for without effort on his part, had time to cultivate that flair for politics so well adapted to the nimble Attic brain, which resulted in decades of intense and exhausting politicalization after the death of Pericles and his coldly logical régime. Early in the fourth century the Athenian polity showed definite signs of political exhaustion, and the poverty of the political life of Athens is a theme monotonously reiterated by her orators. Philip had, at the time we are considering, de-

[1] D. G. Hogarth, *Philip and Alexander*, p. 37.

stroyed her hold upon her last dependencies, lost her the tributes she had formerly wrung from them,[1] and reduced her national income to almost nothing. But the citizens lived on, in a poverty-stricken city now no longer able to care for them, loafers in the market place and on the Hill of Assembly. The citizen declined to give either personal services to the city or permit himself to be taxed for her; his was a sincere belief that the government existed for the good of the citizens, and the height of his desires was that the city should have a circle of dependencies whose tributes and taxes would hire mercenaries to fight his battles, provide free shows and circuses, and support him in idleness. Now that the tributaries had been freed he was little better than a pauper, and without knowledge of how to better his condition.

The world-old cure for civic unrest is war, and the war party in Athens now regarded the city as capable of coping with the Macedonian army if Thebes would help. Philip was much less feared since his failure at Perinthus and Byzantium, and if he were beaten decisively, the restoration of Athens to her place in the sun and to her empire would follow as a matter of course. War need not be declared, merely prosecuted, for the Athenians regarded a state of war as having existed already for two years.

Demosthenes was dispatched to Thebes, where, upon his arrival, he found Philip's envoys urgently requesting either active alliance or permission to march in peace across the Copaic plain. The Thebans were at first inclined to compliance, but after granting two audiences to Demosthenes, in which he persistently worked upon the Thebans' fears, finally agreeing Athens would pay two-thirds of the cost of the war and let the Thebans appoint the commander, the latter agreed at last and swore alliance. The Athenian troops marched to Thebes, where they were joined by contingents from Achaea, Corinth, Megara, as well as several of the islands. They immediately occupied the pass of Parapotamii, a few miles northwest of the village of Chaeronea, to keep Philip from passing from Phocis into Boeotia. They also sent Chares with ten thousand mercenaries

[1] D. G. Hogarth, *Philip and Alexander*, pp. 145–157.

around the head of the Gulf of Corinth to take up his post guarding the passes between Cytinium and Amphissa. During the
next several weeks a few minor engagements were fought, the
allies being the victors. Probably Philip was merely making
tentative tests of strength of the guard forces of the mountain
passes. Athens became jubilant and voted Demosthenes a laurel
crown.

Philip then settled down at Elatea and refrained from pressing
the war while he again began building political fences and making friends. He had once punished the Phocians severely, destroying their towns and scattering the people. Now, because
they hated the Thebans, he re-established their government and
(contrary to the statements of Pausanias, who attributed the
restoration to Athens and Thebes later) re-established and rebuilt their ruined towns, a serious blow to Thebes, bringing
once more into existence a tribal power inimical to her.

At the meeting of the Amphictyonic Council that spring the
two Thessalian members who sat on it were friends of Philip's,
who had accompanied his envoys to Thebes and saw them dis-
comfited by Demosthenes, and the meeting was, as usual, packed
with his partisans. The council voted to create a new executive
body, a College of Treasurers of the temple funds of Delphi, a
committee hardly less important than the council itself. With
the sanction of this committee added to his political power,
Philip could now point out to the rest of Greece that he was
the champion of the Delphic Apollo, and that it was nothing
less than deliberate sacrilege to oppose his punishing the convicted sacrilegious Amphissians.

The Athenian-Theban army remained unimpressed and alert.
With every conceivable legal sanction behind him, Philip prepared to act. He wrote a letter to Antipater at Pella, announcing a revolt in Thrace and his intention of returning there to put
it down. The letter, as he intended, fell into the hands of Chares,
still guarding the Cytinium-Amphissa passes. He, as Philip
anticipated would be the case, relaxed his vigilance. The
Macedonians made a forced night march and fell furiously upon

the defenders of the pass, routing them. He took Amphissa with no difficulty, dismantled its walls, and banished its leaders. He marched on to the sea, rounded Delphi, and made a few tentative advances eastward over the mountain roads toward the valley of the Cephissus River, destroying a few villages and burning a few farms in the rear of the allied forces. With the Macedonians emerging from the passes to their rear, the allies realized their position at the Paropotamii Pass was no longer tenable. They withdrew down the valley and concentrated their forces in the plain near Chaeronea. Philip made a hurried march back to Elatea, seized the pass, and garrisoned it in force.

Yet even now it would seem Philip preferred to settle their differences without resort to war with Athens, and dispatched messages to both enemy cities.[1] In Athens, Phocion, whose service record for honesty and fearlessness was unimpeachable, and in Thebes at least some of the city magistrates, attempted to bring reason into the war-panicked cities. Both met with furious vituperation, and Demosthenes sarcastically asked the Thebans freedom of passage for an army fighting for the freedom of Greece. Demosthenes won again. The allied army was concentrated at the bridge over the Cephissus River in the plain of Chaeronea.

Philip marched to meet them, and there, on the seventh day of the Athenian month Metageitnion, was fought one of the world's decisive battles. There is doubt as to how the month fell — the Greek period computations were subject to inexplicable changes[2] — but the time was either in August or September, 338 B.C. The battle was, even in those days, recognized as marking the beginning of the end of Greek independence. We have no definite description of the struggle itself, and only by inference can we reconstruct the possible outline of the arrays.

On the Macedonian side the Thessalian and allied cavalry were on the right wing; in the center, as usual, was the phalanx, with the heavy armed mercenary hoplites on the right, the

[1] Plutarch, *Demosthenes*, 18; *Phocion*, 16.
[2] D. G. Hogarth, *Philip and Alexander*, p. 127.

Macedonians on the left; beyond was probably Philip himself with his guards, and still farther, constituting the extreme left wing and flankers, the matchless feudal cavalry, the superb 'companions' under command of the eighteen-year-old Alexander. Opposed to them, in the enemy battle line, facing Alexander and the left, or Macedonian, section of the phalanx, was the heavy Theban phalanx, with the Theban Sacred Band in its center front. To the left of them, and opposite the mercenaries of the Macedonian phalanx, was the phalanx of the Athenians with their own phalanx organization; beyond them the Achaeans, the islanders and other allies, and beyond them, on their extreme flank, the light irregular harassers, javelin men, archers, and slingers.

Both sides probably had about thirty thousand men engaged. Philip's discipline and organization were superior to those of the Athenians and their allies, but the Thebans were little, if at all, inferior to the Macedonians in quality. As the opposing armies faced each other that fateful day, they represented the direct antithesis of each other. Governmentally they stood at opposite ends of the poles. The miscellaneous array of the Greeks, half civic, half mercenary, were the last representatives of their ancient freedoms, a freedom they had misused, perhaps, to the point of being no longer able to maintain it, but a freedom they ardently desired nevertheless. On the Macedonian side was represented the ideal of a single monarch, supreme in war and in peace, holding a nation absolutely subject to his own will in every movement of their lives, who lived or died at his whim, to make him a great man and ruler in his own eyes and for his own glorification. And on that day, tyranny demonstrated its superior efficiency over democracy in the art of waging war, and that day has gone down in history as a date to be remembered and mourned by the Greek survivors.

The battle opened when the Thebans' dense phalanx moved slowly forward and was met by the highly mobile and experienced veterans of Macedonia, and a deadly struggle ensued. The Athenian lighter phalanx moved more swiftly and hurled itself upon the phalanx of Philip's mercenaries, cut its way through with unexpected ease, and then, losing contact with the commanders, and not knowing what else to do, the Athenians rushed straight ahead, shouting, 'On to Macedonia!' Philip, quick to grasp the advantage, threw his own phalanx into the gap left by the Athenians between the Thebans and the mercenaries, and Alexander with the heavy companions fell upon the flank of the unwieldy Theban phalanx. There was one perilous moment before this, however, when, it is said, Philip suddenly found a bitter quarrel between the Macedonians and the mercenaries of his own phalanx, the former jeering the latter for having broken under the Athenian attack. Philip was struck down (we are not told how) and was saved only by Alexander's intervention. For that service, and Alexander's later claim that his charge alone had saved the battle, Philip never forgave him, nor did Alexander ever forget or forgive the refusal of the credit he demanded. That charge was the beginning of the end. The Theban leader fell, the Sacred Band had died to a man, the Greeks broke and fled, and Demosthenes proved that he could run, as well as speak, for he flung away his weapons and escaped with the rest.[1] Philip that day won the right for which he had so earnestly striven for years, the power to dictate the policies of Greece.

Contrary to his usual custom, Philip never pursued the flying remnants of the broken allies; indeed, he restrained his men from even the minor barbarities they were wont to inflict upon their captives. That same evening there came from near-by Lebedea an embassy of the vanquished, suing for the return of the allied dead. Several of our authorities tell us this, one stating that Philip refused to receive them. At any rate they were made to wait for the answer. That night Philip gave to his leaders a great feast, a carouse such as his heart delighted in, with women, wine, and song in plenty. In the gray of early morning Philip staggered drunkenly from his tent and out upon the death-strewn field, shouting insulting comments upon his enemies, and Demosthenes in particular.[2] He approached the

[1] Plutarch, *Demosthenes*. [2] Plutarch, *Demosthenes*.

cowering mass of prisoners, and their equally cowering Macedonian guards; the latter knew only too well the murderous temper of their drunken king. But one man, the Athenian orator Demades, dared face the conqueror. He spoke, harshly and incisively, even as was Philip's wont: 'King, when Fate has cast thee for the part of an Agamemnon, art not ashamed to play instead the part of Thersites?' [1] Philip's ingrown sense of inferiority in the face of the culture of Athens arose to the surface through the fumes of the liquor. He tore off his garlands, trampled them under foot, and turned away in shame, ordering the release of the man who had spoken to him.

When the first panic-stricken fugitives from the battle reached Athens, they stirred the population into determination of despair. They resolved to defend their city to the last. Women and children, livestock and portable goods from the surrounding districts were brought in to the protection of the walls. Frontier guards were hastily sent out, and an army for home defense organized. Demosthenes immediately dispatched messengers by the fastest ships to the Propontus to make arrangements to send hurriedly loaded grain ships to Piraeus, the seaport of Athens. Extraordinary measures were adopted to raise money. All men capable of bearing arms were conscripted; all others were put on the public works. The city walls were reinforced. Hyperides proposed, and carried in the assembly, a decree to enfranchise and arm all disenfranchised citizens, resident foreigners, and even slaves, and Suidas (in his *Lexicon*, though admittedly writing at second or third hand) quotes a sentence by Hyperides when he was later impeached for the proposal, to the effect that this decree would thus make available for defense the services of one hundred and fifty thousand additional males. [2] 'In those hours no age held itself aloof from the service of the

---

[1] After the *Iliad*: a warrior who was a blunderer and a fool.

[2] It has been suggested that this number derives from an error in reading in original statement, and should be amended to read fifty thousand male slaves of fighting age, or a total of seventy to eighty thousand male slaves of all ages. See inconclusive argument by Gomme, *The Population of Athens in the 5th and 4th Centuries B.C.*, Glasgow University Publications, Blackwell, Oxford, 1933.

state. It was a time when the earth contributed its trees; the dead their tombstones, the temples their stores of dedicated armor. Some toiled in restoring the walls; some dug trenches; some were building palisades. There was no one idle within the city.' [1]

But when the settlement was made, Philip showed his usual, but inexplicable, magnanimity; he returned to Athens her three thousand prisoners without ransom or indemnity, and sent back her envoys to assure her terrified citizens, crouching behind her newly repaired city walls, a pledge of peace and alliance. He even gave her, from the spoils of the Theban federation, the long-disputed boundary city of Oropus; an excellent way, if the Athenians retained the city, of arousing Theban animus and hostility. With the envoys, as his personal messengers went Antipater and Alexander. The Athenians were, however, compelled to dissolve their recently formed naval league and resign all claims upon the Thracian Chersonese. Also — and here the sword rattled in its scabbard — they must acknowledge the hegemony of the half-barbarian Macedonian king over all Hellas. This was a bitter pill for some of the Athenians to swallow, but under the circumstances they could only acquiesce. But they, who had expected a military invasion with fire and sword, were so overjoyed at this unexpected leniency that they granted Attic citizenship to both Philip and Alexander, and set up a statue of the former as a public benefactor in the Agora.

To Thebes, in contrast with his almost apologetic forbearance toward Athens, Philip was harshly brutal. She had to submit to encouragement of Orchomenus and Plataea, south and north of her, to rise again; she was stripped of her feudal towns in Boeotia; deprived of her own civic autonomy; her leaders banished, and in their stead three hundred men, exiled for adherence to Philip's interests, were recalled and placed in office, and as a crowning insult, a Macedonian garrison was placed in the Cadmeia. Thus, the last city which had long been an obstacle in the way of Philip's realization of his dream of a Hellenic con-

[1] Lycurgus, *Oration Against Leocrates*, sec. 44.

federation, with him at its head, had been reduced to impotency. With the other rebels, he could now be forgiving without incurring the charge of weakness.

While these negotiations were going on, Philip caused to be circulated, officially at last, news of his intention to launch a war against the might of Persia, a holy war of revenge for the invasions Greece had suffered at the hands of the barbarians in the past. In one of his letters to the Athenians he inserted a paragraph 'inviting' them to join with all Greece in a pact for universal peace and to join the League Council or 'Synhedrion' later to be known as the Corinthian League. This partially concealed threat of domination of Athens, for such it would be with Philip as controlling factor of the league, is the first and last we ever hear from the Macedonian toward the city. Philip needed now but to make one more demonstration, against the Peloponnesus. He took Corinth in his stride, and moved into the isthmus, to be joyfully welcomed by most cities; with some who had been hostile to him he made peace on surprisingly easy terms. Only the Spartans, when summoned, refused to join the new crusade. In conjunction with her old enemies, Argos and Messene, Philip raided her fields and towns, and was probably exasperated by the political necessity of refraining from completely destroying her. Had he done so he might have once more outraged the touchy political sentiments of the Greeks; therefore, he contented himself with cutting down her territories to a point reducing her to a negligible military and economic factor. Then, with the understanding that the first league meeting was to be held the following year, Philip returned to Macedonia.

When the delegates from all Greece, except Sparta, met at Corinth the next year, Philip laid his agenda, and proposed program, before them for discussion, and spoke at length of the necessity of union for the sake of successful prosecution of his pan-Hellenic ambitions in and against Persia. The prospect of hostilities against the vast and powerful empire evoked little genuine Grecian enthusiasm, but the delegates no doubt took cognizance of the Macedonian spearmen encamped just outside the walls, and concluded philosophically that now that Philip had so nearly reached his long-sought goal, he would probably take by force what they would attempt to deny him. Philip had achieved a reputation for irascibility, and the master of those iron battalions was not a person to accept lightly the refusal of what he considered a reasonable request. No better summation of this treaty has ever been made than the one quoted:[1]

> Its chief points are as follows. Philip concluded with the Greeks amity and an offensive and defensive alliance (*symmachia*) forever. It is not certain, but not improbable, that even then, as at a later renewal of this treaty of alliance in 302, the Greek states at the same time agreed to friendship and an offensive and defensive alliance with one another. The League of Greeks formed by the alliance (styled 'The Hellenes') was represented in a general Synhedrion (Federal Council), to which the individual states had to send their deputies in number varying in proportion to their military strength. This Synhedrion was to hold its ordinary meetings and sessions at the times and places of the four great pan-Hellenic festivals (at Olympia, Nemea, Delphi, and the Isthmus), while for extraordinary meetings Corinth was probably chosen; and it was there also that the permanent business committee of five presidents (*prohedroi*) no doubt sat. In the first paragraph freedom and autonomy, and probably exemption from military tribute and occupation, was given each member of the league.

No doubt Philip, as duly elected hegemon (captain-general for life) of the league, easily obtained approval of the assembly for retention of his garrisoned hold upon Thebes, Ambracia, Chalcis, and Acrocorinth, as a means of assuring the maintenance of peace in these areas, for the garrisons stayed on. Macedonia he naturally left out of the league, so Philip in his own country and of his own right was left free to do what he might will without the nuisance of being held accountable to anyone. From one motive or another, the delegates acknowledged that Philip should be, and was, the hegemon of the league, and bound

[1] Ulrich Wilcken, *Alexander der Grosse.*

themselves to provide their required quota of military and naval assistance he had always envisioned as necessary to give the forthcoming expedition a genuinely pan-Hellenic character. As a further guaranty to the safety of his rear while he was abroad on his contemplated conquests, Philip forced the delegates to swear eternal alliance and friendship not only with himself but with his descendants, that the realm of Macedonia might henceforth be free from the anarchical state prevailing before and even after his accession. Having secured all he wanted in Greece proper, Philip then rose and proposed that the Macedonians and the Greek contingents the delegates had just voted him open the war with Persia immediately, the war of revenge for which he had already prepared them. In reply they voted for war, and, as the hostilities were not to be directed against any of the Greeks or their allies, gave Philip the title of Strategos, with unlimited power to prosecute the invasion as he saw fit.

Philip returned to Pella, well satisfied at the successful conclusion of the league meeting, and threw all his organizational energy into preparations for the adventure. By the spring of 336 his plans were complete and his army nearly ready to move; all that remained undone was to set the affairs of his own house in order. His break with Olympias the year before was beginning to have repercussions in the west. The cast-off queen was beginning to influence seriously the Lyncestians and the Illyrian hill tribes to Philip's detriment. Storm-clouds of revolt were fast gathering in the west, and Philip hastened to action designed to offset the growing menace before he departed on his long absence from the country. Accordingly he made overtures to Alexander of Molossia, with the intent to render harmless Olympias' intrigues with her powerful brother, offering him the formal tender of the hand of Alexander's sister Cleopatra, and an alliance of friendship. To Olympias' fury the offer was promptly accepted, and Philip in triumph projected a wedding on a scale unheard-of in magnificence. He sent invitations, which were really demands for their attendance, to all the representatives of the league, and to scores of Greek notables in all walks of life, to repair to his old capital of Aegae in the autumn. The greatest actors, musicians, and athletes were engaged, games on a scale surpassing those of Olympus were planned and ordered, shows and banquets of a magnitude that promised to empty the royal exchequer were arranged.

While the arrangements were going forward for the forthcoming nuptials, Philip did not neglect the rest of his plans; and apparently a satisfactory understanding with the larger cities on the Propontus was reached, perhaps an arrangement for their active assistance, perhaps only their benevolent neutrality. Parmenio and Attalus were dispatched with ten thousand men to the Chersonese with orders to cross over into Asia Minor, seize the enemy's seacoast cities there, and prepare for the main body of the army, due to arrive in the late autumn or early winter.

In Epirus, Olympias saw the work of a full year fall into naught upon the announcement of her brother's acceptance of Philip as father-in-law. Her rage knew no bounds, especially as soon afterward the news arrived, a few days before the Aegaean festival, that Cleopatra had borne Philip a child,[1] a son of undoubted parentage, named Caranus. Olympias planned immediate revenge, and returned to Macedonia.

On the morning of the wedding day the great theater of Aegae was thronged with spectators even before daybreak,[2] to see the sunrise procession of the statues of the twelve gods of Olympus, following which was one of Philip himself. At last the royal procession approached, and as it drew near the gate Philip bade his nobles and their entourages to go ahead, and ordered his bodyguard to hang back. He wished to be separated significantly from his retinue so he might, when he entered majestically in his magnificent white robe, be heroically acclaimed by the populace. The nobles walked on, the bodyguard obediently lagged behind, and Philip stalked into the great gateway. At that instant a man sprang from one of the lateral corridors, drove a short sword into the king's body, and leaped away as

[1] Diodorus, XVII, 2.   [2] *Ibid.*, XVI, 92.

he fell. The assassin nearly escaped in the wild confusion, for he had friends waiting near-by with horses. But as he fled, his sandal caught in a vine, tripping him. He was instantly pounced upon, jerked to his feet, and slain by many spear thrusts. When Philip was picked up he was dead.

Though the assassin who wielded the blade was Pausanius, an Orestian, contemporary opinion held that the *cherchez la femme* (look for the woman) principle was just as applicable in that day as it was later. Pausanius, though historically an androgyne, had been insulted by an incredible indecency on the part of Attalus, now high in Philip's favor. Pausanius had been unable to secure redress at Philip's hands, and had long meditated revenge. His rancor had probably been noticed by one of the pro-Olympias factions of the court. The rest was easy. Attalus, the object of his hatred, was four hundred miles away in Asia Minor, beyond his reach, but Philip, whose contemptuous refusal of redress was nearly as bitter, was so near he could be reached by so short a thing as a knife. The knife was provided, the time and place meditated upon and set. The king died in the dust of the gateway.

For the historian it is perhaps well that Philip was cut down when he was, at the moment of the launching of the Persian campaign; it was certainly well for Alexander, for we have reason to believe that the breach between father and son had grown so wide that Philip was contemplating cutting him out of the succession, if not out of existence. Had he done either, the already much injured Olympias could then, with an excellent *casus belli*, have stirred up civil war to rend the kingdom, to the almost certain extinction of its unity and perhaps even of its national existence. Nor is it likely that Philip, subtle politician though he was, would have had the breadth of vision or the utter foolhardiness to carry the war against Persia beyond the confines of Asia Minor. How far he did intend to carry it has been the source of much bootless and fruitless conjecture and rationalizing, and to it there is but one answer: We can never know.

=IV=

ALEXANDER
THE KING

W HEN Philip fell in the theater gateway on that
October morning, the scepter and crown of Macedonia were
snatched out of the indecisive air by the hand of the twenty-
year-old Alexander, and for a few hours the throne of Macedonia
quaked under the imminent gathering of a political cyclone.
Alexander was not the only legal heir to the kingship; the
twenty-five-year-old Amyntas, son of Perdiccas, whose throne
had been taken while he was a baby by Philip, had many sup-
porters, and his newly born half-brother Caranus [1] had many

---

[1] Helmuth Berve, in his monumental work, *Das Alexanderreich* (II), advances the
claim that Caranus was a grown man at that time, the offspring of another irregular
union of Philip in his youth. Other commentators, rather uncritically, we believe,
accept this conclusion, but we have been unable to give credence to this belief, against
the greater weight of more of our ancient authorities and writers. Berve also says
that the child newly born to Cleopatra was a daughter; to this we also cannot agree.
Not infrequently a single obscure allusion or reference will be seized upon and accepted,
historical facts being made to agree, erroneously, with it. We ourselves may be guilty

84

others. Both were therefore legal claimants, and each a grave threat to Alexander's accession and subsequent peace. Alexander's own legitimacy had been impugned by Philip, and there were many chauvinists in the land who railed against him as the son of Olympias, hence half-barbarian, conveniently neglecting to recall that Philip and the two kings before him were also sons of an Illyrian woman. These, the reactionary die-hards, were prepared to appeal to popular prejudice against Alexander's acceptance of the new foreign ideas, his Graecized mode of life, and the new ambitions tending to reach so far into the dim terrors of distant lands. Alexander acted with instant decision, before opposition had even time to formulate. Before any of the others could make a claim, he had assembled his friends and mustered the army in the valley of the Vardar, and there, his godlike beauty clad in complete battle armor, he appealed to the supreme arbiter of the kingship. His dashing gallantry at the battle of Chaeronea and his actions during the regency had already won the army, and at the end of his speech their thunderous acclaim and the clash of spear upon shield served notice to all that a new king had already supplanted the murdered Philip. He then went swiftly to the already ordered assembly of the representatives of his father's allies, and the cynical diplomats, their ears still ringing with the acclamations of the assembled army, agreed unanimously when Alexander informed them expressly of his expectation that they would retain toward him the loyalty they had pledged his father in the Treaty of Corinth. By this expression he showed plainly his intention of preserving his claim and rights as his father's successor as hegemon of the league under its articles.

His accession secured, Alexander turned at once to the vigorous prosecution of his father's murderers, and to clearing away obstacles to his retention of the throne. Two Lyncestian princes, Arrhabaeus and Heromenes, both sons of Aeropus, strongly suspected of at least foreknowledge of Pausanias' intent, were

of the same actions, but we still believe every historian entitled to the conclusions he draws from his researches.

brought before the assembly of the army, accused, tried, sentenced, and stoned to death. The third son of Aeropus, who has gone down in history as Alexander the Lyncestian, had, immediately after the murder of Philip, hastened to do homage to the new king. This, perhaps coupled with the fact that Antipater was the Lyncestian's father-in-law, convinced Alexander that association with the general had probably kept him from any considerable association with his brothers, and removed from him suspicion of complicity in the plot. The security of the throne demanded additional precautions, and Alexander's cousin Amyntas was slain. The newborn son of Cleopatra, sister of Attalus, was a problem which Olympias with cool savagery solved for him. The queen murdered the child in its mother's arms, and forced Cleopatra to commit suicide. As other highborn relatives of Cleopatra might also be trouble-makers, Alexander decimated the clan, killing all the male members of the family. Then he dispatched one of his trusted friends with a small body of cavalry to Asia Minor to seize Attalus, if practicable; if not, to put him quietly out of the way. The Athenians had in the meantime been quick to seize their opportunity now that the terrible Philip was in his tomb. They sent messengers posthaste to Attalus to carry urgent verbal communications, and a letter from Demosthenes himself urging his refusal to recognize the sovereignty of Alexander. Their intent was to secure a declaration for the already dead Amyntas as the rightful heir and successor to the throne. But when, after careful sounding, the old general Parmenio revealed his intent to remain faithful to the new king, Attalus grew faint of heart and hurriedly sent the letter, with fulsome protestations of his loyalty to Alexander; but he had already waited too long. Traveling like the wind, the king's messengers raced along the coast of Thrace, into the Chersonese, and crossed the Hellespont into Asia Minor. From then on Attalus disappears from our history, and none of our biographers record the manner of his passing. Demosthenes, disappointed, again immediately entered into communication with the Persian king.

With the iron-handed Philip dead, Greece seethed with unrest, and many of the cities prepared to shake off the yoke of the hegemony of Macedonia. In Athens Demosthenes was again the leader of the uprising. He had been notified by a special messenger from the Athenian admiral Charidemus, who was then hanging off the coasts of the Thermaic Gulf. Though at the time in mourning for a daughter who had died only a week before, Demosthenes put off his mourning, donned a white festal robe, crowned himself with a chaplet of flowers, and thus appeared before the city council.[1] In a speech filled with rolling oratory he dramatically stated that Athena herself had communicated news of grave import to him in a dream. The goddess, he said, had informed him that Alexander was a stuffed simpleton [2] who would not trust his precious skin beyond the confines of Pella. His oratorical fervor was communicated to the council and the town meeting, and his motion was carried: that the murderer Pausanias was a public benefactor of all Hellas, and further decreed thank-offerings to the gods for the removal of the tyrant.[3] As a rabble-rouser Demosthenes was second to none; as a political prophet, however, he hardly ranks so highly. For the Macedonian army, twenty-five thousand strong, was already on the move, a grim and deadly war machine rolling swiftly southward. The first night out of Pella they stopped at Pydna, the second at the mouth of the river Peneus, opposite the vale of Tempe. Here the Thessalian commander bade Alexander wait outside the entrance, while he sent to Larissa for instructions. The time-honored way of getting through what was deemed the only possible route would have been either an immediate assault to carry the pass by storm or the purchase of passage by gold. Alexander did neither. He put his men to cutting a path along the seaward face of Mount Ossa,[4] rounded

---

[1] Plutarch, *Demosthenes*.

[2] Literally a Margites, after a character in a poem ascribed to Homer; a boy who grows up but never attains the sense or wit of a man. The reference is given by Plutarch.

[3] For the attitude of the Athenians, see Arrian, I, 10; Aeschines, *Ctesiphon*, 77; Plutarch, *Demosthenes*, 22.   [4] Polyaenus, IV, 3.

it swiftly, negotiated the hills and gorges, passed along the slopes, and swept down into the plains of Thessaly and up to the gates of Larissa before the news of their coming could run before them. The shocked inhabitants took a good look at the machine-like array of Macedonian spearmen, and from somewhere resurrected an astonishing amount of enthusiasm for Alexander's cause. They elected him as archon of Thessaly, and affirmed him as their choice as hegemon of the league. Thessaly and its famous cavalry belonged to Alexander, secured without a blow.

In the meantime Demosthenes had issued the clarion call of freedom to the other cities, with the hope that Athens could secure the hegemony Philip had held. The Aetolians recalled their citizens exiled by Philip; the Thebans took steps to expel the Macedonian garrison from their Cadmeia; the Ambracians successfully expelled theirs; and several of the Peloponnesian cities meditated revolution. Alexander marched the seventy miles from Larissa to Thermopylae in less than three days, and immediately summoned the members of the Amphictyonic Council, received their renewed assurances of loyalty, then marched swiftly into Boeotia, reached Thebes, and encamped on the southeast side of the city, opposite the Cadmeia. Athens, fifty miles away, went into a panic, the country people fled to the protection of the city walls, and defense preparations were hastily begun. A town meeting was promptly called, retracted its former acts, and dispatched an embassy to beg forgiveness. Demosthenes was included in the embassy, but when the little group reached the Cithaeron, his nerve failed him [1] and he turned back. Alexander, however, resolved to maintain his father's attitude toward Athens, and assured the ambassadors of his desire for friendship and peace, and while they were still speechless before the young king, he guaranteed continuance of their local autonomy, and summoned them to meet him later at Corinth. Upon return of their ambassadors, the overjoyed Athenians awarded two golden crowns to Alexander, and voted him benefactor of the city. Other opposition in Hellas and the

[1] Plutarch, *Demosthenes*.

88

Peloponnesus vanished. When the representatives of the league met again at Corinth to repledge to Alexander the assurances they had given to his father, the only missing city was Sparta, still stiff-necked and aloof in her fading glory.

The visit has given us, if true, a story of one object lesson that, however, failed to change the course of the young autocrat. To him with due homage came soldiers, statesmen, the great, the near-great, and the sycophantic would-be-great of all Hellas. But one day, as Alexander was walking through the market-place, he noticed an old man sitting silently upon the ground in front of a great cask. On inquiring who he was, the king was told this was Diogenes, the apostle of poverty, of self-sufficiency, the exponent of the art of doing without. Alexander, surrounded by his glittering suite, walked up to him. Diogenes ignored him. Presently the king ventured to introduce himself. 'I am Alexander,' he said. 'I am Diogenes the Cynic,' was the reply. Alexander waited, but Diogenes was silent. The conversation had bogged down. Presently Alexander renewed it, asking Diogenes if there was anything he wanted of him. 'Yes,' came the reply: 'Stand out of my sunlight.' Alexander marveled, but upon a moment's reflection perceived the worth of the man. 'By Zeus,' he said, 'if I were not Alexander, I would be Diogenes.'

Time pressed. Alexander had much to do, and it was already November. All he needed now out of Greece was the sanction of the gods upon his self-imposed task, and he marched to Delphi. But already the sun god Apollo had yielded his seat in the sanctuary to Dionysus, here god of the fallow earth and sleeping nature, and traditionally the mouth of the oracle of Apollo was closed. Tradition, however, often means little to the man who has the sanction of many battalions behind him, and in order to get the oracle, Alexander seized the arm of the Pythian priestess and tried to drag her to the famous tripod seat of augury. The unwilling priestess resisted a bit, then reluctantly said, 'My son, thou art irresistible!' Alexander instantly recognized the value of the statement, and released her at once. He was glad to accept it as the oracular augury of his future.

Alexander réturned to Pella in the early winter, to be met with reports of warlike restlessness on the part of the outlying tribes in and just beyond his frontiers. These numerous and warlike people were, he considered, the only remaining possibility of menace to his rear or flanks when he should ultimately get the long-prepared anti-Persian crusade under way. There was no central power over there, and only periodic and severe castigation would assist their short memories and force the tribesmen to the unwilling conclusion that peaceful pursuits were a happy means of obtaining a livelihood. They had given Philip a great deal of trouble, and now Alexander would have to read them a severe lesson in order to convince them that he was other than 'painted to resemble iron.' The Illyrians and Thracians near-by were watchfully biding their time against the new king's proof of his mettle, and farther north, the Getae, the 'Scythians,' and the perennially troublesome Triballians were arming and raiding. They were the tribe with whom Philip had fought his last skirmish on his return from punishing the Danube chief, and to the Macedonians the loss of their valuable booty to the tribesmen was a sore memory. No doubt the tribesmen were still chuckling over their exploit, up in the plains between the Haemus (Balkans) Range and the Ister (Danube) River, and counting upon fate to be equally kind to them when they should sweep out of the rugged hills into the rich and fruitful lowlands of Thrace and Macedonia.

In the early spring of 335 Alexander left Amphipolis, marched along the coast to the Nestus (Masta) River, followed up its valley, crossed the pass between Mounts Rhodope and Dunax, which separate the drainages of the Nestus and Hebrus Rivers, and in ten days reached the Kotcha Balkans. The army climbed the narrow route between modern Bulgaria and eastern Rou-melia, famous today as the Shipka Pass, at seventy-eight hundred feet altitude. Here they found the heights occupied by a tribe of Thracians, who were, Arrian says, masses of tradesmen and bands of free clansmen. They had collected their wagons and lined them up at the top of the declivity, intending to use them as ramparts, and where the descent was steep, as missiles.

Alexander's military caliber is noticeable here, on his first campaign, in his instant willingness to abandon old for new methods, when faced by circumstances where blind adhesion to precedent would mean failure or heavy losses. He had the gift of immediately improvising new tactics, new formations, new and instant adaptations to the pressing needs of the moment, which we find in him time and time again, never at a loss, and never guessing wrongly. Quickly realizing the potential destructiveness of the poised wagons high on the hill above, Alexander gave orders [1] that, when the loosed vehicles came thundering down, those men in the array where the ground would permit should open their ranks, creating lanes for the unhindered progress of the ponderous vehicles. The other formations, unable to move aside, were ordered to lie down in a solid mass, lock their shields together over their heads in a solid roof, thus letting the swiftly moving wagons pass over them. So it turned out; not a man was injured beneath the flying wheels. The Macedonians rose to their feet and charged with their battle-shout. The ill-armed tribesmen broke at the first shock, and the rest of the battle was more of a footrace, though Arrian reports they suffered fifteen hundred casualties. Much booty was captured, including large numbers of women and children, who were dispatched to the seacoast, where they would find ready sale in the slave markets.

Alexander descended the mountains and, near the small Lyginus River, fought another short engagement, in which the tribesmen, under their king Syrmis, were seriously defeated. The Macedonian war machine simply rolled over them. The survivors fled in panic to an island in the Ister River, three days' march distant. Grimly the Macedonians marched after them. When they arrived at the river, Alexander there found several small ships, which Byzantium had sent to co-operate with him, awaiting his coming. As many as possible of the soldiers were embarked and the island assaulted, but what with the limited

[1] Polyaenus, IV, 3, 11.

number of attackers and the high, steep banks they had to scale, the tribesmen beat off the attack. On the opposite shore during the engagement, numbers of the people of the tribe, transcribed down to us as Getae, had come to the river's edge as if to resist an invasion. Here, Arrian tells us, as he so often tells us later, Alexander was seized with a 'longing' to cross to the other shore. Also it occurred to him that he could, by a brilliant demonstration on the other side, break the will-to-resist of the fugitives on the island. After nightfall the army prepared to cross, and before morning, by the use of seized fishing boats, the Byzantine ships, and hides stuffed with hay, a sizable force of fifteen hundred cavalry and four thousand infantry was ferried over. On the opposite bank the army assembled under cover of the high corn (this places the action as having occurred late in May or June) and advanced, bent over, until within a short distance of the enemy, where the grainfields ended. The Getae, in amazement at the appearance of the southerners, whom they still imagined on the other side of the mighty Ister, fled without offering resistance to their village, about four miles distant. Alexander, throwing out a screen of mounted advanced guards as a precaution against ambuscade, followed them. The Getae, watching in amazement, realized they were facing an unparalleled situation, abandoned their village as untenable, and fled to the steppe. The Macedonians came up, and finding little of value within the place, unnecessarily and gratuitously burned the village. This done, Alexander set up altars and offered sacrifice to Zeus the savior, Heracles the demigod, and also to the Ister river god in thanks for permitting a safe and easy passage.

Before nightfall the Macedonians had recrossed the river and gone into camp. Thither came several embassies from local tribes, including the Triballians on the island. From all Alexander accepted homage, and made alliances, the Triballians later providing him with valuable contingents of excellent fighting men for his army. From as far as Hungary, embassies came from the Celts, a people, says Arrian, big and strong of body and of a haughty spirit. With them, too, Alexander made peace, they swearing,[1] 'We will keep faith unless the sky fall and crush us, or the earth open and swallow us, or the sea rise and overwhelm us.' Alexander, knowing the terror of his name had reached to and beyond their country, asked the Celtic chief what they feared most, imagining and intending they should answer: himself. The haughty Celt, with thinly veiled sarcasm, replied that they feared only the sky falling, such a remote possibility that he was really saying they feared nothing. Alexander was somewhat abashed at the reply, but he treated them kindly nevertheless; however, when he afterward mentioned them he always would say that the Celts were an arrogant and braggart people.

Alexander marched for Macedonia by the western route through Paeonia, but in the country of the friendly tribe of Agrianians, from whom he drew his best light javelin and spearmen (near modern Sofia), he was surprised by a messenger bearing news of the revolt of the Illyrian chieftain Clitus, whose bellicose father, Bardylis, had been slain by Philip twenty-four years before. Clitus himself, in his first revolt fourteen years before, had been thoroughly defeated by Philip, but permitted to retain his power. Now that a new, young, and untried king had taken the reins of Macedonia, he had made alliance with one Glaucius, king of the Taulentians (somewhere in the vicinity of modern Durazzo in Albania), and revolted. With a hastily gathered reinforcement of Agrianians, Alexander marched, immediately and swiftly, toward Clitus' frontier fortress of Pellion, commanding the pass from upper Macedonia into Illyria, two hundred miles away. When the Macedonians approached the city, Clitus offered a sacrifice of three boys, three girls, and three black rams, then, assured of being generously requited in kind by the gods, prepared positions and posted his men on the mountain over against the city. Alexander made a feint and the mountaineers precipitately abandoned their sacrifices and fled to the shelter of the city walls. The Macedonians moved up, invested the place, and prepared for a siege. The following day, however, intelligence was brought that Glaucius, with a considerable

[1] W. W. Tarn, *Cambridge Ancient History*, VI, 355.

army, was on the way to bring relief to his ally. Philotas was placed in command of Alexander's own heavy cavalry and sent to harass and deter the oncoming enemy. Philotas, naturally being unfamiliar with the mountainous terrain, scouted about, and upon trying to return, discovered that in some way the crafty Glaucius had managed to occupy a pass in his rear, cutting him off from the Macedonian army. Alexander, hearing of the blockade, drew off a body of the Agrianian light spearmen and archers and hastened to Philotas' assistance. Glaucius, who seems to have had an excellent scout organization, was apprised of Alexander's approach, but dared not offer battle. He retreated and the beleaguered force of cavalry was rescued. The Taulentians brought up their whole army and were joined by Clitus. Alexander, seeing his army heavily outnumbered by the enemy, made a feint attack with a small part of his force, and while the enemy were occupied with it, drew the main body of his army across the river. There they set up the light artillery, and under cover of a barrage of stones and arrows, the rest of the force was disengaged and taken over in safety. Three days later came his chance for revenge. He was informed that his enemy's camp was carelessly guarded and unfortified. That night the Macedonians fell upon the sleeping camp, slew many of the enemy and drove the others forth in panic, with the Macedonians in hot pursuit. Clitus set fire to his city and escaped.

As long as Alexander stayed in Macedonia the Greeks remained quiet, but it was now midsummer, and the king had been gone from home for five long months. He was now about three hundred miles away, through a wild and mountainous country in which news traveled but slowly from the political centers of Greece. The country was suddenly filled with wild rumors of Alexander; he had been disastrously defeated, his army broken up, and he was a fugitive hunted from hill to hill by the vengeful mountaineers; he was killed, said another. The country seethed with unrest and excitement, and Alexander's enemies became more and increasingly more voluble and convincing.

Meanwhile, in Persia, Darius III, who had ascended the throne in May, 336, had received authentic news of the forthcoming attack upon his empire, both from Demosthenes in Athens and from his own satraps in Asia Minor who were fighting the vanguard of the Macedonian army. Parmenio had passed the Hellespont, captured several seacoast cities, and driven inland. He passed Ephesus and reached Magnesia on the Meander, and there met a Persian army under the Rhodian Memnon, who defeated him in one pitched battle, then maneuvered him back to the Hellespont. Some of the Macedonians had even been forced back into Thrace. Memnon, we judge from our fragmentary accounts, seems either to have been the better general or to have had a greatly superior army. Darius had, of course, been informed very fully of the war resolutions passed by the Corinthian League, and whether or not the Great King was, his advisers had been, wise enough to take the matter very seriously. They decided to have, not recourse to armed force, but the old political stand-by, gold. The political democracies of Greece had always been easily swayed by the will of the Persian king, their chief men yielding to the secret lure of Persian gold. Therefore, during the summer of 335, Darius had dispatched agents throughout all Greece, with authority to finance any revolt from, or war against, Alexander which might be slumbering from lack of money. Though Philip first, and Alexander after him, had tried to assure the governments of the cities, except Sparta, being in friendly hands, it is still certain that many anti-Macedonian elements received Persian money, and used it effectively to Alexander's detriment. King Agis of hostile Sparta openly accepted the Persian subsidy, and more secretly, though neither he nor his partisans ever denied it, Demosthenes received three hundred talents of Persian money. Later, the orator Aeschines accused his oratorical opponent of having retained one-third of that sum for his own fee and use. The accusation can neither be proved nor disproved. It is a little difficult to determine the fee or percentage of money a paid corruptionist should retain for himself, or to decide where lay the dividing line between private and public use of such a fund. We do know that eleven years later Demosthenes received twenty-three talents from the vast treasure stolen by Harpalus, and that, as he was unable to show any but the private use of the sum, he was convicted by the trial court, fined fifty talents, and imprisoned. If the reader thinks this work unduly and unnecessarily blackens the fame of a great man, this commentator can merely offer in rebuttal that in his opinion Demosthenes was neither better nor worse than the other politicians of his day.

As the summer drew on, the plans of the plotters were perfected. Demosthenes produced a wounded Athenian in the forum who testified to having received his wound in the battle with the Triballi, where, he claimed, he had seen Alexander slain with his own eyes. Demosthenes made a great speech. He fairly outdid himself. It was so good that Demades says, 'He all but showed us the corpse of Alexander there on the bema before our eyes.' In the continued absence of news of the Macedonian, the plot reached a crux. In Elis Macedonian sympathizers were banished the town. Aetolia was in ferment and several towns there were preparing for revolt. Athens began arming in furious haste. The belief was now universal that Alexander was dead, so in passing judgment later it must be borne in mind that, the Macedonian removed from supreme power, the Treaty of Corinth, in the absence of legal issue by Alexander, was null and void, and the Greek cities returned to the status they had enjoyed before the battle of Chaeronea.

One night a body of Thebans, who had been living in exile in Athens, quietly returned home, proclaimed the death of Alexander, and sounded the call for revolt. The Macedonian garrison in the Cadmeia had long offended the rather insensitive Theban civic conscience; a mob formed, caught and murdered two Macedonian officers who happened to be abroad in the lower city, threw a cordon around the Cadmeia, and began to build a double rampart around it to prevent a sally by the garrison and to prevent supplies from entering. Citizens who soberly considered the situation and protested against excesses were roughly handled. A hastily summoned mass meeting of the citizens voted immediate expulsion of the officials appointed by the Macedonians, and named a board of *boiotarchi* to resume again, as of old, supreme control of the city. Freedom of the city from the Macedonian yoke was officially proclaimed. Next day wagons loaded with arms, paid for by the Persian insurrection fund handled by Demosthenes, arrived in Thebes. From Athens messengers hurried throughout the country, north, south, and west, to call the people to arms. An Arcadian army was the first to be ready, and despite a message of grim warning from the dour Antipater in Macedonia, it marched north from the Peloponnesus, with Athens only awaiting its arrival to join in. War! *War!* WAR! The senseless hysteria of war was setting all Greece into a fever of action. The Hellenic empire of Alexander was swiftly falling into madness and dissolution, and he was three hundred miles away in the tumbled mountains of wild Illyria.

News of the revolt reached Alexander immediately after his night attack upon the insurgents. He turned abruptly from pursuit of the fleeing Illyrians, and led his army southward by forced marches. He passed through the rough mountain wilderness of Eordaea and Elimiotis, marched down the Haliacmon valley, crossed the Kambounian ridge, and on the seventh day halted his march to make night camp at Pellene (close to modern Trikkala) in northern Thessaly. The next day he pushed on across the Thessalian plain, crossed the pass near modern Domokos, passed Lamia and Thermopylae, through the hill country, and entered Boeotia, after making one hundred and thirty miles in six days from Pellene, traveling so fast that only when he reached Onchestus, in the immediate vicinity of Thebes, were there heralds of his swift advance. When the report reached the Thebans that Alexander, at the head of the Macedonian forces, was very near, the leaders of the revolt insisted that it must be Antipater in command, or perhaps that other Alexander, the one from Lyncestus, merely a case of mistaken identity. It is

97

possible that the Thebans really believed in the report of Alexander's death — propagandists are often believed — and thought he might have been succeeded by the Lyncestian, but if so, they were soon disillusioned.

Thirteen days after he had left Illyria, Alexander appeared before the southern gates of Thebes and went into camp a short distance away. He was, remember, not there in the capacity of the king of Macedonia, but as hegemon of the Corinthian League, deputed by it to maintain the league intact, keep the peace, and if necessary punish refractory or rebellious members, and restore order to the country. As hegemon, he was promptly joined by contingents from Phocis and Plataea, members of the league, and rabid with hostility and hatred for the cruel oppressions Thebes had for years inflicted upon them.

Thebes was then a city of something over forty thousand population, built on the gentle northern slopes of a low range of hills, its walls having a circuit of about four miles. The famous Cadmeia was a citadel built upon a long, low hill in the southeastern part of the city, near the Electra, the southern gate where the road came in from Athens. The town itself was a solid place, rather well-to-do and given to easy living as a result of wealth acquired by grinding tribute exacted from conquered and oppressed neighboring small cities. The public square was said to have been surrounded by colonnades, and the city boasted of several temples within its environs. Anciently the Thebans were considered 'piggish' in their eating and drinking, and for the crudity of their manners, many instances of which come to us *passim* in our histories.

Alexander tried for a peaceful settlement (we are not told the terms). He preferred to use means calculated to antagonize as little as possible the people of Greece, and run less chance of insurrection in his rear when he at last should leave on his Persian conquests. But the Thebans rejected his proposal, immediately sending out a detachment of cavalry who attacked his outposts and had to be driven off. Next day Alexander moved his camp closer to the wall, next the Cadmeia, but still hoped for a peaceful reconciliation. In the town, the more sensible citizens, foreseeing the inevitable disaster, proposed to send an embassy to Alexander, make submission and beg pardon for the revolt. They were shouted down by the exiles and the war party and treated with opprobrium by the instigators of the revolt and the nobility. In reply to a demand by Alexander that they cease the revolt and surrender the ringleaders, they countered with a demand for the surrender of Antipater and the Macedonian commander of the Cadmeia. They even sent a herald to cry from the city wall that all who wished to free Greece from the yoke of the Macedonian tyrant should join Thebes and the Persian king. Still Alexander waited, unmoving and yet hoping for peace.

About this time, however, Perdiccas, commander of the advance guard close to the walls, being exasperated beyond endurance by the taunts of the Thebans, launched an assault, forced a breach in the wall, and stormed in. Another commander, seeing them enter the city, gathered his troops and hastily followed. Alexander, seeing this, to prevent his friends being cut off, quickly ordered the Agrianians and archers through the breach to support them. The invaders pushed forward for a while, though suffering heavy losses, until the rallied Thebans counter-attacked and drove them precipitately into flight. They poured out of the city in headlong rout. In the meantime the rest of the army had been assembled, and when the Thebans poured out of the gates in pursuit of the first attackers, the Macedonian phalanx fell upon them. Pressing hard upon the heels of the instantly disorganized Theban rout, Alexander drove them back into the city so fast that they had no time to close the gates behind themselves. The Macedonians stormed through, followed by their allies; the garrison of the Cadmeia, raging at the humiliating plight to which the hated Thebans had reduced them, rushed out to join their friends. The Thebans retreated to their colonnaded public square and there made their stand. The phalanx crushed their resistance, they broke and fled, only to be hunted through the narrow streets and alleys and killed like rats. The battle degenerated into little more than a massacre. Six to eight thousand of the Thebans were slain. As Arrian tells us: 'Then indeed the Thebans, no longer defending themselves, were slain, not so much by the Macedonians, as by the Phocians, Plataeans, and other Boeotians, who by indiscriminate slaughter vented their rage against them. Some were even attacked in their houses, others as they were supplicating the gods in the temples, not even women and children were spared.'

The conquered city was a problem, as were the surviving Thebans. They were a stiff-necked people who had made much trouble before and had been forgiven. But their psychological conditioning was such that they would remain uncoercible, perpetual revolters, unlike the nimble-witted Athenians, who had understanding enough to know when adversity had beaten them. Thebes had transgressed too greatly this time for forgiveness, and must suffer the consequences. Alexander had needed an opportunity and reason to make one thunderbolt stroke in Greece as a terrible object lesson, to end sedition and revolt, and here, in the universally hated Thebes, he had both. As Alexander the Macedonian king, however, he could do nothing in retaliation, but as Alexander, hegemon of the League of Corinth! ah, that was different. A hastily summoned council decided the question, and from the mouths of her oppressed 'little peoples' the Thebans heard their sentence pronounced. And out of the bleak hatred they bore for their old oppressor, the sentence was doom indeed. The city, except for the house of Pindar [1] the poet, was razed to the ground, a garrison of the allies placed in the Cadmeia, and the city's lands, except that set aside for sacred uses, were apportioned to Alexander's auxiliaries. The people, with exception of the descendants of Pindar, the known friends of Macedonia, and the priests, to the number of over thirty thousand, were sold into slavery, the

---

[1] Dion Chrysostom gives us as the reason for sparing the house of Pindar, that Alexander enjoyed the poet's works and read them constantly. Perhaps gratitude had also something to do with it, for it is also true that Pindar had celebrated in song that earlier Alexander and his victories at the Olympic games.

glut depressing the slave market throughout the Aegean for a considerable time. A decree was also passed outlawing all Theban fugitives in any territory under supervision of any of the members of the league.

The news of the overthrow and destruction of Thebes swept like the wind over all Greece. Sedition was paralyzed. The Arcadian troops in the isthmus halted abruptly and disbanded. The Arcadians at home pronounced the death sentence against all persons who had assisted Thebes with men or money. The people of Elis recalled Alexander's exiled friends. Now that Alexander had visited the terrible punishment upon Thebes, he could, without laying himself open to suspicion of weakness, pardon the rest of the innovators, and did so.

When the news of the Theban disaster reached Athens, it came as the people were just completing preparations, late in September, for celebration of the Greek mysteries. Athens was panic-stricken. Thebes had transgressed before, but had been forgiven, now she was destroyed. Athens had also transgressed before, several times even more greatly, and had also been forgiven, but now surely Nemesis was upon her, and the day of reckoning come. The people of Attica fled to the shelter walls, a war loan for a final desperate defense was raised, the city walls strengthened. But the political wheels went round, the anti-Macedonian party of Demosthenes was ousted, and the party of Demades came to power. A committee of ten was elected and appointed to congratulate Alexander upon his safe return from among the barbarian Triballians and Illyrians, and for his punishment of Thebes. When the ambassadors appeared with the letter, the fawning sycophancy of its contents disgusted even Alexander, accustomed as he was to such missives. He tore it up and threw the pieces on the ground and turned his back upon the deputation. Later, however, he recalled them and dismissed them with a letter to the Athenians in which he asserted his willingness to grant them pardon upon the following terms: first, they must expel the Theban fugitives sheltered by the city; second, they must surrender to him the following politicians and militarists whom he regarded as having been the fountain-heads of all opposition and insurrection of the last three years: Demosthenes, Lycurgus, Hyperides, Polyeuctus, Charetes, Charidemus (of whom we hear later as an ally of the Persian king), Ephialtes (who was later killed fighting the Macedonians at Halicarnassus), Diotemus, Merocles, and Chares, the *condottiere* admiral.

The demand produced great excitement in Athens, and the matter was brought before a town meeting to be thoroughly threshed out. Many voices were raised in opposition to the proposal on grounds that surrendering their own citizens to the young autocrat was abasing and degrading. The old general Phocion, whose integrity, patriotism, knowledge of military matters, and past conduct was such that none could impugn his motives, advocated that were Alexander's anger unleashed against the city its destruction was inevitable: it was, he said, better that the few should be willing to sacrifice themselves for the many, rather than that the whole should perish. But again Demosthenes' golden tongue swayed the people. He and Hyperides pleaded that the citizens should pluck up their courage, assert their national dignity, and care now for those who had in the past spent themselves in caring for the city. In other words, the great orator found himself now looking into the face of the death his conniving political stupidity had brought to many others; and as most other warmongers, he cringed from the face of justice. Then Demades suggested a counter-proposal, that another embassy be sent Alexander, offering to try the accused men under Athenian law, and promising punishment if they were found guilty. Regarding the Thebans, they had already been terribly punished, and the embassy begged mercy upon the few survivors. The proposal was adopted by the meeting, and the second embassy, led by Phocion, elected. When they again visited Alexander, he agreed to their own terms, with the exception that he would grant no amnesty to Charidemus. The Persian attempt had failed, Greece was at peace internally, and Alexander free at last to devote his energies to prosecution of the long-planned, oft-delayed beginning of the campaign against Persia.

He returned to Pella late in the autumn of 335 and immediately began to push the final stages of his preparation. Parmenio was recalled from Asia Minor and he, Antipater, and Alexander began to work out the details of the army organization and organization of the home government. Antipater was the abler of the two old generals; Alexander therefore made him regent in charge of Macedonia and Greece during his own absence. Parmenio, though overcautious and without initiative as a *strategos*, was nevertheless a splendid organizer, rigidly loyal, and could be relied upon to follow instructions and orders to the letter. Alexander needed such a man, and took him along. Then there was another problem at home, Alexander's hell-cat mother, Olympias, whom he loved, but recognized as a definite liability. All he could do was to hope that Antipater would be firm enough to keep her from doing too much damage, and diplomat enough to avoid too much conflict and clash of wills. That the arrangement, though it did work well for a while, created a great deal of trouble in the home government is shown by the fact that soon after Alexander's departure into Asia, Antipater begins to write him, more and more insistently and bitterly as time goes by, of Olympias' interference in affairs which she should have left alone.

Alexander gathered his company. With him he took Eumenes (whom Philip had found as a boy in Cardia and made his secretary) as chief of his secretariat; Callisthenes of Olynthus, nephew of Aristotle; Anaxarchus and Pyrrhon, professional philosophers of the Skeptic School, to perform duties vaguely similar to those of the modern army chaplain; a group to handle the religious ceremonies under Aristander as chief soothsayer; another group called *bematistae*, whose duties it was to make records of the routes taken and distances traveled, and another very considerable group of students of the various sciences.

Before his departure, though Olympias was outspokenly annoyed at his generosity, Alexander made large gifts from the public funds and lands to many who had served him well, but were not going with him, as compensation for having no part in the spoil and great treasures they were going to take from the Persians. Parmenio and several others refused his grants and gifts. One of the recipients of his prodigal bounty is said to have asked Alexander what he was keeping for himself, 'My hopes,' answered the young king. To which Perdiccas, who was standing near, is said to have rejoined, 'In this your soldiers will be your partner.'

=V=

ORGANIZATION AND
FINANCE OF THE ARMY

WHEN Philip ascended the throne of Macedonia he found the country little more than a regional name, inhabited by a narrowly insular population noted mostly for their rude barbarianism and disunity. The citizen army was little more than a bare rabble of unorganized, ill-disciplined, poorly armed tribesmen, fighting on foot, assisting the real army core of several hundred mounted men led by a king whose real status was hardly more than that of a mere tribal chief. When he died twenty-three years later, the country was firmly molded into a national entity high in morale and fighting spirit, with the best organized, best equipped and disciplined army the world had ever known, and the kingship was firmly seated in absolute autocratic authority. Philip's original intention, later fulfilled, of making himself master of Greece, caused him to see clearly that in order to master his southern neighbors his military machine must be at least equal to any logical combination of allies in numbers and *matériel*, and superior to them in psychological preparation. For years his every effort had been bent toward attaining this objective, which, when accomplished, presently became supplanted by another, greater and more grandiose in conception, breath-taking in scope and magnitude, the projected conquest against the Persian Empire. Philip stands out in history as a shining example of grim determination and single-mindedness of purpose, a militaristic organizer and empire-builder head and shoulders above any historical figure who preceded him. Theopompus, the historian, was one of the few ancients who correctly gauged the monumental stature and caliber of the Macedonian, for he says, 'Taking him all in all, Europe has never borne another man like Philip, son of Amyntas.' [1] And indeed, until the birth of Alexander, Europe had never borne a better.

In Greece, with the tyrants firmly in power in most of the cities, the enormous number of slaves owned by them and the ruling cliques, had caused the gradual but complete pauperization of the great mass of citizens. For years they had been supported by the slave-owning oligarchy, growing more slothful and corrupt as the poverty-stricken but politically powerful wards of the state. The decline of the material welfare of the citizens had coincided with the decline of their patriotic love for their city-states; they would still shriek for it in the forum, but not fight for it in the field. The dispossessed and disinherited of the earth never make good fighters for the property rights of others. Thus, with few exceptions, the cities of Greece relied heavily upon hired mercenary soldiers with a slight leaven of citizens to fight their battles. The best fighting organizations of the time were the Thebans, with the Athenians a poor second, and the once proud Spartans a poorer third.

The dense Theban phalanx under Epaminondas had broken the hitherto invincible power of the Lacedaemonians by sheer weight of numbers and density of formation. Philip was quick to recognize that the Thebans were massed too closely, their

---

[1] Theopompus, *Fragmenta Historicorum Graecorum*, frag. 27.

formation too unwieldy to be effective against a commander not utterly imbued with the idea of victory through sheer over-whelming weight of numbers, or not so woodenly unadaptable as the conservative Spartans. The heavy Greek hoplite was armed with the oblong or rectangular shield (*hoplon*), curved to protect the body, a two-edged short sword, and a thrusting pike of eight to ten feet in length. Philip invented, or at least adapted, the two-handed spear, a massive weapon variously cited as eighteen to twenty-one feet long, most commentators citing Polybius as their authority for the latter figure, he quite definitely stating the *sarissa* as being fourteen cubits in length. At any rate the long Macedonian spear accomplished what Philip desired, it outreached the shorter weapons of the Greeks and it won victories for him.

Contrary to the usual conception that the phalanx was a fighting organization developed about this time, archeologists have found records in southern Babylonia proving that the Sumerians there had employed the phalanx as early as two thousand years b.c. The Assyrians had adopted it in turn, for later records relate its use by them in overthrowing the Hittite empire about 1350 b.c. It seems to have fallen into disuse until it was revived and perfected by Epaminondas, who formed his phalanx as deep as thirty-six ranks. Considering the numbers of men involved it was inefficient, but effective against the Spartan parallel or quadruple line. It was, however, even at its best, unwieldy, and could not be maneuvered over broken ground without breaking into a useless mob. Philip modified the phalanx greatly, making it much lighter, only sixteen ranks deep, so drilling it that it could, at word of command, instantly re-form eight ranks deep with a front of doubled length. Alexander's phalanx was the same as that of Philip, efficient against similar organizations, but, as he discovered later, much less so against the mobility of the irregular Persians. Not only was it never the decisive factor in any of his battles, but on at least two occasions, to be told later, the phalanx was so hard pressed that it had to be rescued from its predicament by the heavy cavalry.

After the battle of Arbela we hear no more of its use and we are told that Alexander, shortly before his death, had planned a new, more mobile and efficient organization to supplant it.

The basic unit of the phalanx was a file or *lochos* of sixteen hoplites, whose leader, the *lochagos*, occupied the place of command, honor, and danger at the head of the file. The last man was a kind of second-in-command and was known as the *uragos*. The man directly behind the lochagos received extra pay, as did also the man in front of the uragos, the inferior men being placed in the center of the file. Four files (*lochoi*) of sixty-four men constituted a *tetrarchia* commanded by a *tetrarch*, whose post was in front of the right-hand file. Two tetrarchiae constituted a *taxiarchia* of one hundred and twenty-eight men, whose commander was known as a *taxiarch*. Two taxiarchiae constituted a *syntagma* or *xenagia* of two hundred and fifty-six men, commanded by an officer seemingly interchangeably called either *syntagmatarch* or *xenagos*, and a duplication of appellations occurs in the title of uragos who was second-in-command. There was also an adjutant, a color- or standard-bearer, and a trumpeter. These last transmitted commands by various movements of the standard or by trumpet blasts when oral commands were impractical. The syntagma, when massed sixteen ranks square, was the basic striking unit of the array. Four syntagmata were a *chiliarchia*, frequently referred to by the elastic title of *taxis*, which was also used to denote a detachment of almost any size, commanded by a *strategos*. Four chiliarchiae of sixteen syntagmata in a single massed unit of command were the striking unit known as the simple phalanx of four thousand and ninety-six spearmen under a *phalangiarch*. Two phalanxes were a double phalanx under a *diphalangiarch*, and two of these constituted the heaviest massed military striking unit the world has ever known, the 'grand' phalanx of sixteen thousand three hundred and eighty-four heavy armed hoplites and their officers, under a *tetraphalangiarch*. These divisions and numbers must be regarded more as theoretical than practical. In the old days when an army was far afield it faced nearly insurmountable difficulties in recruiting to maintain its strength. Losses from disease were usually greater than battle casualties, and it is obvious that though units may sometimes have been recruited to full strength they cannot have long remained so. The phalangists were known as *pezhetairoi* or 'foot companions,' a designation formerly carried by the small unit who had really been the king's guard. As Philip expanded the numbers of the footmen of his army he used the guards as their nucleus, and passed the privileged title on to the whole of his heavy infantry.

In battle order in the syntagma (the tactical unit of the taxis) the individual soldier occupied a space about three feet square. The first five ranks leveled their sarissas, those of the front rank (granting that the figure of twenty-one to twenty-four feet for length is correct) protruding fifteen feet; those of the second rank would project twelve feet ahead of the first rank; those of the third, fourth, and fifth ranks, nine, six, and three feet, respectively, ahead of the front rank. The front rank, therefore, was protected by a bristling hedge of spear-points through which nothing penetrable could pass, and live. The last eleven ranks, seemingly to order, either held their long weapons erect or sloped forward at an angle, both for ease in holding and to help ward off flying missiles. When these latter were arriving in appreciable numbers, the front rank sometimes knelt behind their shields, the second rank raised theirs at an angle in front of and over their heads, the other ranks raising theirs horizontally over their heads. Sometimes, when the arrow fire was particularly severe, the entire group tightened and closed their intervals, the raised shields presenting a solid missile-proof roof called a 'tortoise,' against the deadly hail. The phalanx might advance with a solid front of massed taxeis, or it might, as was Alexander's usual custom, be moved into action with them echeloned one behind the other to the right or left as circumstances dictated. The taxis might in turn be broken into echeloned syntagmata, formed into either a solid block or open square, into a wedge formation for attack, into circles of various sizes, or any one of several other formations at word of command.

The phalanx could wheel through any segment of an arc to face any direction, double their front by stepping the even numbers to right or left into the interval, closing up, and giving way right and left from the center, files were broken in two and the rear half detached for service to the rear in case of attack from that direction, or to be moved elsewhere; and several other maneuvers could be ordered and several other formations were available at word of command. There is excellent reason to believe that Alexander generally used his phalanx eight ranks deep rather than Philip's customary sixteen, but it must be remembered that there was no set rule. One of Alexander's greatest qualities was his instant recognition of the need for changed tactics, and his ability to make them upon the spur of the moment. For instance, Arrian tells us, in the narrow gorges about Pellion Alexander formed his phalanx into a wedge one hundred and twenty ranks deep. At Granicus he used his conventional echelon of taxeis; at Arbela he formed two assault wings and a highly mobile reserve. The phalanx with which Alexander began the invasion of the Persian Empire was, as near as we can judge from a careful compilation of the data of our ancient authorities, composed wholly of native Macedonians, and was, if we grant that the heavy hypaspists were not included in it, nine thousand strong, divided into six taxeis. The commanders at the outset were Perdiccas, Meleager, Amyntas, Coenus, Araterus, and Ptolemy (who was killed at the battle of Issus and replaced by Polysperchon). Later many changes were made, as promotions were granted or governmental posts were created which Alexander felt safe in filling only with his most trusted men.

Complementing the heavy-armed and comparatively slow phalangists was the unit of hypaspists, so called from their round shields, the aspis, numbering about three thousand, under command of Nicanor, second son of the veteran general Parmenio. Of generally superior caliber to the heavy hoplites, they were trained to be equally effective in the phalanx, or operating as separate units of various sizes. They were excellent in the assault, in the field, in the van or rear-guard, or as hard-hitting fighters in front of the phalanx before the opening of the battle. They were divided into five chiliarchiae, of which one, a *corps d'élite*, was the royal bodyguard of foot known as the *agema*, and sometimes historically as the 'Silver Shields.' They seem to have been an aristocratic unit, for they usually referred to the others of their type as 'the other hypaspists.' They were armed with short spears, long swords, and protected by helmets, breastplates, and greaves.

Other heavy hoplites or hypaspists were four thousand Greek auxiliaries under Antigonus, and six thousand mercenaries under Menander. Information is wanting as to their exact status, and the conclusion that they were troops of the hoplite type is based solely on the data that two thousand additional auxiliaries are definitely referred to as being lightarmed troops. Alexander seems to have had a no doubt justifiably poor opinion of the league men, or perhaps our authorities wrote partisan histories, for they are never mentioned as having distinguished themselves outstandingly. One gets the impression that they were used as garrisons and to keep open the long lines of communications. It is not improbable that many of them were also used as military colonizers along with the failing and convalescent, for we find that soon after Alexander's death, a large body of Greek colonizers, making their way homeward from the inhospitable plains of arid Sogdiana, were destroyed as deserters from their posts.

In the third category of footmen were the *peltasts*, light skirmishers and harassers armed with lances, short swords or daggers, and protected only by small round arm shields and cuirasses of quilted linen or leather. There were two thousand Greek auxiliaries and mercenaries of this type. It is also probably correct to include in this category the *psiloi* or light irregulars, the Thracian and Agrianian spear and javelin men. The final category included about five hundred Cretan archers and the same number of Macedonian archers and slingers. The foot soldiers of Alexander's army thus numbered about thirty thousand.

Despite the forbidding array of the massed spearmen, however, it was the notable heavy Macedonian cavalry, the *hetairoi*, who carried off signal honors in battle. Chosen from among the wealthier classes, the democratic cavalryman was at first practically the social equal of the king. It was only in Philip's reign that the line of social demarcation became sharp, and when Alexander obtained the throne he was king first and 'companion' second, if at all. Thus, though the whole of the heavy cavalry were called 'companions,' only one, the squadron known as the *agema*, the mounted royal bodyguard commanded by his boyhood friend Clitus, and whom the king himself was often wont to lead, were on the old friendly and democratic footing with the king. The whole body, under Philotas, first son of Parmenio, numbered, according to conflicting data, from twelve to eighteen hundred, and were divided into eight squadrons (*ilae*), from one hundred and fifty to two hundred and fifty strong, with the probabilities favoring the lower figure. A description of the conventional Greek cavalry tactics and organization would be of little value in our history, for we have little reason to believe, and much reason to disbelieve, that Alexander cared much about the conventional formations. In general, however, it can be said that the Macedonian cavalry command was called an *ilē*. The Greek basic cavalry unit was also called an *ilē*, or platoon, of sixty-four men in sixteen files four deep; eight ilae constituted a *hipparchy*, two of these an *ephipparchy*, and four ephipparchiae an *epitagma*, a grand cavalry phalanx of four thousand and ninety-six men. This was the technical Greek formation, which the Macedonians seem to have ignored. The other heavy cavalry, the Thessalians, were little, if any, inferior to the *hetairoi*. They, too, were divided into eight ilae and numbered about twelve hundred. Their armament consisted of a metallic helmet, a cuirass of quilted linen or leather covered with metal scales, and high Macedonian boots; they rode without saddles and carried two-edged swords and a stabbing lance about eight feet long, but were without shield or javelin. The light Greek auxiliaries numbered about four hundred, the light

Macedonian, Paeonian, and Thracian auxiliaries and lancers about six hundred each. Besides these we find mention of an unknown number of other cavalry called *sarissaphors*, armed with the long weapon of the hoplites. It is difficult to imagine the use to which mounted men armed with this massive spear might be put, but the impression prevails that they were probably used by the provost marshal as guards for the large numbers of prisoners captured and to protect the train. The cavalry, therefore, numbered at least forty-six hundred and perhaps as high as fifty-two hundred strong. The whole fighting force, cavalry and infantry combined, was a few hundred more or less than thirty-five thousand strong, an apparently pitifully small army to pit against the Great King backed by the might of the Persian Empire.

In the battle array the center was always the massed syntagmata of the six taxeis of the phalanx. To their right, generally but not necessarily invariably, were the five chiliarchiae of the hypaspists, with the royal agema always on the right of the hypaspist formation. Sometimes they were posted to the rear of the phalanx to act as a reserve to be thrown in where necessary as the battle developed. To their right were the eight squadrons of the hetairoi, with Clitus' squadron always on the extreme right. The extreme end of the right wing were light cavalry, and sometimes archers and slingers ready to move out in a screen of harassers and skirmishers and open the action. When these were driven back by the advance of the heavy attackers they ran to the rear through lanes opened for them in the phalanx. On the left of the phalanx were the heavy Thessalians, to their left additional light auxiliaries. In opening the battle the heavy 'companions' usually moved forward first, squadron by squadron in echelon, left refused. When the cavalry impact broke the enemy line, the phalanx moved forward in the same formation, with the Thessalians riding alongside to prevent or break a flank attack from the as yet untouched right wing of the enemy. The position or uses of the four hundred Greek cavalry is open to conjecture. Owing to the thinly veiled animosities existing between the various national groups, it is doubtful that they were brigaded with the other units. Certainly the fiercely nationalistic hetairoi would never have tolerated them, and it is improbable that the scornful Thessalians would. They, therefore, probably operated as a separate unit where small numbers of hard-hitting cavalry would be invaluable. On the march the light cavalry, notably the Thracians, played the part of scouts, in the service of intelligence, and as royal messengers.

To supplement the fighting men proper we find them using light catapults throwing javelins (*euthytona*), others throwing stones (*palintona*). These of course had to be taken along, as had also an extra supply of arms and tools and perhaps certain parts of the siege towers and battering rams so freely used in Asia Minor and Phoenicia. We find an occasional reference to the existence of a supply train, and this, together with the artillery park, especially in later years when the army's strength multiplied and it operated in arid or mountainous countries, must have grown to a size sufficient to have sometimes constituted a serious drag on the column. The fact that Alexander's army marched twenty-two thousand miles with a serious shortage of supplies reported only in the deserts of barren Gedrosia (Makran) bespeaks not only a huge supply train, but a degree of efficiency and planning hardly to be equaled, certainly not surpassed, even today. This column varied greatly in size and numbers from time to time. Each mounted man was allowed one slave in attendance, who, to keep up with his master, must have been mounted. To carry rations, spare arms and armor, tents and other necessaries for both, would require at least one, possibly two additional packhorses. Each ten men of the phalanx were allowed one slave. Their equipment and rations would require at least two horses for transportation. We therefore would have a column, including spare animals and remounts, of several thousand horses, mules, and later, camels. Later also there must be added to these an immense quantity of booty that was carried along, thousands of captives and slaves, and still later, large numbers of women and children of the men, plus the increasingly luxurious ménages of the officers, and we find the trains swollen to monstrous size.

We thus find Alexander at last ready to take the field in earnest against the world's most powerful monarch with the resources of half of Asia at his command. The question of how many troops Darius had at his disposal for use against Alexander is one which cannot be answered. The Persian Empire, with its estimated population of fifty millions of persons, stretching as it did from the Carian coast to the Indus River, and from the Caspian Sea to the Indian Ocean, theoretically could provide the Great King with almost unlimited numbers of fighting men. In actual practice, however, the vast distances from Babylon to the outposts of his empire limited very definitely the number of men he could levy; as did the fact that his lax hold on much of it precluded forcing large numbers of recalcitrants into objectionable service. Though we may disregard as fantastic the numbers tradition gives us of Darius' army, it is still undeniable that in each of Alexander's pitched battles, the three of Granicus, Issus, and Arbela, his army was outnumbered in increasing ratios. Besides his own picked troops from his own personal areas of Iran, Media, and Parthia, conscripts from the rest of his empire, Darius had also thousands of Greek mercenaries who still served him, many to the death, despite the decree of the Council of Corinth against Greeks taking service with foreign rulers.

Alexander's financial position was markedly worse than his military one despite the marked disparity in the size of the two forces. The Great King had an almost unlimited wealth of gold and silver in his various treasuries scattered throughout his wide-flung empire. Thousands and thousands of talents of both metals had been gathered by his predecessors of the previous two hundred and fifty years, and stored away in an ever-increasing horde against contingencies. He had an annual personal tribute income of seventy-six hundred talents, besides the tributes due for the army and governmental expenses, plus tributes in kind, amounting to scores of thousands of cattle, horses, sheep, and slaves.

Alexander had, upon his accession to the throne, found but sixty talents of ready money in the treasury, and a public debt of five hundred talents, to which must be added his own personal debt of eight hundred talents. However, the young king seems not to have done so badly in his brief one and a half years' reign, for we are told that when he left for Asia he owed but seven hundred talents and possessed seventy talents in money, and supplies barely enough to last for a month. Without his supreme confidence in his destiny he might be considered merely an adventurer, but he must have received very accurate information of the country and must have known he could live off it until supplies and treasury both could be replenished, a confidence that afterward proved justified.

The whole question of the coinages upon which were built the campaigns of Alexander is much too complicated and subject to too many variables to be discussed at length. Occasionally our records and histories tell us of sums captured or dispensed, and some historians, inaccurately informed of the actual coin or weights involved in these transactions, refer in awe to their vast values. Such impressions are wholly erroneous in the matter of translations or comparisons. That the sums were considered vast in that day, when all metals were comparatively scarce and possessed of a relative value inconsonant with modern conceptions of equivalent amounts, is intelligible. We have, unfortunately, few guides to an estimate of equivalent values, and must each form his own opinion of them in so far as his scope of knowledge extends or his imagination will substitute for the lack of specific data.

The Philippian gold stater, when it first appeared, was struck in such numbers as the result of the immense increase of the output of the mines of Mount Pangeum, that they caused a fall in the market price of gold in relation to silver from a high of about 13.3 to 1, and apparently an average of 12 to 1, to as low as 10 to 1. Thus a gold stater was a coin of about 135 grains

(8.6 grams) weight, and was equated in value with the familiar Persian gold daric of about 133 grains (8.34 grams) weight. By Philip's intent the stater was tariffed at twenty-four silver drachmae of 67.5 grains. As the ratio of gold to silver fell to 10 to 1, a new drachma of 56.5 grains was struck to replace the heavier coin. As his basic silver coin Philip adopted the so-called Phoenician stater of about 224 grains (14.5 grams) weight, the common coin of the islands, the Chalcidic peninsula and the Thracian seaboard. The gold stater bore a head with long hair, usually regarded as that of Apollo, but there is reason to suspect that it was really supposed to represent that of Philip as Ares, the war god of Macedonia and Thrace.

The stater was exchangeable according to the following scale: The gold stater (135 grains, 8.6 grams) equaled six tetradrachmae of 224 grains, which was also the weight value of twelve didrachmae of 112 grains (7.25 grams), and twenty-four drachmae of 56.5 grains (3.62 grams). There was also another coin in the series, the dekadrachma, which seems to have been little used; at any rate, it seems so rare today that we have been unable to secure information other than to verify its existence. There was another common little coin of silver, called the obol, of 11.4 grains (.73 grams) weight and an octobol, or eight-obol piece, of 66 grains weight, equivalent in value to the older heavy drachma.

In Persia the gold daric of 133 grains (8.34 grams) was a more stable unit of currency, the exchange value of which, 'like the law of the Medes and Persians altereth not,' simply due to the vastness of the empire and Oriental resistance to change. This was based upon the silver unit known to us commonly as the silver shekel (Greek, *siglo*) of 86 grains (5.57 grams) and exchangeable at the rate of twenty shekels to one gold shekel or daric.

The widely misunderstood *talenton* or talent,[1] a large slab of copper or bronze, was an even more ancient and primitive unit of metal value. In the old days it was usually shaped like a

[1] Charles Seltman, *Greek Coins*. London, 1933.

spread cow-hide with the neck and tail cut off, and in earlier periods was equivalent to one good cow in exchange value. The actual weight of the base metal talent varied with the standard adopted by various localities, but the standard adopted in Attica was that of early Achaea, of 57.58 pounds, or 26.26 kilograms. As the other and more precious and more easily transportable metals, silver and gold, came into usage, they were equated in value with the heavier copper or bronze ingot. Finally the talent was considered to have a gold value represented by the tiny pellet of 133.5 grains, or 8.6 grams of the precious metal; thus the gold stater was actually a gold 'talent,' but definitely and specifically not a talent of gold. We have the authority of an Alexandrian scholar [1] of the Hellenistic period for the statement: 'The talent of Homer was equal (i.e., weight) to the latter daric, or two Attic drachmae,' of 67.5 grains each. As the Persian daric scaled exactly twice as heavy, or 8.34 grams, the base metal equivalent of this small gold coin was the big crude ingot of copper. Thus the Persian daric and the Philippian stater were both a talent in value, and a talent of silver was a weight of 1348 grains, or 87.3 grams, when the exchange value was on a 10 to 1 base.

In Persia, too, there existed a double weight unit similar to the smaller Grecian gold talent and the great copper or bronze talent. The gold shekel or daric was the small unit, the large unit the *biltu* of about 30 kilograms. In between these there was a medium weight, the *mna* or *manah*, usually known as the classical *mina*. This gives us the following scale of values: 1 shekel, 8.34 grams; 60 shekels, 1 mina of 500.40 grams; 60 minae, 1 biltu of 30024.00 grams. The Greeks were made acquainted with the biltu and mina through intercourse with the Phoenician traders, and presently they adapted and adjusted the weight and value of their own talent system to that of the Persians.

Of the system of payments for services we can glean little from

---

[1] Hultsch, *Metrologicorum scriptum reliquiae*, 1, 301.

our direct narrators, and other sources are very contradictory.[1] Thus we hear that in Attica, which was the pace-setter for all Greece in most respects, at one time the money allowance for the food and maintenance of each soldier and sailor amounted to two obols per day. In this regard no other information has come to our attention. While the Egyptians were endeavoring to maintain their independence after their successful revolt against Persian domination, individual mercenary commanders were offered personal pay as high as ten staters per day, and of the soldiers' pay we are told nothing. At one point in his narrative of the expedition of Alexander, Arrian mentions a ten-stater man, but this reference tells us absolutely nothing else. Whether he received ten staters a month, year, or what! we are unable to determine. Cyrus the Persian, in 401, paid each of his heavy mercenary infantrymen a daric or gold Phoenician stater per month. Demosthenes, in one of the *Philippics*, makes the statement that the pay of an Athenian hoplite was ten drachmae (the light 56.5 grain coin) per month, but there was an agreement by the Athenians to pay mercenaries from Argos at the rate of one 67.5 grain drachma of Aegina to each cavalryman, and three obols for each light infantryman, per day. Two cities along the coast of the Euxine Sea offered Xenophon's army a gold Phoenician stater per month per man, another offered a daric. Droysen (*q.v.*) does indeed offer tentative figures for the probable rate of pay of Alexander's army, ranging from three hundred drachmae per month per man for the hetairoi, downward through a graduated scale to a minimum of eighty-four drachmae per month for each light infantryman. But the figures he offers are manifestly absurdly high. No army since the beginning of time has ever been paid upon such a munificent scale. Until, if ever, more light be shed upon this subject, it will have to be acknowledged as unsettled and unknown.

[1] See also Andreades, *Les finances de guerre d'Alexandre le Grand. Annales d'histoire économique et sociale*, pp. 321–334. Paris, 1929.

=VI=

THE CAMPAIGN
IN ASIA MINOR

Finally all his plans were completed, and in the spring of 334 Alexander moved out of Pella upon the beginning of the long journey which was to carry him to what the Greeks visioned as the ends of the world, a journey from which he was never to return. A twenty-one-year-old king, godlike in his physical beauty, and even now convinced that he was the son of Zeus-Ammon, with the last words of Olympias in his ears reminding him of his divine birth. He marched to Amphipolis, inspected his newly gathered fleet harbored on Lake Cercinitis, gave them orders to sail at once to the Propontus, and marched away on the most ambitious project ever undertaken by any man, before or since. He passed Phagres and Pergamum, skirted Mount Pangaeus (Rhodope) to Abdera, went on through Dicaea, Maronea, Messambria, and Aenos, and rounded the Gulf of Melas (Saros) to Cardia (today ruins on the promontory of Bakla-burun), and arrived at Sestos in the Chersonese after covering three hundred and fifty miles in twenty days.

Here where the Hellespont is narrowest (about three quarters of a mile) Xerxes had built his famous double bridge of boats and crossed, nearly a century and a half before. Here also Leander — one can only guess how long before — had nightly swum the strait to his rendezvous with Hero, priestess of Aphrodite. And here, too, Alexander proposed to cross his army. The fleet, of one hundred and sixty ships, had arrived, and these, with a number of local craft, were put to the task of ferrying the men over the narrow water to Abydos, on the Asiatic side near the point where the Turkish fort of Nagara stands today. The Persian fleet, which certainly must have been forewarned of the attempted movement, was unaccountably lax in failing to be on hand to make an attempt at least at barring the passage. Their four hundred ships, efficiently manned by Phoenicians and Cypriots as well a large number of Greek mercenaries, could certainly have delayed, perhaps even permanently blocked, the attempt, had the commander been equal to the task. Their failure to do so is one of the many inexplicable things and circumstances which time and time again played Alexander's game for him.

Alexander left the task of overseeing the passage to Parmenio while he himself went, with a small group of friends and the bodyguard, about fifteen miles down the coast to Elaeus (Eski Hissarlik), to a small cairn of stones on the Chersonese coast, legendarily reputed to be the grave of Protesilaus. He was said to have been the first Greek to land, and the first to be slain in the Homeric attack upon ancient Troy, just across the strait. Alexander paused at the tomb and sacrificed to his *manes* to save him from a like fate. He then crossed from Elaeus, steering his own ship until in the middle of the strait. Here he relinquished the tiller and sacrificed a bull to the gods of the sea, and poured out a libation from a golden cup to the Nereids, with, no doubt, a little extra piety to his ancestress the sea-goddess Thetis,[1] mother of Achilles.

---

[1] Wife of Peleus, *Iliad*, I, 538, XVIII, 35; also XXIV.

When the ship neared land, he flung his spear ashore and leaped after it to the beach where a thousand years earlier Agamemnon himself had drawn his fleet to the shallows, crying in a loud voice that he claimed all Asia as 'land won by the spear' according to the custom of the early Greek tribes. Behold him now, this romantic young descendant of Achilles and Heracles, a slightly unbalanced young king, whose ambition was even now nothing less than to dispossess Darius of his vast dominions; probably already planning to force upon a reluctant world acknowledgment of his godly origin, and to establish his own pan-Hellenic empire in all the world's lands. It is perhaps necessary to emphasize this, for many others have overlooked the obvious fact that, after all, Alexander was but the product of his age, when the greatest thinkers of all Greece gave their sanction to enslavement of the 'barbarian' and custom gave to him, who possessed the might to take it, the moral right to all lands and peoples his sword could conquer and force to acknowledge. Any lesser action than the uttermost limit of desires was looked upon with astonishment and hailed as magnanimity. His motives were very simple. Philip had spent his life building up to this invasion, and the boy's entire life had been spent in an atmosphere of war and conquest for acquisition. He had inherited Philip's army, Philip's generals and staff, and Philip's self-set ambitions. He automatically carried them out; to have done otherwise would have been unthinkable. Darius' vast dominions were his goal now. Ultimately his goal expanded, as will be later seen, transcending the primary intent, to include the whole world. But at this time we cannot credit Alexander with creating, or attempting to create, a political condition beyond the conception of the greatest minds of the day, nor dare we credit him with consciousness and conscience in advance of his epoch or beyond his own few years. To claim that he was actuated by an overwhelming desire to advance and spread Hellenism for its own sake over the bounds of the world for its regeneration is sheer absurdity, and to say that he planned in advance the great changes the Hellenes would later accomplish in those far lands to suit their own selfish ends would be to rank him with the foreseeing gods. It were better to look upon him rationally, as a young man eager for battle and conquest, very sure of himself and seeing the world through the rose-light of youth and large-hearted consciousness of his kingly power, which none might gainsay.

There is, in the statement that Asia was claimed as his, won by the spear, the only preliminary announcement we have that his desires transcended the mere freeing of the Greek-founded cities of the seaboard of Asia Minor, and it is easy now to read into it the intention that only became manifest later, his intention to subdue the whole of Asia. It is hardly credible that he had as yet made this known to the army as a whole, though it is entirely possible that the matter had been spoken of to some of his closest friends. For public consumption and information the expedition had been referred to as limited in its scope to Asia Minor, for it is doubtful if the insular Greeks or the still more insular Macedonians would have so whole-heartedly co-operated had they had even an idea that wider conquests in his own name were contemplated. In view of his actions in the earlier part of the campaign, it is possible that he specifically exempted from his intention the Greek areas of Asia Minor, for he did, it seems, in adherence to the promises made in the Treaty of Corinth, free the western coastal regions. However, at this date and distance, in the wording of our authorities, we have no assurance of even this fact.

At the landing-place Alexander erected altars to Zeus, Athena, and his ancestor Heracles and offered sacrifices to them. He then went with his friends and bodyguard to the tombs of the illustrious dead, those of Ajax, Hector, and Priam; and with very special veneration to the two barrows, one large, the other smaller, beneath which were supposed to lie the remains of Achilles and Patroclus. One report is that he stripped himself and ran naked around the tomb of Achilles, and then laid a wreath upon his stele, saying as he did so that Achilles was fortunate in life to have had such a friend as Patroclus, and after his death such a herald as Homer to perpetuate his fame.[1] His bosom friend and companion, Hephaestion, took the hint, and as a Patroclus to his Achilles, he too ran around the tomb of Patroclus, afterward laying a wreath upon it also.

By this time a messenger arrived from Parmenio with the news that the army had been safely ferried over the Hellespont at Abydos and lay in waiting and ready to move, at the near-by town of Arisbe. But first Alexander must further indulge his romantic nature by visiting and paying homage to the sacred soil of ancient Troy. At the village of New Ilium, upon the site of the heroic city, stood a small temple, a shrine of Athene Polias, whose palladium had guarded the citadel of Pergamum. In this temple was the altar of Zeus, before which Neoptolemus, son of Achilles, had sacrilegiously cut down the old king Priam. Alexander, as a descendant of Achilles, made a great sacrifice to the *manes* of the king, as an offering of propitiation. Then he dedicated his armor on the altar of Athene and took thence an ancient votive shield said to have dated back to the heroic days of the Trojan War. This was the shield carried by or before him in all his battles, and long years later saved his life in his suicidal attack upon the Mallians of central India. Aristander the soothsayer declared that sacrifice must be made to Athene, afterward announcing that it had been accepted, and henceforth Athene herself would lead the army even as she had done that other Greek army which had invaded Asia nearly a thousand years before. To Alexander now came Chares, the exiled Athenian ex-admiral and commander of the Athenians at the battle of Chaeronea. He made submission and was forgiven his hostility to the Macedonians.

The king then rejoined his army and moved eastward, reconnoitering as he went, toward Zeleia (Sarikoi), seventy miles away, where a Persian army was awaiting him. He advanced by the way of Percote, passed Lampsacus (Lapsaki), which sent

---

[1] It is obvious that Alexander had no intention of leaving the heralding of his own fame to chance. His taking Callisthenes the historian, and the task he gave Eumenes of keeping the 'Ephemerides,' the daily chronicle of the expedition, is warranty of the fact.

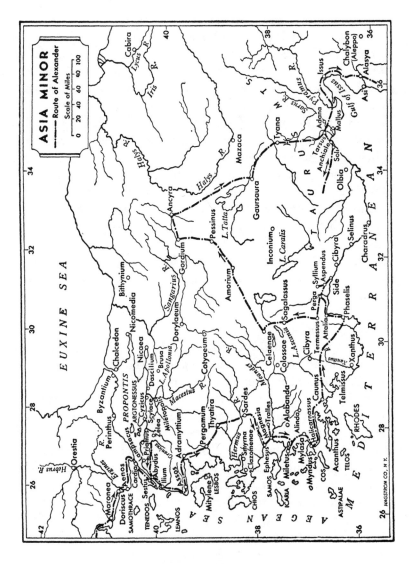

ASIA MINOR
Route of Alexander
Scale of Miles
0 20 40 60 80 100

him an embassy, and received other ambassadorial representatives from the small towns of Hermoton and Priamus. He halted at the latter place and sent out a body of light scouts far in advance, then, to support them in case they contacted the enemy, he added four additional companies of scouts and a troop of his own hetairoi, following them up with the main force. Early in the afternoon of the fourth day after leaving Abydos he reached the valley of the Granicus (Chan chai). There at a point about fifteen miles from the sea, near modern Bigha, where today the road from Brusa (ancient Cierus) to the Sea of Marmora crosses the stream, the enemy awaited his coming.

The satraps of the region, as the most concerned, had assembled their forces and joined Memnon, the Rhodian, and his troops. The satraps and the generals then held a council of war at Zeleia, in which Memnon argued strongly against offering battle at that time. No doubt he knew perfectly well that the untrained provincial nobles and their half-trained retainers, which constituted the cavalry of the satraps, were inadequate to the task of backing his own forces. He also knew well the fighting qualities of the grimly disciplined Macedonians. Had he not fought and finally defeated the Macedonian Parmenio and the murdered Attalus? He proposed to retire ahead of Alexander and lay waste the country as he went, destroying the crops and estates and finally forcing Alexander's retirement from stringency of supplies. This eminently practical plan, betraying as it does an exact knowledge and accurate summation of Alexander's precarious situation, was received with disdain by the proud Persians, who resolutely refused to permit the destruction of a single farmstead. Believing themselves superior to the barbaric invaders, they finally decided upon a pitched battle in which they planned, by a crushing defeat and the deliberate intention of killing the Macedonian king, to eliminate forever the recurrent threat of continued invasions. They then marched to the small Granicus River near-by, and there, with the stream opposing an obstacle to frontal attack, they confidently awaited the coming of the Greeks.

They took position in the flat country east of the river, posting their cavalry close to the bank, their own Greek mercenary infantry being posted some distance to the rear upon a level elevation. Alexander, apprised by his heavy scout screen of the mobilization of the Persian array, arrived from the northwest, and while the army was still in marching order, rode forward to survey the enemy. His eyes must have gleamed when he noted their glaring tactical error of placing their cavalry so close to the steep bank as to lose the inestimable factor of ability to charge. It was so outstanding a piece of stupidity (surely none of Memnon's doing) that he determined an immediate attack before the error was corrected. The cautious Parmenio advised him to encamp and rest the troops and attack the next morning. Parmenio had excellent strategic reasons for the delay, but he had also sixty years to teach him undue prudence. Alexander was young, relatively untried and personally courageous to the point of foolhardiness. But he had, too, the faculty of being, as we see demonstrated time and again, almost infallible in judging instantly and accurately all the angles of any military situation. Now, as he plainly saw, the twenty thousand Persian cavalry were no obstacle at all to his army; and the only enemy troops worthy of consideration were the Greek mercenaries, also numbering about twenty thousand, but posted too far away to be a menace. He instantly ordered the army into line of battle from column of route. Here for the first time he employed the 'oblique battle array' developed by his father Philip and based upon the tactics of Epaminondas, the Theban. The army was divided into an offensive right wing of which he took command, the left or defensive being given to Parmenio. This was the first time he had had to employ this means of attack; his next great battles, those of Issus and Arbela, being started the same way, with, however, local variations dictated by circumstances.

The glitter of Alexander's armor and the attitude of his attendants revealed to the watching Persians the presence of their enemy and the position he had taken, and they hurriedly massed dense squadrons of cavalry on their left wing where they ex-

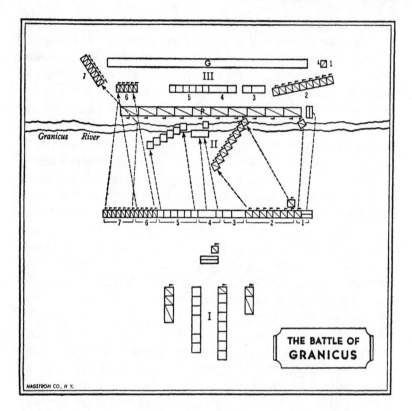

THE BATTLE OF
GRANICUS

HAGSTROM CO., N.Y.

pected his attack. Amyntas was sent off first with a command to engage the enemy's extreme left wing; first with light cavalry skirmishers followed by a troop of the heavy hetairoi, which in turn was supported by a taxei of the hypaspists. This was intended to draw the enemy line farther to the left, thinning and weakening it at the center of the left wing where Alexander proposed to attack. The fundamental idea was to penetrate the enemy's left wing by a heavy cavalry charge, then to turn left and roll up the enemy's flank. The echelon of the phalanx, covered on their left by a heavy protective screen of light cavalry, would roll up irresistibly and complete the destruction of the enemy line.

The two armies paused an instant and faced each other in silence and as if in dread of the action to come. Alexander made a swift survey, noted that all was as he had ordered and gave the signal. The trumpets blared, and at the head of his hetairoi, Alexander moved off. He led the squadrons obliquely across and down the stream half left so that they should present as broad a front as possible when they contacted the enemy. The first arrivals fared hard. The river was fairly deep in places and the bank high and muddy. The horses slipped and stumbled and jammed in a confused mass at the bottom of the bank. Finally the struggling mass of attackers cleared the stream and fell upon the Persian cavalry who seem not to have charged, contenting themselves with hurling darts down upon their advancing enemy. In no other way can the infinitesimal Greek casualties be explained. The Greeks swarmed out of the river and hurled themselves upon the Persian line. Farther to the left they gradually contacted the enemy as a door closing and took up the battle also. They pushed their way steadily forward, the long Macedonian spears of tough cornel wood stabbing their passage deep into the masses of their adversaries. The shorter enemy weapons were outranged; the Persians simply could not reach them. Alexander, storming along like a thunderbolt, was a shining mark and soon found himself beset by several Persian noblemen. His lance broke and he fought on with the fragment until Aretis, an aide, handed him another. That too broke, and another aide, Demeratis of Corinth, gave him his own.

'No sooner had he taken it than, seeing Mithradates, the son-in-law of Darius, riding up at the head of a squadron arranged like a wedge, he rode forward and, striking him full in the face, threw him to the ground. Thereupon Rhoesaces charged full upon Alexander and smote him a blow with his scimitar. A piece was broken from the helmet, but it held against the blow. Then, in turn, Alexander threw him to the ground, driving his lance through his breastplate into his chest. And, just then, as Spithradates had swung his scimitar aloft to bring it down upon the head of the king, Cleitus, the very one whom Alexander six years later in his anger slew, anticipating the blow, smote him through the shoulder, cutting off arm, scimitar, and all.' [1]

It may not be amiss to pause a moment at the thought of how greatly the history of the world would have been changed if Cleitus had not blocked the deadly blow and Alexander had died here on the threshold of his conquests. Alexander's men gradually forced their way into the Persian mass, fighting fiercely all the while. He then turned left and pressed toward the center of their line. Parmenio came up, crossed the river, resisted and broke, with the help of the Thessalian cavalry, a hostile attack, and the ponderous phalanx moved irresistibly across the plain. The Persian center felt the first impact. They began to waver, then retreat, and soon the wings, seeing the center broken, joined the rout. They had had relatively light losses, about a thousand men, or five per cent of their total strength, yet as a fighting force they were finished. Panic ended what the long sarissas had started and the survivors fled pell-mell. Starting to pursue them — like his father Philip he aimed at the annihilation of the enemy — Alexander came upon the Greek mercenaries, the best of the army, by some incredible stupidity relegated to uselessness during the battle and now abandoned by their employers and commanders to the wolfish mercy of the Macedonians. While the cavalry attacked them on the flank the phalanx attacked them in front. And so it was that this body of first-class Greek soldiery was totally destroyed with the exception of two thousand prisoners, and, as Arrian says grimly, 'those who escaped by hiding among the bodies of the dead.'

The Persian defeat was overwhelmingly complete. Thus in a few hours on the afternoon of a spring day was proved not only Alexander's superiority as a leader, but the superiority of the Macedonian weapons and discipline. The Macedonian losses were astonishingly light, for Arrian says that the hetairoi lost only twenty-five men, the other cavalry sixty, and the phalanx

[1] Arrian, *Anabasis*, 1, 15.

thirty. These numbers have a suspicious sound, but it enumerates only the dead. There must have been hundreds of wounded, many of whom certainly would die later. The light losses of the phalanx, which were used only against the mercenaries, give the impression that the latter must have swiftly become an unorganized mob and were simply massacred.

Contrasting the Greek losses, the Persians lost at least nineteen thousand men, including many of their greatest personages in this area. Among the slain were Arbupales,[1] grandson of Artaxerxes; Spithradates, satrap of Lydia and Ionia; Mithrobuzanes, governor of Cappadocia; Mithradates, son-in-law of Darius; Pharnaces, brother-in-law of Darius; and Omares, commander of the mercenaries. It is probably correct to add to the battle's toll also Arsites, governor of Phrygia, for he later committed suicide in atonement for his part in the loss of the battle through the rejection of the advice of Memnon. The wily Rhodian fled the field and went to Ephesus.

We cannot, in retrospect, and in anticipation of the future of the campaign, admit that Alexander was, as seemed at the time, a hare-brained adventurer or, as later seemed, a mere opportunist. He knew, for we have abundant evidence of the fact, that the hold of the Persian king upon much of his vast empire was tenuous; that his far-flung satrapies were held together more by sheer inertia than otherwise. They were too far apart to hope to act in unison against an invader, and no single section was strong enough to fight their battles alone. Alexander knew that to make himself master of the empire he had only to break the Persian army and he was certain that his own compact, hard-hitting force could do it. He also must have had a fairly exact idea of the lack of cohesiveness and unity of the heterogeneous elements composing the Persian army. They were as mixed an army as ever took the field, some, such as the Greek mercenaries, fighting for pay only, the Persians mostly because they had to. There were no ties of national patriotism, of religion, or indeed

---

[1] These are obviously not Persian names, nor are they Greek. It must be assumed therefore that they are the Greek rendition of Persian names.

any other sentiment to bind them. They fought well, but not well enough to save Darius' empire against the calculating hammer blows of the cohesive Macedonians. War to the Persians, or at least the aristocracy, was looked upon in the light of a sport to be played according to rules of the game, with many of the chivalrous tenets which were to re-emerge in the attitude of the European knights a thousand years in the future. But before the grim deadliness of the Macedonian ranks their nerve broke, as that of many equally brave soldiers have done before and since in the face of some new or deadly military novelty.

After the battle Alexander ordered the burial of his own dead with their arms and accouterments. Then he went among the wounded, examining their wounds, seeing that they were attended and, as Arrian says, 'allowing each the free liberty of being the herald of his own praise.' As soldiers have never been noted for their reticence as heralds of their own praise, it is not improbable that the young king was soon heartily weary of their boastfulness. He next ordered the slain Persian noblemen and the dead Greek mercenaries buried, sending back the survivors as captives to slave in the mines and farms of Macedonia, because they, as Greeks in opposition to the decrees of the Corinthian League, had borne arms against their own country. He also ordered Lysippus, the sculptor, to make statues of each of the twenty-five fallen hetairoi, these to be set up in the holy temple town of Dion in Macedonia, and granted to the children and parents of the fallen freedom from any and all public taxation and exactions. Then as a final shrewd shot aimed at publicity, he dedicated three hundred sets of Persian armor to the temple of Athene Polias, over which was to be inscribed: 'Alexander son of Philip, and all the Greeks, excepting the Lacedaemonians, have devoted these spoils, taken from the barbarians of Asia.'

He had, apparently, time to consider and deprecate his rash and unconsidered total destruction of the Greek mercenaries. Had he simply forced their surrender his magnanimity would have had favorable repercussions throughout Greece, but in the excitement of the battle this political angle had been overlooked. Now we note, however, for the first time, that the necessity of considering phases other than the purely military destruction of an objective was receiving attention. The dedication of the spoils shows him diplomatically stressing the result of the battle, not as a victory of the Macedonians nor of himself as their king, but of the Alexander who was hegemon, the generalissimo of the allied Greek and Macedonian army acting in behalf of the Corinthian League. He is also at some pains to sneer at the sulking Spartans living aloofly in dreams of their past glories. In this way he sought not only to still the very vocal doubts of himself in Greece, but also to create or widen any ideological rift between the rebellious king Agis of Sparta and the rest of the country. However, we soon see that though he pays lip service to the idea of the league, the actual military services he renders them are but stepping-stones to the attainment of a vastly greater ambition. He may or may not have acted as representative of the league in his dealings with the Greek-founded coastal cities.[1] We presently see him capturing them or accepting their surrender one after another, possibly joining them to the league, restoring their ancient freedoms, save perhaps to him, and their pre-Persian laws and customs. Often he remitted the tributes they had formerly paid their Persian rulers and ordered that they be used instead for local improvements,

[1] W. W. Tarn (*Cambridge Ancient History*, VI, 363–371) admits the impossibility of carrying purely Grecian theories into practice in this region, but in the above (and in his *Alexander and the Unity of Mankind*, British Academy, XIX, 1933) he gives reasons for believing Alexander did hand over the Greek cities to the Corinthian League. Further, he says (*C. A. H.*, 372) Alexander neither claimed nor exercised authority beyond what the league gave him. The latter is true, but subject to this modification: Alexander, if acting only in the capacity of captain-general of the league, had it in his power to act as he saw fit. As captain-general he was appointee of the league, but as king of Macedonia he was dictator to the league, hence masterless and above all laws. To consider him as otherwise is failure to consider facts. Ehrenburg, in his *Alexander and the Greeks*, *op. cit.*, takes the viewpoint that Alexander never joined the coastal or other Asia Minor cities to the league at all. His citations and summaries of their status is more convincing than the opposite viewpoint expressed by Tarn. The matter, however, is purely academic, for the reason just cited, that it made no practical difference whether he did or not. In the final analysis they were wholly subject to his will, as expressed either by him personally, or through the satraps as his representatives.

but his acts did not exclude the king from interfering with their political and economic life at will, disregarding, and unrestricted in his actions, by the League of Corinth. But here along the Hellespont he considered himself in purely Persian territories and immediately began to rule over them as king. For Phrygia, whose governor had just died a suicide, he appointed Calas as satrap,[1] giving his vacated command over the Thracian cavalry to Alexander, son of Aeropus, usually called by history Alexander the Lyncestian. Thus he gave to the inhabitants the government, even to the title of the governors, to which they had been accustomed, and it does not appear that his rule was either more or less tyrannical. The tributes they were called upon to pay him seem to have been the same in amount and value as they had paid their old lord and master. Parmenio was sent, temporarily, for soon we hear of him rejoining his king, to take charge of the capital, Dascylium (Yaskili), eighty miles eastward, which, since the Persian garrison had fled, was surrendered without fighting.

From the battlefield on the Granicus, Alexander marched to Sardis (Sart), the famous old capital of the Lydian kingdom. Most of our ancient authorities and historians say no more. There were two routes open to him. The most direct would take him on eastward past the islanded Cyzicus and on to Miletopolis (Mikalich?) on the lower reaches of the Macestus (Susugirlu) River, up that stream's valley and over the mountains to Thyatira (Akhissar), then southeast through the mountains and past the Lake Gyges of Homer to Sardis, about two hundred and twenty miles from the battlefield. That is the route he would have chosen if he were in a hurry. But Strabo[2] says (and he is the only one of our ancient writers to mention any route at all) that he returned to Ilium. This commentator believes we can accept his statement. He then returned to Ilium, and there ordered Chares to rebuild the ancient city upon its ancient site.

---

[1] Satrap: Graecized version of the Persian title: '*kshatrapavan*, protector of the country.'

[2] Strabo, 593.

Then, to encourage the gathering of a population there, he remitted all taxes and imposts to new settlers in the region. There was neither economic nor military advantage in the site, for Antiochus, a few decades later, was forced to build a militarily advantageous city on the seacoast to the southward, Alexandria Troas, which rose to power while the lesser village of New Ilium remained in comparative obscurity.

He took the seaboard road south through Assus, then skirted the coast of the Gulf of Adrymittium (Adramyti keurfezi) and passed east through Antandrus (ruins near Papazli) and on to the gulf-head town of Adrymittium (ruins of Edrimid, near Kemer), then to the city which was soon to rise as royal Pergamum (Bergama), thence to Thyatira (Akhissar) and on to Sardis. It is far more likely he took this route than the first mentioned. At this time he was still trying to impress the Greek-founded cities, all along the seaboard, with the fact that he had just released them from the centuries' old domination of the Persians. Also his supplies must have been almost at the vanishing point, and these could be more easily replenished here than in the relatively unsettled lands farther inland.

The governor of Sardis met the invaders several miles from the city and threw its gates open to them, surrendering the almost impregnable citadel and the treasures therein, of which Alexander was in desperate need. Asander, son of Philotas, was placed in charge of the Lydian satrapy and the government of the great Sardian citadel itself was given to Pausanias, Alexander's boyhood friend. He abolished the oligarchy at once and restored popular government under the old Greek laws and codes, and ordered the erection of a temple and altar to Zeus upon the citadel, in order that they also might live under the old Olympian gods. Here, says Plutarch, among other captured state documents, the Macedonians found letters written by Demosthenes after the battle of Chaeronea, begging help from the Persians.

While the changes were being made and the army rested at Sardis, the fame and the noise of the young conqueror spread fast. At Ephesus (ruins near Ayusoluk) the oligarchs read aright the fate which would soon be upon them. The panic quickly spread to the garrison of mercenaries, and they seized two triremes and fled under command of one Amyntas, a renegade Macedonian, to Phoenicia.

Alexander marched out of Sardis, crossed the Tmolus (Boz Dagh) Range at whose foot the city nestles, descended into the Cayster (Kuchuk Menderez) River valley and followed it down to Ephesus, covering the sixty-five miles in a little over three days in the breathless heat of the Asia Minor June weather. This ancient and important city had then fully a quarter of a million population, standing at the head of a bay (now a swampy alluvial plain silted up since that day), the administrative and commercial center for half a dozen other prosperous towns and cities along the bay shore. As the young king advanced, Memnon, who had fled the invader at Granicus, fled again, going southward to Halicarnassus. First Alexander abolished the oligarchy, restored the old Greek *demos* and ordered that the exiles be recalled. The instant the populace were relieved of their fear of the 'first families,' riot broke loose. The people, suffering from ancient wrongs and continued oppressions, started in to pay off old scores. Many of the oligarchs were dragged out and stoned to death before Alexander restored order by clamping down martial law and putting summary end to the rioting.

It will be recalled that the sanctuary of the great temple of the Ephesian Artemis (equated in the Greek mind with the huntress-goddess Diana) had been burned some twenty years before, reputedly on the night of Alexander's birth, by a notoriety-seeking youth named Herostratus. Alexander offered to rebuild and restore the glorious old temple at his own expense, but evidently the Ephesians could not see themselves obligated to him to that extent. They must have also been rather an independent lot too, for they replied ironically that it was not meet that one god should build a temple to another. This is the first reference we have to the presumption that the young man aspired to more than human honors. Unluckily we have only the bare statement that this really occurred, but nothing more. He seems to have taken the answer in good part, however, perhaps humorlessly seeing no undercurrent in the remark, perhaps ignoring it entirely. Anyhow, he gratuitously ordered that the tributes be remitted and used for the restoration. It is possible, however, that he later insisted upon being accorded the honors he desired, for in after-years it is reported that Apelles, the great Ephesian painter who alone was permitted to paint his picture, later painted him on the temple wall, depicting him grasping in his hand the thunderbolt of Zeus. The green jasper columns used in the restoration were removed centuries later and now are still in use to support the great dome of the mosque of Saint Sophia. He also made great sacrifices to the goddess Artemis and held a military review in her honor.

Ambassadors arrived from Magnesia and Tralles, twenty and forty miles distant in the Meander (Menderez) River, bringing submissions from their cities. The king dispatched Parmenio with five thousand men to consolidate them, and another expedition was sent to the cities of Aeolia and Ionia to bring those areas under domination.

He took the road southeast through Magnesia (Manessa) and Priene (ruins, Samsun), though no mention is made of the latter town in our histories. There was no other way he could have gone.[1] Then it led around the Gulf of Latmus (now a rich but unhealthy plain, the whole gulf having been silted up by the muddy waters of the Menderez) to the ancient and strong city of Miletus, whose extensive ruins today are called Palatia. Hegisistratus, the commander of the Persian forces there, had written the king several letters offering surrender of the strong-

[1] On the north side of the Mycale promontory near Priene was the great temple of Poseidon, where the pan-Ionic festivals were held. It is hardly likely that Alexander would pass this famous spot without even visiting it. Priene was a small seaport in those days, though their harbor was already silting into uselessness. The city was abandoned not long afterward and sank into ruin. In 1868 a party of European antiquarians, excavating in a temple there, found the following inscription upon its lintel: 'King Alexander dedicated this temple to Athene Polias.' The lintel is now in the British Museum. The account will be found in *Century Magazine*, May, 1901.

hold and commercial mart, but receiving, falsely, intelligence that a Persian army was on the way and preparing to meet the invaders, he had a change of heart and decided to hold the city for them. Alexander hurried on to visit condign punishment on the place. Nicanor, temporarily in command of the whole fleet, sailed swiftly and unexpectedly down the bay and anchored at the island of Lade,[1] some three miles from the city's waterfront. That same day Alexander arrived by land and took up his position along the waterfront to cut the city from any possible communication with the sea and the Persian fleet, now gathering at Samos. Three days later, however, the Persian fleet, over four hundred sail, arrived, but finding the haven of Lade already occupied and garrisoned by four thousand of Alexander's mercenaries to support his fleet there, they withdrew and anchored off the promontory of Mount Mycale, some eight miles westward. During these three days Alexander established his camp along the foreshore and a number of smaller camps as outposts around the city, closely investing it. Parmenio then marched in with his detachment to join the besiegers.

That evening a council of war was held in the king's pavilion, and Parmenio, with his usual unhappy faculty of ruffling Alexander's feelings, strongly advised Alexander to a naval battle, arguing that victory on the water would so intimidate the Miletans as to frighten them into suing for peace without the necessity of a trial of arms on land. Parmenio was a fighter of battles, but unluckily saw, seemingly, no further than the armed clash of forces. He was therefore somewhat taken aback when the king, usually so willing to fight, declined to permit his fleet to do so. He could see no reason to risk nearly certain defeat which would be the result of an attack with his greatly inferior number of ships, inexperienced seamen, and unreliable allies upon the Persian's greatly superior numbers of experienced and sea-hardened fighters. Defeat would hearten his enemies in

---

[1] Lade Island and another small island mentioned by our historians are now part of the mainland. The river delta has built up, by silting, over eight miles since the days of the conqueror.

Asia as well as at home, 'for,' he said, 'the Greeks might take heart and start a revolution,' and as a naval disaster would minimize his possible threats to the Peloponnesus, revolts would certainly break out there. Even a naval victory and the destruction of the Persian fleet would be empty, gaining nothing of importance. And if his losses should be heavy enough, as no doubt they would be, the possibility of using his fleet to maintain a constant naval threat to Greece would be removed just as effectually and not improbably with the same result as if he were defeated. The Greek city-states wanted their freedom — a freedom they would use to squabble or fight insanely among themselves, but freedom nonetheless. They were already chafing against the restrictions of the none too diplomatic Antipater. That dour old warrior was obeying his young king to the letter — and the Greeks didn't like it. Therefore, until he could capture the whole of the Mediterranean seaboard, vanquishing the Persian fleet by the simple process of depriving it of its bases, he would decline to fight a naval battle if possible. Time itself would fight for him on water; he could do his own fighting on land.

Miletus as a great commercial seaport city had been allowed a considerable degree of freedom by the Persians and had become prosperous. Prosperous peoples seldom see any reason to fight, an attitude which also seldom makes for a continuance of prosperity; more often conduces to its loss. Therefore, as soon as a decision was made to press the siege without risking a naval engagement, the people of the city sent out one of their leading citizens with the proposal that Alexander raise the siege and leave their harbor neutral and their walls alike free to him and the Persians. Exasperated at such spinelessness, Alexander ordered him to return and tell the citizens to prepare at once for an assault. The siege was pushed with fury. Great engines were assembled and started beating at the walls. When this began, the Greek fleet left the island of Lade and took up positions side by side, beaks outward, across the harbor, interposing a barrier between the city and the enemy fleet in case the latter should make a sortie.

After several days of steady pounding at the city walls the great siege engines beat a number of breaches in them and the Macedonians poured through in force. A fierce and sanguinary battle was fought in the streets before the defenders broke and scattered. Many were cut down or captured, but many escaped by swimming, using their wicker shields as floats, to another small island in the bay, among them three hundred Greek mercenaries. Numbers of others took to small boats and tried to escape by water, only to be pursued, caught, and slain by sailors from the ships. The fugitives on the island threw up barricades and prepared to defend themselves to the last. The Macedonians embarked and moved over to attack them, but Alexander, considering that he now had the city and seeing no reason for continuing the slaughter, stayed the assault and offered the mercenaries pardon if they would take service with him. The Greeks, now that their cause was lost, their paymasters destroyed, and having no reason for continuing the senseless struggle, accepted the amnesty. They were incorporated into the army. The surviving Miletans were pardoned, ordered to return to their homes, repair the damage to their city, and resume life under a new régime.

In the meantime the Persian fleet had been drawing their water supply from the Meander River. Alexander sent a strong force to the river mouth to block them from it, and another to the promontory to prevent them from landing there. Almost at once their fleet ceased to be an asset to the Persians and became a liability instead; they were almost literally besieged in their ships. It can be assumed that the crew of a war vessel, a trireme, numbered about two hundred, of whom some one hundred and seventy were rowers, and at least ten more were officers; there were therefore hardly over fifteen men who could be counted as fighters. If this is correct, the fleet could have had no more than six thousand fighting men in the four hundred vessels, a force far too small to dare a land attack against the invaders. They sailed at once to the island of Samos, a score of miles distant, took on all the water they could transport and returned to the roadstead off Miletus. For several days they maneuvered off the harbor mouth, attempting to draw the Macedonian fleet into a naval action, but as the latter persistently refused to bite at the opportunity, they gave up at last and sailed back to Samos.

By this time Alexander had given serious thought as to the value of his own fleet, and soon after the conclusion of the siege he disbanded it, save for twenty Athenian triremes which were held as hostages. Winter was coming soon with its attendant storms and high winds when the narrow, island-studded seas were dangerous to the most skilled seamen. Also Alexander was moving the scene of his activities farther southward, which would bring his vessels into waters at present controlled by the Phoenicians, Cypriots, and Rhodians, and ever farther and farther from their own bases. Then, too, one hundred and sixty ships required a force of over thirty thousand men to maintain them at any acceptable degree of efficiency, practically as many men as he had in his army. The military results of their existence was very much less than that of the army, and the cost was higher, an item which no doubt entered seriously into the calculations of the young king. It may be seen that here Alexander marks a turning-point in his career, changing from the reckless and exuberant youth who had led his army into Asia Minor, barely three months before, into a calculating man of the world. The cities of the coast which he had believed to be Greek in sympathy and culture had demonstrated to him that they had become Persianized, and preferred to remain that way. Also in Hellas the Greeks were demonstrating that not only were they indifferent to the ideas of pan-Hellenism, but they were actively in opposition to him. The islands which he had considered as Greek opened their ports to the Persian fleet. And despite the existence of the great enemy fleet and their obvious threat to the young pan-Hellenic champion, no fleets put out from Hellas to assist him. His boyish illusions begin to vanish, and in their place a sterner resolution rises.

Marching on southward, Alexander received the peaceful submissions of several cities, but at the ancient fortress and capital city of the Carian kingdom, Halicarnassus (modern Budrum), he again clashed with that tough old soldier, Memnon of Rhodes, who, as military commander under Orontobates, satrap of Caria, was in charge of the defense of the city. He had been appointed admiral of the Persian fleet and military governor of the whole coast. In preparation against the Macedonian attack he had greatly strengthened the garrison, repaired and added to the defenses, and brought part of the fleet into the harbor. The invaders moved warily up the peninsula and beleaguered the ancient city. On the first day of the siege Memnon sent out a strong sortie force of mercenaries from the east gate. This was under command of Alexander's old enemy, Ephialtes the Athenian; a surprise assault which was beaten back only after severe fighting in which Ephialtes himself was killed. A day or so later several Greek sympathizers of the little city of Myndus (Gumschlu-liman), some seven miles farther out on the tip of the peninsula, entered into secret negotiations with Alexander to surrender the city to him, provided he come secretly and under cover of darkness. The king knew the immense value of Myndus as a *point d'appui* and realized the great psychological effect of its capture upon the Halicarnassians when they should learn that Myndus was in his possession. He therefore took his hetairoí, three regiments of the phalanx, the archers and Agrianians, and moved ostentatiously around to the west side of the city as if planning an assault there. They slipped away at night under cover of darkness and marched off to Myndus. Arriving there he found no one to open the gates as he had been promised; the plot seems to have miscarried. Although he had neither siege engines nor scaling ladders, in his wrath he ordered the phalangists forward to start saps and undermine the walls. The men threw themselves to work with a will and presently one of the towers fell, but without weakening the wall itself. By this time, however, the Macedonians were the target of concentrated fire from above as the aroused garrison fought back. Shortly afterward several Persian ships arrived and their crews swarmed out to engage in hand-to-hand conflict.

Alexander, seeing his forces outnumbered and in danger of annihilation, withdrew and returned to Halicarnassus.

The archers and slingers were posted along the west side of the city to maintain a heavy missile rain against any of the defenders who should expose themselves, and under cover of the barrage, other workers were busily engaged in filling the wide moat. When this was accomplished, siege engines were erected and started beating at the walls. After several days of sorties and assaults, in which both sides suffered heavily, one corner of the wall was beaten down. Memnon and his Persian co-commander, Orontobates, son-in-law of Darius, anticipating that the town would soon fall, set fire to it one night and took refuge with all their troops in the two citadels which still tower today, two thousand years later, above the ruins of the city. Alexander sent a heavy detachment into the town with orders to put out the fires and seize the place, but with strict injunctions to harm none of the citizens who remained in their houses. When daylight came the king entered also, to make a survey of the citadels, when, impressed with their great height and strength, he concluded that only formal siege of considerable duration would reduce them. Their existence was a matter of little importance, however, for as long as he held the town itself, the fortresses would in due time be reduced to impotency and compelled to surrender through being isolated and deprived of supplies. He left a force of three thousand footmen and two hundred cavalry to invest them and they later capitulated, though Memnon once more escaped, fleeing to the island of Cos, there to continue his defiance. Orontobates disappears from our histories thereafter.

Alexander left Halicarnassus and marched back to the fortified plateau city of Tralles (Aidin Guzelhissar) in the Meander River valley, an Argive foundation, which, though history is silent, must have offended greatly since its submission; certainly it incurred his extreme displeasure in some way, for he leveled the city to the ground and distributed its population over the countryside. He went on to Alinda (ruins near Yenibazar, ten miles farther up the river valley), where, to show how little he cared for precedent, he then made a woman, the old queen Ada of Alinda, satrap of Caria. She had formerly ruled as the widow of her brother and husband Idreus until she had been supplanted by Pixodorus, whose rule, upon his death, had passed into the hands of Orontobates. She met Alexander as he entered Caria, did homage to and adopted him as her son. He restored to her her city and accepted the adoption, thus placing himself in line as hereditary heir, and removing for the Carians the sting of being ruled by a foreigner.

During these sieges and battles the summer had passed and autumn was well advanced. Many of the young Macedonians had married just before Alexander's expedition moved; to these were given furloughs to spend the winter at home with their wives and families. They were sent away under command of three of the king's trusted lieutenants, themselves also young benedicts, with orders to rejoin the army in the spring at Gordium in Phrygia. His magnanimity seems designed to serve the double purpose of popularizing his victories in Macedonia and Greece, and attracting thence the desired type of young and adventurous recruits to his ranks. Alexander had several times publicly showed a thoughtful kindliness to his men here in Asia Minor (Arrian says this deed endeared him greatly to him) quite at variance to the attitude we later find in him as the years pass, his conquests increase, and his powers grow greater and ever greater. One of his friends, Cleander, was dispatched to the soldier marts of Hellas and the Peloponnesus with orders to bring back as many mercenaries as he could obtain. We see him rejoining Alexander fourteen months later at Sidon on the seacoast with four thousand men, the small number as the result of so much time spent forcing the conclusion that the service lacked popularity and appeal with even the hard-bitten soldiers of fortune.

Parmenio was sent off with the league troops and trains through Phrygia, apparently with orders to subdue specified yet unreconciled areas, and rendezvous at a given time at Gordium (Pebi), a central point on the Sangarius (Sakaria Irmak) River, about one hundred and fifty miles from the Sea of Marmora, and on the royal road from the sea to the interior of Persia. Alexander himself marched on south and reached the heavily fortified and determinedly hostile city of Caunus, today in ruins near Dalian. He surveyed the place thoroughly, and concluded it far too strong for the small force he had with him. He sent back orders to his siege garrison at Halicarnassus that they should, when they had completed the reduction of the citadels there, next attack and reduce the refractory holders of Caunus. He went on to the Lycian frontier fort (unidentifiable) of Hyparna, where a small garrison of mercenaries surrendered quietly. Passing on into Lycia he received and accepted submissions from Telmissus, Xanthus, Pinara, Patara, and, says Arrian, about thirty other cities. This was the seacoast march he had been contemplating since dismissing his fleet at Myndus, the reasoned intent being to deprive the Persian fleet of their bases along this stretch of seaboard, and incidentally, perhaps, cause the natives of the coast on the fleet to become dissatisfied with the service and return home to the cities now free of Persian rule. He advanced along the coast as far as the western border of Cilicia where the Taurus Range meets the water's edge, then made that range, which cuts straight across Asia Minor, his eastern boundary, thereby completing his military security in that area west of it.[1]

Turning northward in the dead of winter he reached the mountainous area of Milyas, a small sub-satrapy governmentally attached to Lycia. To him there came a number of Lycian envoys, bringing submissions of their several cities. He accepted all, and in most cases found it necessary only to order them to deliver their governments into the hands of those whom he should send

[1] Plutarch says that at this time Alexander's mind was unsettled whether to drive straight ahead through the mountains and across country, hunt for and offer battle to Darius directly wherever he might be found, or whether to continue his campaign on its present lines, to subdue the whole of Asia Minor and consolidate it and the seacoast to his rule, thus rendering the Persian fleet relatively innocuous. Luckily his good sense, or the advice of others, prevailed, and he pursued the latter course, by far the wiser of the two.

for that purpose. Phaselis (Tekirova), a large coastal city some fifty miles eastward, not only sent submission, but also a heavy golden crown of curious workmanship. He turned and marched there, and took his first rest since leaving Macedonia nine months before.

The results of his first year's campaign are remarkable. He was, by virtue of victory at the battle of the Granicus and the immobilization of the only sizable enemy force remaining in existence, that at Halicarnassus, master of Asia Minor as far as the Sangarius River. The coasts were clear of the Persian fleet as far as Cilicia; the Greek cities he had come to free were free and as hegemon of the Corinthian League he had incorporated them into the league.[1] From now on, though there may have been doubts of it before, we find him definitely fighting for his own glory and increasing his own empire. He had perhaps filled to the letter his obligation to the league and he marches ahead on his own. Later we find him still hegemon of the league to the Greeks, their king to the Macedonians, Pharaoh and son of Ammon to the Egyptians, and emperor of the vast dominions of Persia and India, maintaining all his dignities with a curious parallelism that is never permitted to overlap, save once, and that when he made the egregious error of attempting to be a god also to the Macedonians. As yet he appears, however, to be still a Macedonian only, with the hardihood, the ideals, and ambitions one would expect of the prince of a simple country people. But little by little he was changing, his eyes were gradually seeing and his mind beginning to understand the scope and magnificence of the Persian Empire; and when he saw the Persian camp at Issus a new and grandiose world opened to him. It was a world incomparably grander and wider and richer than any he had conceived. He had eaten of the fruit of the tree of knowledge and for it his ambitions were to grow until the world itself was too small for the satiation of his overweening greed for more and ever more power and conquest.

[1] Ulrich Wilcken (*Alexander und der korinthische Bund*) adheres to the thesis that he did incorporate the Greek cities into the league. Contra, Ehrenburg, *op. cit.*

While the king's detachment was resting at Phaselis, he received a message from Parmenio carrying intelligence of the discovery of a plot against his life, by the young Lyncestian prince Alexander, son of Aeropus. The Lyncestian had been gravely suspect of complicity in the murder of Philip, but had managed to convince Alexander of his whole-hearted loyalty. So great was the trust in him that when Calas was made satrap of Phrygia, he had been elevated to the rank of commander of the Thracian cavalry, at that time attached to Parmenio's army. The circumstances of the discovery of the plot were thus: A renegade deserter fled to Darius, carrying letters, said the accusation, from the young cavalry commander hinting at the latter's willingness to betray his king. Darius had taken the offer seriously and he dispatched a courtier, one Asisines, by devious ways, to communicate with the traitor and with instructions to offer him, for the compassing of the king's death, the throne of Macedonia and one thousand talents of silver.[1] A patrol captured the courtier-messenger, found the communication, and brought him to Parmenio, who obtained a confession. Asisines was sent to Alexander and made to repeat the confession. The king immediately called a council of war and laid the matter before them. The findings of the council were that the best part of the king's allied auxiliary cavalry was in dangerous hands and that it was necessary to remove the Lyncestian immediately. A trusted messenger was disguised as a peasant of the country and dispatched to Parmenio carrying intelligence by word of mouth. The traitor was seized and committed to safe-keeping. Four years later we find him still under guard with the army in Afghanistan. Up to that time either lack of definite proof of his guilt or deference to his father-in-law, the aged general Antipater, still ruling faithfully at home, had caused him to be spared. But when the alleged plot of Philotas against the king was discovered, in the hysteria which followed, the surprised and stammered denials of the Lyncestian, before the officers'

---

[1] Robson's translation of Arrian (1, 25, 1–5) says one thousand talents of gold.

court-martial trying him, were deemed sufficient proof of his guilt and he was summarily speared to death.

Meanwhile, much was occurring in the west, in the islands and Greece, to endanger Alexander's continuation in the region. After his escape from Halicarnassus, Memnon, now that he was free of the necessity of consulting with other and less able Persian commanders, determined to execute a plan which was part of the one he had proposed and had been turned down at Zeleia; namely, to seize and consolidate all the Aegean islands, establish naval bases on a number of them and thence carry the war direct to Macedonia and Greece, by means of the full strength of the Persian fleet. The island of Chios was betrayed to him by the oligarchs; this was followed by a swift attack upon Lesbos, of which he quickly gained control of all but Mytilene which he closely besieged. The news spread rapidly through the Cyclades and Greece. In Athens there was open rejoicing, Demosthenes exultingly preaching the approaching downfall of his pet hate, Alexander. Sparta prepared for war, sending ambassadors throughout the land asking alliances. Other cities began agitation against the yoke of the Macedonian. Antipater in Macedonia grimly prepared to move south to quell the insurrection. But by an almost inconceivable stroke of fortune for Alexander, Memnon was taken suddenly ill, and died, on his deathbed turning over command to his nephew, Pharnabazus. News of the capture of the islands had filled Alexander with deep concern. Realizing that the Persian fleet under the command of the astute old Rhodian would be a real menace, he immediately dispatched Amphoterus and Hegelochus to assemble another fleet in the Sea of Marmora. Memnon's death, however, restored the king's tranquillity; the other Persian commanders were so slothful as to be unworthy of consideration. Darius must have thought so too, for he abandoned Memnon's plan of attack, recalled Pharnabazus and his mercenaries and prepared to prosecute the war on land. Though the Persian fleet later extended their successes somewhat by the capture of Mytilene and Tenedos, these were mere flea-bites which, now that Memnon was out of the way, could have no bearing upon the war as a whole. The problems of the islands could be left to the newly reconstituted fleet and time itself, and those of the mainland to old Antipater.

Alexander left Phaselis, sending part of the army northward over the mountain road. He himself with a much smaller unit went by way of the coast, on a less-used route which at some points was exceedingly rough and precipitous. It was wintertime and the winds were high. Along the foot of Mount Climax (Takhtali Dagh, a few miles up the coast from Tekirova) the route skirted the coast at the foot of the abrupt cliffs, and sometimes, when the wind blew strongly from the south, it was under water and impassable. A south wind had prevailed for some time, but just as Alexander reached there the wind changed and blew violently from the north, blowing back the water and permitting the detachment to pass dryshod.[1] Alexander reached Perga (ruins, Balkiz, sixteen miles northeast of Adalia), where he was met by ambassadors from Aspendus who surrendered their city to him on the condition that he garrison no troops on them. Alexander agreed to the request, countering with the requirement that the citizens raise a voluntary donation of fifty talents and send him the horses formerly exacted of them as a tribute to Darius. He then marched on around the bay to the important seaport of Side (Eski Adalia), where he left a small garrison. He then turned inland to Syllius. The place was very strongly fortified and garrisoned. Alexander inspected it carefully and made plans for a formal siege, as its strength plainly precluded reduction by assault.

While this was being planned, indignant messengers, in the form of those he had sent to Aspendus to receive the guaranteed money and horses, arrived at camp. The Aspendians had had a change of heart, refused the tribute, gathered stores within the city and barred their gates to Alexander's representatives. The

---

[1] Much has been made of this incident, it being frequently cited as proof of the gods' regard for Alexander. It seems to this commentator, in view of these and other citations, necessary to call attention to the fact that it is not uncommon in many places to have areas flooded by water under pressure of high winds, or to have a shallow body of water blown from its normal bed by the wind.

king immediately raised the siege of Syllius and swiftly returned to Aspendus. As he approached, the inhabitants abandoned the lower town upon the plain by the Eurymedon (Keupri su) River and fled to their citadel. He marched into the lower town and surrounded the stronghold. The citizens, in dismay at the unexpectedly prompt punishment being visited upon them, sued for peace and promised immediate fulfillment of the terms demanded of them. Alexander cannily considered the strength of the citadel and concluded he was not in a position to undertake the siege necessary to reduce it, but likewise took cognizance that the terrified Aspendians were unaware that such was the case. He agreed, therefore, to leave them in peace, but not on the former terms. First they must give a number of leading citizens as hostages, next the horses promised must be promptly delivered, the fifty talents war contribution were increased to a hundred, they must accept a garrison, pay annual tribute to the Macedonians over and above those due the crown, and accept arbitration in the matter of some farmlands they had taken by force from a neighboring settlement. These conditions being agreed to, he raised the siege and returned to Perga, no doubt promising himself that sooner or later he would have the Syllians attended to in a manner befitting their defiance. Turning northward he reached the strongly fortified city of Termessus and besieged it for a while, but apparently decided a successful conclusion of the siege worth neither the time nor the energy required to force its submission.[1] At Sagalassus (modern Aghlasan) a bitter battle was necessary to reduce the city, which he garrisoned afterward. He then turned into Phrygia, passed the salt lake Ascania (Lake Buldur) and in five days camped before the walls of Celenae (Deneir) twenty-five miles north. The city and its garrison of

---

[1] Count von Lanckoronski, in his *Stadte Pamphyliens und Pisidiens*, verifies the remarkable strength of this citadel, stating that of all the ancient sites he visited, this place had the most imposing appearance. Alexander could have reduced it in time, but spring was now at hand, and he soon would have to be in Gordium to reassemble his army. He seems to have had little esteem for the peoples of the interior of what is now Anatolia, for we are told nothing of troubles there nor of organizations he built to govern them.

eleven hundred surrendered. He placed another garrison of fifteen hundred men in the place, rested ten days; and after writing Parmenio to join him at the city of Gordium, one hundred and forty miles to the northeast, marched there himself.

Parmenio came in from some unspecified duty. Shortly afterward the young Macedonian married men arrived from their winter furlough, bringing with them three thousand infantry and six hundred cavalry recruits. Here also came Athenian ambassadors entreating him to release such of the captives of Granicus as were Athenian citizens. They failed in their mission, however, because Alexander wished to make a harsh object lesson of them to discourage other Greeks who might be inclined to take service against him. He merely told the ambassadors that they had his permission, when the Persian war should be over, again to request release of the slaves.

In the temple of Jupiter (Zeus) at Gordium, so the story runs, was a chariot, dedicated by the long-deceased king Midas as a thank-offering to the gods for raising him from a poor farmer to the kingship. Arrian says that a strange story began to gain credence, to wit: whoever could untie the cornel bark cord that bound the yoke pin to the pole should become king of Asia. The knot was so made that neither end could be seen. Alexander, it was said, examined the knot carefully, then drew his sword and cut it in two. At any rate, whatever he did with it was assumed to be acceptable, and conforming to accomplishment for fulfillment of the prophecy.

Darius in his capital of Susa, now that his only real strategist in the west, Memnon, was dead, became aware that there was no obstacle to the furtherance of Alexander's conquests, even to the heart of the empire if he so desired. The Great King (this story is from Diodorus) called a council of war and referred to them the question of what steps to take to stem the tide of the invader's conquests. His Persian advisers were unanimous in their opinion that he should raise a large army and personally lead it forth to annihilate the young Macedonian upstart. In the old days the Persian kings had always led their own armies,

but with the increase of their power and wealth the kingly line
had softened and fallen into the custom of delegating command.
Darius seems to have been a good king, as Persian kings went,
but he certainly lacked the hardness and courage to make a
great military leader in a day when the leader's personal courage
in combat was not infrequently the deciding factor of victory or
defeat.

Among those present at the Persian council was a single dis-
senter, the old enemy of Philip and Alexander, the Greek
Charidemus, recently in the pay of and outlawed from Athens.
He had for thirty years been a stormy petrel of both Greece and
Persia, pirate, freebooter, soldier of fortune, mercenary general,
and since his proscription by Alexander, military adviser to the
Persian king, the most experienced and crafty soldier in the
empire. His advice was to raise an army, by all means, but one
of not more than one hundred thousand men, to include the
thirty thousand Greek mercenaries already in the pay and
service of the Great King, and place it in the hands of a competent general. A force of this size, he argued, would have great
striking power, outnumber the invaders at least three to one,
and yet not be so large as to be unwieldy in maneuver or difficult
to supply. They could operate on a simple scheme of elementary
strategy. First they could approach Alexander, then as the
latter followed, they could retreat ahead of him, laying waste
the country as they went, until the Macedonians should be
straitened by lack of supplies and entangled in the vastness of
the country. Then a single decisive battle, forced at the will
of the Persians, should destroy the invaders and put an end to
their menace.

The obvious logic of this plan was so clear that the Great
King was at first inclined to agree with it, but the haughty
Persian nobles furiously accused Charidemus of wanting the
command himself, which may have been correct, for certainly he
was the only general in the empire with sufficient patient
sagacity to carry the scheme to its fruition. His detractors went
even further; hotly resentful of the implication that they were

unequal to the Macedonians, they were at last guilty of the error of accusing him of meditating treachery. The irascible Greek lost his temper then, and proceeded in forcefully undiplomatic language to give expression to his accurate but highly unflattering opinion of the courage and fighting qualities of the Persians. Apparently he carried his denunciation of them to an extreme, a most unwise thing to do in the presence of an Oriental despot; it reflects too greatly upon him. Darius was so incensed that he himself laid violent hands upon Charidemus and ordered him away to execution. Whatever may have been the shortcomings of the Greek filibuster, he cannot be accused of lack of courage, for as he was being led away to death, he turned and flung a final bitter taunt at Darius, promising him that his stupidity in ordering his, Charidemus', death, was flinging away his empire, a prophecy which events soon justified. The king was bitterly to regret his hasty action later, for he realized then that he had slain the only real military leader he had. However, he mustered his army in Babylon and set forth at last upon the long journey into upper Syria.

News of the approach of Darius reached Alexander when he was at Ancyra (modern Ankara), some sixty miles east of Gordium, creating local governments for Galatia, Paphlagonia, and the western part of Cappadocia which had recently come under his suzerainty. From Ancyra two great routes led to Persia, one the great royal road from Sardis through Gordium, and eastward through southern Armenia; the other the ancient migration and trade route straight south to the seacoast of Cilicia. When Alexander received definite information that Darius was marching into Syria, he hurried south by the road passing between the salt lake Tatta (Tuz Chellu) and the Halys (Kizil Irmak) River. He reached the foothills of the Taurus Range and struck straight for the age-old pass known as the Cilician Gates, the Geul Boghaz. It is a curious commentary upon the utter slackness of the Persian commander of the region that he failed to guard the pass substantially, for we know (from Xenophon, who marched that way with the famous

expedition of the Ten Thousand Greeks in the year 401 B.C.)
that it was then a carriage road just wide enough to permit four
men to march through abreast. The rugged cliffs on the sides
were impassable, and any really determined resistance could have
been broken only by the most determined efforts by the invaders.
But as the Macedonians moved up for a night attack, the small
Persian guard at the pass abandoned their post and fled precipitately back to Tarsus. The attackers moved swiftly through the
Gates and descended into the plain of Cilicia in the flaming heat
of the seaboard August. There they were met by a delegation
of the citizens of the town who begged Alexander to hurry to
the city, for they said Arsames the governor, hearing the passes
less than twenty-five miles away had fallen and Alexander
through them, was preparing to flee, but they were afraid he
would loot the place before he went. Alexander took the
hetairoi and some of the light infantry and hurried onward,
making such speed that the Persian garrison fled in haste ahead
of them, leaving the city unharmed. It fell to him without a
blow.

Here Alexander fell seriously ill, the result, according to one
account, of the toils and hardships he had undergone; according
to another as a result of a bath while overheated from exertions,
in the cold river Cydnus (Tarsus, or Terso) which flows through
the city. Both may be right, one reporting the time, the other
the place and circumstances. The illness, says Arrian, was
characterized by 'nerve pains,' a high fever and insomnia, so
grave that most of the physicians accompanying the army despaired of his life. In one, however, a certain Philip of Acar-
nania, he had great confidence, and ordered his attendance.
While Philip was preparing the medicine a letter from Parmenio
was delivered to Alexander stating baldly that Philip was in the
pay of Darius, with instructions to poison him. Alexander
handed the letter to Philip, and while he was reading it, took
the cup from his hand and drained the potion. The imperturb-
able physician, without changing color, merely entreated the
king to take any medicine he offered, assuring him if he did so

he would recover. Alexander did recover under his ministrations and later publicly showed his esteem for Philip and conferred many favors upon him.

Cilicia, a strip of land some two hundred and fifty miles long, varies in width from thirty-five to fifty miles. It is hedged in on the north by the lofty range of the Taurus, on the west by the Imbarus Range, on the east by the high Amanus, and on the south by the sea. It is divided into two parts, the western, the rough mountainous Issaurian Cilicia (Cilicia Trachea), and the eastern Cilician plain which is the vestibule of Syria. The southern part lying along the seaboard is the old Aleian plain of the classical period, the 'Plain of the Wandering' where Bellerophon roamed inconsolably after losing his winged horse Pegasus. Parmenio was sent eastward to occupy the passes of Mount Amanus to guard against an irruption of possible invaders from Syria, while Alexander turned westward to overawe the inhabitants there. In one day he reached Anchiale (Mersin, eighteen miles from Tarsus) and without pausing moved on to the ancient Ionian city of Soli (ruins, ten miles west of Mersin, today called Mezetla) whose inhabitants spoke such corrupt Greek that they are responsible for the modern word 'solecism.' He occupied the city without resistance, but fined the people two hundred talents, because although they were of Greek descent they had become Persianized. Utilizing the town as a base, he made a seven-day excursion to the mountains to the north (the Chamurlu and Bulgar Dagh) to overawe the hill tribes and frighten them into refraining from any attempt to block or bar the Cilician Gates, now a bottleneck in the life-line of communications of his growing conquests. Here, too, he abolished the long powerful oligarchy and restored democracy and popular government.

Time had been flying. It was late in August, when messengers raced in from the west bringing tidings of victories by the forces the king had left behind to reduce Halicarnassus, Myndus, and Caunus. In the battle at the former town the enemy had lost a thousand prisoners and seven hundred slain. The last remnants of the forces of the Persians west of the Taurus had been swept out of existence, and the land completely freed of their sway. Also the fleet under Hegelochus and Amphoterus had forced the surrender of the islands of Cos and Triopium. The pincers were closing upon the Persian fleet, and soon the eastern Mediterranean would be untenable for them. In celebration, partly of the victories and partly of his restoration to health, he held another festival at Soli and offered great sacrifices to Aesculapius. This method of celebrating seems to be wholly Greek, and roughly amounted to giving the gods a feast and inviting themselves to it; then of course it was necessary also to provide the gods with entertainment, contests of skill and strength, musical contests, torch and other races, review of the troops, anything considered conducive to the enjoyment of their invisible guests.

Alexander then turned back toward Tarsus, sending Philotas with the cavalry through the heavily populated Aleian plain in a convincing show of military might. He went on to Megarsus, where he paused briefly to make sacrifices to Minerva, then proceeded to Mallus, an ancient but unimportant little town on a hill east of the Pyramus (Djaihun Irmak) River mouth. The inhabitants of the latter town claimed to be descendants of a colony founded about the time of the siege of Troy by Amphilocus and Mopsus of Argos, and as Alexander himself claimed descent through Heracles Argivus and was anxious at all times to advance his claim, he sacrificed to Amphilocus as one of the semi-divine heroes.

Again fateful news seeped over the passes of Mount Amanus. Darius had reached Syria and was encamped at a place called Sochoi, only two days' journey from the other side of the mountain, east of the pass we know today as Bailan. Alexander immediately summoned a council of war of his commanders and in a brief summation of the situation laid the news before them. Unfortunately our sources are scanty of detail of the whole of the campaign just completed, and it has been necessary to delve into many strange places for the information we possess of it. Many things which occurred are untold. Thus we are not informed as to the details of any of the subsidiary and side expeditions made by Parmenio and other commanders, what they accomplished or where they went, if it was necessary for them to fight battles or sieges. That these may well have occurred is a foregone conclusion. That Alexander fought several engagements is known, that he left garrisons behind him at several places is also recorded. In those days too, Asia Minor was certainly no more healthful than it is today and there were certainly losses through disease as well as battles, sieges, and skirmishes. The forces had therefore suffered an unknown number of losses, which must certainly have outnumbered the recorded number of additions to the ranks. It must then be considered that Alexander's army, if no additional recruits were received other than those accounted for, was several thousands short of the number engaged at the Granicus, but just how many short there is absolutely no way of calculating. No doubt these matters were thoroughly discussed at the war council, and the decision was for an immediate attack upon the Persian host.

They gathered their whole force and marched along the coast to Issus. From here two routes led into Syria, the northern through the Gates of Amanus (modern Koprak Kalessi), the other the Syrian Gates (today a long poverty-stricken village of a single street), eastward of Myriandrus (Alexandretta). Alexander chose the southern route as the most practicable and marched through the narrow hill road called the Cilician Gates of Myriandrus. There, as they were preparing for the climb over the mountain pass, a severe storm delayed their march into Syria, and when it was over, electrifying tidings arrived which instantly changed all of Alexander's plans.

=VII=

Darius had indeed, as Alexander had been informed, camped at Sochoi (in the plain of Sinjerli) and there awaited the coming of the young Macedonian, upon a great plain perfectly adapted for the employment of his huge force, of which cavalry formed a great part. Amyntas, the renegade, had joined the Persian forces, and been appointed to a position of command with the Greek mercenaries. He had access to Darius, and was trusted. He endeavored to persuade the Great King to remain there, as the best possible place to meet Alexander, who, Amyntas assured the monarch, would certainly come to any place where Darius should await him. Alexander's illness had interfered with his intention to make an immediate attack, and after his recovery the expeditions in the lowlands of Cilicia to impress and intimidate the cities there, the reduction of the mountain tribes, holding the games, and the excursions to the various shrines to offer sacrifices created a delay irksome to the impetuous Persian aristocracy. Finally the nobles managed to persuade Darius, who (says Arrian), after the manner of weaklings, preferred to accept as truth that which was pleasantest to believe, that Alexander had turned poltroon and feared to face the Persian host. Indeed, such a conclusion would be not wholly unjustified. Alexander had left Ancyra in July to take up the Persian challenge and now, four months later, he had not yet arrived. Why, said the sycophantic advisers, the Persian cavalry alone were sufficient to ride down and trample underfoot by sheer weight of numbers the small Macedonian force. Amyntas, fully aware of the falseness of this premise, redoubled his entreaties to the Great King, but to no avail. Offered both good and bad advice, Darius had the unhappy faculty of always choosing to accept the latter. He became convinced of the truth of the specious reasoning of the courtiers. The palatial tents were struck, the treasures and harems and other unnecessary baggage were sent off to Damascus, two hundred and fifty miles to the south, and the great and straggling army moved off.

They passed east of Mount Amanus to the Lion Pass (Toprak Kalessi), then turned southwest through the Gates of Amanus (Bailan Pass) and reached the plain of Issus on the same day Alexander reached Myriandrus, thirty-five miles to the south. Having taken Issus, the Persians found there a large number of wounded and ill Macedonians, whom they mistreated and slaughtered. Had Alexander remained there but a single day longer, the two armies would have met head on. It is no discredit to his tactical skill that he departed southward leaving the vast Persian army to march peacefully into possession of Cilicia. In those days military intelligence was gathered in a rather haphazard fashion, and, besides, he probably never for an instant credited the possibility that Darius would be guilty of such consummate folly as to abandon the open battlefield he had so long ago selected in favor of the narrow foreshore and limited flatlands available on the plain of Issus. Alexander's only strategic error here seems to have been in rating Darius' intelligence too high.

When the news of Darius' passage of the mountains reached Alexander at Myriandrus, he could not credit the veracity of his own scouts. He accordingly dispatched a thirty-oared boat back along the shore line to Issus for verification. These returned with the news that it was indeed so, they had sighted the Persian myriads and tents upon the shore of the bay; the gods had delivered his enemies into his hands. Alexander's luck was holding amazingly. On the open Syrian plains his army would take a desperate gamble against the clouds of Persian cavalry; he would willingly have dared the hazard there; how much more would he here where, in this strait plain, the Persian masses would not have room to deploy. The overwhelming numbers of Persians, instead of being an advantage, would be detrimental to intelligent movement. Verily the gods had delivered the enemy into his hands. Alexander called his officers together and reviewed the situation to them. They were to meet a foe whom they had met before and vanquished, even as that other Greek army (Xenophon and the Ten Thousand in 401 B.C.) who, though small and without auxiliaries, had met and vanquished a Persian host under the walls of their capital city, Babylon. They were a nation of freemen, fighting voluntarily for honor and glory, against a nation of impressed slaves. There was evidence that the gods were on their side, for had they not put into Darius' mind to leave the broad plain and come here where his multitude would be useless, while the compact Macedonian phalanx would have plenty of room to maneuver? The might of Asia, with Darius himself, was before them; and when they had subdued the Great King in a single battle, all Asia would be theirs, its riches in their hands and their labors ended. These and many other arguments inflamed the minds of his listeners to battle fever, and when he had ceased speaking they crowded forward, taking his hand and begging to be led against the foe.

This done, Alexander ordered his men to take their dinner and get some rest, for evening was near. A scouting party of light cavalry and archers was sent back to the Cilician Gates, a narrow passage barely fifty feet wide between the hills and the sea, eight miles north. Near dark the army moved up to the pass and camped for the night after posting a heavy guard.

When the Persians arrived at Issus and found that Alexander had just passed, they believed that he was trying to avoid battle. But now, knowing they were between Alexander and Greece, and him hemmed in between the sea and the mountains of Lebanon, they thought they had him trapped at last. Polybius,[1] with Callisthenes as his source, says that when Darius learned that Alexander had gone to Syria, he, perhaps thinking that after all the battle would be fought on the Syrian plains, followed after him, approached the pass, and encamped for the night on the Pinarus (Deli tchai) River. This sounds logical, and reasonably accounts for the Persian position being nine miles south of Issus. The plain of Issus from the Pinarus River was about five miles long, wedge-shaped, and widening from about fifty feet at the Cilician Gates to about a mile and a half [2] at the river where the Persian army drew up. Alexander knew this. He had passed there only two or three days before, and he hastened now to make use of his knowledge. As they drew out of the narrow pass and the mountains opened a bit, Alexander moved the army, part by part as space permitted, into the usual tight phalanx, extending from the sea-side sands on the left to the mountain-side on the right. The cavalry ranged behind. When open country was reached, the army immediately swung into line of battle. The right wing, rubbing against the mountain-side, was composed of a regiment of hypaspists and a body of lightarmed infantry under Nicanor, then the Thessalian and Macedonian heavy cavalry, the phalanx in the center, but divided into two commands and assigned equally to the left and right wings, this latter under Alexander. The left wing under Parmenio was composed of the allies, the Cretan and Thracian

[1] Polybius, XII, 17.

[2] Today a mile wider. If this figure, said to be given by Callisthenes who was very probably a spectator of the battle, is correct, it means the Persian forces actually engaged could not have exceeded 70,000, simply because the space was too narrow for more.

archers under Sitalces, with Craterus as second-in-command, leading the left wing of the phalanx. Parmenio had special instructions to hold tightly to the seashore to prevent the enemy from attempting to break through his flank there. Later Alexander grew doubtful of the safety of the shore line and sent the Thessalian cavalry and archers as reinforcement to the left wing.

Darius' army, which (though the fantastic figures of six hundred thousand, as given by ancient historians, are certainly erroneous) did undoubtedly outnumber the Macedonians by five or six or more to one, was drawn up north of the Pinarus, which on its upper courses has steep banks. Against the seashore their right wing was composed of a heavy mass of cavalry poised for a charge, for there the low flat banks were no obstacle to the movements of the heavily armed fighters. Darius avoided the glaring error perpetrated by his commanders at the battle of the Granicus and placed the disciplined mercenaries against the riverbank, flanked by his best native troops, the Cardaces, in the center, and even further protected them by palisades on top of the steep banks. His left wing was composed of miscellaneous troops, whose extreme flank was posted high on a hillside from which they could swoop down upon the Macedonian flank. Before the battle opened, Alexander recognized the menace of these and sent against them a force of archers and the Agrianians who soon drove them off under a cloud of arrows. He then withdrew these troops and sent them to reinforce the wing against the seashore, leaving only three hundred cavalry in the foothills to guard the extreme right flank. Darius had also thrown a screen of thirty thousand cavalry and twenty thousand infantry across the river as a shield against attack before completing his battle array to his satisfaction, but this accomplished, they were withdrawn again. Behind the Persians' battlefront were large numbers of additional massed forces, cramped into immobility and useless in the confined space between the gullied and rocky hillsides and the sea.

Alexander's array being disposed of satisfactorily, he rode

along their front, exhorting his own men, calling upon the leaders and commanders by name. To his own men he spoke of their former victories against the Persians; the Greeks he reminded that here was their chance for revenge for the indignities that other Persian Dariuses had heaped upon their cities and ancestors, until presently the soldiers were shouting in battle fervor to be led against the enemy. Alexander rode leisurely back to his hetairoi and gave the signal for the advance. Slowly, to keep his lines intact and the massed phalanx in perfect order, the Macedonians moved forward with measured tread; slowly, but with the relentless efficiency of a well-tuned machine. As soon, however, as they came under the Persian arrow hail, there was a surge forward at the double-quick. Ahead of the phalanx, now swinging into its usual oblique echelon formation, thundered the magnificent hetairoi. They splashed into the shallow river and in a swirl of mud and water dashed up the bank and fell upon the enemy left wing. The furious assault caved in the Persian front and they wavered uncertainly backward from the glittering swords and forest of lances bearing down upon them. Alexander himself here received a sword thrust in the thigh, but in a few minutes the Persians' left wing broke and fled in panic. Meantime other parts of the line were not faring so well. The phalanx entered the river under a hail of javelins, but upon reaching the opposite bank, which was naturally steep and reinforced by a palisade, were assailed from above by the Greek mercenaries of the Persian phalanx. The close-knit lines were broken in the river, and their right left unprotected when Alexander's cavalry vanished in the battle. High on the banks above the Macedonians the Greeks pushed down at them with their spears, the height even offsetting the reach of the long sarissas. Here it was Greek against Macedonian, the years of Philip's oppressions rankling in the former, the latter battling upward under the urge of their nationalistic contempt for their southern enemies. The Persians on the left having broken in route, Alexander found himself on the flank of the Greek phalanx. Turning to the left he fell upon them like a thunderbolt and cut his way through, then, seeing Darius far ahead of him in his great four-horse chariot, he turned toward his imperial enemy. The Persian nobles and bodyguard threw themselves in the path of the attacker, only to be swept aside or cut down and trampled underfoot. Our chroniclers say that the bodies of the Persian dead piled high before their king. The raging Macedonian king, now that his enemy was at least within range of his eyes, would not be halted. Oxathres, brother of Darius, threw himself upon Alexander, who slew him as casually as if he were merely a minor obstacle in the way of an accomplishment. Arsames, who had fled from Alexander at Tarsus, fell under his hand. Sabaces, satrap of Egypt, and many other great Persians, fell in the mêlée. As his gleaming Nemesis swept forward, Darius could stand it no longer; he turned his chariot and drove away at top speed, accompanied by only a few of his bodyguard. He fled away across the plain in his chariot, but as soon as he reached the rough foothills, he abandoned the vehicle, and, leaving in it his mantle, shield, and bow, continued the flight on horseback. On the left, near the seashore, the Persians definitely had the best of it; they had crossed the river and hurled themselves upon the Thessalian cavalry. A fierce equestrian battle ensued, the Thessalians being driven back until the Persians received intelligence that Darius had fled and the Greek mercenaries were routed. In disgust, the cavalry broke off the engagement and joined the rest of the Persian army in headlong flight. As soon as the rout was complete Alexander started in pursuit of the Great King, and Ptolemy Lagus, who accompanied him, later wrote that so great was the number of slain that in the pursuit they crossed a ravine on a dam of corpses. They rode furiously, but although Alexander found the abandoned chariot and weapons, Darius escaped when falling night forced the pursuers to desist and turn back. Darius fled back to Sochoi, where of all his great army he could gather only four thousand men. With these he moved swiftly eastward, crossed the Euphrates at Thapsacus, and took up his *via dolorosa* back to Babylon. His army had completely disintegrated.

When Alexander returned from his unavailing pursuit of Darius, he found that among the booty of the Persian camp were also Darius' mother, sister, wife, two daughters and six-year-old son, as well as a great number of other women, wives, and concubines of the nobles of their army. Arrian says that, as the Persians had sent off most of their valuables to Damascus, the camp of Darius at Issus was worth *only* three thousand talents. According to Plutarch, Alexander did not immediately learn of the presence of the women, but went immediately into the king's quarters.

'Here when Alexander beheld the basins and water pots and bathtubs and ointment flasks, all of gold, wondrously wrought, and smelled the divine odors with which myrrh and spices filled the room, and from thence passed into a pavilion marvelous for its height and breadth and for the magnificence of its couches and the feast that was spread, he turned to his companions and said, "Well, this, I take it, is royalty."'

Plutarch goes on to say that that night, as Alexander and his friends occupied Darius' tent, he heard the wailing of women near-by. On inquiring who the women were and how it happened they were so near, he was informed that they were Darius' family, who, having heard that his chariot, mantle, and weapons were captured, were bewailing him as dead. Alexander sent Leonnatus, one of his boon companions, to reassure the women that Darius had escaped unhurt. He was told also to add that they were to be treated as queens and retain their retinue and other forms of rank; that what he did was not out of personal hatred for Darius, but that he was conducting war in a regular manner for the conquest of Asia. It may not be amiss to note here that he adhered to his promise to the letter, even after Darius was dead. It seems, however, that he could have been more humane with them, for we find him, two years later in Persia, still forcing his queenly captives to accompany him and his army. His peculiar ideas of chivalry even went so far, it was said, as to refuse to look upon Darius' consort Statira, who was considered the most beautiful woman in Asia. We

know that, years later, in Babylon he married one of Darius'
daughters; it can therefore safely be assumed that he, who
could have had his choice of all the women of Greece, Egypt,
and all Asia, must have been rather impressed by his captives.
Arrian adds that the following day Alexander and his friend
Hephaestion visited the queens. Darius' mother, not knowing
which was the king, went to Hephaestion, who was the taller,
fell at his feet and saluted him. Hephaestion, unwilling to
receive the homage due Alexander, retired. Someone near
showed her Alexander, upon which she was covered with confusion, but he raised her gently, and assured her that she was
not mistaken, that Hephaestion was another Alexander.

The day after the battle, Alexander, though his own wound
had stiffened overnight, visited the wounded, and ordered the
burial of the dead, giving them heroes' honors with the whole
army standing in battle array. Exactly how we are to take that
statement about the burials must be left to conjecture, but as we
know that at Granicus and later at Arbela the Persian dead were
left unburied, we are justified in the assumption that such was
the case here also. Gifts of money were then given to those who
had particularly distinguished themselves in the fight, and
altars were erected, in celebration of the victory, to Zeus,
Heracles, and Athene.

As the numbers engaged on the Persian side were certainly
enormously exaggerated by the old biographers, the reports of
the casualties suffered by them must be equally suspect. Arrian
says that one hundred thousand were slain, including ten thousand cavalry; Curtius says one hundred thousand infantry and
ten thousand cavalry; Diodorus goes further, saying one hundred
and twenty thousand infantry and ten thousand cavalry; Justin,
sixty-one thousand infantry and ten thousand cavalry plus forty
thousand prisoners; Orosius, eighty thousand infantry and
ten thousand cavalry and forty thousand prisoners. Of Alexander's army the casualties reported are equally absurd. Diodorus
says four hundred and fifty killed; Curtius, four hundred and
fifty-two killed, five hundred and four wounded; Justin, two

hundred and eighty killed. Arrian says only that in the fight between the Greek mercenaries and the phalanx the latter lost one hundred and fifty men. It is exceedingly difficult, save through sheer rationalizing, to arrive at a conclusion that remains tenable. According to General Dodge, the ratio of killed to wounded in battles around the turn of this century was seven to one, and he believes that in ancient times, when the lethal weapons were propelled only by brute force, infinitely less efficient than our modern explosives, the ratio was probably nearer ten to one. Thus we read that during a night sortie of the besieged at Halicarnassus the Macedonians lost sixteen killed and three hundred wounded; at Sangala, one hundred killed, twelve hundred wounded. Diodorus says that in the battle of Paraetacene Eumenes lost five hundred and four killed, nine hundred wounded, while Antigonus' defeated forces lost nearly as many killed as wounded. Thus our figures vary so widely that decisive conclusion is impossible. A careful study of Greek and other ancient histories and comparisons of the figures given leaves us with the same viewpoint.

> In respect to the number of killed the loss of the defeated army was, in ancient battles, out of all proportion to the victor's losses, on account of the massacre which followed the unprotected retreat. At Granicus Alexander lost one hundred and fifteen killed in an army of thirty thousand men, while the Persian cavalry of twenty thousand lost one thousand men, and the division of Greek mercenaries, twenty thousand in number, was entirely scattered or destroyed. At Arbela, Alexander, from an army of forty-five to fifty thousand men, lost from three to five hundred killed, while the loss of the Persians was so enormous as to leave room only for the wildest estimates. Curtius sets it at forty thousand; Diodorus at ninety thousand; Arrian reports only a hearsay estimate of three hundred thousand. . . . In the battle of Megalopolis, two years later (331 B.C.), the defeated Spartans and their allies lost fifty-three hundred of their twenty-two thousand men, while the forty thousand victorious Macedonians lost only one thousand (Curtius). A loss of one man in four, such as the Spartans suffered, is a terrible ratio, but one to be expected among the

Spartans, if defeated. At Leuctra they lost, from four battalions numbering about twenty-four hundred men, one thousand killed, and of the seven hundred Spartiatae — i.e., genuine Spartan citizens — four hundred were killed. So at Lechaeum they lost two hundred fifty out of six hundred. While ancient battles, therefore, contrast a loss of from one to two and a half per cent among the victors with one of, say, from ten to twenty-five per cent among the vanquished, modern battles with their completer organization show a much closer relation of loss.[1]

After the battle of Issus a great change comes over Alexander. He grows more mature and perhaps slightly embittered by the attitude manifested by the Greek cities in sending their envoys to the Great King. Also instead of being merely the king of Macedonia, overlord of Asia Minor, and hegemon of the Corinthian League, he is now, in his own opinion, also entitled to call himself ruler of the far-flung Persian Empire.[2] He sent Parmenio to seize the treasures and baggage Darius had dispatched to Damascus. We hear a short time later that Parmenio has captured the city, and overtaken and captured the treasure train. According to Athenaeus, Parmenio wrote a letter in which he reports to Alexander, 'I found flute girls to the king, three hundred twenty and nine; men who plait crowns, six and forty; cooks, two hundred seventy and seven; makers of cheese, thirteen; boilers of pots, twenty and nine; mixers of drinks, seventeen; strainers of wine, seventy; makers of perfume, forty.' Curtius reports also the capture of twenty-six hundred talents in coined money, five hundred talents in silver, seven thousand pack and riding animals, thirty thousand men, fair women without number, and a mass of other valuables. Plutarch tells us later that of the women captured, one of them, Barsines, widow of the dead Memnon, bore Alexander an illegitimate son, who was to become a bone of contention after Alexander's death. Alexander ordered Parmenio to convey the treasure to Damascus and guard it there; however, it must have either been brought

[1] Benjamin Ide Wheeler, *Alexander the Great*, 1900.
[2] Athenaeus, XIII, 607–608; XII, 548–549.

to Alexander or the commander of the treasure guard changed, for we soon find Parmenio back with his king again. Alexander marched south, pausing to found a city, known today as Alexandretta, on the site of Myriandrus, to guard the Cilician Gates, then went on. Marathus, property of King Gerostratus, who also owned the island city of Aradus (modern Ruad Island), was surrendered to Alexander by Stratus, the son of the king, who was then with his ships in the Persian fleet.

In the meantime the Persian fleet had been lying at the island of Chios. During the summer ten of the ships had lain at anchor in Syphnus, while Pharnabazus intrigued with the Greeks, and waited a favorable moment to be of assistance to any city or alliance strong enough to start an insurrection. Presently a small Macedonian squadron gathered at Euboea and launched a carefully prepared surprise attack upon the Persians, destroying eight of their ships.

In the meantime Hegelochus had gathered a fleet in the Sea of Marmora and lay there on guard against an attempt of the remainder of the Persian fleet to cut Alexander's long line of communication. In the autumn he sailed out and recaptured Tenedos. Then, there being little love lost between the two countries, Hegelochus, probably needing supplies, seized several Athenian grain ships homeward bound and fully laden with wheat from the ports on the Euxine (Black) Sea. An immediate storm of resentment broke loose in Athens. An assembly was hastily convoked and a vote taken. It was ordered that a hundred war vessels be sent to protect the Athenians' vital lifeline through the Hellespont. Hegelochus, no doubt a little surprised at the hornets' nest he had stirred up, in view of the slights and outright *casus belli* the Athenians had overlooked from Philip, released the grain ships. Rupture with Athens would have given the Persians the opportunity they needed and wanted and would have cost the Macedonians dear. As it was the Persian fleet promptly sailed back to Syphnus and immediately war fever flamed again in Hellas.[1] The Athenians sent

[1] Aeschines, *Ctesiphon*, p. 552. Josephus, in *Antiquities*, XI, 7, 3, confirms this attitude at this time.

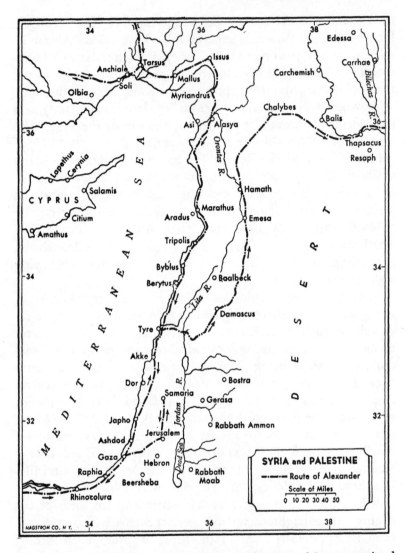

them envoys and began intriguing. King Agis of Sparta arrived with a single trireme and begged funds to prosecute the war and was given ten triremes and thirty talents, with which he sailed for Crete to use that troubled island as a base for operations against the Peloponnesus. While the conference was going on, messengers arrived in Greece carrying tidings of the astonishing disaster to the Persian arms at Issus. That changed things completely. The would-be plotters vanished. The Athenians beat a hasty retreat, thankful they had carried the revolt no farther. Pharnabazus, with twelve triremes and fifteen hundred mercenaries, hurried back to Chios to prevent a revolt, and the rest of the fleet withdrew to other islands for the winter. In the spring, as news of Alexander's increasing successes in Phoenicia reached them, the admirals and kings of Phoenicia hastened away to join the conqueror whose star was in the ascendancy, and the Persian fleet, as Alexander had foreseen, broke up.

While Alexander was at Marathus, Darius sent ambassadors with a letter, and also to entreat verbally for the release of his family. To quote Arrian:[1]

> The letter itself mentioned the league which Philip, his father, had entered into with Artaxerxes, and that... Arses, the son of Artaxerxes, had ascended the throne, the same Philip, without any damage received from the Persians, or other provocation whatsoever, had first of all unjustly invaded his dominions; and how Alexander, from the time he had begun his reign, had never sent ambassadors to confirm the ancient league and treaties between the two nations, but, on the contrary, had passed over into Asia with his army, and committed numerous depredations upon his subjects; that he only took up arms to defend his own rights, and protect his dominions; however, the event of war must be according as the gods had determined: in the meantime, he, a king, sought his wife, mother, and children from him, who also was a king, offering to enter into friendship and alliance with him, and to that end desired that when Meniscus and Arsimas, the two ambassadors, returned, he would send others with them, who both might receive the terms proposed, and agree with them.

Alexander, without troubling to send ambassadors, sent only a single messenger bearing a letter, but with orders to refuse to

---

[1] Arrian, II, 14. Regarding the probable authenticity of the conqueror's letters to Darius, see Pridik, *De Al. Magni epistolarum commercio*, p. 39 ff. He critically accepts them as, at least, including the general meaning of the originals.

discuss either the situation or the letter. The letter, again quoting Arrian:[1]

Your predecessors have entered Macedonia, and the rest of Greece, in a hostile manner, and injured us, before they had received any injury from us. I, at my advancement to the Empire (?) of Greece, willing to avenge my country's wrongs upon the Persians, have passed over into Asia, having received sufficient provocation from your former ravages. You aided the Perinthians [2] in their unjust wars against my father; and Ochus [3] transported an army into Thrace, to disturb the peace of our government. My father was slain by traitors,[4] whom you hired for that purpose (as you have, everywhere, boasted in your letters); and at the same time, when you had taken care that Arses should be dispatched by Bagoas,[5] you usurped the empire unjustly, and in open defiance to all Persian laws. You have, moreover, wrote letters into Greece, encouraging my subjects to rebellion,[6] and to that end have sent money to the Lacedaemonians, and others, which nevertheless all Grecians, except the Lacedaemonians, loyally rejected; by which means, you strove to withdraw my friends and followers from me, and to dissolve that firm league which I have entered into with all the states of Greece. Wherefore I have invaded your realms in a hostile manner, because you were the first author of hostilities. And now, when I have met your governors, and captains, and afterward yourself and your whole army, in pitched battle; and have already, by permission of the gods, gained possession of Asia; as many of your soldiers as sur-

[1] Arrian, II, 14, Rooke's translation.

[2] A false statement. The Perinthians were defending their city against Philip's unjustified assault in an undeclared surprise attack.

[3] Verily a case of visiting the punishments of the father's iniquity upon his children, except that Darius was not even a relative of the late king Ochus, as the Greeks called Artaxerxes III.

[4] Alexander's statement that Darius was responsible for the murder of his father was wholly false. There is indeed far more reason to believe that Alexander or Olympias, or both, were instrumental in bringing it about.

[5] True. Darius had seized power by the murderous connivance of the eunuch Bagoas, who acted the part of kingmaker and rebel against his imperial master Arses.

[6] Also we have reason to believe this untrue. The Thebans, Athenians, and perhaps the inhabitants of Euboea, it is reasonably certain, took Persian money to stir up rebellion.

rendered themselves into my hands, after the battle, I protect; neither do they tarry with me against their inclination, but freely and voluntarily take up arms in my cause. To me, therefore, as Lord of all Asia, come and apply yourself: But if you are afraid of any harsh usage upon your coming, send some of your friends, who may take an oath from me for your safety. When you come into my presence, ask for your wife, your mother, your children, and whatever you will besides, and you shall receive them; and nothing shall be denied you. However, when you write me next, remember to entitle me King of Asia, neither write to me any more as your equal, but as Lord of all your territories. If you act otherwise, I shall look upon it as an indignity of the highest consequences; and if you dispute my right to the possession of your realms, stay and try the event of another battle; but hope not to secure yourself by flight, for wherever you fly, thither will I surely pursue you.

A careful study of the foregoing, which we have no reason for assuming to be other than authentic, discloses Alexander to be by no means the nobly magnanimous person many of his pane-gyrists would have us believe. Not only does he hold Darius per-sonally responsible for the actions of his predecessors, but the coldly ferocious threats in the last lines seem calculated to force any self-respecting man, let alone a haughty Persian king, to resistance to the ultimate degree. Not that Darius was angelic on his own part, however, for his machinations and rise to power over the murdered bodies of his predecessor and his family will be excused by no manner of explanation. Too, history, as it unrolls in these pages, will show that, although Alexander did become Lord of Asia in years to come, he was somewhat pre-mature in claiming it then. He had still to conquer the coasts of Phoenicia, take and consolidate Egypt, cross hundreds of miles of Syria and Assyria, fight another and still greater battle against Darius, and then spend years forcing the hard-fighting tribes-men of Turkestan, Afghanistan, and India into submission. Yet it does speak volumes of his confidence in himself and his destiny that he so proclaimed himself now, and his extraordinary self-control that he spent two years thereafter in conquering and

consolidating his newly won territories along the Mediterranean seaboard and Egypt, before pursuing Darius to press the
proof of his assertion; two years in which he knew Darius would
and did use every resource of his great empire to raise and equip
an enormous army in a stupendous effort to block the meteoric
career of the young invader. There must have been a strong
temptation to pursue Darius now before the army could be
raised and before Darius could recover from the demoralization
of Issus. Unfortunately, however, the Persian fleet still held
the Aegean and most of the islands, and it was only in the following spring that it started to break up. Also as evidence of
the unpopularity of the Macedonian cause in Hellas, there were
captured at Issus ambassadors to Darius from Thebes, Athens,
and Sparta. They had arrived just before the battle, in other
words, during his campaign, when he was at war with them.
The two Thebans were freed because, Alexander said, they could
not be held blameworthy in attempting to restore their city-
state after the miserable conditions to which they had been reduced by the Macedonians, even to the extent of applying to
Darius for money and assistance; the Athenians because of the
respect he bore for that city; but the Spartan ambassador, for
his stiff-necked attitude, he ordered held, releasing him only
long afterward.

Alexander was now leaving behind him the area of Greek
colonization and influence and entering a civilization of the
Semitic peoples, psychologically conditioned in the north
first by the ancient Assyrio-Hittite, later by Persian, Canaanite,
and Aramaic influences; in the south by Nabataean (Arabic) and
Egyptian. The Phoenician cities, old and prosperous, were his
first aim for the bulk of the Persian fleet derived from them.
Byblus freely opened its gates to him. The people of Sidon, still
smarting under the city's destruction by fire when Memnon
captured it by treachery (Diodorus says Mentor, his brother)
eighteen years earlier, welcomed him wildly. The hereditary
kings of both cities were left in power, practically autonomous,
subject only to the will of Alexander. Tyre, however, was a

different proposition, and gave the young king the most savage resistance he was ever to encounter. The city at first offered to surrender, but when Alexander announced his intention of entering the city to offer sacrifice, permission to do so was refused. The explanation is that the local god of Tyre was Melkarth (or Melkart), long identified by the Greeks as equated with Heracles. Nothing, therefore, was more natural than that Alexander should wish to sacrifice to the god he recognized as Heracles, whom he claimed also as one of his own ancestors. But whether or not he understood it, also nothing was more natural than for the Tyrians to refuse to permit it, for according to the Oriental viewpoint, only the king or priests could offer sacrifice, and permitting Alexander to do so would have automatically proclaimed their acceptance of him as king of Tyre. Besides, there was a tradition of the world-old city that no foreign conqueror had ever entered the gates (twice Assyrian sieges, one lasting four years from 701 to 697, another nine years from 671 to 662, had failed, as had that of Nebuchadnezzar the Babylonian in his twelve-year siege, 585 to 573 B.C.) and the pride of the city would not allow it now. From the dawn of time through many vicissitudes, the city, impregnable behind its high walls, and located upon a rocky island two miles in circuit and half a mile offshore, had successfully repelled all attempts at invasion. They had never had a foreign ruler, and would have none now. Azelmicus, king of Tyre, was absent with the Persian fleet, and his son, with perhaps a council, ruled as regent in his father's absence. Whether the king would have surrendered the city at Alexander's demand must remain conjectural, at any rate the son would not. Alexander, who could see only contumaciousness in the suggestion that he could sacrifice to Melkarth in the temple in the old city of Tyre, now falling into ruins on the mainland, prepared to besiege the city. He dared not leave it unsubdued with its powerful navy in his rear when he marched on to Egypt. The date was January, 332 B.C.

The island upon which the city was built was separated by a

channel about twenty-five hundred feet wide, the water near the shore being shallow with a soft mud bottom; farther out near the city the depth increased to eighteen feet with a bottom of hard clay. The abandoned city of old Tyre on the mainland furnished a quantity of stone, while the quarries of the hills furnished more, and the Anti-Lebanon, hard by, supplied timbers for piles and siege engines. Alexander began to build a mole from the mainland toward the island, driving a double line of piles and filling in between with stone and earth and rubble from the old city. Diodorus claims to know that it was two hundred feet wide when it was finished. It remains today, an isthmus broadened by the silting and detritus, still connecting the island and mainland. Alexander himself carried and threw in the first basket of earth, then, amid wild clamor, men and officers alike fell upon the task. The work went well until deep water was reached, and the head of the mole advanced to within range of the artillery upon the city walls, then the Tyrian ships became active also. Filled with archers and slingers protected by superimposed high bulwarks, they rowed swiftly past the head of the works bringing the laborers under deadly fire, making it necessary to build high movable barricades to protect them. Additional defenses were constructed on the mole in the form of towers several stories high filled with archers and catapults for throwing stones and javelins, and protected by thick walls from missiles and a sheathing of green hides against the torch. These held the ships of the attackers at bay for a while, then the ingenuity of the Tyrians found a way to combat the towers. They took a large horse transport scow and filled it with combustibles; a mast with two derrick-like arms was erected and on each was hung a great cauldron filled with highly inflammable fluids, probably turpentine or naphtha. They then loaded the scow's stern heavily to bring the bow high out of water, and with a fair wind and two other boats pushing, the scow was run high up on the mole. The two cauldrons were swung out and emptied on the towers, a torch applied to the combustibles, and the whole roared up in flames. The Macedonians who swarmed out to stem the conflagration were simply targets for the catapults and ship's archers and slingers. The whole of the wooden fortifications went up in flames, ruining the work of months.

Nothing daunted, Alexander set to widening the mole to carry larger towers, and building anew. Then he realized that without a fleet to help him, the same disaster could be easily wrought again. Leaving the engineers to their work, Alexander went back to Sidon, where he found himself again favored by fortune. The kings of Aradus and Byblus, finally hearing that their cities were in Alexander's possession, deserted the Persian fleet and, with the fleet of Sidon, came to offer submission to Alexander; then came ten ships from Rhodes, from Soli and Mallus, three more, from Lycia ten, and one even arrived from Macedonia. Soon afterward, the kings of Cyprus, terrified at the Persian downfall at Issus, came hurrying anxiously with one hundred and twenty more ships to ally themselves with the winning side. Now Alexander found himself master of a magnificent fleet two hundred and twenty-four strong. While the ships were preparing to take part in the siege, Alexander, with a detachment of archers and light infantry, made a surprise raid of ten days into the Anti-Lebanon, the Iturean tribesmen (ancestors of the modern Druses) readily submitting to Macedonian authority. This widened his territories, till then a narrow road along the seashore only, and is indicative, not only of his amazing energy, but of his methodical intent to leave behind no city or tribe in a position to interfere with his lines of communications. When he returned to Sidon he found there Cleander, whom he had sent fourteen months before for reinforcements, waiting him with four thousand Greek mercenaries, a welcome addition to the army, no doubt, but hardly a good showing for an able recruiting officer backed by ample money.

A few hours' sail brought the fleet to Tyre, where Alexander ordered it into line of battle, himself in command of the right, Craterus of the left wing. The Tyrians, whose king had returned with his fleet, had intended to offer battle, but when they saw from their walls the size of the fleet opposed to them, they realized, to their surprise and dismay, that they were heavily outnumbered. They had not considered the possibility of having the Cyprian kings to face also. But now it was patent that they would have to secure their harbors and prepare for siege in deadly earnest. They immediately brought their ships to the mouths of their northern and southern harbors, mooring and lashing them in the entrances, beaks outward. Alexander's fleet crept slowly in, but considering an attack upon the harbor mouths too costly, he contented himself with a display of strength. Three of the Tyrian ships lay somewhat exposed, however, and several Phoenician vessels dashed in and rammed them, the Tyrian sailors easily escaping their sinking craft by swimming either to friendly craft or into the near-by harbor. Alexander then divided the fleet, placing the Cyprian ships to blockade the harbor on the north, the Phoenician ships the harbor on the south, where his royal pavilion was also erected.

Alexander's siege-craft was unequal to the task he had set himself at Tyre, and he called upon the Cyprians and Phoenicians for assistance. In the art and science of the siege and defense, the people of Phoenicia and Syria were, due to longer and greater experience, measurably far superior to the Greeks. When the requested engineers arrived they immediately began building new and larger siege appliances. Some they placed upon scows lashed together to provide a wide platform and to support their immense weight, some upon the decks of ships best able to carry them, others upon the head of the works. Huge towers were erected upon the mole to carry the heaviest possible missile weapons. The Tyrians immediately erected still higher towers upon the walls and opened fire with flaming arrows and javelins upon anything inflammable within range. Finally all was ready and the triremes and the scows bearing towers closed on the wall, only to find their way blocked by stones cast from the wall, partially filling the channel. Ships were brought up with derricks on them and the stones were fished out one by one and dropped again in deep water, a perilous task under fire from the walls, made slow from the insecure footing on the decks. Tyrian ships with high bulwarks faced with rawhides slipped in and cut the cables of the stone-re-movers. These were countered by similarly covered triremes set to watch and ram the cable-cutters. Still the desperate defenders were successful; they sent out divers who swam under water and cut the cables there. Iron chains were substituted for the cables and the Tyrian divers were at last defeated.

Finally the channel was cleared, the engine-carriers moved in and started battering at the walls. Meanwhile, the siege had been pressed from the mole. The beleaguered garrison in the city swarmed over their ramparts, hurling javelins, arrows, stones, and fire-balls at the workmen toiling below, getting back these same missiles, with compound interest, from the fighting men in the towers. At last the besiegers got their rams into position, great metal-weighted beams that swung far across the water gap, and began hammering at the solid stone walls. The Macedonians were in a terrible rage at their long impotency before the city and every day their fury grew. And every day the hopes of those within the city sank. Every day prayers were offered in the temple of Melkarth for the long-awaited succor which the king had asked of Carthage, but when at last news came, it was in the form of a single trireme bearing word that the Carthaginians had their own hands so full in Sicily that they were unable to render assistance.

The plight of the besieged was now so desperate that they resolved upon a naval attack upon the Cyprian fleet off the north harbor. Their preparations were made quietly (Arrian says they spread sails across the mouth of the harbor to prevent the Macedonians from seeing them; an unlikely story); the ships were manned with the intention of starting the raid about noon. At this time most of the sailors of Alexander's fleet were busied ashore, bringing water, collecting food and fuel, and it was Alexander's habit, as the besieged could plainly see from their walls, to retire to the royal pavilion for a noonday siesta; this then was the best time for the attempt. Thirteen of the best Tyrian ships — three quinqueremes, three quadriremes, seven triremes — manned with picked oarsmen and fighting men were moved up and lay waiting just inside the harbor mouth. At the time selected, silently, with only the low objurgations of the boatswains instead of the steady drumbeat used to guide the rhythm of the long oars, the desperate craft of the forlorn hope got under way. They cleared the mouth of the harbor in silence and turned eastward toward the drowsing and nearly deserted Cyprian fleet less than half a mile away. Once clear of the harbor, the oar rhythm was picked up, and with a great shout the rowers leaped to their fullest power and sweep, racing to the attack. It so happened that that particular day, unfortunately for the Tyrians, Alexander had, as customary, retired to his tent, but after remaining only a short time, returned to the Phoenician fleet, just in time to witness the onset. Almost immediately a great quinquereme, a war vessel with five banks of oars, belonging to Pnytagoras, king of Cyprian Salamis, was rammed and sunk, as were also two other ships. Confusion reigned supreme for a few minutes as the attackers swung back to assault other vessels before those with their crews aboard could recover from their surprise and offer effective resistance. The Tyrians drew up to the Cyprian ships and swarmed aboard, frenziedly wreaking all possible damage on them. Then, as discipline reasserted itself, from all directions men raced toward the mole to fight back. Alexander with the Phoenician fleet sent orders for ships on the north side of the mole hurrying to the harbor mouth to blockade it and prevent the emergence of more attackers and to block the return of those outside. He had a few quinqueremes and five triremes ready manned on the south side of the mole. Boarding one, and ordering the others to follow, he set out at full speed on the three-mile journey around the outside of the island, hastening to attack the daring raiders. The people on the wall, seeing the immediate preparations for the counter-attack, and noting with dismay that Alexander himself was leading it, shouted for their compatriots to return. The bedlamic uproar of the conflict drowned out their cries, and when at last their signals were understood and the Tyrians finally broke clear of the engagement, they were already too late. Alexander had made the circuit of the walls in less than twenty minutes, and was surging swiftly in like an avenging Nemesis. Several of the Tyrian vessels were rammed and sunk, others were driven into the rocks of the mole or at the base of the city walls and wrecked, and two, a quinquereme and a quadrireme, were overtaken, boarded, and captured almost at the mouth of the harbor. This was the end of the menace of the Tyrian ships; most of those from the north harbor were destroyed, those in the southern harbor were afterward so closely invested that they dared not repeat the attempt to carry the war outside. It was the last fight that Persian sea power was to attempt in the Mediterranean, and it was the first and last sea battle in which Alexander ever engaged.

Alexander now ordered the attack upon the walls carried on with redoubled energy. Ships mounting engines were moved up to the side of the city facing the mainland and started beating at the solid walls. These were soon found to be so strong it was impossible to make much impression upon them. The ships moved around to the north wall. That, too, was very strong. They moved farther around to the western wall. That also defied their efforts. Again they moved, this time to the south wall. This was found to be much less solid. Additional rams were moved up, and ships with towers loaded with archers and catapults were brought up to protect the rams with a barrage of arrows and stones. Other ships rowed slowly along the circuit of the walls and maintained a heavy fire against all who showed themselves above the battlements. The assault from the mole was increased in magnitude. The siege-weary garrison was thus dispersed all along the wall and were beset from all sides. A breach was beaten into the south wall and the Macedonians threw up scaling ladders to help them over the fallen stones, and attacked. After a sharp battle the Tyrians drove them back. The breach was too narrow. On the third day after that the sea was like a millpond. The ram ships advanced to the assault and soon tore great gaps in the walls. The rams were then withdrawn, and two great ships, jammed with armed men, carrying scaling ladders and bridges like gangplanks, were moved in. The first assault party, an auxiliary company of hypaspists, swarmed to the attack, led by Admetus, the first to land, and the first to die. Alexander, in another ship, led his foot agema up, followed by heavy armed phalangists carrying hoplons and their long sarissas. A fierce conflict followed, but the Tyrians were driven from the breach and cleared from the entire south wall between the towers. Alexander formed up his guard and a few phalangists and marched along the top of the wall, fighting every foot of the way against the Tyrian defenders rendered desperate in trapped and hopeless fury. Reaching the royal palace he descended the ramp and carried the battle into the narrow streets.[1]

Meanwhile, Alexander's fleets had crashed their way through the harbor defenses and captured or destroyed the Tyrian ships. The Phoenician sailors, who also brought Coenus' regiment of phalangists, then left their ships and joined with the attackers on land, while the remaining soldiery, arriving on the other ships, swarmed into the city at every possible entrance. The Tyrian defenders, driven from the walls, rallied at the shrine of Agenor (legendary founder of the city) and faced the attackers, but Alexander drove in on them, slew many and put the rest to flight. Coenus and his forces made a great slaughter in the narrow streets, for the Macedonians were furious at the long

[1] This is the story as Arrian gives it. Plutarch gives another version, not, however, wholly incompatible with Arrian's fuller account: 'One day when Alexander, with a view to resting the great body of his army from the many hardships recently incurred, was bringing only small bodies against the walls, and that more to keep the enemy busy than with any prospect of advantage, it happened that Aristander, the soothsayer, was engaged in sacrificing. After inspecting the entrails, he announced to the bystanders with all assurance that the city would be taken that month. This produced considerable merriment and derision, for the day happened to be the last day of the month. The king, seeing the embarrassment of the soothsayer, and being always anxious to maintain the credit of their predictions, gave orders to set the calendar back one day, and made a more serious attack than had been planned. So brilliant was the assault that the other troops in camp could not deny themselves joining in; whereupon the Tyrians gave way, and the city was taken that day.'

siege and burning to revenge a number of their compatriots who were captured at sea while coming from Sidon; they had been displayed from the top of the ramparts, then murdered and cast into the sea. Of the number of Tyrians slain we have two figures, Curtius says six thousand, Arrian eight thousand, Diodorus giving no figures for a total, but says, in which Curtius concurs, that two thousand young men were nailed to gibbets by the Macedonians, though both fail to give any reason for this particularly vicious piece of barbarity. Some of the Tyrian nobility and King Azelmicus had sought sanctuary in the shrine of Melkarth, and these, the major cause, by reason of their stiff-necked obstinacy in the beginning, of the destruction of the city and its population, together with the Carthaginian priests, were given pardons. The rest of the survivors, to the number of thirty thousand men, women, and children, were sold into slavery, this marking the end of the ancient commercial and naval power of Tyre. Arrian gives the number of Macedonians killed in the siege as four hundred; granting that we take this absurdly low figure as correct, we must nevertheless add to it, on the basis of seven killed to one wounded, a list of wounded of not less than three thousand. Alexander after this offered at the shrine of Melkarth (remember that to the Greeks the god was Heracles) the sacrifice he had proposed to offer seven months before, at which solemnities his army and navy assisted. The ram which had made the final breach in the city wall was dedicated to Heracles and placed in the temple, as was the Tyrian sacred ship which he captured. Alexander then held a gymnastic festival, with a grand review of the army and fleet, the inevitable games, torch parade and torch races, in celebration of his victory and in honor of Heracles. Thus fell the city of Tyre, Alexander's most difficult military feat, after a seven months' siege, in August, 332 B.C., when Alexander was twenty-three years old and in the third year of his reign. The city was resettled under a Macedonian, and it again became a naval base, this time of a fleet hostile to the Persians.

While the siege of Tyre was being carried on, other ambassadors came from Darius, making an even better proposition than the first. Darius offered him ten thousand talents of silver as ransom for his family; [1] also if Alexander would become his friend and ally Darius would give him the hand of his daughter in marriage and cede to him all of his kingdom that lay west of the Euphrates River. This proposal was carried to the council, and during the debate Parmenio said, 'If I were Alexander I would accept these terms now that the reason for going to war has been gained, and secure peace.' Alexander replied coldly, 'So should I, if I were Parmenio, but as I am Alexander, I must act like Alexander.' The ambassadors were sent away with this curt reply: that Alexander wanted neither part of Darius' money nor part of the empire; he was determined to have the whole of both, and that as for Darius' daughter, if he wanted to marry her he would do so without Darius' consent. Darius received the reply, and, knowing it meant a continuation of his conquests by the implacable Macedonian, at once redoubled his efforts of raising an army to oppose him. Josephus [2] tells an interesting story of this period. He says that during the siege of Tyre Alexander sent a message to the high priest, Jaddua, of Jerusalem, ordering him to send a contribution of money, provisions, and auxiliaries. The high priest replied that he had sworn fealty to Darius and would never, as long as the king lived, commit any act detrimental to him. To which Alexander, whose imperious will could brook no opposition, replied with the threat that he would soon come to Jerusalem and teach the Jews to whom they should make oath.

After the fall of Tyre, Alexander turned south again, meeting no resistance until he reached Gaza, one hundred and fifty miles away. The city, about two miles inland from the seacoast, was

[1] This is Arrian's version. Diodorus, XVII, 39, says that Alexander, at the council, made report of a less generous offer, desiring the refusal of acceptance by the council. If Diodorus is correct, the only inference to be drawn from his action is that Alexander knew how far his real intentions and aims differed from those of the officers and army, and intended to keep yet secret his own plans.

[2] Josephus, Book XI, chap. XII, and Niese's *Geschichte der griech. und makedon. Staaten,* p. 83.

located upon an artificial mound sixty feet high, upon which rose the city walls to a still greater height. It was then, even as it is today, the meeting-place of the great trade routes out of Syria, Arabia, and Egypt, populous and wealthy. Alexander summoned the city to surrender, and met abrupt refusal. He marched down and invested it, camping, after a careful inspection, on the south side, which seemed most amenable to assault. His officers, noting the height of the walls [1] and the great height of the mound from which they rose, expressed the opinion that the place could not be taken by assault. That, too, was evidently the opinion of the commander of the city, the fat black Ethiopian eunuch Batis,[2] a stubborn giant of a man, who believed, despite the terrible object lesson of Tyre, that he could hold the city for his Persian master. Before Alexander's arrival he had garrisoned it strongly with Nabataeans (Petra, south of the Dead Sea, was their capital city), provisioned it for a long siege, and considered it impregnable. Alexander did not concur with the belief; he couldn't afford to consider the possibility of an impossibility. As candidate for the world empire which he proposed to conquer he obviously could not let a single city defy him with impunity. He therefore ordered a mound raised against the wall, and while this was being done, the engines from the siege train were placed in position and started beating against the walls. At this time a delegation of fifteen special commissioners arrived, sent by the Corinthian League, which, at a meeting held during the Isthmian games, had voted to send Alexander a golden crown in honor of his victory at Issus, an honor which to the young king, who was now Lord of Asia Minor, Syria, and Phoenicia, was a mere bagatelle, testimony now, a year after Issus, only of the fickleness of the components and members of the league.

The light engines of the siege train were slowly wearing their

---

[1] Arrian says specifically the walls were two hundred and fifty feet high, an obvious absurdity. Curtius gives no figures, nor does any other ancient chronicler whom we have read.

[2] Curtius calls him Betis, Josephus refers to him as Babameses.

way into the wall despite the strenuous resistance of the city, too slowly for Alexander, too fast for the citizens. The defenders launched a strong counter-attack which Alexander rushed, at the head of his guard, to beat back. An arrow shot from a catapult on the wall crashed through his shield and breastplate, wounding him severely in the shoulder. While he was convalescing, the great engines used in the siege of Tyre were brought down by sea. The earthen mound was increased to a width of twelve hundred feet and the heavy engines brought into action. These started beating the walls down while sappers assisted by undermining their foundations. Soon a breach was beaten in, and the Macedonians rushed in to the assault. Three times they were beaten back. Then the breach was enlarged and a fourth assault carried the city after desperate fighting. Batis himself was captured alive, and (according to Hegesias of Magnesia [1]) brought to Alexander, who detested the sight of him, as he was big and grim and black. The captive was tied by the feet to a chariot and dragged to death. The survivors were sold into slavery, the city being recolonized by people drawn from that area, and a garrison placed in it. The siege had lasted two months.

He sent to his mother Olympias and sister Cleopatra several loads of jewels, perfumes, spices, and rare fabrics, and the inevitable letter to his mother, telling her the story. He also sent a consignment of incense to his old tutor, partly as a rebuke for an occurrence of many years before. Plutarch tells us:

> As Alexander was sending off to Olympias and Cleopatra and his friends great quantities of booty he had taken, he also sent along, for his pedagogue Leonidas, five hundred talents of frankincense and a hundred talents of myrrh, in memory of a boyish dream of his youth. For it so happened at a sacrifice that as Alexander seized both hands full of incense and threw it on the fire, Leonidas called to him and said: 'Sometime, if you get to be master of the land of spices, you can throw incense lavishly like this, but for the present be economical of what you have.' So now Alexander took

[1] Hegesias, *Fragmenta Historicorum Graecorum*, 142, frag. 5.

occasion to write to him: 'We send you frankincense and myrrh in abundance, so that you make an end of economizing with the gods.'

Alexander then, recalling the refusal of the high priest of Jerusalem to render assistance during the siege of Tyre, next turned toward that city, a bare three days' march distant. As the army neared, the people of the city were panic-stricken, but, acting on the advice of the high priest, the citizens, with the priests at their head, met the king outside the gates of the city. Alexander was so impressed at the meeting, especially when shown one of the ancient prophecies that a Greek (literally a man from Javan, i.e., Ionia) would at last come and free the people from the Persian rule. This prophecy he read to mean himself. He therefore permitted the people of the country to live on under their own laws and system. Josephus says that he then made a short excursion northward into Samaria where he conscripted several thousands of the inhabitants and took them with him. Upon his arrival in Egypt, continues Josephus, he sent the Samarians to garrison the upper Nile post of the Elephantine. He then turned back to Gaza and prepared to march on to Egypt. The time was November. He had spent a whole year in the sieges of the two cities, and that was but a tenth of the time he had left to reign upon this earth.

==VIII==

FROM Gaza Alexander moved west along the seacoast over the ancient caravan route and in seven days marched one hundred and thirty miles to Pelusium, the fortified guard city of the eastern frontier, upon the eastern arm of the Nile. History is silent regarding the passage past Arsa Aspa, later Rhinocolura (now Arish), the Biblical Brook of Egypt, and now the Wadi El Arish. For centuries before and after this time, the little town was the key to Egypt, and the meeting-place of the caravans out of Nabataea and Arabia. Arriving at Pelusium (now only two great mounds, almost unknown, in a nearly inaccessible area of desolate salt marsh) the city surrendered without resistance. Mazaces, ruling Egypt as lieutenant of the satrap Sabaces, slain at Issus, ordered the gates thrown open to the Macedonians. Persian rule in Egypt collapsed without a blow. It can, of course, be argued that Egypt had been swept clean of fighting men by Sabaces in the service of his imperial master, but Mazaces had had time to create a new army during the year-long sieges of Tyre and Gaza. It is a matter of record that the Egyptian garrison at Pelusium had been strong enough to annihilate an invading army of eight thousand mercenaries under the renegade Amyntas. Amyntas had escaped at Issus with his command, gone south to Tripolis, sailed thence to Cyprus, and later to Egypt in an ill-fated attempt to subdue that country for himself. Though most commentators report Amyntas as having been slain also, there is reason to believe that he again escaped and continued his anti-Alexander activity by joining King Agis of Sparta in Crete. More probably the deciding factor in Mazaces' apparent inaction was the wild enthusiasm of the populace for the conqueror, as well as an accurate knowledge that the army, such as was left, was pro-Greek and in sympathy with Alexander. The temper of an aroused people often makes the levying of a reliable army impossible, and the Egyptians, after Alexander's amazing victories over the Persians, hailed him as their deliverer. For threescore years they had succeeded, by prudently taking advantage of disorders within the Persian Empire and with the assistance of well-paid Greek mercenaries, in keeping a pharaoh on the throne. But in 344, just twelve years before, the last native prince (whose name is transcribed as Nectanebo by the Greek historians) had been deposed by Artaxerxes III, and Persian rule restored. Perhaps fortunately for them, the Egyptians could not foresee that Alexander came, not as an ally, but as a master; that he was merely substituting for the rather lax and lenient Persian rule, an iron-handed government that was to be the beginning of a thousand years of Greco-Roman misrule and exploitation. Never from that time on would a native prince ever sit upon the throne of Egypt as pharaoh. And when the thousand years had passed, the Egypt that was to come under the sway of Islam was a new Egypt, with a greatly changed people, new social customs, a new organization, new religion, and even a new language.

After putting a garrison in Pelusium, Alexander marched up

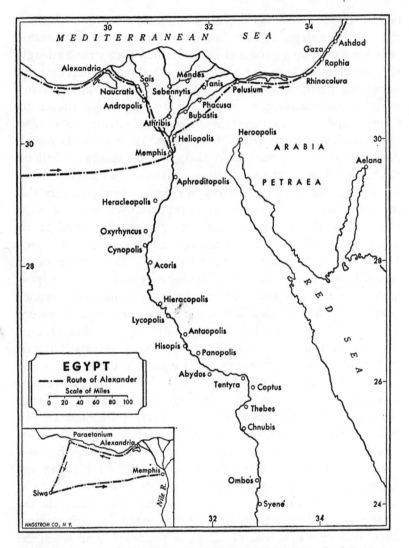

the eastern arm of the Nile, through the Biblical land of Goshen, crossed the Nile at Heliopolis, and entered Memphis. Here Mazaces surrendered the citadel, the garrison and eight hundred talents, and the treasures of the King's House. The *Romance of Alexander*, probably written in the third century A.D., states that

Alexander was enthroned in the temple of Ptah in Memphis, following the age-old rites used by the pharaohs. This statement may be, and very probably is, correct, and embodies historical fact as handed down in the form of a legend. It is certain that Alexander in Egypt either showed perfect understanding of the psychology of conquered peoples or acted upon excellent advice in adopting the course of action that he did. He officially and publicly offered sacrifice to the gods and to the bull Apis, who was not a god but a sacred animal of the cult of Ptah. It may be that Alexander, though officially offering sacrifice to the gods of Egypt, was really sacrificing to the gods of Greece. The Egyptian gods had long been equated in the Greek mind with their own, Ammon with Zeus, Osiris with Dionysus, Horus with Apollo, and so on. Therefore, when officiating at the sacrifice he was fulfilling his duty and obligations as king of Egypt. Further proof comes to us in the form of hieroglyphic writings which testify that he bore the traditional royal titles.[1]

Of the five titles customary from the middle of the third millennium B.C. the first, fourth, and fifth were given to Alexander. As 'Horus' (1) he was called 'the strong prince' (2); also with the addition 'he who hath laid hands upon the lands of the foreigners,' or 'the protection of Egypt' (3). As 'King of Upper Egypt and King of Lower Egypt' (4), he was called 'beloved of Ammon and selected of Ra'; and finally as 'son of Ra' (5), he was called 'Alexandros.' Here the Horus title, 'he who hath laid hands upon the lands of the foreigners,' seems to have been invented for Alexander, whereas the other titles are frequent before his time. These titles prove two things of Alexander, his special sovereignty over Egypt and his consequent deification.

By these and subsequent acts, such as ordering the rebuilding of the sanctuary of the temple of Karnak and the temple at Luxor, Alexander identified himself with the preservation of the gods and religions, thereby removing immediately a very possible seed of rebellion and discontent. Molestation of established forms of worship in a conquered country has, both before and

[1] Ulrich Wilcken, *Alexander der Grosse*.

since, proved a constant source of trouble to the conquerors. Rebellion had flared and been brutally suppressed more than once in the last ten years, though the Persians were, on the whole, not oppressive in their treatment of the people. But when Artaxerxes arrived, he, as a follower of the austere creed of Zoroastrianism, had been disgusted with the animal, reptile, and insect worship of the Egyptians. Callously disregarding the political dictum that a people can be enslaved with a degree of ease as long as their spiritual pabulum is left them, he had violated every precept making for internal peace. He had defiled their temples, plundered their holy treasures, stabled an ass in the shrine of Ptah, and as a crowning enormity ordered the bull Apis slaughtered and served for his dinner. Bevan [1] holds that the Macedonians acted as they did in Egypt through awe and veneration of its traditions and antiquity, its learning and sciences, the mystery of ancient and inscrutable gods and their vast temples. It *may* be, of course, that they did feel that in this land, which they had heard of for centuries in connection with esoteric wonders, they must, to be on the safe side, pay adequate deference and due to its ageless gods. This commentator prefers to believe that the hard-headed Macedonians acted from what they considered military and political expediency; and that the notable toleration to the native gods which they displayed both here and elsewhere was simply recognition of the political necessity of such a policy.

Immediately after the sacrifices to the Egyptian gods, Alexander held at Memphis a gymnastic and musical festival. Some of the most renowned athletes and musicians of the Greek world were participants. Alexander had then been in Egypt hardly more than a month or six weeks, yet these famous entertainers managed somehow to be here in Memphis. Certainly there was insufficient time for the news of the capture and consolidation of Egypt to be conveyed to Greece along with a summons to the games, yet these competitors had received the summons, crossed the sea, and ascended the Nile to Memphis. The only hypothesis

[1] Bevan, *Ptolemaic Egypt*, pp. 2–6.

left us today is that the summons went forth before Alexander left Gaza, which in turn justifies the assumption that Alexander knew that he would encounter no resistance to his seizure of Egypt. In short, it permits more than a suspicion that long before he had made arrangements with Mazaces for the peaceful surrender of the country.

Alexander realized that as soon as he departed for Persia to continue his quarrel with Darius, Egypt would be the most difficult to defend adequately and the most certain of assault of all his conquests. Its peaceful and industrious population, its riches of soil and the large numbers of skilled and docile artisans available rendered it the glaringly logical point of attack by an enemy needing a naval base and a source of supplies of food and war stores. To assure against attack he needed a base for his own navy, and to bring into being the commerce necessary to permit Egypt to grow out of its isolated provincialism he needed a seaport as well. Down the western arm of the Nile and some forty miles from the sea lay the Greek traders' city of Naucratis (near present-day Nibireh). Though then nearly three hundred years old, it had never risen to any degree of power or affluence; it was too far inland and the Nile too shallow and variable for building into a great seaport. Alexander left Memphis by boat, attended only by a small force of hypaspists, archers, Agrianians, and the royal squadron (agema) of hetairoi. Proceeding down the western arm of the Nile, he reached Naucratis, paused there briefly, and went on to Canopus. He then turned west. Eastward was the one-hundred-fifty-mile width of the marshy delta of the seven mouths of the Nile, past that the barren desert coast. And along that coast a current set toward Phoenicia, promising to fill with Nile silt any harbor, natural or artificial, that might be built. Already the western arm on which Pelusium lay was so badly silted even then that only fishing boats or other small craft could enter. And even at this early date ships, notably warships, were as long as one hundred and fifty feet with drafts of eight and ten feet. The Phoenicians now manning his navy could hardly have failed to have known and notified him of these conditions. Then, too, the Greek scientists he carried with him were far enough advanced to predict eclipses with considerable accuracy, and persons of such mental astuteness must have known much of this and other natural phenomena. Be that as it may, however, Alexander turned west to the neck of land lying between the fresh-water lake Mareotis (now a swamp) and the sea, where lay the fishing village of Rhacotis, or Rhakoti.

> As for the site of the city, it has often been pointed out why the little Egyptian Rhacotis was selected to be transformed into a world capital. The Canopic mouth of the Nile had long served for the comparatively little seagoing commerce (nearly all of it in the hands of the Greeks of Naucratis) with the alien Levant, which Egypt had hitherto had. Of the other (there were seven) the Pelusiac alone remained open to anything larger than a fishing boat. Even the Canopic had a dangerous bar. Entry, exit, and conditions ashore (near Canopis) which made neither for health nor security, were against it. But at Rhacotis, a few miles farther west, Alexander found a dry limestone site, raised above the delta level, within easy reach of drinkable water, and navigable inland water to be taken by a canal off the Nile (this canal followed much the same course as the modern Mahmudiyeh canal) and covered by an island, which, if joined to the mainland by a mole, would give alternate harbors against the sea winds, blow they whence they might. It was the one possible situation in Egypt for a healthy open port to be used by the Macedonian seagoing fleets and particularly warships, already tending at that epoch to increase their tonnage and draft.[1]

Strabo states that besides the fishing village of Rhacotis there was also a military post here to forestall pirate raids upon the region. Homer's *Iliad*, Alexander's favorite work, had also referred to the harbor, and Menelaus the Hero had visited here. Therefore we can be sure that before Alexander even saw the site he knew all about it. Soldiers could not have failed to be impressed by its very obvious military, if not commercial, possibilities. However, it was genius that selected this site as a place

[1] D. G. Hogarth, 'Alexander in Egypt,' *Journal of Egyptian Archeology*, 1915.

whereon to build the city that Alexander willed to become the commercial center of the earth. In the selection of the site Alexander had the advice of those who had previously seen the possibilities of the place, yet in the final analysis the decision and the praise or blame for it rested upon his head. No doubt he was impressed strongly by the great productivity of the country in contrast with the relatively barren Greece and Asia Minor and the barren coasts of Phoenicia, and foresaw at least some of the enormous trade within the potentialities of Egypt. The first part of the campaign, that of occupying the ports of the eastern Mediterranean, was a *fait accompli* and now he proposed to turn a military necessity into a commercial convenience. So successful was he that for hundreds of years Alexandria was the most important port on the Mediterranean coast.

The city was planned as an oblong rectangle about two miles wide by four miles long, upon the style introduced by Hippodamus of Miletus a hundred years before. The architect was Deinocrates of Rhodes. Two broad streets were laid out crossing each other at right angles and other streets were drawn parallel to them so that the whole consisted of regular blocks of houses. Alexander took an active part in the planning and himself designated the position of the market and the temples, and as pharaoh he ordered a temple built to Isis. A stone tablet, formerly set in the town wall and dating about 311 B.C., reads: 'The fortress of the King of Upper and Lower Egypt, Alexandros, on the shore of the sea of the Ionians. Rhacotis was its earlier name.' The foundation feast of the city was held on the twenty-fifth day of the month Tybi; it was therefore about January 20, 331 B.C., that the actual founding ceremony took place. A mole was built to the island of Pharos to provide a breakwater against coastal winds; in succeeding ages the rubbish and detritus of the city has built the mole up solidly, more than a mile wide, until now, to the casual eye, the onetime island of Pharos is seemingly part of the mainland. It is difficult to trace with real exactitude the city and area as it was of that day. A subsidence of the soil of Alexandria of at least seven and one-half feet has occurred since then, and at least at one point the land has subsided as much as twenty feet and risen again eleven feet. Thus today a considerable part of early Alexandria actually lies below the surface of the water.

Recently,[1] however, researches of M. Gaston Jondet, Engineer in Chief of the Ports and Lighthouses of Egypt, has given history a new and sensational problem. For he has discovered under the sea, reaching in some places to a quarter of a mile beyond what was in ancient times the island of Pharos, remains of a large and massive harbor works, moles and quays; and it is still a question whether they were part of Greek Alexandria, or whether they were works of a far earlier epoch, abandoned and fallen into ruin long before Alexander passed that way. M. Jondet himself is disposed to think that the submerged harbor was made by the great Rameses as a defense against the marauding people of the sea. 'The mass of materials used is colossal, as in all pharaonic buildings; its transportation and construction must have presented graver problems than piling up of the stones which form the pyramids.'[2] Another French scholar, M. Raymond Weills, has advanced the theory that the works in question are a relic of the 'mysterious Cretan sea power in the second millennium B.C. which held at some time or another this bit of Egyptian coast.' This discovery adds greatly to the speculative possibilities of the problem of the building of the city, and it may at last be found that Alexander was decidedly second fiddle to an even greater builder on the same site in the dim past. It seems wise, however, to withhold judgment until perhaps more enlightenment dawns from additional study of these things. Disregarding that, it is plain that the planning of the city, in its military and commercial aspects, was the work of Alexander's staff, and the work of construction, though started immediately, was yet very incomplete upon Alexander's death, nine years later.

[1] Bevan, *Ptolemaic Egypt.*

[2] Gaston Jondet, 'Les Portes submergés de l'ancienne Isle de Pharos,' from *Mémoirs présentés a l'Institut Egyptien*, IX. Cairo, 1916.

While Alexander was still on the coast, his admiral, Hegelochus, arrived with the joyful news that the fleet once more controlled the Aegean, and that after the break-up of the Persian fleet Tenedos, Lesbos, Chios, and Cos had all been recaptured. He now took a decision, which may give us an insight into his relation at that time with the Corinthian League. About a year before in a document preserved to us he had determined, according to the arrangement in force with regard to Chios, then under siege, that the traitors, when captured, should be brought to the Synhedrion as the regular tribunal of the league — as it was to the Synhedrion that he formerly had referred the punishment of the Thebans. Notwithstanding, when Hegelochus brought before him the captive traitors of Chios, he did not send them to the Synhedrion, but in exercise of his own authority, commanded that by way of punishment they should be transferred to the Elephantine, the most southerly city of Egypt above the first cataract. This justifies the conclusion that in the interval he had won a more independent position in reference to the league, so that now he denied to the Synhedrion a right he had expressly recognized to it a year before. If we inquire into the psychological basis for such a change the conjecture suggests itself that his great successes in the interval — the occupation of Syria and Egypt, the dissolution of the Persian fleet and recovery of control of the sea — must have largely increased his feeling of power. Perhaps it did not fail to impress the king, who was only twenty-four years old, that to these many Egyptians he had become a god.[1]

Now over in Greece, Sparta alone remained hostile. King Agis, when we left him last, had obtained ten ships and thirty talents of money from the Persian admiral, had fled to Crete and there raised the banner of revolt. While Alexander was reducing Phoenicia, Agis was consolidating Crete, planning to turn it into a military stronghold and naval base from which he hoped to control the Aegean. After the battle of Issus (where Agis' ambassador fell into Alexander's hands) numbers of mercenaries, fleeing from the rout, reached Crete and were warmly welcomed into Agis' army. The following winter (332–331) he openly

[1] Ulrich Wilcken, *Alexander der Grosse.*

raised the standard of revolt in the Peloponnesus, and the Achaeans, Eleans, and the Arcadians, except the city of Megalopolis, swarmed to him. In the spring a small punitive expedition of Macedonians was sent against him and annihilated. At this time another revolt sprang into being in Illyria, and Antipater had his hands full, trying to quell this tribe of irrepressibly turbulent mountaineers. The movement instigated by Agis grew larger until Alexander (remember that we have really got a year ahead of our main theme), then marching through Assyria on the way to his last battle with Darius at Arbela, received news of the disaffection. He is reported to have remarked to his companions, 'While we are here conquering Darius, it seems they are having a war of the mice in Arcadia.' [1] His composure, based on faith in Antipater, was not groundless. Antipater had just put down the Illyrian insurrection, and marched south into the Peloponnesus. Here he found Megalopolis besieged by the Spartans, and in one last fierce battle, crushed the Spartan army, killing fifty-three hundred of them, including King Agis himself. Sparta never recovered from that defeat, never again regained the power she had once had.

Alexander marched westward toward the Cyrene. At Paraetonium he was met by Cyrenaean envoys who made submission and brought costly gifts and many horses. Arrian says nothing of this, and the statement is based on Clitarchus, usually an untrustworthy guide, but in this case Clitarchus follows the history of Callisthenes, and is probably correct. Certainly Alexander would never have left the Cyrene in unfriendly hands, its resources available for hostile action. He seems to have regarded Carthage, still farther to the west, as unimportant, or it may be that he knew he could rely upon their traditional enmity to the Persians, and the fact that they were still engaged in a death struggle upon the island of Sicily at the time, as ensuring their non-co-operation with his enemy.

Arrian tells us that while he was founding the new city, a 'longing' seized Alexander to consult the Oracle of Ammon (at

[1] Plutarch, *Agesilaus*, 15.

the oasis of Siwah) seemingly for confirmation of his reign over Egypt and perhaps for godly sanction of his plans for the future. But had he desired merely this, the desert road from Memphis offered a more logical route. However, by the way he went he could accomplish two things, secure the submission of Cyrene and cut several days from the desert journey. Alexander may have wanted, or thought he wanted, the sanction of the gods in his rule of Egypt, but he was hard-headed enough to know that the gods favor those who are foresighted in preparing against military exigencies and building political safeguards.

It could not have been wholly as an Egyptian pharaoh that he visited the Oracle of Ammon; already he had been crowned as pharaoh, and there were many other Egyptian oracles, notably that at Karnak, he could have visited in Egypt. Nor could it have been merely as an anti-Persian demonstration to prove himself in opposition to the Persian Cambyses (Kabujiya) who had dispatched, to destroy the oracle, an expedition which had been overwhelmed and annihilated by a sandstorm. We know that for centuries the Greeks had deemed the oracle infallible, usually ranking above those at Delphi and Dodoma. Pindar wrote a hymn to it; Aristophanes writes of it as comparable to, but greater than, the other two; the Athenians had several decades past constructed a shrine and sanctuary to Ammon, whom they worshiped. Thus we can understand and rate the effect, upon the growing group of dissidents in Greece, of a favorable oracle from Ammon to the young king. Callisthenes adds that Alexander had also had ambition (which we see again when he reaches Afghanistan) to rival the semi-deities Heracles and Dionysus, who were reputed traditionally to have consulted the god. In view of what we know to have been his attitude, his refusal to brook a superior in deed or manner, this becomes credible. There is also another possibility not wholly beyond the bounds of conjecture. We know that Alexander firmly believed himself to be descended from Heracles (born of a mortal mother and sired by Zeus, as was also claimed of Dionysus), and we know that at least on one occasion Philip is reported to have called him a bastard. Our biographers claim that Olympias herself had told Alexander that he himself was sired by Zeus (or Ammon) who visited her one night in the form of a great serpent. Into his emulation of Achilles at Ilium, his ferocious killing of Batis at Gaza (*vide* Achilles and Hector at Ilium) may be read significance of his identification of himself with the Homeric hero, and it is not beyond the bounds of credibility that his romantically mystic nature genuinely accepted as truth that he was, even as those heroes of old, god-begotten by a mortal woman. If this hypothesis be accepted as possible, it is not asking too much to consider the possibility that he may have also counted himself as half-brother already with Heracles and Dionysus, in consideration of their common fatherhood, that is, Zeus himself.

From Paraetonium (modern Matruh), an age-old caravan route (now a two-hundred-mile motor road via Bir-(well) Kenayis, Bir-Gellaz, Bir-el-Istabl, and the low Bayud Pass) runs to Ammon, requiring about seven days for the journey. The many troops on foot in the heavy sand greatly slowed up the rate of travel. The journey was terrible, but just as the water carried in skins on the backs of camels [1] failed, a heavy and unseasonable rainstorm supplied them with water. A simoon or sandstorm came up and obliterated the route. Then two crows or ravens flew ahead of the column and pointed the way when they were lost in the sand. These factors were looked upon as miraculous by the Greeks, terrified by the grim and barren desert, as signs of the favor of the gods. However, even unseasonable rain is not phenomenal in the Sahara, and desert ravens flying, when the general direction of the oasis was known, could surely be relied upon to be going toward a source of food and water. The guides, without whom they certainly would not have undertaken the journey, would know the value of the direction of the birds' flight. It was also said that two serpents 'uttering a voice' went before them and showed them

---

[1] Lest some reader state that camels are not mentioned in the ancient histories, I quote Curtius: 'Aqua etiam defecerat, quam utribuss *cameli* vexerant.'

the way. They probably did see snakes also, but their guidance is certainly one of the myths that have since sprung up about Alexander.

Today at the oasis of Siwah there are two villages, Aghurmi and Siwah, huddled upon rocks about two miles apart. The remains of the temple of Ammon are at the former. In the temple was the god.

> Like all prophetic images, this one, too, was constructed so as to be able to make a limited number of gestures, move its head, wave its arms or hands. A priest pulled the string which made the image move, and uttered the oracle. Everyone knew him, and nobody charged him with fraud. He was an instrument of the god, an unconscious instrument. At a definite moment the spirit seized him; he made the image work and moved his own lips; he lent his hands and his voice; but it was the god who impelled his actions and inspired his words.[1]

Callisthenes gives us a complete description of the temple and the ritual of the oracle which differs little from the ritual at that of the temple of Thebes.[2] We are told further that when Alexander came to the shrine:

> The king alone was suffered to enter the temple in ordinary dress; his retinue was compelled to change their clothes. All others stood outside to listen to the delivery of the oracle, Alexander alone inside. Oracles are not given here, as in Delphi and Branchidae, in words, but for the most part in gesture and symbols, the prophet assuming the character of Zeus (Ammon). This, however, was said distinctly in words by the prophet to the king, that he, Alexander, was the son of Zeus.[3]

Plutarch has a word to say on this subject also:

> Some say the prophet, wishing by way of courtesy to address him in Greek and intending to say 'pai dion' (my boy) made a slip of the tongue on the last sound and said 'pai Dios' (son of

---

[1] Maspero, *Etudes de Mythologie et d'Archéologie Egyptiennes*, VII. 1912.
[2] Strabo, XVII.
[3] Strabo, *loc. cit.*

Zeus) instead. Alexander, they say, welcomed the blunder, and the word went out that the god had addressed him as son of Zeus.[1]

When Alexander returned to the court, in answer to the eager questions of his friends he only replied that he had 'heard that which was according to his wish.' Clitarchus later quotes a series of questions posed and answers received, reporting these imaginative fabrications as authentic. It is doubtful, however, that Alexander ever told anyone exactly what the oracle really said. The secret was well kept, for though he wrote his mother Olympias soon after, he simply told her he had received secret instructions which he would impart to her upon his return to Macedonia.[2] As he died in Babylon it is unlikely, despite the fictioneers and romancers of a later age who profess to reveal the story of what happened in the shrine, that Alexander ever told anybody. The probability is that the questions dealt with existing or future military plans. He had already at Issus, prematurely perhaps, assumed sovereignty over the whole of Asia, but whether his questions related to this and his coming struggle with Darius, or that he very possibly had then, as he certainly had later, an intention to subjugate the whole world, we will never know. As we have historically proved knowledge of the not infrequent bribery, or partisanship, or outright coercion of most of the noted Greek oracles, it may not be amiss to remark that what was possible in one country might be duplicated elsewhere. Indeed, some later commentators say that he dispatched before him from Paraetonium messengers to the priests to insure receiving the answers he wanted. One lone priest or temple would indeed be guilty of a singular species of personal folly were he to attempt, alone of a great nation, to bar from his set course the iron-willed commander of a victorious invading army. Certainly the priest of Ammon made no such attempt.

We can never know how much of this was psychological stage-

---

[1] See Lamer, *Alexanders Zug in die Oase Siwa*, Bd. 24, pp. 63–69. Klio, 1930.
[2] Plutarch, *Alexander*, 27.

setting designed to impress his entourage and the rest of the world; as, judging from the quick results he obtained, as indicated later, much of it was. The fact that Alexander was permitted to enter the sacred Holy of Holies, the inner shrine, in ordinary dress while his retinue were compelled to change clothing completely before being admitted to the outer courtyard was cleverly designed to enhance his claim upon godship. Later, his amazing successes and victories, the worship of the conquered and the adulation of his own Macedonians, aggravated by his heavy drinking and other excesses, including the thrills and excitement of personally participating in the dangers of battle, made him really paranoid to the extent of making an attempt to force the hard-headed Greeks to worship him as a god. Certain it is that he continued publicly to show absolute faith in the Oracle of Ammon, for he sent messengers long distances, even from Persia, to consult with the god.

One rationalistic and excusing viewpoint of this tawdry affair is that from time immemorial the pharaoh of Egypt had been officially deified and hailed as the son of Ammon-Ra. Therefore the priest was merely adhering to age-old custom in so treating Alexander, who, though a foreigner, was nevertheless the pharaoh, also a pharaoh likely, when crossed, to be forcefully abrupt in removing obstacles from his path. Hereafter the appellation was continued, and the coinage of Alexander shows him with the curly ram's horns of Ammon protruding through his wavy hair. His Greeks even took up the appellation, at first seemingly in ridicule, but later they appear to have recognized its political value, for they then enforced the belief upon conquered peoples. Be that as it may, it is yet a fact that his spectacular career and personality were so impressed upon the people of Egypt and Asia that a thousand years later he graduated into the Islamic Koran as 'Dhulkarnein' the 'two-horned.'

Ptolemy's history says Alexander returned to Memphis by the eastern (Gara and Megara) route. Here he at once plunged into the business of creating an effective administration for his new kingdom. Several embassies from Greece awaited him, and his regent, the old general Antipater, had sent him a new levy of three hundred Greek mercenaries and five hundred Thracian cavalry. He held a review of the army, and organized another musical and gymnastic competition, during which he offered sacrifices to Zeus the king, whom the Greeks believed identical with Ammon, and thus another link was forged in the belief that was to merge the authority of Alexander the conqueror with Alexander the son of Ammon-Ra. Then came ambassadors from Miletus who reported that the spring in the temple of Didyme, dry since the looting of the temple in the time of Xerxes, one hundred and sixty years before, had begun flowing again, and the oracle had confirmed Alexander as the son of Zeus, as had also the Sibyl of Erythrae. This is another example of the quick conveyance of news so frequently mentioned by our biographers and gives the impression that Alexander had recognized the value of and maintained intact the highly organized courier system [1] of the Persians.

While in Egypt Alexander dispatched to the south an expedition to settle a question which had long been a lively subject of speculative conjecture among the Greeks, namely: why did the Nile, contrary to the rivers of Europe, which rose only in the winter or spring, rise in punctual, mysterious summer floods? How far they went we are uninformed, but they returned with the correct answer, which was that the Nile floods were caused by summer rains in the mountains of the country we now know as Ethiopia. We also know that he wrote a letter about it to his old teacher, Aristotle, saying that this was no longer something unknown.

In the organization of Egypt we find Alexander was fully

---

[1] Herodotus says of this courier system, whose service networked the entire Persian Empire: 'Nothing mortal travels so fast as these Persian messengers. The entire plan is a Persian invention; and this is the method of it. Along the whole line of road, they say, there are men stationed with horses, in number equal to the number of days the journey takes, allowing a man and a horse to each day; and these men will not be hindered from accomplishing at their best speed the distance which they must go either by rain, or snow, or heat, or the darkness of night. The first rider delivers the message to the second, and the second passes it to the third, and so it is borne from hand to hand along the whole line...'

aware of the easily defended position of the country, bordered by deserts and separated from Greece by the wide seas. He now feared no external attack, but realized that the real possibility of trouble lay in internal insurrection and seizure of power by rebels, who, once in authority, could be ousted only by himself and that by military force. We see now that he is preparing to go a far distance, that even now he is envisioning the conquest of India and even the ends of the earth. And he did not propose to be forced to return to put down rebellion in this, his most fruitful province. He therefore decentralized his administrative authority, appointing two Egyptians to head the civil administrations of Upper and Lower Egypt, and assigned the eastern frontier district, Heroopolis, and adjacent territory to the Greek Appolonius; the western frontier, the Delta, and Libya to Cleomenes of Naucratis. Appointment of the two Egyptians was obviously a sop to popular feeling, for he coupled them with monitorial Macedonian military governors. He also appointed Cleomenes to head the whole financial administration, feeling, though after his departure we hear many complaints of oppression and extortion, that he could rely upon the personal faithfulness of his appointee. We know the complaints received short shrift and no action was taken upon them, and Cleomenes, whether or not justly accused, was left in power.

It seems Alexander left Egypt in late April or early in May, having apparently waited until the Egyptian crop season furnished him with supplies sufficient to last the army to Palestine and southern Syria where the harvests are gathered late in May or early June. He then marched back to Phoenicia and stopped for his first rest at Tyre.

═══IX═══════════════════════════════

THE CONQUEST OF
PERSIA—FIRST PHASE

PART ONE

A T TYRE Alexander again offered sacrifice, at the
shrine of the Tyrian Melkarth, to the demigod Heracles, now
his god-acknowledged half-brother as well as ancestor. Then
he held another great festival, immediately thereafter plunging
into the details of consolidating his western conquests before
going forward to enforce his claim upon the East. Two more
financial posts were created, and appointees placed in office as
tribute and tax collectors, one for the satrapies west of the
Taurus Range, the other for Syria, Phoenicia, and Cilicia.
Nearchus, boyhood friend who was later to distinguish himself
as the admiral of the fleet on his history-making voyage from
the Indus to the Euphrates, was made viceroy of the lands west
of the Taurus. A shipload of envoys arrived from Athens again
to prefer a request that had been denied them before, but which
was granted this time — release of the Athenians captured at

the battle of the Granicus, and since kept as slave labor in the farms of Macedonia and the mines of Mount Pangeum. This clemency, Alexander hoped, would help create a favorable and pro-Macedonian reaction in turbulent Athens, for now he needed all the good will he could get in Greece. Almost simultaneously messengers arrived from Antipater, bringing tidings of increasingly serious disturbances as the result of the rebellious activities of King Agis in the Peloponnesus. He dispatched Amphoterus with the fleet to aid Antipater in quelling the insurrection, and ordered his Phoenician allies to prepare and outfit another hundred ships to sail to Amphoterus' assistance as soon as possible. Amyntas, commander of one of the taxeis of the phalanx, was sent (though one narrator places this action just after the siege of Tyre) to Macedonia to bring recruits, and was replaced in his command by Simmias.

The army then marched to Damascus, where Arsimmas, governor of Assyria, was replaced by another, for, Arrian says, he had shown tendencies, and adopted a mode of life, causing suspicion that he aimed at sovereignty. Here in the ancient 'city of many rushing rivers' the vast captured treasures of Darius had lain for sixteen months awaiting the expression of Alexander's will. Apparently so had the captive women and girls, and these seem to have been not unwelcome to their captors. Alexander took to bed Barsines, widow of the dead general Memnon, and she bore him an illegitimate son, who, as Alexander IV, was to reign briefly and unhappily in the deadly game of imperial shuttlecock that was to be waged over the fragments of the dismembered empire of his dead father. Here, too, we are told, the hetairoi commander, Philotas, became so deeply enamoured of one of the girl captives that he was loath to be separated from her even to the extent of taking sufficient time off to fulfill his ordinary duties. He is alleged to have told her one day that without him, Alexander would amount to nothing, as Philip before him would have amounted to nothing without the able assistance of Parmenio, his father. The gossipy little featherbrain, no doubt boasting of the great leader who had succumbed to her allure, told this to others. Proverbially, a secret once told is carried by the wind to all ears, and it was not long before the boast reached the ears of Alexander. The king listened, but said nothing and continued to say nothing for two long years. But his silence did not mean that he forgot, and, no doubt, when, in the wastes of far Drangiana, Philotas was at last charged with treason, the remarks were remembered and held against him. The club-footed Harpalus, friend of Alexander's boyhood, who had already deserted once and returned only at Alexander's earnest solicitation, was appointed treasurer of the army chest, and placed in charge of the captured treasure. By this time the grain crops of the Hauran, south of Damascus, were gathered, and very probably were wholly acquired by the army. The matter of food supplies attended to, Alexander marched north in the terrible heat of early summer, through a land today but a bleak and stony desert raped of its fertility and destitute of the dense population it then supported. He went by the way of Hemessa (Homs), Epiphania (Hamath), Chalcis (Kinnesrin), to the city the Greeks knew as Beroea or Chalybon (Syrian Halyb, or Steel, modern Aleppo), a populous place long famous even in that day for the manufacture of fine edged weapons. From here they turned eastward on the ancient caravan road to Thapsacus (Dibsi) on the Euphrates.

Alexander's advance guard and pioneers had been sent ahead some time before to repair the river bridge destroyed by the retreating Persians. The work had started well, but before they reached the eastern bank, they were forced to suspend it by the appearance of a threatening body of three thousand cavalry under Mazaeus, satrap of Syria and Mesopotamia. The builders had for a while been afraid that the Persians themselves would complete the bridge and come over to attack them. But it soon appeared that the enemy was there less as a threat than to watch and report on the movements of the invaders. Upon Alexander's appearance they had the news for which they had been waiting, the crossing of the Euphrates. Without bothering their oncoming enemy, they galloped away to the east, laying waste the land by fire [1] as they went, and impressing for Darius' already huge army all the male inhabitants of the country. The bridge repairs were swiftly completed, and the Macedonians marched eastward. Near the mouth of the Bilechas (Balikh) River, Alexander founded the frontier guard city of Nicephorium (Ragga or Rakka), then turned northward through what was then a well-populated and fertile wheat-raising country. Though our narrators are silent on the route taken, our knowledge of the historical conditions permits us to piece it out of the brief statement of Arrian,[2] who simply says: 'From Euphrates, he took his way toward Babylon, but not by the direct route, because another was not only more convenient for drawing up the army, but afforded greater plenty of forage and other necessaries; and besides, the heat was not so great as in the countries through which he had just passed.'

Alexander, true to his invariable custom of subduing all possible enemies who might constitute a menace to his flanks or rear, cannot have failed otherwise than march straight north to Carrhae (Harran, legendary birthplace of the patriarch Abraham). It is unthinkable that he left untouched this city of prime military importance sitting astride his main line of communications from Greece and Asia Minor, the world-old caravan route from Cilicia through the Syrian Gates via Carchemish (Zormara, then the center of the North Syria grain region), and on to the Tigris through Resaina (Ras-el-Ain) and Nisibis. This consolidation of the line of communications is attested by the passage of at least two months' time on the march through Mesopotamia, a distance of hardly over two hundred and fifty miles. Arrian also says Alexander kept the mountains of Armenia close upon his left; thus the army hugged the foothills closely to take advantage of the numerous small streams that issue from them soon to be lost in the thirsty sands of the arid plains. The army, in the pitiless summer heat of the semi-desert at latitude 37 north, required an enormous

[1] Curtius, IV, 9.
[2] Arrian, III, 7.

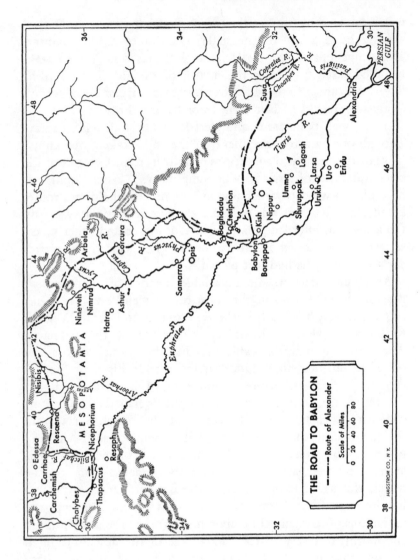

THE ROAD TO BABYLON

----- Route of Alexander

Scale of Miles
0 20 40 60 80

quantity of the life-giving water, which this route alone could supply.

As they marched through the northern part of Mesopotamia, apparently in the vicinity of Nisibis, where Alexander seems to have intended to turn southeast along the caravan route which reached the Tigris at Eski-Mosul, a body of his far-ranging scouts captured a number of Persian scouts. Questioning of these elicited the information that Darius had assembled a huge army, far greater than that of Issus, on the Tigris, and was prepared to resist his crossing. Alexander immediately altered his line of march to slightly north of east, and reached the Tigris in the vicinity of modern Djesire-ibn-Omar. They found the river fordable, but very swift, indeed, its name in the country dialect means 'arrow,' today flowing with a current at six miles an hour. A line of cavalry was posted above the ford to break and retard the current, and another below it to prevent the men from being swept away. Alexander himself, on foot and carrying his own armor, led the van into the river, and waded, more than waist-deep, through the rushing water to the opposite shore. So carefully, in spite of the need for expedition, was the crossing carried out that not a man was lost. Alexander rested the army a few days, to give both men and animals a short respite from their labors, and to recuperate from their long march in the summer heat. While they were encamped and resting here, there occurred an evening eclipse of the moon. This is one of the dates in our history that has been accurately determined, astronomical calculations setting the time as of the evening of September 20, 331 B.C. Had this been interpreted as usual, this would have been looked upon as a portent of ill omen. The army was excited and uneasy. To quiet the superstitions of the untaught soldiers, Alexander, who knew perfectly the cause of the phenomenon, ordered Aristander, the soothsayer, to make explanation to the army on something like the following lines: The eclipse, he declared, was, indeed, a portent of ill fortune, but not for the Macedonians. They worshiped Apollo, represented by the sun. It was the moon, Astarte, worshiped by many of the peoples of the Persian Empire, which was obscured, and even as the moon was eclipsed, so too would the empire of the Persians be eclipsed. This heartened the uneasy, and Alexander took advantage of the occurrence to further cement the friendly attitude of the gods. He erected altars and offered public sacrifice to Helios, Selene, and Ge (Sun, Moon, and Earth), definite proof that his own knowledge was sufficiently advanced to be perfectly aware that these bodies were responsible for the eclipse.

Breaking camp, they marched again, skirting the outthrust serpentine spurs of Gordyaen (Kurdish, Djebel Behehr, Djebel Abaid, Dohuk Dagh) Mountains, following the ancient military and trade road, trodden for hundreds of years by the feet of untold millions of fighting men, lusting for battle in conquest or defense, for territory, loot, or religion, by traders and slaves in wholesale migrations of captured peoples. This part of the Assyrian Triangle had in those days an adequate rainfall and excellent climate, and supported a far greater population than it could today, as attested by hundreds of ruin mounds of once prosperous villages and cities that line now dry watercourses. Dehydration of the whole land is proceeding, not swiftly enough to matter greatly in the span of a single lifetime, but, over historical periods, to a degree sufficient to give rise to trepidation to a thoughtful student of a changing and deteriorating world. We have archeological records of the Assyrian kings, of less than a thousand years before Alexander's advent, hunting elephant, aurochs, and lions in this area, another pertinent and disturbing piece of evidence of the increasing desiccation and aridization of the country. For the existence of these beasts is possible only on the coexistence of an enormous amount of wild and easily obtainable food; for the first two, of herbage, for the lion, of flesh. Today these arid regions support little of wild life, other than a few desert gazelles and hardy jackals.

The Macedonians marched southeastward. On the fourth day, September 24, mounted scouts galloped back to report that they had sighted several bands of horsemen, of unknown numbers, who, however, could be only Persians. Alexander halted the army, drew it up into battle formation, and advanced slowly. Soon additional intelligence arrived; the enemy horsemen did not exceed a thousand in number. The king immediately called forward the Paeonians and mounted auxiliaries. When they reported, he ordered them to accompany him and the royal squadron, told Parmenio to follow slowly with the rest of the army, and led off at a gallop.. The army further closed up in parallel columns, with the cavalry on the right flank of the now tightly massed footmen. The Persian squadrons hesitated whether to fight or fly as the Macedonians thundered down upon them. They hesitated too long, for when they did start to flee, their enemies caught and killed a number of them and captured several more. From the prisoners Alexander learned that Darius, with a force so great that we can scarcely credit the figures given, was encamped only a few hours' march farther on. This little action must have occurred in the neighborhood of the hamlet of Nisara, and five to ten miles south of Dohuk Dagh. Here also the Macedonians went into camp, probably on the little Khoxer su near Baldri, for Arrian tells us it was sixty stadia (about seven miles) from the battlefield. Immediately the slaves and prisoners were set to work to fortify the camp with an outside stockade, a wide and deep ditch, and inside that a rampart was built of earth dug from the ditch. Here Alexander prepared to leave the vast and valuable booty, the baggage, the prisoners, and all the wounded and ill. This done, he would move forward to battle with only his able fighting men, encumbered only by the arms they were going to use. Four days' idleness were given, to rest the men from the ardors of the march. Darius had long awaited the coming of the little army of invaders; he had chosen the battlefield himself. He would wait, this time, with a grim and terrible patience, perfectly confident of the outcome, as long as necessary. Alexander knew what was going on in Darius' mind. Therefore he would accept the gage of battle only when he too was ready, for he knew he was, paradoxically, perfectly safe almost within eyesight of the Persian host. He had marched six thousand miles and spent three and a half years in warfare and sieges, all in preparation for this, what he hoped would be the final encounter in which he would break the might of Persia. He was no longer the impetuous and rollicking youth who had led the army light-heartedly eastward from Macedonia. He was now a battle-tried, hardened, and wary veteran, and he would not be hurried. For now he was faced with the necessity of playing the deadly game of war according to the place selected by his opponent; he himself would select the time. Darius had, with much of his vast empire from which to select, chosen this place as the battlefield he considered perfectly adapted to the requirements of his vast army, and he had no intention of leaving it, or committing a second time the blunder of which he had been guilty in leaving the open plains of Sinjerli for the strait shore land of Issus. He would not again allow his impatience to imperil the opportunity to use the masses of his army in the way he planned.

In the twenty-two months since his amazing defeat at Issus, Darius had bent his every effort toward assembling and arming a force which, he determined, would definitely crush and destroy, once and forever, the almost impertinently small army of the invaders. When Alexander at Tyre refused his final offer of friendship and alliance, swift messengers had immediately sped forth to the farthest corners of the great empire, summoning the fighting men once more to the service of their lord paramount. Kings and satraps, feudal princes and tribal chieftains, from all quarters of the compass, all had received the summons to assemble their armies and retainers, equip and supply them, and dispatch them to Babylon. And they had answered! From faraway India a contingent of bearded Pathans, Rajputs, and Punjabis, with fifteen armored war elephants, stalked through the passes south of Kabul, marched down the Helmand River to Sistan, crossed the mountains and deserts between there and Babylon, and reported for service with their king. Out of Afghanistan and Turkestan, from Bokhara and the steppes of Kara-kum, poured the wild horsemen of Bactria and Sogdia under their satrap Bessus. With him came the Massagatae and the Dahae from the sandy wastes of Khiva and Trans-Caspia; they came as his allies, not his subjects, men who fought for the love of battle and danger. They were armed with curved swords and U-shaped reverse bows of deadly accuracy and enormous range. From northern Baluchistan and Afghanistan the satrap of Arachosia led his tribesmen and mountaineers. From the satrapies of Aria, Parthia, and Hyrcania shaggy tribesmen upon shaggy ponies trotted for weeks along the desert roads, all converging upon Babylon. From the mountains and plains of Iran and Media they came; from the Red Sea countries came dark Arabs, lean and rangy men with the eyes of zealots and fanatics, dressed in long brown robes and mounted on rangy desert camels; the Uxiian mountaineers, and men from Susa, the capital city; those exiles who had fled from Asia Minor joined the Babylonians; from the north came contingents from Armenia and Cappadocia, and even Scythians from the lands north of the Caucasus Range, desert men of the Qidri (Kedar), and the army of Mazaeus with his impressed men from between the Euphrates and the Tigris. Men in such numbers as the world had never seen before, and has rarely seen since.

Darius had assembled his army at Babylon and armed it with double-edged swords and, mistaking the cause of his defeat at Issus, with spears far longer than the customary Persian javelins. He could not, however, provide his men with that inestimable factor that they wholly lacked, and the Macedonians possessed in abundance, discipline, and the *esprit de corps* and morale that only community of interest, plus the personality of the commander, plus discipline, can bring into being. There was, even had he possessed the caliber, personal qualities, and magnetism, insufficient time to bring even a portion of an army of that size to any considerable degree of efficiency, even had they been a single homogeneous people instead of a heterogeneous mob, excellent individual fighters though they were. Unfortunately for the empire, Darius showed he had learned nothing beyond the fact that a long spear outreaches a shorter one. He had, we have reason to believe, assembled his great force and marched into the plains of Mesopotamia, between the Tigris and Euphrates, where the lie of the land was eminently suited to the deployment of the horde, then about-faced and marched out again. It seems, in retrospect, an inconceivable stupidity on his part that he should have, as he did, permitted Alexander to cross the Euphrates, the whole of Mesopotamia, and the Tigris, without the slightest molestation, when a constant guerilla warfare by mounted raiders should commend itself as being one of the most elementarily desirable courses. The Macedonians could have been harassed for months, their lines of communications endangered, their trains destroyed, supplies rendered unobtainable, outriders slain, and their morale endangered, besides making their river crossings murderously expensive. Why Darius had none of these things done, or, in fact, why he had nothing at all done, is one of the wonder-provoking questions that must remain forever unanswered. He crossed the river at or near Eski-Mosul, and marched southeast to the even then ancient 'city of the four gods' Arbela (Erbil), and there deposited his treasures and his officers their harems and baggage. He then turned back north, crossed the Lycus River and went to the village the Greeks have erroneously reported down to us as Gaugamela (now Tel Gomel, on the river, or *gau* Gomel), on the stream whose name is historically recorded by them as the Bumodus. He chose his position carefully, on the north bank of the stream. The bushes were cut down, stones removed, and all inequalities of the ground were leveled to allow free and unhampered movement to his cavalry and scythed war chariots.

The tale is told by at least one of our sources that Darius' wife, Stateira, died sometime before this; in childbirth, according to rumor. Alexander, presumably as a courtesy from one king to another, notified Darius of her death. He, touched by the courtesy and by the humane and kindly treatment of his family by their captor, again made a bid for peace. This time he offered Alexander half his kingdom, the hand of his daughter in marriage, and thirty thousand talents of gold as ransom for his family. Alexander is said to have carried the proposal, as a matter of routine, to the council, who were greatly impressed by the magnitude of the offer. He immediately grew suspicious that the proposal was made, not to him personally, for he presumed the Persian was by now convinced of his adamant intention of pursuing the conquest, but with the hope that the offer might corrupt some of his friends, whom the Great King could approach in no other fashion. Alexander dismissed the council, and of his own initiative drove the Persian messengers forth with contumely.

During their four days' wait, the Macedonians made preparations for the coming struggle. Weapons and armor were carefully inspected, repaired, and strengthened. Extra liberal rations were issued. Councils of war were held almost continually. About midnight the army silently filed out of the fortified camp, formed into column, and marched southward in the darkness, intending to attack the Persians at daylight. There were numerous delays. The plain of Arbela today is covered with the ruin mounds of ancient hamlets and villages, some of which were no doubt in existence then. Their inhabitants would have been removed and the places probably occupied by Persian scouts or patrols. These would have to be avoided or captured. And it is possible that, as with all armies moving in darkness, disorders occurred in units, commands were misunderstood and contacts broken, and other common but irksome delays slowed the movement. It was only in the gray light of early morning that Alexander rode over the rolling ridge four miles north of the battlefield and saw, through the morning mists, the Persian host, aware of the Macedonian's approach, already drawn up into squares of prodigious depth, waiting to accord him a fitting reception. Mazaeus and his cavalry had occupied the ridge and retired before the Macedonians, carrying intelligence to Darius of his enemy's impending arrival. The young king halted the army, and sat quiet on his horse, studying the terrain and the panorama of military might spread before his eyes. Another council of all the higher officers was called, and the question posed: Should they attack immediately, as many of the younger officers advised, or should they, as the maturer Parmenio advised, reconnoiter the field thoroughly to ascertain if the Persians had set pit traps or spike-filled covered ditches, and acquaint themselves with the disposition of the enemy's forces? The latter view prevailed, and the army camped in battle order.

Alexander took the hetairoi and the light auxiliary cavalry and spent several hours in undisturbed traverse and painstakingly accurate survey of the battlefield and the enemy line. Returning shortly after noon, the officers were again called into conclave. The king made them a short speech, telling them that it was not his intention, for indeed, it was unnecessary, to stir up their ancient warlike valor by anything he could say, the memory of their own heroic achievements of the past would be incitement enough to call for duplication of those memoried deeds. He only asked that each commander should acquaint his men with the knowledge that the action facing them was not a battle for a mere city or province, but for the mastery and possession of all Asia; and that that could be the only outcome of the conflict. There must be, however, a last reminder that the various units must act instantly upon receipt of orders and maintain silence to receive them without error; and to remember that upon the gallantry and bravery of each individual soldier and officer rested the fate of the army and the fate of empire, and only by such individual behavior could the victory be gained. The army then went into bivouac to enjoy a good meal and a long rest.

That evening Parmenio came to Alexander's tent to urge a night attack. The young king listened, and replied briefly that he would steal no victories; probably replying so partly for effect, for others were listening, but partly because he realized the dangers inherent in night operations to a small force in the confusion of darkness. As Arrian says, strange and unaccountable accidents happen by night, as well to those who are prepared for battle as to those who are not, which not uncommonly bring defeat to the stronger and victory to the weaker. Also he knew that if he were to gain such a victory, Darius could afterward reasonably contend that the Macedonians had stolen the victory by a species of cowardice and fraud, and it would be greatly lacking in the moral force of a defeat inflicted by day. Furthermore, if the Macedonians were to suffer defeat the remnants of the ruined army would be lost in the vastness of the Persian Empire, knowing nothing of it save the narrow route they had traversed, and their enemies could, with their knowledge of the country, cut off and destroy the survivors at will. Another factor worthy of consideration was the possibility of their great body of captives and slaves in the fortified camp staging an uprising which would be almost certain of success in the confusion of a night battle. Alexander slept soundly until awakened by Parmenio at dawn. This last is made much of by the various commentators to prove Alexander's absolute equanimity regarding the coming battle. Psychologically it might prove just the opposite, that his nervous system was completely exhausted by concealed worry over the possibilities of the situation, and the deep sleep resulted from exhaustion.

Darius, in the meantime, had made his forces stand to arms ever since the previous morning. During the long hot day they awaited the attack that failed to materialize, and when it did not, he became convinced that a night attack was inevitable. As the Persian camp was unfortified, they had remained under arms all night in battle formation, while Darius himself, with his bodyguard bearing torches, made a tour of inspection to keep them in a state of wakefulness. The long weariness of twenty-four hours of waiting and watching in their heavy armor had worn the Persians down physically, and the sickening apprehension all veterans know as the prelude to a great battle had sapped their courage and morale.

The host was placed in battle array (for we have, from Aristobulus, who was present, via Arrian's account, almost a verbatim copy of the Persian 'orders of the day' captured after the battle) according to the following: On the left wing were the Bactrian cavalry under Bessus, along with the Daans (Dahae) and Arachosians, behind whom were Persian foot with a stiffening of cavalry; next was the Susian contingent, and behind them the Cadusians, mountaineers from the country between Lake Urumia and the Tigris; these composed the left wing up to the center of the army. On the right wing were the cavalry of Mazaeus, with the contingents of Coele Syria and Mesopotamia, behind them were the Medes; next were the Parthians and Indians, backed by the Sacae; next them were the Tapurians from the Elburz Range and the Hyrcanians from the shores of the Caspian Sea, and behind them the Albanians and Sacessinians. In the center was posted the chariot of Darius, surrounded by his 'kinsmen' bodyguard, fifteen thousand strong, and the Persian guard, the select 'apple-bearers,' their spears butted with golden pomegranates. On both sides of these were ranged the Greek mercenaries, thirty thousand strong, placed opposite the Macedonian phalanx, as the only troops sufficiently steady and reliable to pit against that grim formation; next were the Indians, the Carians, and, inexplicable in the line of battle, the Mardian archers, these last touching the inner right wing. Behind the center in great masses of reserves were the Uxiians, the Arabians, and the Sitacenians. In front of the Persian left wing were a thousand each of Bactrian and 'Scythian' cavalry, and a fearsome line of a hundred scythed chariots. In the center, ahead of Darius, were the royal cavalry, one thousand strong, under Nabarzanes, and ahead of them, what must have been a terrible sight to the Macedonians, a line of fifteen Indian armored war elephants. To the left of the elephants were aligned another fifty scythed chariots. Before the right wing were the Armenian and Cappadocian cavalry and to their left another fifty chariots. Mazaeus commanded the right wing, Bessus the left, with, of course, Darius in command of the center.

Of the numbers of the Persian army we have been given several figures. Arrian (III, 10) states that: 'Darius' whole army was *said* to consist of a million of foot, forty thousand horse, two hundred scythed chariots, and fifteen elephants.' Curtius is, as usual contradictory and unreliable, for he says (IV, 12–13) that

Darius had forty-five thousand cavalry and two hundred thousand foot soldiers. But he had already said (IV, 9, 3) that the Persian force here was stronger by half than that of Issus; yet he had previously (III, 2) made the statement that Darius there had sixty-one thousand and two hundred cavalry, two hundred and twenty thousand native foot, and thirty thousand Greek mercenaries. These statements and purported data are wholly unreconcilable, for according to the figures the army at Issus was much larger than that at Arbela, or three hundred and eleven thousand for the former as against two hundred and forty-five thousand for the latter. Justin and Orosius very nearly agree, the former reckoning (XI, 12) the cavalry at one hundred thousand, the foot at four hundred thousand. Orosius (III, 17) gives the same number for the cavalry strength, but the curious figure of four hundred and four thousand for the foot. Diodorus (XVII, 39, 53) says there were two hundred thousand cavalry and eight hundred thousand foot, for a total of one million. Plutarch simply says that the total of all forces were a million. These figures are cited, not with the intention of giving the reader a specific number as the Persian strength, but to give him an idea of a few of the difficulties confronting the conscientious historian who might attempt the not infrequently impossible task of reconciling the writings of widely divergent ancients into an acceptably intelligible account. We can be sure of but one thing, namely: that the Macedonian army was marching into battle against odds that were at least ten to one, and, not improbably, more than twenty to one.

Early in the morning, after a night's rest and a good breakfast, the Macedonians marched down from the hillside to the plain below and formed their line of battle. Though a little vague on two points the best description of the battle plan comes to us from the soldierly Arrian. It is so simple and direct that narrative purpose and clarity can be best served by quoting:

> Alexander's army was thus marshaled: On the right wing stood his auxiliary troop of horse; before those the royal bodyguard, commanded by Clitus; next stood those [hetairoi] of Glaucus;

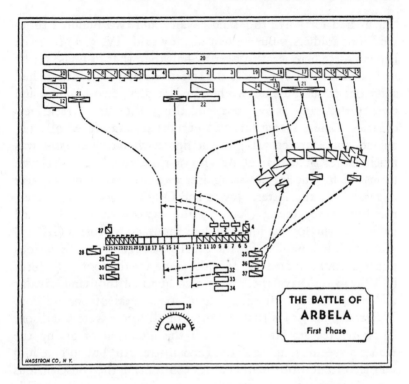

THE BATTLE OF
ARBELA
First Phase

CAMP

HAGSTROM CO, N.Y.

and then that of Arsiton; after which we have that of Sopolis; next that of Heraclitus; then that of Demetrius, followed by that of Meleager, and last, by the last of the royal troops [hetairoi], was that commanded by Hegelochus [long since recalled from the fleet]. But the command of all the auxiliary [hetairoi] belonged to Philotas [why should this unnecessary statement have been thrown in bodily at this point?]. The first rank of the Macedonian phalanx, which was joined with that of the horse, consisted of the hypaspists under Nicanor; next these was the taxis of Coenus; then that of Perdiccas; after this stood that of Meleager [note *two* commanders of the same name]; then that of Polysperchon; next that of Amyntas, with Simmias in temporary command. On the left side of his taxis was posted that of Craterus, who was in command of the whole body of foot on the left [that is, of the hoplites of the phalanx]; next was the auxiliary horse, under Erigyius;

next these, still toward the left wing, were the Thessalian horse, now commanded by Philip. The whole body of the horse on the left wing was under command of Parmenio. Round these the Pharsalian horse were posted [as bodyguard to Parmenio], who were both the best and most numerous of all the Thessalian cavalry.

After this manner Alexander ranged his army in front; but he added another phalanx [this sentence must be read in the light of what follows it], which should be a kind of flying party, or squadron, having given orders to the commanders thereof, that if they perceived any of their own countrymen surrounded by the Persian army, they should suddenly turn backward and charge the barbarians, and contract or dilate their phalanx as occasion warranted.

On the right wing, next to the royal bodyguard [Arrian calls it the royal cohort] was posted a body of Agrianians, under command of Attalus; behind these the Macedonian archers, led by Briso, to whom were attached those troops named the 'foreign veterans' [?] commanded by Cleander [no doubt a chosen body of mercenaries this officer brought with him when he rejoined Alexander at Sidon during the siege of Tyre]. Before the Agrianians stood the forlorn hope of horse, and the Paeonians, headed by Aretes and Aristo. Before the rest stood the mercenary troops of horse under command of Menidas. But before the royal bodyguard were the remaining part of the Agrianians, archers and javelin men, under Balacrus, placed to front the scythed chariots. Orders were given to Menidas, and the troops under his command, that if the enemy should surround the wing, they should strike the attackers' flank. This was the disposition of the right wing. On the left, in a half-moon, were the Thracians, commanded by Sitalces; next the auxiliary horse under Coeranus; after these, the Odrysian horse, under the command of Agaton. But to front all, on this wing, stood the foreign mercenary troops under Andromachus. The Thracian foot [javelin men] were posted to the rear as a guard upon the baggage. The whole army of Alexander, thus disposed, constituted about seven thousand horse and forty thousand foot.[1]

This description, as given by Arrian, is the best we have. In some respects its ambiguous wording leaves the position of the

[1] Arrian, III, 12.

defense wings somewhat controversial. However, vague though Arrian is, other writers are more so. Curtius, frequently cited, writes in such a fashion as to wind himself into a maze of inconsistencies and outright impossibilities. The accompanying diagrams (pages 222 and 229) can, however, be taken as correct in essentials, and, in the main, conform reasonably well to the reported movements and probabilities during the battle.

The Macedonians advanced with measured tread, maintaining their perfect alignment, and keeping silent until they drew near the ominously waiting Persians. Alexander called his army to a halt, and rode slowly along its front on a final tour of inspection and encouragement. We are not told what he said to the Macedonians, but one tale runs that when he reached the Thessalians, they cried aloud that he should lead them against the foe. In reply, he stopped his horse, changed his spear to his left hand, raised his right to the heavens, and prayed in a loud voice that if he were really the son of Zeus, the gods should assist the Hellenic army. He thus showed publicly at least his public belief, and it must have been his private one too, that he accepted as authentic the accuracy of the expressed oracle of Ammon.

As he rode back to his post, Arrian says, a movement was noted in the Persian ranks, as Darius was seen to place himself with his guards and the 'apple-bearers' directly opposite to Alexander. The latter, noting the movement, which left a gap in the Persian line to the left of center, instantly grasped the possibility of enlarging it, and abruptly inclined his line obliquely to the right, partly because the tremendous Persian battle line was twice the length of his own, and, as before stated, partly to cause the Persian wing to stretch farther until their line, at the juncture of the left wing and the center, where he proposed to strike with the full force of his massed hetairoi, was perceptibly weakened. True to his expectations, the Persians also lengthened their line, taking ground to their left. There can be little doubt that Alexander, lightning-quick to see and take advantage of every possible move which would tend to his benefit, acted from this reason. He obliqued still farther, until the obliquing Macedonian line, with the three detachments of the light cavalry on the extreme right, almost touched the opposing 'Scythian' cavalry. Nevertheless, Alexander continued the movement until they approached one of the places leveled off to facilitate the chariot attack. Farther to the right the brush and stones forbade the use of wheeled vehicles. Darius, to prevent Alexander moving this far, ordered the extremity of his left wing to wheel round and block its continuation. As the ponderous Persian line swung into motion to obey their king, Alexander opened the battle by ordering the squadrons under Menidas to halt the enemy movement. Their attack was instantly met by the combined 'Scythians' and Bactrians, posted in front of the main line, for just such a contingency. The heavily outnumbered Greeks were halted and forced back. Aristo with his Paeonians and Aretes with his lancers thundered out to their assistance, and after a short, sharp battle, the Asiatics were forced back upon their own lines. Another body of Bactrians, the famous cavalry of Bessus, fourteen thousand strong, better armed and wearing more complete armor than the Greeks, trotted up, rallied and turned back their broken comrades, and a bitter cavalry battle ensued, the Greeks losing heavily. But they returned fiercely to the assault, and the Persians began to give ground.

In the meantime, Darius had played one of his trump cards, launching the war chariots into their thundering charge. They were met in the center of the field by small groups of skirmishers and javelin men, who hurled themselves upon the attackers. Some of the horses were slain with javelins, the reins of others were cut, a hail of stones, arrows, and javelins toppled the fighters and drivers; many of these were slain by nimble skirmishers swinging themselves onto the back of the chariots to cut down their occupants. Several, however, could not be stopped, and dashed on toward the phalanx. The hoplites coolly opened lanes in their ranks, and the horses, maddened by wounds, the unaccustomed violence, and the shouts of the soldiers, raced through. Behind the phalanx, the horses and charioteers were expeditiously captured or slain by the Thracians, ending in costly futility the arm upon which Darius had heavily relied to produce confusion and sow death in the Macedonian ranks.

After the end of the chariot fiasco, and while the cavalry fight clear of the Macedonian right was raging, Darius ordered forward his dense body of footmen in the center. These, however, took some time to get under way. Alexander, watching the progress of the battle with the eyes of a hawk, sat his horse still in his original position, keyed to the highest pitch of physical and mental tension. As he noted the preliminary movements of the dense block of Persians confronting him, he saw at the same instant the first signs of breaking and panic in the cloud of enemy cavalry being violently charged and hammered by the squadrons of his light cavalry. They suddenly broke and recoiled upon their own second line, throwing it into confusion, with the lancers pressing hard after them, furiously slaying everyone within reach.

When the cavalry of Bessus moved out of their line they had left uncovered the left of their own center. Now the cavalry were breaking into a rout, and were too disorganized, momentarily, at any rate, to be a menace to the next movement. A few swift orders, a trumpet signal, and the massed squadrons of the hetairoi, echeloned to the left, and bearing very slightly right, hurled themselves at the left flank of the massed Persian phalanx. Behind them the six compact taxeis of the hypaspists moved forward in their echeloned wedge to strike the enemy line to the left of the hetairoi's point of impact. The first five taxeis of the phalanx also immediately moved forward in echelon, leaving only the taxis of Craterus to assist the mounted left wing. With a roar, the hetairoi struck the left of the enemy phalanx, turned left, and started cutting their way along the dense ranks as a husbandman cuts his way along rows of grain. For a short time the mass resisted, while javelins and arrows sang, spears glittered bright, then red, and swords whirled in the air. The Macedonians simply could not wield weapons fast enough to make any great difference in the masses confronting them. The hypaspists swept up, led by the agema, and their grim spear lines started hewing at the dense mob of Persians. After them and to arrive in a few minutes rolled the terrible war machine of the phalanx, behind and under a forest of long metal-pointed sarissas. Alexander and his men redoubled their efforts, thrusting their lances into the faces of their foes, and the bodies of the enemy dead began to pile high in front of them. The full force of the hypaspists were now engaged, cutting their way deep into the Persian ranks. The taxeis of the phalanx, roaring their deep-throated battle-cry, were very near. The fifteen war elephants broke from their posts despite the efforts of their mahouts, and panicked back through the Persian ranks, escaping ahead of the massed spears moving in upon them. Darius, from his high chariot, again saw, what he had seen before at Issus, the face of death confronting him, as his flank crumpled and his front caved in, in shrinking apprehension of the approaching phalangists. His heart turned to water within him. A thrown spear hissed through the air and transfixed his charioteer. Darius turned in terror and fled like a poltroon. The huge Persian host was again leaderless.

Meanwhile, as the phalanx moved forward, Mazaeus, the Persian commander of the right wing, saw his chance. Into the gap left by the phalanx hurtled the Indian and Parthian cavalry, while Mazaeus, with the Armenian and Cappadocian cavalry, drew his men into deep masses, and drove with concentrated fury headlong at the Macedonian left flank. These received him fittingly. They were the Thessalians, proud men with a reputation as disciplined and stubborn fighters, and already restless because they had been left out of the battle so far. They wheeled half-left, and met the Persians halfway, the Pharsalian squadron, the first to contact the enemy, suffering heavily in the stubbornly contested assault. Slowly the weight of overwhelming numbers began to tell, and Parmenio sent an urgent plea for assistance and reinforcements to Alexander. The message arrived at a crucial moment when victory itself hung in the balance. 'Tell Parmenio,' replied the king, 'if we gain the victory here we shall regain everything lost elsewhere. If we lose here, all he can do is fight to the end and go down sword in hand.' However, the same message reached Simmias, whose taxis, last in the echelon of the phalanx, was not yet in contact with the enemy. Seeing that all was going well in the center and realizing at once that his services were more needed on the left, Simmias wheeled and went back. Another unexpected factor had developed from this last attack also. The Indian and Parthian cavalry, who had galloped straight through the Macedonian position, had not wheeled right, as they certainly must have been ordered, to catch Parmenio's wing between two forces. Instead, they saw the plain perfectly clear between them and their enemy's camp. Being bandits by natural proclivity, they instantly dismissed all ideas of fighting, and pounded straight toward the camp in a scrambling rush for loot. A number of the Thracian camp guards were overrun in the rush; others, the convalescents and the wounded who were able, hastily seized weapons and fought desperately, while the Thracians formed ranks, and offered disciplined resistance. Many of the prisoners, wild with joy at the arrival of friends and allies, hastily armed themselves and fell upon the rear of the defenders, while others, joining the attackers who evaded the fighting, rushed about seizing everything of value they could lay hands on. Coeranus, Agatho, and Andromachus, stationed far to the left and behind the Macedonian front line, had seen the irruption of the attackers' cavalry and its assault upon the camp. They may have hesitated a moment to choose the foe they would encounter, but if so, the hesitation was soon ended. They wheeled and came galloping to the assistance of the hard-pressed Thracian guard, and falling upon the disorganized looters, slew many of them. Then the enemy rallied, and realizing the precariousness of their situation, courageously started fighting their way back again.

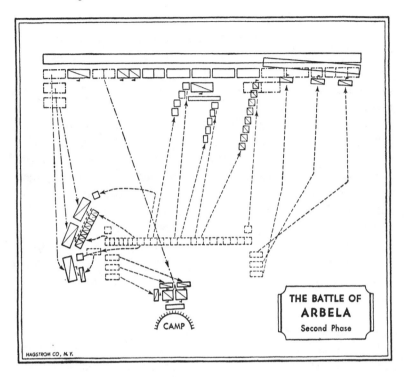

THE BATTLE OF
ARBELA
Second Phase

CAMP

HAGSTROM CO., N.Y.

The struggle had developed in a curious way. Far over on the right flank, the lancers of Aretes, Aristo, and Menidas were still hammering away with repeated charges at the cavalry under Bessus, waging a desperate but winning battle against what would seem to be overwhelming odds. Nearer the center, the hetairoi had nearly completed the destruction of the juncture of the Persian center and left wings, and the dense masses of Asiatics behind this section, only now aware of the flight of their pusillanimous king, were beginning to break and flee. The hetairoi were just putting the finishing attacks upon the rapidly demoralizing army that was here fast degenerating into a mob, and Alexander was preparing to withdraw them for use elsewhere. To the left of the hetairoi, the hypaspists, and still farther left, the phalangists, were engaged in what was now more nearly butchery than battle. Still farther, far over on the left wing, the third wholly isolated battle was raging where Craterus' and Simmias' taxeis of the phalanx, the Thessalian cavalry and Sitalces' mounted Thracians, were battling furiously, but making no headway against the repeated determined attacks of Mazaeus' forces. To the rear, near the camp, the flying column from the left wing was locked in a bitter struggle with the Parthians and Indians. Four different battles were taking place, each widely separated from the other; and as yet hundreds of thousands of the Persians had never been engaged, or indeed moved a foot from the positions they had occupied for thirty hours.

The Persian center was crumpling fast. Alexander withdrew his hetairoi from the line, leaving the final blows to the spearmen, and turned to help Parmenio, intending to sweep around and fall upon Mazaeus' right wing. On the way, however, they encountered the slowly retreating Indians and Parthians, still courageously facing the light cavalry, though the latter was now reinforced with the taxis of Coenus, but being slowly driven backward. The hetairoi fell upon their backs, and the enemy, desperate but undaunted, faced about to meet the new foe. Here the fighting was the bitterest in the whole battle, for Arrian says: ' ... and then there was no casting of javelins, nor dextrous management of horses, as is common in cavalry battles, but everyone strove to dismount his foe, and, as if their whole safety had depended on their success that way, they proceeded to give wounds, and receive them, to smite, and be smitten, as if each person had endeavored to procure a victory for himself, and not for another. In this conflict about sixty of Alexander's forces were slain, and Hephaestion, Coenus, and Menidas wounded.' If sixty of the hetairoi were killed, their casualties in this short engagement alone, if we consider acceptable a ratio of seven wounded to one killed, means that four hundred and twenty, at least, suffered non-fatal injuries of more or less severity. A loss in a few minutes of nearly five hundred of all casualty categories, out of a force which may not have exceeded twelve hundred, is a spectacularly high percentage, evidence more vivid than words of the deadly ferocity of the conflict. This is easily understandable, however, if it be remembered that the Persians were caught between two attacking forces, and were forced by sheer desperation to go the limit and exert every possible effort to cut their way out of the trap. Presently their courage, that had kept them in disciplined ranks, deserted them, and those who could, fled. It is unlikely that many could. Alexander drew clear of the fray, and again turned toward the left wing. By this time, however, the entire Persian host was fast breaking up, and Mazaeus' forces, under the hammering of the Thessalians, were becoming discouraged; when Alexander appeared, they too broke and galloped away.

Alexander, seeing his assistance no longer required, turned south and galloped back to the battle line. He gathered a body of his hetairoi and mounted auxiliaries, and rode hard in pursuit of Darius. The masses of the panic-stricken Persians were so great they impeded his pursuit by sheer numbers. In utter demoralization, thousands were killed on the brandished weapons of their friends or ridden down by the mounted men. And so great was the mob that their flight raised a cloud of dust so thick that nothing could be seen in it, and only the cracking of the whips of the fleeing horsemen and the frantic shouts of those on foot could be heard. The only part of the Persian force that escaped in good order was that of Mazaeus. With about twenty-five thousand cavalry he crossed the Tigris near the ruins of Nineveh, about twenty-five miles from Gaugamela, and marched swiftly south to Babylon.

Here again we are faced with incredible figures when we try to check the casualty lists of the combatants of this important battle. Arrian says only that about one hundred of the Macedonian cavalry were killed. If this has reference to the hetairoi only, as is likely, for the other cavalry was usually referred to in other words, this figure seems roughly correct. If so, however, they were virtually annihilated, if, as before, we agree that the ratio of killed to wounded was one to seven. This, then, would

give us a casualty list, of the hetairoi, of eight hundred men, or
two-thirds of the entire strength. It admittedly sounds unduly high, yet Arrian has previously given us the number of
sixty slain, with the implication of four hundred and twenty
wounded, in the mêlée with the Indians and Parthians only.
He has, unfortunately, no more to say on the subject. Diodorus,
whose account seems less biased in this particular, says the
Macedonians lost five hundred slain, implying thirty-five
hundred to five thousand wounded, or a loss of eight to ten per
cent. Of the Persian losses Arrian refuses to be specific, simply
reporting, 'three hundred thousand were *said* to have been
slain.' As a soldier, he realized the incredibility of the statement; as a historian, he reported it. That an army numbering
less than fifty thousand effectives should kill more than six
times its own number in one conflict, however stubbornly contested and sanguinary, is incredible, and must be rejected.
Curtius places the Persian losses at forty thousand, Diodorus at
ninety thousand. It is refreshing to find Curtius, usually utterly
unreliable, the narrator, this time, whose report is the most
believable. Whatever the actual numbers were is, however,
relatively unimportant. The main thing is that the Persian
army, as a fighting force to be reckoned with, was utterly destroyed. The date was October 1, 331 B.C.

When darkness fell, Alexander had reached the Lycus (Great
Zab or Zab-el-Kebir) River, twenty-five to thirty miles from
Gaugamela, and his detachment went into bivouac for a few
hours' rest. A little after midnight, when the moon rose, they
mounted and trotted onward toward Arbela (Erbil), six hundred stadia, about seventy miles, from Gaugamela, where Darius
and his officers had deposited their valuables. Darius was not
there, in fact had not come that way, but again Alexander
captured his royal chariot, shield, and bow. He seized the Persian base and sat down to await the arrival of Parmenio with
the rest of the army. The latter seized the Persian camp and
large numbers of captives, the Indian war elephants and many
draft animals. Then, as quickly as possible, spurred by fear of

an epidemic from the intolerable stench arising from the dead on the battlefield, he hurriedly departed for Arbela.

When Darius left the battlefield, he fled eastward into Media, taking with him a few of his 'kinsmen' bodyguard, a few of the 'apple-bearers,' a small group of Bessus' cavalry, and about two thousand Greek mercenaries under their own commander, the Phocian Paron; a total of about six thousand foot and three thousand cavalry. He turned east through the mountains along the old road, believing, in view of Alexander's previous actions, that he would, in order to profit from and secure the spoils of his victory, immediately make haste to seize the great cities of the south, and with them control of the rich and populous delta. Darius therefore marched toward Ecbatana (Hamadan, the 'meeting-place of the roads'), the ancient Median capital, there to gather another army. Darius seems to have had little tactical judgment, or perhaps he was personally demoralized, for as a native of the satrapy of Persis proper, he should have known that it was still feasible to attempt what might have been a possibly successful defense of the remainder of his kingdom, in the strait passes of the tumbled mountains of southern Luristan and Arabistan. These, constituting one of the most formidable barriers on earth to the passage of an invading army, were populated by mountaineers, who, under proper persuasion, would have probably fought well for their king. The plateau of Iran and Persis were still able to supply men for an army also. Darius disregarded these and other possibilities; he seemed to have paid much more attention to the preservation of his own life and comfort than to pressing, at all costs, war against the invaders.

PART TWO

While waiting at Arbela for Parmenio to finish the task of reassembling the army and caring for the booty, Alexander made magnificent sacrifices to the gods for the unexpectedly easy and complete victory. Parmenio marched in, and Alexander granted the army a few days' rest for celebration. He sent captured booty of considerable value to Croton, in southern Italy, because this town was the only one of the Greek-Italian cities to be represented and fight on the side of the Hellenes at the battle of Salamis. And Croton was represented by only one man! Also it is a matter of record that he again patently ignored the Synhedrion, for he sent orders back to Greece that in all the territories of the allies — meaning all Greece with the exception of Sparta, for though the battle of Megalopolis had been fought a few days before, he, of course, had not yet received the news of it — all tyrannies must be eliminated and democracies substituted. The rise of the tyrannies in his absence had created a great deal of inter-city ill-will, for genuine democracies are never belligerent and genuine tyrannies always are. It was partly to quell this rising threat to the peace of the land, and partly to prevent the possibility of continuing defections to the aegis of the rebellious Spartan king. These acts not only served his own ends in Greece, but were a not particularly subtle way of reminding those who might have short memories that the winner of Arbela was also still, and intended to remain so, hegemon of the League of Corinth, to all intents and purposes the master of all Hellas. Alexander also instigated a number of his friends to propose to the army in assembly that he be elected, proclaimed, and acclaimed, as king of all Asia. This was done, and now, as king of all Asia, he gave the order to march again — this time against his rebellious subjects, wherever they might be in all the broad land.

The Macedonians started south on the three-hundred-mile march toward Babylon, the almost mythical city of which they had for long heard so many fabulous tales. Some commentators profess to point out the exact route they followed and ignore the one most logical, the seventy-eight-foot-wide great royal road from Asia Minor, running directly from here to Susa. The possibility that any other way was chosen is largely nullified by the existence of the even more greatly augmented baggage-trains laden with loot and captives. No other route would be nearly so practicable. We assume he followed this down to the vicinity of modern Kifri, at which point he detached a strong body of mixed arms, and gave the command to Philoxenus, with orders to proceed post-haste to Susa to seize the city, prevent possible disorders and uprisings and assure the safety of the imperial treasury. He himself turned from the road, crossed the Tigris to the Euphrates and followed it down to the ancient city that had arisen to power as Ca-Demissa of the pre-Sumerian Acadians, and to world fame as the Semitic Bab-ili, the 'Gate of God.'

As the army approached the city, Alexander drew it up into battle array, and advanced warily behind a heavy screen of cavalry scouts. But as they neared the blank and menacing walls it became patent that they were manned only by curious sightseers, and that the great gates were open. Mazaeus and his highest officials, followed by the priests of Bel (erroneously transcribed down to us as Chaldeans by the Greek historians), and thousands of people scattering flowers in his path, met the new king outside the gates. Mazaeus had given full and loyal service to Darius, but now that his former master was definitely vanquished and fugitive, the doughty commander philosophically accepted the new state of affairs. Kings may come and kings may go, but the people live on, and as long as one serves a king there will always be a people to govern. Resistance now would have been worse than criminally stupid. The great city of the law-giving Hammurabi and the semi-mythical Semiramis was surrendered without a blow.

Babylon, when Alexander entered it, was still the greatest city in the world, though Susa had long supplanted it as the capital of the empire. It was still the spiritual center, the grand old wicked city that was the cynosure of all hearts of the people of the country. For over long centuries in which it had reigned supreme as the trade center of the world and the imperial seat of power of the long long lines of her kings, Babylon had, whatever name she bore on the tongue that was speaking of her, the glamor of her storied years and her mighty being. The seventy-five-foot-high walls of sunbaked brick, thirty-two feet wide on top, that enclosed the city were ten miles in length on each side, though the whole enclosure was not completely populated. Part of the land just inside the walls was devoted to farms, a not uncommon condition in many of the cities of that period (and found in North Africa even after the twentieth century, of which Kano in Nigeria and Timbuctu are examples) when long sieges were to be anticipated at one time or another by most large cities. These farms were then of great value in providing much-needed additional food supplies to eke out the hoarded grain. The Euphrates flowed almost diagonally through the square city, and was then, according to Xenophon's report, two stadia wide (twelve hundred feet), though today it is less than half that. From the river, canals radiated right and left through the city, serving as supplements to the commerce-carrying main streets, fifty in number, and each one hundred and fifty feet wide. In the northwestern portion of the city, where the Euphrates entered, both its banks were lined by royal palaces and fortress arsenals. On the east bank, each perched high on its individual artificial mound, were two vast citadel palaces, one built by Nebopolasser, the other by Nebuchadnezzar, world wonders of three centuries earlier. South of these towered the gigantic tiered structure, the Esagil, known as the temple of Bel or Belus, who, since the time of Hammurabi, as Marduk (Mithra) had been the chief or city-god of Babylon. This god, for a score of centuries, had been worshiped as supreme, and in the olden days had conferred upon the occupant of the Babylonian throne lordship over 'the four quarters of the earth' and thereby the title of 'king of kings.' He alone was accounted as king by the people, who, upon the day of the beginning of New Year's festival, climbed the encircling ramp to the temple upon the top of the tower, and there, nearly five hundred feet above the city, clasped the hand of the god. For long after the beginning of the sway of the Achaemenid line, successive monarchs had catered to this custom in indulgence of the beliefs of the Babylonians, and had borne the title of 'king of Babylon,' and main-

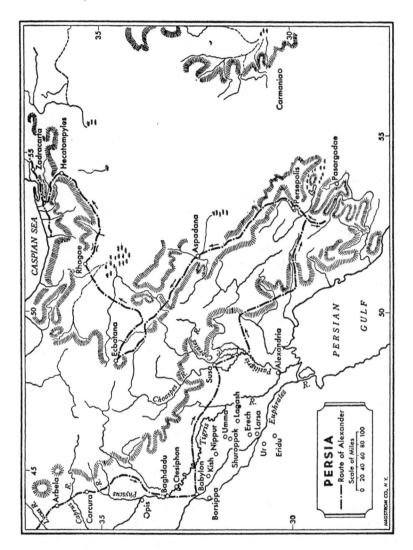

tained the rituals. Xerxes (one of several to bear the appellation) in 479 had, in disgust at exhibiting subservience to a demonological religion contrary to the precepts of the severe Zoroastrians, which was the official court religion, had destroyed the temple, carried away the image of the god to Susa, and put an end to Babylon as a separate kingdom. On the north side of the river was the royal park, in it the mass of palaces wherein Alexander, less than eight years later, was to die. Close to these, and nearer the river, were the world-famous 'hanging gardens,' lifted from the earth on brick piers, and rising in terraces to a height of seventy-five feet. That the historical descriptions of this ancient city were, in the main, correct is amply attested by its mighty ruin mounds that loom today, depressing reminders of the transience of 'greatness,' above the plain north and south of Hillah. Alexander occupied one of the royal palaces, the first time in history that a conqueror from the West had done so.

According to Curtius and Diodorus (neither Arrian nor Plutarch mentions it, and it is fairly certain that they were willing to write anything which would so redound to the credit of the spirit of generosity they claim for Alexander), he gave the Macedonians, out of the vast captured treasures, rich gratuities. This, they say, amounted to six minae to each heavy cavalryman; to each of the light cavalrymen, five minae; each infantryman, two minae; and to each of the peltasts and other psiloi, two months' extra pay, though the latter amount is not stated. Whether or not this was done must be left to the judgment of the reader, taking into consideration the weight of metal constituting a mina, then the number of men in the army. It will be seen that the sum is incredible for that day. Alexander also gave orders that the Esagil, and on it, the temple of Bel, should be restored, and true to his custom of deference to all, even foreign, gods, offered rich sacrifice to and worshiped Bel. He seems to have had no intention of neglecting or belittling any god whatever or wherever.

Mazaeus, who had been a good servant to Darius and would

doubtless be equally faithful to Alexander, was made satrap of Babylonia, though, as customary, two Macedonian officers were placed as checks upon the improper use of his authority, one as commander of the garrison, the other as collector of taxes and tributes. Mithrines, who had surrendered the citadel of Sardis, was dispatched northward as satrap of Armenia. Another Macedonian was appointed viceroy of Cilicia, Syria, and Phoenicia, and given the duty of keeping open the ever-lengthening lines of communications, this being now dangerously threatened by yet banded groups of raiding freebooters from the scattered remnants of the Persian army. After what was a busy month for himself and a good rest for his soldiers, Alexander completed the task of organizing Babylon and the delta country into a base of operations, a rich source of supplies, money, and men, wherewith to pursue the conquest.

He left Babylon and marched east to Susa (whose ruins lie about twenty miles south of modern Dizful), capital city of ancient Elam, now winter capital of the ruling Achaemenids. On the way, letters were received from Philoxenus, announcing the surrender and pacification of the city and the safety of its treasures. Susa was reached in twenty days, probably about the middle of December.

The treasure seized here was enormous for that day, totaling over forty thousand talents in silver and nine thousand darics in coined gold, and, of course, many other valuables in the form of the fittings and furniture of the several royal palaces. Alexander also found two brazen statues of Harmodius and Aristogon, carried away from Athens by Xerxes. These were restored to their Attic homeland. Arbulites, the Persian governor of the city, was restored to power, though the commands of the garrison and the citadel were placed under the control of two Macedonians. Apparently hearing that his latest appointee to the government of Cilicia, Syria, and Phoenicia was abusing his position, or because his services were unsatisfactory, the king dispatched Menetes to replace him. Menetes was also given three thousand talents in silver, with instructions to send to

Antipater as much of that sum as the latter required to carry on the struggle with King Agis, proof that the news of Megalopolis had not yet arrived. Amyntas marched in with reinforcements from Macedonia, and though Arrian gives us no figures, Curtius says the recruits numbered fifteen thousand, including fifty pages, the proportion of horse and foot not being mentioned. Knowing that the incorporation of the new forces into the ranks of his decimated units would temporarily check their close-knit adhesion and *esprit de corps*, the king considered he might as well use the time to put into effect several changes in their organization of such a type as would later facilitate, as he saw would be eventually necessary, the incorporation of Asiatics as additional replacements. The taxeis of some of the most capable of some of the phalangist officers were enlarged, cavalry squadrons divided into two commands, and a number of other changes, referred to but not detailed, were made. New methods of signaling were adopted; hitherto this had been carried on exclusively by trumpet blasts or movements of the standards. Against possible contingencies a uniform system of additional signals over long distances were put into effect, using smokes by day and lighted torches or fires by night.

Alexander may have been personally convinced of his star and destiny, but there was little use in pursuing it alone, therefore another great festival was held, to thank the gods for past, and insure future, favors. He needed some additional assistance, for the wide mountain chain that lay across his road ahead was one of the worst barriers on earth to military passage. It was midwinter; there were several large fast-flowing rivers to cross; the mountains themselves rose in several successive terraces from the lowlands of Susa to a height of fourteen thousand feet, with many of the passes buried in deep snow, a broken labyrinth of precipitous heights and stony valleys. The most logical route to Persepolis, the capital and citadel city of the satrapy of Persis, which was his next destination, lay south along the foothills, crossing the Pasitigris (Karun) River at modern Ahwaz, thence to Behbehan and on to Shiraz, and across the Rud Band-i-Amir.

Some narrators consider this to be the route he took. This however, disregards several factors of the story of the march. Others consider he went first to the Coprates (Dizful) and on by the way of Shustar; also hardly tenable. The tribesmen of the plains submitted to Alexander without fighting, but the strong and turbulent tribe of the Uxiian mountaineers, of modern Kuh-i-Mangasht and perhaps Kuh-i-Bangistan, were of sterner stuff. Brigands from the beginning of time, harsh and intolerant of others, they had successfully resisted domination by the Persians, and had even succeeded in forcing Darius to pay tribute to them for a free passage through the defiles of their mountains. They sent word to Alexander that he too could pass to Persia proper only upon payment of the same sum of which they had formerly mulcted Darius for his passage. We can imagine the cold fury of the arrogant young king toward the equally arrogant tribesmen when they gave him the message. But he swallowed his fury and dissembled his feelings and received them courteously, and sent them back with word that the army would reach the pass upon a certain day, with their toll ready in their hands. As soon as they left, he moved swiftly into action. Quickly gathering the royal bodyguard, the hypaspists, and a few thousand others, he impressed several Uxiian guides by threats and promises, and made a swift night march by a little-used route to the pass, destroying several villages on the way. When the Uxiians arrived, they found the invaders already in possession of the pass, and Craterus' taxis holding the heights above the defile. In consternation at the unexpectedness of the action, they fled without striking a blow, under grim pursuit by the cavalry and the psiloi. Many were slain and their force dispersed. It was Alexander's intention to deal with them with extreme harshness, but they got Darius' mother to intercede for them. Finally, under the pleas of the old lady, the conqueror consented to change his will and restored their territory to them, but exacted a tribute of one hundred good cavalry mounts, five hundred pack animals, and twenty thousand sheep, goats, and cattle. The tribute was exacted in kind because the Uxiians had no money; their lands were unsuited to extensive farming, and their wealth was counted only in domestic livestock. Apropos of the story previously told of the theft and recovery of Bucephalus, it is probable that this occurrence took place about here.

From the land of the Uxiians, the army marched on south to the vicinity of Behbehan. Here Parmenio was sent on, via Kazarun, to Shiraz and Persepolis, a distance of about two hundred and forty miles, the longer though much easier route, but, according to Arrian, the only road practicable for chariots, that is, the baggage and siege trains. Alexander, with the hetairoi, the lancers, and mounted bowmen, and the Agrianians and archers, turned off to take a much shorter but rougher road. On the fifth day, after a march of a thousand stadia, or about one hundred and fifteen miles, out of a total, if we reckon from Behbehan, of about one hundred and seventy-five miles, he approached the Persian Gates. Here he found the pass, now known as the Kaleh-Safed, or 'the white fortress,' was held in force by the enemy. The defile, about four miles east of the modern village of Falhiyan, is the key position to the entrance to the plateau of Iran, difficult of approach, and, with the proper type of defenders, impregnable. Here Ariobarzanes, satrap of Persia, had built a wall across the defile, and posted nearly fifty thousand men to hold it.

Alexander went into camp at the mouth of the defile, and, next morning, reconnoitered the position. Ariobarzanes had foreseen every contingency, and prepared for it. Alexander sent his men into the defile in a frontal assault. At the narrowest part, where the sides of the defile rose high above them, and even before they had reached the wall built across the neck of the pass, a deadly rain of arrows and stones poured down on top of them, slaying many. The Greeks were mountaineers from boyhood in their own rough lands, accustomed to maneuvering and fighting in broken terrain. They, therefore, grimly considered this but another mountain battle. They raised their shields above their heads, and turned to attempt to scale the almost vertical walls that hemmed them in, and searched for hand-holds to climb. These were few and small, but many started up. Heavy stones crashed down upon the climbers and knocked them from their precarious holds, and arrows slew them as they slid down. They could make no headway at all, and Alexander, seeing his men uselessly destroyed, reluctantly sounded the retreat. The Macedonians had in some way contrived to capture several prisoners, and these were questioned until one, a Lydian slave who had been employed as a shepherd and pastured his flocks in this place, told them there was another way, a hazardous footpath over the steep cliffs, to the other end of the defile. Alexander personally talked to the man and ordered him to guide a strong detachment over the trail, promising him a great reward if he would — and a terrible death for failure or refusal.

The king left in camp Craterus, with his own and Meleager's taxeis, with a number of archers and light cavalry, with orders to make continued active demonstrations in the daytime and to keep the proper number of campfires burning at night, to prevent the enemy from becoming aware of the diminution of the attackers, and, finally, when they should hear the sound of Macedonian trumpets from the other side of the wall, they should launch a determined attack and carry the front of the wall. Alexander took his own bodyguard, the taxeis of Amyntas and Perdiccas, the hypaspists and the Agrianians and the rest of the archers, together with about a hundred carefully chosen auxiliary cavalry, and followed the guide into the darkness. During the night they made about a hundred stadia, or fourteen miles, an excellent showing under such conditions, but one which leads one to the conclusion that the road or trail could hardly have been as bad as our sources would have us believe. They passed through the range, and daylight showed them, ahead and far below, the Araxes (Rud-i-Kurr or Rud Band-i-Amir) River, which must be crossed to reach Persepolis. It would soon be broad daylight and the enemy alert and watchful, and attack now would be unnecessarily expensive in casualties. A strong detachment under Philotas was sent down to throw a bridge over the river, and, the task completed before evening, they returned. They went into bivouac for a few hours' rest, then arose and pushed on at all speed. Just before daybreak they reached the last Persian outpost at the rear of the defile. These were slain silently, the next post being similarly treated. At the third post, most of those on duty, seeing the Macedonians appear in the gray of the morning like evil genii, promptly fled in consternation. So fear-stricken were they that not one carried the news of the approaching onset to their camp. Therefore the Macedonians arrived, and fell upon an unarmed and unsuspecting enemy. Ariobarzanes, even if he had known of the existence of the other route, must have believed it impassable. Ptolemy, with three thousand men, and another and independent body of cavalry, were sent around the enemy to take him from behind. The hetairoi were sent around the other way to attack from the left front. It was just after daybreak, when the hetairoi, urged on by the screaming trumpets, fell upon the enemy from the left front, Alexander from the right, and Ptolemy and the cavalry from the rear. Craterus and his command, aroused by the shrill voice of the trumpets, stormed the wall, swarmed over, and drove the defenders back into their camp, and almost onto the spearheads of Ptolemy's three thousand attackers and the swords of the cavalry. Attacked on all sides at once, the enemy broke and fled in disorder, many falling to their death over the precipices. Ariobarzanes gathered together four thousand infantry and forty cavalry, cut his way out of the trap, and fled into the mountains. Alexander left Craterus to attend to the aftermath of the battle, and, with the hetairoi and light troops, hurried to Persepolis (Takt-i-Taus and Takt-i-Dshemshid), speeding to prevent the garrison from learning of the defeat of Ariobarzanes in time to loot the royal treasures and escape.

The Macedonians were now in ancient Persis itself, the homeland of the Achaemenid royal family. Parsagadae (Takt-i-Suleiman), a short distance south of modern Mashad-i-Murghab, was the citadel city which Cyrus I had built for himself near the battlefield whereon he had won a victory — and kingdom — from Astyages, the king of Media, when that once-great kingdom went down to defeat and ruin. This place, to the Achaemenid dynasty, was their Mecca where they had had their spiritual beginning. There they built their palaces and sepulchers, the king's 'Gate of Forty Pillars,' temples, and gardens of exotic flowers terraced into the hillsides. They made the site a thing of beauty. Darius I had been the first to break from the place. To leave his name as a creator to his posterity, he built the citadel city of Persepolis about twenty miles south, a citadel within whose frowning walls he and his successors built their royal palaces, and the great colonnaded audience hall on a high artificial terrace reached by two great curving flights of richly carved steps, upon which are chiseled in deep relief, still legible today after the lapse of two and a half thousands of years, the following boast: 'Thus sayeth King Darius: this land of Persia, which Ahuramazda has granted me, which is fair, rich in men, and rich in horses, according to the will of Ahuramazda and of me King Darius trembles before no enemy.' The day when that was true had passed, even as had passed the author of the utterance, and the great royal palaces were now beneath the iron rule of a rude conqueror from a far land.

Curtius gives us a strange tale here, but one which will hardly bear up under reasoning; the following being an abridgment of what he draws out to a whole chapter: 'When Alexander drew nigh Persepolis he saw a miserable spectacle; for almost four thousand Greek captives met him, whom the Persians had used barbarously, by cutting off the feet of some, the hands or ears of others, and branding them all with a hot iron, whereon were Persian letters, for a perpetual brand of their slavery.' Neither Arrian nor Plutarch tells the story, and it is highly improbable that the report had any truth except in the imagination of Curtius. The Persians did often practice mutilation as punishment, but hardly upon prisoners of war. These were always able-bodied young men, valuable property as slaves, but only when they were able to work, as certainly men so maltreated could not. Nor were the Persians altruists; they would not gratuitously keep alive hated and crippled enemies, by providing them with food which they could not provide for themselves. If it be considered that they were recently captured, it is inconceivable that the Persians would, in anticipation of Alexander's imminent arrival, have been guilty of acts so calculated to infuriate the Greeks and lead to certain and terrible reprisals.

In Persepolis Alexander came into the centuries' old treasures of the kings, amounting to one hundred and twenty thousand talents, and in Pasargadae, six thousand more. This was incredible wealth in that day, amounting, if of gold, to a metal weight of one thousand and eighty-three kilograms; if of silver, to ten or twelve times that weight. It was said that the other valuables in furniture, utensils, rugs, and fittings were enough to load ten thousand mules and five thousand camels, doubtless an exaggeration, but still indicative of the way the vastness of the loot affected the minds of all Greece. Plutarch says Alexander remained here four months, the remainder of the winter, to give the army a rest, and to wait until the snow melted from the road he contemplated taking over the mountains on the continuation of his journey northward.

Before he left Persepolis, Alexander caused the greatest of the palaces, that of Xerxes, to be burned. The reasons given for the act vary, as much as do the accounts of the degree of premeditation shown. Arrian simply says it was done, against the advice of Parmenio, 'who entreated him to leave it untouched, not only because to spoil and destroy what he had gained by his valor, but that he would thereby disoblige the Asiatics, and render them less benevolent to him; for they would then suppose that he would not keep Asia in his possession, but abandon it as soon as it was conquered and laid waste. To which Alexander made answer that he was resolved to revenge the ancient injuries his country had received by the Persians, who, when they arrived with their army in Greece, subverted Athens, burned their temples, and committed many other barbarous devastations there. But this, in my opinion, seems to have been no prudent or politic action in Alexander, and was no revenge upon the Persians at all.'

This brief account can be accepted as possibly basically correct, with, no doubt, much abridging from the original. Plutarch, who, with Curtius and Diodorus, tells us the destruction of the palace was the result of a drunken orgy, passes the story on to us in a more complete form:

When he was about to set forth from this place against Darius, he joined with his companions in a merrymaking and drinking bout, at which their inamoratas were present and joined in the debauch. The most celebrated of them was Thais, a girl from Attica. She was the paramour of Ptolemy, who afterward became king of Egypt. As the license of the drinking bout progressed, she was carried so far, either by way of offering Alexander a graceful compliment, or of bantering him, as to express a sentiment which, while not unworthy of the spirit of her fatherland, was surely somewhat lofty for her own condition. For she said she was amply repaid for the toils of following the camp all over Asia that she could this day revel in mockery of the haughty palace of the Persians. But, she added, it would give her still greater pleasure, if, to crown the celebration, she might burn the house of Xerxes who had once reduced Athens to ashes, and might with her own hand set the fire under the eyes of the king; so the saying might go forth among men that a little woman with Alexander took sorer vengeance on the Persians in behalf of Greece than all the great generals who fought by land or sea.

Her words were received with such tumults of applause, and so earnestly seconded by the persuasions and zeal of the king's associates, that he was drawn into it himself, and leaping from his seat with a chaplet of flowers on his head and a lighted torch in his hand, led the way, while the rest followed him in drunken rout, with bacchanalian cries, about the corridors of the palace. And when the rest of the Macedonians learned of it, they were delighted, and came running with torches in their hands; for they hoped the burning and destruction of the palace was an indication that his face was turned homeward, and that he had no design of tarrying among the Persians.

During the stay at Persepolis, Alexander made an excursion into the mountains south of Shiraz, and reduced the tribes of the area, erroneously transcribed down to us as the 'Mardians.' This required only a month despite the fact that the mountains were deep in snow above a certain level. After he returned to Persepolis, welcome news at last arrived from Antipater of the final crushing of the Spartans and the death of Agis, at Megalopolis. Antipater had also seized and sent to Alexander, for judgment, a number of hostages and prisoners. When these arrived, the king forced them under coercion to consent to Sparta joining the League of Corinth. On a visit to Pasargadae, he paid his regards to the tomb of Cyrus (still in existence today) and, noting that it had fallen into a state of disrepair, showed his admiration for the great conqueror and empire-builder by ordering it restored and redecorated. In this connection it is worthy of note that Darius was still alive, and at large, hence Alexander could not feel wholly that he was definitely yet the heir of Cyrus. It is possible, however, that his unbounded confidence in his destiny caused him to consider the matter as being absolutely certain of fulfillment according to his own desires and intentions, and that he would be able shortly to come into the possession of the monarch, and thereby succeed in all respects in forcing his claim to the kingship of the entire country.

By spring Alexander was ready to march again. The deep snows on the mountains were melting, and the road open. In Ecbatana, Darius was gathering another army, but, the people of the country having lost faith in him, slowly and with difficulty. He had, however, according to Curtius, who alone gives us figures, thirty-seven thousand men of all arms; and several of his best and ablest commanders still adhered to him. Among them were Nabarzanes, commander of the thousand royal mounted bodyguards; Autophrates, satrap of the Tapurians; Phrataphernes, satrap of Parthia and Hyrcania; Barsaentes of Drangiana; Bessus, cousin of Darius and satrap of Bactria; and Artabazus, commander of all the Greek mercenaries, and his three sons. These were all brave men, of such caliber that, had

Darius been the equal of them in military perspicacity, his army, reduced though it was, could, under their capable leadership, even now be a greater obstacle to Alexander's continued conquest than was the inchoate horde at Arbela. With any real degree of skillful and determined leadership they could have, in fact, halted the advance, and by a guerilla warfare of attrition, possibly have even made the halt permanent. They could have saved the entire eastern part of the empire beyond the mountains, and force Alexander to retrace his steps to Babylonia. For Ecbatana lay only three hundred and fifty miles from Babylon by way of the easily traversed valley of the Gyndes (Zab-el-Asfal) River, and Susa about the same distance by the valley of the Choaspes, the Diala su. Threats of invasion along either of these routes would have driven Alexander hurriedly back to meet them, and skillful tactics from then on might make it possible to force him to remain west of the mountain barrier and out of Iran and Media. That nothing was done must have been the fault of Darius, vacillating between several possibilities.

Alexander marched north, and, without pausing, received the submission of a tribe called the Paritacae (they cannot be located today with any degree of accuracy) and hurried on. Plutarch tells us he covered three thousand and three hundred stadia in eleven days, or about thirty-seven miles a day, and was still three days' march from Ecbatana. The distance is approximately correct, being nearly five hundred miles, a terrific march, and an amazing pace, even for cavalry, to say nothing of foot soldiers. When still three days out of Ecbatana, Bis-thanes, son of the dead king Artaxerxes III, a deserter or fugitive from the Persian cause, came into camp, bringing information that Darius (whose spy and courier system seems still to be working perfectly) had fled ahead of the Macedonian approach five days before, going eastward into Parthia, in company with only eight thousand men. The Cadusians and 'Scythians' had deserted him over, a period of time; at first many had left in disgust at his procrastination, later the remainder had abandoned him rather than flee to the east. Darius had previously sent his reconstituted harem and baggage ahead, intending, if necessary, to flee as far as Bactria.

At Ecbatana, Alexander made arrangements to discharge the time-expired Thessalian and Greek cavalry, and those Macedonians who had faltered through age or disability on the tremendous march to the city. They were paid in full, and a bonus totaling two thousand talents distributed to them.[1] Epocillus, with a guard of Thracian cavalry under (another) Ptolemy, was detailed to convoy them back to the Syrian coast, and Menetes was sent orders to provide them with ships to carry them back to Euboea. Many accepted their discharges, but many re-enlisted, their status thus changing from allies to mercenaries. By dismissing the Greek allies Alexander thus served notice of a complete change in his own status. He had freed the Greek cities of the seaboard, put an end to the Persian rule of Egypt, conquered all the land which the Greeks believed to constitute the empire of Persia, captured all the capital cities of the rulers, and finally had destroyed the palace of Xerxes of execrated memory. He had accomplished the uttermost limits of the task for which the Greeks, in congress assembled as the League of Corinth, had appointed him as 'strategos of all the Hellenes.' *The pan-Hellenic war was over.* The wars that he proposed to carry on in the future, and the conquests he intended to make, were to be exclusively his own, untrammeled by any obligation to the rest of Greece. Therefore the troops they had given him were no longer to be taken as allies, but if they wished to follow his star, it would be as mercenaries only. He would, however, remain as hegemon of the league, as well as king of Macedonia, and king of all Asia besides, and remained in that capacity the rest of his life.

Alexander's next task was to organize a government to control this turbulent satrapy. Harpalus, hitherto treasurer of the military chest, was now made treasurer of the empire, and placed in control of the captured monies now deposited in the citadel

---

[1] Diodorus, XVII, 63. He says the bonus consisted of one talent to each cavalryman and ten minae to each footman.

of Ecbatana. To Parmenio, now seventy years old, was given the responsible and honorable position as military commander of the lands east of the mountains and the task of safeguarding the treasure. Parmenio was too old to continue longer arduous service in the field, but he seems to have felt slighted at what he must have considered virtual retirement. This attitude may have been justified, for there seems to have been a gradual coldness and estrangement between the aged officer and his king. The two represented points of view often opposed to each other, and Parmenio's harshly learned military caution, as well as his inherent conservatism, frequently grated upon Alexander's impetuous nature. He was glad to be thus honorably rid of an often annoying mentor. The first duty he set the general was to take a cavalry command, pacify the Cadusians, and subdue the country to the Caspian littoral, probably as far as modern Resht. Six thousand Macedonian phalangists were left in Ecbatana to guard the treasure citadel against Parmenio's return. Several reliable junior officers were also left behind to establish a base camp for handling and forwarding new levies of recruits and, by inference, to brigade them into units of such types as might be desired and called for. Letters were sent to Clitus, captain of the hetairoi agema, left behind ill and now convalescent in Susa, to repair to Ecbatana, take command of the treasury guards, and, upon Parmenio's return from his raid, to bring his new command to Alexander with all possible expedition. Curtius says Alexander here received a new levy of six thousand men from Greece. If true, this is an excellent commentary upon Menetes' guard upon and the condition of the country between Ecbatana and the sea; that such a comparatively small number of men should be able to march, unmolested, through such great distances of a newly conquered land and the as yet unpacified Kurdish mountains. Too, the new men came as mercenaries, not as Hellenes to the standard of a Hellenic champion, but to the service of the conqueror of Persia, ready to plunge ahead into the terrors of far and unknown lands upon a continuation of his conquests. His work was finally finished in Ecbatana, and Alexander, with the auxiliary cavalry (the hetairoi now gradually fade from our history), the mercenary troops of Erigyius, the rest of the phalangists and hypaspists, the archers and Agrianians, struck for Rhagae (five miles southeast of Tehran) by forced marches.

There is reason to believe that neither Alexander nor Darius proceeded by the most direct route between the two cities. We must put together the statements of two writers, Arrian and Curtius, in order to consider which way was chosen, for Curtius tells us: ' ... with his army he [Darius] deviated from the military road, after he had given the order that the baggage should proceed.'

The Parthian military road to Rhagae runs through a mountainous country, and though a little less than two hundred miles long, is so rough as to be passable to wheeled vehicles only with considerable trouble. Darius may have, indeed, dispatched his baggage over that road, but it is specifically stated that the train was sent out some days ahead of him. There was another and much easier route, longer by about seventy-five miles, running southeast from Ecbatana toward modern Sultanabad, south of the Salt Lake, Tuslu Gol, where it turns northward to Saveh, then northeasterly to where, near the village of Pik, it joins the military road and runs on to Rhagae. Alexander proceeded so fast that men dropped and horses were foundered in the heat of early July, and, according to Arrian, arrived in Ecbatana in eleven days. He never marched so slowly (and all our sources note the losses through exhaustion on this march) as to require eleven days to cover less than two hundred miles, but two hundred and seventy-five miles in this period, and under a ferocious desert midsummer sun, is hard traveling. It would seem, therefore, taking into consideration the statement of Curtius, and the time of Arrian, that the latter route was the one followed. When the Macedonians reached Rhagae, the fleeing Persian king had already disappeared, racing southeast toward the Caspian Gates and onward into Parthia.

Alexander waited five days for the rest of the army to arrive, to give his own force a chance to recuperate, and to form a new local government. Oxydrates, a Persian who had been imprisoned by Darius, was appointed satrap of Media, replacing the fugitive Autophradates, the reason being, as Arrian quaintly says, 'for this confinement of his, by Darius, gained him credit with Alexander.' He then turned again to the pursuit of Darius. Arrian says the Caspian Gates lay about one day's journey distant from Rhagae, *as Alexander marched his army*, but he says that upon the evening of the first day they camped somewhat short of the Gates — probably near the site of the modern village of Aivan-i-Kif. This appellation, the Caspian Gates, was the Greek name for the defiles of Sialek and Sirdara, about forty-eight miles southeast of the ruins of Rhagae. They cut through the Kuh-i-Namak, or Salt Mountains, a low range thrusting south from the parent Elburz Mountains. The northern, Sialek, defile is now blocked by a landslide, probably caused by an earthquake, and has been for over three hundred years. The southern, Sirdara, defile is still open and in everyday use, and is believed to have been that most commonly used in ancient times. It is somewhat over six miles long, and only twenty to twenty-five yards wide at both entrances, with an undrinkable salt stream running down the center. The military and commercial importance of the defiles result from the impassable character of the extraordinarily rough hills and tangled ravines through which, other than the defiles, military passage is virtually impossible.

On the other side of the defiles, there were habitations, but Alexander was told that the country ahead was barren and unsettled. The army halted and Coenus was sent out to search for supplies. The king was pleased to find that Darius' small escort was swiftly becoming yet smaller. Many of his men were deserting daily and returning to their homes, and many of these fell into the hands of the Macedonians. Among them were two noblemen, Bagistanes, a noted Babylonian, and Antibelus, son of Mazaeus. These came to Alexander with the astonishing information that Darius was no longer a free man. Nabarzanes, Bessus, and Barsaentes, the leading men of the fugitive group, had become desperate as the situation had become steadily worse, and finally despaired that Darius would do anything at all to protect his kingdom or crown. They had seized the person of the king and were holding him prisoner. Only the Greek mercenaries, desperate and outlawed men without a country, remained faithful to the fallen king. The seizure of the king had been carried out without their knowledge, but they soon noticed that a screen of mounted men surrounded his chariot by day and tent by night, with the obvious intent to cut Darius off from all communication with them. Wise and subtly aware of the vicissitudes of war, and accustomed to plot and counterplot, the Greeks soon realized what had happened, and aware of the hopelessness of their own situation if the abduction was permitted to be carried on to its logical conclusion. If they allowed the king to be carried into the satrapy of Bessus and accompanied him there, the small body of mercenaries, thousands of miles from home through alien and hostile lands, would inevitably be reduced to sheer slavery by the Bactrian or exterminated if they refused to be reduced to that status. Their leader took his life into his hands one day on the march, forced his way through the close-ranked Asiatics despite their scowling wrath, and addressed Darius in Greek, which the king, but not Bessus, could understand. He warned Darius of the peril in which he stood and implored him to trust himself to the care and attention of the Greeks. Bessus was within earshot, and, though he couldn't understand the individual words, he nevertheless grasped the import of the warning. That night the plotters quietly surrounded the king's tent, put him in fetters, flung him into his chariot, mounted immediately and set off with him to Bactria. A few of the Persian officers accompanied the renegades, but many of the more intelligent, realizing that death probably waited them on the long road to Bactria, threw in their lot with the Greeks and pushed northward toward the friendly shelter of the mountains.

When Alexander heard this, he realized instantly that expedition was necessary. It was not now a case of seizing the Great

King, but of rescuing him. He took the hetairoi, the light cavalry, and the strongest of the footmen, and without waiting for the return of the foragers, he gave command of the rest of the army to Craterus with orders to follow at a moderate pace. Then, taking only two days' rations and their weapons, his pursuit force hurried away.

Beyond the defiles they crossed the district of Kars, anciently called the Choarene by the Greeks, and camped, possibly in the vicinity of modern 'Aradan. Near here is a famous ancient site known as Altigash, or the 'Place of Fire,' that was formerly a temple of the Zoroastrians. If we consider this place as the starting-point the next day, it works out well with the description we are given of the pursuit. Thus, we are told, 'all that night they continued their march until noon the next day,' say eighteen hours elapsed time, of which fifteen hours represent the actual marching time, with the cavalry going no faster than could the armored footmen, in desert midsummer heat. The ancient road east of 'Aradan winds through dry hilly country — and we have already heard it described as barren in that day — flanked on the north by high stony mountains; on the south by salt swamp and the wide salt desert — which is to say, there is not, nor can be, any other route. About seventeen miles east of 'Aradan is the hamlet of Dey Namak, having brackish water only. About twenty-six miles farther is the village of 'Abdullahabad, on an ancient site, with a somewhat better water supply. About eighteen miles farther is a stream of fresh water upon whose banks now stands the caravanserai called Lovur. It is probable, however, that the stop was made at or near the former place, as only supermen could travel farther than that in fifteen hours through rough hilly country. Here the soldiers were allowed a few hours' rest during the sweltering heat of the afternoon, then — 'he again marched all night, and early in the morning entered the camp from whence Bagistanes came, but found no enemy.' Here, though it is not specifically stated to be the case, it is probable the camp may have been made at a town. It is hardly likely that the pursuers could have covered more than forty-five miles, though the country is all plain except for one low hill pass, from 'Abdullahabad to the village of Lasgird, which is built upon a high and very ancient mound, obviously the ruins of what was once an important place. Here, Alexander was told, was the place from which Darius had been carried away as a prisoner in his chariot. Bessus, by virtue of his cousinship to and the complete demoralization of Darius, had assumed the erect tiara, and with the Bactrian cavalry ranged at his side, proclaimed himself as king. The Greeks, refusing to recognize his claim, had left the great road, marched away up the river valley to cross the first range and reach the road running through the Elburz Mountains to the Caspian littoral. Alexander's informant told him, further, that it was the intention of the rebels, if pursuit came too near, to abandon Darius and flee; but if it did not, Bessus planned to convey Darius to Bactria as a prisoner, there to raise an army and take the field himself in the endeavor to carve himself a kingdom out of the northeastern portion of Darius' former dominions.

Alexander pushed on again with all the speed his nearly exhausted men and horses could make. Many dropped out of the column during the night and the next morning. At noon they arrived at a village where Darius and his captors had camped the day before. This village could have reasonably been only in the Rion River valley or Vardamek Mountains, a spur thrusting southeast from the Elburz. Here he was told that the Bactrians evinced uneasiness over the pursuit and that they had spoken as if they too planned night marches. Evidently they had ill-used the villagers, or gained their animus, for when Alexander inquired if there was a shorter way than that taken by the fugitives, information was immediately forthcoming. He was told that there was such a road, but it led through a barren and waterless country. It was so bad that it was impassable to men on foot in such heat, they could not stand the rigors of the desert there. Mounted men could pass, however, and by taking it they might overtake the king and his escort. About five hundred of the lightarmed cavalry were ordered to dismount, and an equal number of the heavily armed infantry were mounted in their stead. Nicanor was ordered to take the hypaspists, Attalus the Agrianians and other light troops post-haste along the great road (the ancient Parthian road) along which Bessus and his people had fled. The other infantry were to follow them. Late in the afternoon Alexander led his men away on the desert road, and drove on so hard that they covered four hundred stadia, forty-seven miles, during the night; and at dawn they came within sight of the long straggling column far ahead.

Let us assume, as we must, for there have never been roads other than those about to be described, that Alexander passed south of modern Samnan, on the present road from the Rion River or Vardamek mountain villages. From this area there are three roads to the city the Greeks knew as Hecatompylos, and today is called Damghan. The northern, the old Parthian military, road crosses the mountains by the hamlet of Ahuan, and goes on to the village of Gusheh, sometimes called Sultana-bad, in the district of Qumish, the ancient Comisene, then on to Damghan. Along this route today only the steppe between Ahuan and Gusheh is without water. A second road, farther to the south, crosses the mountains through a succession of dry hills and low passes. On the eastern slope of the Vardamek Range two small springs are the only water obtainable between here and a point not far from Gusheh, where it joins the northern road. The third road, yet farther south, runs around the Kuh-i-Sultan Shah Rukh Mountains and the Benober Mountains and thence straight to Frat. Bessus took the old Parthian road, Alexander the next road to the south. He therefore overtook the Bactrians not far from and southeast of Damghan. The valley was probably in the southeast side of the Sefid-Kuh Mountains north of the modern villages of Taziabad and Ahazabad.

There was no time for the Bactrians to prepare for, nor, indeed, much thought of defense. Some of them hastily formed ranks as if to offer resistance, but the majority, plying whip and spur and voice to their mounts, fled at the first sight of the pursuing Nemesis. Those who resorted to arms were ridden over and cut down. The mere sight of Alexander paralyzed their weapon arms. The king spurred hard straight along the long column, traveling so fast that only about sixty of the best-mounted of his followers could keep near him. Bessus and his commanders, riding at or near the head of the column with their captive, instantly grasped what had happened when they saw the onrushing Macedonians far behind. For a few moments they tried frantically to persuade Darius to mount a horse and fly with them. The king obstinately refused to leave his chariot. Finally in exasperation they drove javelins into his body, hastily gathered six hundred men into a squadron, and galloped away. The Macedonian king pounded swiftly along the line of the caravan, now a riot of confusion. Says Plutarch: 'They rode over abundance of gold and silver that lay scattered about, and passed by chariots full of women which wandered here and there for lack of drivers, and still they rode on to reach the van of the flight and find Darius there.' Ahead of them they saw the fleeing squadron mass into a tight unit, and spur away at a pace their own jaded mounts could not possibly make. The few of the pursuers reined up and turned slowly back. Presently someone sighted Darius' chariot, the two mules wandering driverless beside a small stream in a near-by valley. When Alexander reached it, the only cargo it carried was the dead body of Darius. He gazed for a moment at the poor corpse that alone was the spoil of the long race, then took off his cloak and wrapped it around the body of his predecessor upon the throne of Persia. So thus, in the fiftieth year of his age, Darius died a fugitive from his enemy and his own, a king imprudent and inept both in war and in peace, who succeeded to the throne by fraud and murder, and left it the same way. With the honors due to his rank, the body of Darius was dispatched to Persepolis and laid by the side of his forebears. The date was late in July, 330 B.C.

X

THE CONQUEST OF
PERSIA—SECOND PHASE

U<small>P TO</small> this point the path of Alexander has been traced with little difficulty; most of the routes were well known even in that day, but hereafter the task is less easy. The writers and ancient geographers, who are our main sources for this narrative, often had little idea of the exact locations of many of the places of which they wrote and of the locations of places in relation to one another, and were often so wrong in their identification that the results would be weird indeed if we were to accept them unquestioningly. For instance, they had no knowledge of the existence of the Sea of Aral; and the Amur Darya River, the classical Oxus, and the Sir Darya which they called the Jaxartes was the one they believed to be the river they knew and called, along its lower reaches, the Tanais (the Don), emptying into the Palus Mareotis, the Sea of Azov. They believed the Hindu Kush Range to be a spur or continuation of the Caucasus, and the Indus, despite assertions to the contrary, to be the upper Nile, because, forsooth, there were crocodiles in both. Many of them were little trammeled by their ignorance, however. When their personal knowledge failed, they drew largely upon their imaginations to supply the deficiency, and kept on writing, not seldom enlarging philosophically upon some occurrence until it is with difficulty that the grain can be threshed from the chaff and the facts deduced; or, what was worse, abridging the story to the detriment of clarity, creating gaps which are difficult, and sometimes impossible, for us to fill. Sometimes we are given names which no amount of research identifies for us; but fortunately many of them have survived translation through two or three languages and yet retain their sounds sufficiently well to be philologically identifiable with the European corruption of what we know as either the ancient or modern name. Where this is not the case, modern archeological, scholastic, or geographical knowledge permits us to fill the gap with a considerable degree of exactitude; but occasionally all resources fail us and we have to fall back upon reasoning, not always with perfect results. Infrequently it is impossible, in view of deficient or conflicting descriptions and place names, plus very considerable physical changes in the countries involved (as later detailed, *passim*), to construe the data given us into a wholly acceptable narrative. Certain questions later arise which must remain unanswered, and, until more light is shed upon the subject by research and discovery, unanswerable. It is worth while at this point to remark upon what will be henceforth a frequently recurring fact, the report of the founding of a number of cities, many of them even yet of considerable importance, all named Alexandria. The attribution of the 'founding' of these places to the Macedonian king is undoubtedly more complimentary than accurate. Alexander was almost always moving at too fast a pace to allow for a halt of sufficient time to found a city; and, most cogent reason, these Alexandrias were invariably located logically and strategically along routes already ancient and well traveled, and always in areas rich enough in natural resources and agricultural land to support a very considerable population. It is very unlikely that the Asiatics, a social and highly intelligent people, engaged in frequent wars for untold centuries, would have, or indeed could have, permitted these perfectly obvious sites to remain unoccupied, while they, the original inhabitants, themselves occupied the less desirable places. It is therefore most probable that Alexander simply gave his own name to existing cities (as he had already done at Myriandrus and Rhacotis) whose central location or strategic value was patent to his discerning eye, and that their ancient names are thus lost to us forever.

According to Diodorus, Plutarch, and others, Alexander led his exhausted followers to the near-by city of Hecatompylos (at present believed to be Damghan), for a much-needed opportunity to recover from the effects of their tremendous exertions in the midsummer cross-country race, and to await arrival of the rest of the army. Arrian says nothing of the city, simply that he was rejoined, before continuing the advance, by those he had left behind.

Alexander's luck was still holding amazingly. Now that Darius was dead without the stigma of his death falling upon Alexander, so far as the western satrapies were concerned, he held indisputable right to the throne. Bessus, the renegade traitor and regicide, had the support of his own satrapies only. To keep the western provinces quiet, Alexander could (and did), by skillful use of propaganda, keep them quiet, by playing upon their native patriotism and regard for the dead king, by proclaiming his intention of pursuing the Bactrian wherever he might run to hide.

But now his own Macedonians concluded that they had won the empire of Persia, or, at any rate, all of it that was worth holding. It was time to turn back and enjoy the possession of the rich cities and lands they had seized by force, for which many had paid with their lives, many more with their blood and illnesses, and all with labors certainly no less than those of the storied heroes. They were physically weary of the long road they had followed, and they wanted none of the desert lands that lay ahead of them to the east, beyond which, the soldiers believed, were the ends of the earth. Alexander knew better, and he was not taken at a loss. By glowingly painting to them a flaming word-picture of their heroic deeds and promising them future rewards greater than those of the past, he at length stilled their grumbling and won their promise to go onward in pitiless pursuit of the man who dared slay his king and set himself in line for the throne of the ruler of all Asia. But first, in order to secure their flanks and rear, the tribes living in and beyond the frowning mountains whose snow-capped heads loomed north of the city, the range they called the Caucasus (Elburz), and on the shores of the Hyrcanian Lake (Caspian Sea), the Tapurians and Hyrcanians, and the now frightened and desperate Greek mercenaries, must be brought into subjection or coerced into innocuity.

Alexander divided his army into three columns, choosing his own command carefully, for he was to take the shortest but most difficult way. Craterus was given a column of his own and Amyntas' taxeis, together with a few archers and light cavalry, and was assigned the western route. Erigyius, with the mercenaries and the rest of the cavalry, was ordered to escort the baggage and siege trains, and, according to Arrian, 'the rest of the multitude' by the great road into Hyrcania, via modern Shahrud, Bagh, and Astarabad. Alexander marched together up the river valley to the vicinity of Ostanek or Chashmeh-i-Amir, and there parted. Craterus turned toward the northeast and disappeared over the pass. Alexander (this is deduced from Curtius' description) turned north, crossed the divide, passed through the defile of Shah Kuh, turned left, and passed down into the broad valley of the Nikha (called the Ridagnus by the Greeks) River, in the vicinity of Radkan. Here he rested his men four days, then proceeded down the valley, moving with his troops drawn into squares (syntagmata), for the warlike character of the people, as well as the broken terrain, rendered Alexander uneasy. At several points where it seemed politic, he left strong bodies of men to guard the passage and discourage the inhabitants from harassing tactics. Curtius says: ' ... it is one long uninterrupted valley down to the Caspian Sea, into which, as it were, two horns of it project, enclosing between them a bay of moderate curve that greatly resembles the moon when the disk is not full and the horns project.' The description fits perfectly the Nikha Valley and the Bay of Astarabad. Alexander left the valley, perhaps near present Barkala, for there is the only place that fits so perfectly with the history of the march, crossed the densely forested ridge, and passed down to the low hot plains of Mazanderan, reaching the town of the Arvae, which might be — there are many reasons pro and con — on the site of, or certainly in the vicinity of, Bandar-i-Gaz, and camped in a plain near a small river. He then called in the guards he had left behind to prevent excursions on his rear, all of whom withdrew safely, only one group of Agrianian javelin men having to fight their way out. The fugitives, Phrataphernes, former satrap, under Darius, of Hyrcania and Parthia, Nabarzanes, and eighteen other Persians of high rank, came in and surrendered unconditionally. Alexander marched toward the capital of the country, Zadracarta, there to be shortly rejoined by Craterus after he brought the country through which he had passed into subjection. Erigyius marched in a day or two later after having made slow time with the ponderous trains, but meeting no hostile action en route.

Zadracarta must be located wholly by conjecture. Our ancient accounts are confusing to the point of incoherence, and no series of factors, *as they are related* by any of our sources, can be reconciled with either of the three most probable locations; namely, Astarabad, Ashraf, and Barfarush. Of these, after careful analysis of the type and locations of the ancient ruinous sites at these places, together with the routes in use during the period, and many other factors too long to cite in detail, acceptance of Astarabad as the site of Zadracarta is indicated as that most probable of authenticity. Thus we assume Alexander marched to the latter place. To him here came Artabazus the Persian, and his three sons, Cophen, Arsames, and Ariobarzanes, whom (despite Curtius' account, which has not the ring of truth, that this doughty commander was killed near Persepolis) we like to consider the officer who so stoutly resisted Alexander's passage through the Persian Gates. Artabazus and Alexander had known each other at the court of Pella many years before, when the former was a temporary fugitive and exile from the intrigues of the Persian court, and the latter a boy of seven. Autophradates, the fugitive satrap, surrendered also, and was immediately restored to power, acting on the principle that he would give him the same faithful service he had rendered to Darius, in this case, however, a service that fell far short of expectations, for Autophradates later betrayed his trust. Emissaries also came from the band of fugitive mercenaries, lost and bewildered in this hostile land of giant mountains, begging for the amnesty and friendship that had been granted to so many others. Alexander would enter into no compact with them, however, because they had borne arms against Greeks in the service of a foreign ruler and in contravention of the decree of the Council of Corinth. To them he offered nothing but the demand for unconditional surrender, failing which, he concluded ominously, they could look out for themselves. They came, abjectly, now reduced in number to fifteen hundred, and brought with them men who had been ambassadors to the court of Darius, four Spartans, one Athenian, one Carthaginian, and several from Sinope on the southern coast of the Euxine Sea. These last he freed immediately, because they were not Greeks, and there was no reason their cities should not have emissaries at the Persian court; but the Spartans and the Athenian were placed under arrest as rebellious subjects. We are not told what was ultimately done with them. The mercenaries who had been in the service of Darius before the formation of the league were unconditionally freed, the others forced to join his army under the same terms of their service to Darius. A certain Andronicus was placed in command of the contingent.

Alexander then made an expedition against the Mardi, a tribe somewhere on the Caspian littoral of Mazanderan. There has been a great deal of speculation about these people, and several conjectures advanced as to their real identification and location. They have been placed from the Talar River in the east to as far west as the neighborhood of Resht; this latter hypothesis will, however, not bear scrutiny. The most tenable possibility, in the writer's opinion, is as follows: historically, the greatest credence can be given the statement that they lived on and west of the Charinda River, which has, erroneously in my opinion, been identified with the Rud Seh Hazar. It was said that their country could be easily reached from Parthia. Today, and probably in that day, the route runs from Tehran (or ancient Rhagae) through the defile of Kuh-i-Namak (the Caspian Gates), into the district of Kars (Choarene), up the Hableh River to Firuzkuh, thence over the easy Gaduk Pass, and then follows the Talar River down to the plains of Mazanderan. According to Strabo, on the Charinda River was the citadel town of Talarbroca; and it is conjecturable that the Talar anciently took its name from its connection with the district of the Choarene, and later, after Greek influence passed, from the town of Talarbroca. If this abridgment of the reasoning is correct, the Mardi occupied a limited area on and west of the Talar, with the possibility that they may have extended as far as the Rud Seh Hazar. East of the country of the Mardians was the land of the people the Greeks called the Tapurians, occupying the Caspian littoral and the mountains behind it, a small people possessing only a limited area. Curtius says Alexander required only five days to subdue the Mardians. He then returned to Zadracarta, held a great festival, and rested the army for fifteen days.

The army marched eastward along the valley of the Sarnius (Atrek) River toward Susia, a city of the Arians, the ancient Tus, about twelve miles north of Meshed. The way led through a land rich and with plentiful supplies, and the road, to permit easy passage of the huge trains, must have been good. Curtius gives us the story that the train, what with the addition of huge quantities of loot and large numbers of women, had grown to such size that it constituted a serious impediment to the freedom of movement of the army. Alexander concluded that it would have to be greatly lessened, and ordered all unnecessary baggage burned, and made a holocaust of his own as an example.

At Susia, he was met by Satibarzanes, satrap of Aria, who made submission, and, though he was one of the murderers of Darius, Alexander nevertheless deemed him suitable to retain his post, which was later to be proved another mistake in judgment. Unlike the king's previous appointments, in which brakes were put upon the authority of the civilian satrap by coupling him with one or more military monitors, Alexander here in Susia merely assigned one of his friends, Anaxippas, with forty mounted archers, to the police duty of preventing thefts or other depredations by his army in this territory. It would seem that here, too, he made the first radical departure from his former mode of life. Hitherto he had only been king of Macedonia and hegemon of the Council of Corinth, and had lived and dressed at least in accordance with his rank. Now he was, by virtue of the declaration of his army and the death of Darius, king of all Asia, and slowly his manner of dress and mode of living was changed to correspond to his new and more exalted rank. Plutarch gives us the account of the beginning of the change: [1]

> From here he marched into Parthia, and as he had not much to do here, first put on the Median dress, probably with a desire to accommodate himself to the usages of the country, in recognition of the influence which conformity to the usual dress and costume has in the work of civilizing a people; or perhaps it may have been a way of insinuating upon the Macedonians the usage of prostration through accustoming them to tolerate this change in the conduct of his life. He did not, however, assume the ultra-Oriental style of dress, with all its odious features, the trousers, the sleeved jacket, or the tiara, but a compromise between the Persian and the Macedonian, more quiet than the former, but more imposing than the latter. At first he wore it only when meeting barbarians or with his friends at home, but later he appeared in it

[1] Plutarch, *Alexander*, XLV.

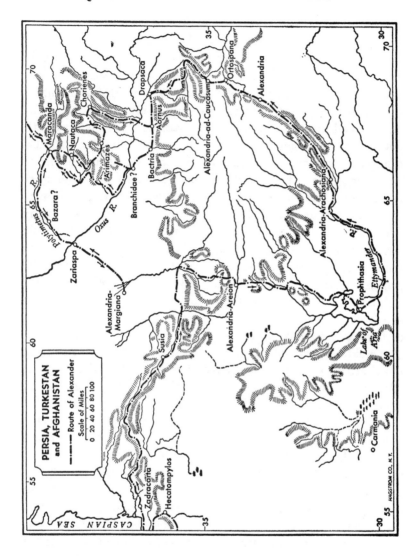

PERSIA, TURKESTAN
and AFGHANISTAN

------ Route of Alexander

Scale of Miles
0 20 40 60 80 100

publicly, when he drove out, or at public audiences — a sight which the Macedonians viewed with much distaste.

That the hardy peasant warriors of Macedonia should be harsh judges of the changes they saw taking place in their young king is understandable, when even in this presumably enlightened day, we note the narrow insularity and national hatreds and bigotry of much of the world. There is also little doubt that the disaffection, first coming into the open at Hecatompylos, was yet unstilled, and perhaps intensified by Alexander's adoption of Oriental customs. The lessening number of independent and outspoken Macedonians, their ranks thinned by discharges, death, and special service detachments, was being overshadowed by the increasing percentage of more servile Greeks and self-abasing Asiatics, both in the court and in the army itself. Their privileges were becoming less, their independence curtailed, and their hope of personal profit from their rich conquests on this, what was after all a robbers' expedition and banditry on a cosmic scale, fading. Praise for the actions of heroes is poor compensation to a man being asked to face continual dangers and hardship with little prospect of anything but death in a hostile country far from his homeland. Not that Alexander can be greatly blamed with the onus of unjustified assault upon a people with no other excuse than a desire for personal glory and to add to his dominions; other rulers have repeated this type of international atrocity hundreds of times since his day — and the end is not yet. But we have indications that the impulsive youth the Macedonians had so gladly and willingly followed over the narrow Hellespont was, here in the mountainous deserts of central Asia, becoming an irascible and temperamental despot, whose undoubted courage was turning into mere foolhardiness, and whose personal disregard for discomfort or even pain, degenerating into sheer cruelty. Alexander hereafter shows definitely increasing deterioration, at first as a man with the attributes of humanity, and seemingly too as a strategist and commander. This last is reckoned by some students as due to the removal of the long experienced

Parmenio from his councils, though later we find indications of an able councilor again at the helm, probably the man who later filled the post we would today designate as field-marshal, Craterus. We find less and less to admire in Alexander as time goes on and history unrolls.

While the Macedonians were still in Susa (Tus), intelligence was brought that Bessus in Bactria had formally proclaimed himself king of Persia, adopted the robes of royalty, placed the erect tiara upon his head, and changed his name and title to Artaxerxes IV. He was now engaged in raising an army, and had called upon his old allies, the 'Scythians,' to come to his assistance. The matter was threatening, and Alexander prepared to deal with it immediately. Before the army could move, Nicanor, second son of Parmenio and commander of the hypaspists, died. Much to Alexander's grief, the revolt was dangerous, and its suppression urgent; he must move without delay. He left behind Philotas and twenty-six hundred men, sufficient to give Nicanor a burial with military pomp and display suited to his rank and station. Philotas buried his brother, and, like a good soldier, proceeded by forced marches to overtake the army. He had hardly disappeared over the eastern hills when Satibarzanes reversed his newly declared allegiance in favor of Bessus, exterminated Anaxippus and his little police force of mounted archers, and ordered his own and Bessus' adherents to assemble in Artacoana, preparatory to moving east to join the Bactrian. Alexander, proceeding east by the military road skirting the desert, received the news on the border of Russian Turkestan and Afghanistan, perhaps in the vicinity of the modern Kushk (ancient Margus) River. Hereabouts he was also joined by a considerable reinforcement from Ecbatana, consisting of the re-enlisted Thessalians, the Greek mercenary cavalry, and the recruits under Andromachus, the whole under command of Philip. The king halted his swift advance toward Bactria, and, with the auxiliary cavalry, the newly formed corps of mounted javelin men, the archers and the ever-valuable Agrianians, together with the taxeis of Coenus and Amyntas, turned abruptly south, leaving the rest of the army, under Craterus, to follow. He marched along the Kushk River, over the Ardewan or Baba Pass, and two days later, having marched six hundred stadia, about seventy miles, he stormed into Artacoana. When the swiftly moving column approached the city, Satibarzanes, in complete dismay at the extreme promptitude with which punishment was being visited upon him, precipitately abandoned the city, and fled, with a few of his friends, to Bessus. Alexander entered the city, seized and put to death all persons found with weapons in their possession, and sold the rest of the people into slavery. Arsames, son of Artabazus, was made satrap.

Artacoana, built upon one of the most valuable strategic sites in the ancient world, was even then ancient beyond knowing, and the capital city of the Arians, the original Aryans. Alexander instantly recognized its worth, and, with the view to improving, enlarging, and strengthening it, ordered additional building and fortification, and gave it his own name as Alexandria-Areion, today surviving both physically and philologically as Herat. Here, today as then, center trade routes from all directions, out of Afghanistan, Turkestan, from India and far-away China, including the ancient and well-trodden caravan road, up the river of Aria (the Hara Rud) into Bactria. However, Alexander was informed that in Drangiana or Zarangeia (so-called from the lake of Aria, Palus Aria, the modern Lake of Sistan), the satrap Barsaentes, another of the murderers of Darius, was raising an army of defense. If he turned north into Bactria now, there would be nothing to prevent Barsaentes from moving into Aria in his rear. Accordingly, to isolate Bessus, Alexander turned south via Sabzawar and Farrah. Certain commentators state their belief that he again turned at Farrah, following the caravan road eastward through the rolling country to the village of Girishk on the Helmund River, thence striking straight for the site of Kandahar. The following brief summary does much to refute this theory.

Within the last few decades it has been discovered through various means that the Drangiana (Sistan and southwest Afghan-

istan) was, in that day, a rich land with a vastly greater population than today. The lake itself was correspondingly greater,
including the whole of the desolate sink today known as the
Gaud-i-Zirreh, now a great curved depression, partially occupied by salt swamp. The whole of Asia was, in that period,
demonstrably much less arid than today, a truth especially
applicable to this section. The rich lake delta and lowlands
were an obvious source of large food supplies, the many populous villages and towns an equally prolific source of potential
enemies. Both of these would have remained untouched had
Alexander bent his steps along the Farrah–Girishk caravan road.
The food was needed for the army, and the population must be
subdued and subjected if for no other reason than the necessity
of again leaving only chastened and cowed peoples in his rear.
Farrah is, due to its great antiquity and the similarity with the
name passed down to us as the city of the country, often accepted
as the place variously transcribed to us as Phra, Phrada, or the
most commonly called Prophthasia. Here, however, is where
unqualified comparisons, based only on similarity of sounds,
leads astray, for *farrah*, *fahraj*, and their phonetic variations
mean nothing but ‘town,’ of which the Hindu variation is the
repetitive suffix -*pur*, -*por*, and -*pore*, appearing in endless numbers of place names. Of the scores of deserted towns and town
sites of Sistan, the most probable site of the ancient capital is
the ruin known today as Shahristan, some sixteen or eighteen
miles southwest of modern Nasratabad. As Alexander's army
marched south, Barsaentes fled from the pursuing Nemesis into
‘India’ (?), where he was seized and delivered back to the conqueror, who had him slain. The story is told that somewhere
along the line of this march, a small but inimical tribe was encountered. There was a short fight, and the tribesmen fled up
the forested slope of a mountain whose other side was a preci-
pice. As the wind happened to be blowing strongly up the slope,
Alexander had the forest at its foot fired in several places, waited
until the fire formed an impassable barrier, and marched away,
callously leaving the tribe to perish in the flames.

At Prophthasia was discovered the oft-disputed facts of the so-called conspiracy against Alexander's life, involving Philotas. The ominous appearance of symptoms of revolt in the heart of his own army, the Macedonians grouped about the king, has attracted the attention of many students and writers, both ancient and modern,[1] and its significance must needs be understood to make a fair estimate, not only of the king's attitude, but that too of his army as a whole, or at least that of his own Macedonians, an attitude which can probably be attributed also to the Greeks.

Parmenio, now in semi-retirement in Ecbatana, was seventy years of age, a man of the most conservative school, but from the death of Philip the most faithful servitor of the young king. His calm assurance, and, if we judge correctly, his eminent fairness to his men — unusual in that day — had given him, and through him to his relatives in the service, great influence with the Macedonian soldiery. Apropos of this, Plutarch declares (claiming Callisthenes as his source) that at this period Parmenio was viewing with no kindly eye Alexander's growing power, his heightened ambitions, and the Persian ceremonials to which he was taking with such obvious liking. Parmenio's brother, Agatho, was commander of the valuable Odrysian (Thracian) cavalry; Philotas, his eldest son, the trusted leader of the hetairoi; Nicanor, his second son, to whom had been entrusted the command of the most valuable of the infantry, the hypaspists, had already died of fever contracted in the unhealthy lowlands of Hyrcania; Hector, his youngest son, was drowned in the Egyptian Nile. Phalangist-Commander Coenus was his brother-in-law. Many other kinsmen held other positions of lesser rank in the army. No other family group held so much power, or were so placed that their positions permitted them, if they felt so disposed, to form a nucleus about whom the discontented could build a concrete expression of their feelings.

[1] The most complete study of this affair that has come to the author's attention is an article by Frederick Cauer, 'Philotas, Kleitos, Kallisthenes,' *Jahrbücher für Class. Philol.*, Supplement-Band XX, 1894, pp. 1–79.

In the Macedonian camp, uneasiness began to be manifest. The older officers and men, especially the former, began to feel that the Macedonian general with whom they had left Europe was gradually drawing apart from them. They had not liked his assumption of semi-divinity in Egypt, and their bleak reception of the claim had caused it to be relegated to the background for two years. Now they felt they had real grievances, and, true to the — already dead, though they did not yet know it — spirit of the old tribal democracy, they voiced them, loudly and publicly. The army had left Macedonia to fight for and free the Greek cities and lands of Asia Minor from the Persian rule; first they had carved out a new and reasonably secure province out of the western lands, this should have been enough; but they had gone on, unquestioningly, down the Phoenician seacoast and into Egypt, which had been added to the territories of their king. Afterward they had crossed Mesopotamia, fought the battle of Arbela, penetrated to Babylon, Susa, and Persepolis; they had captured there treasures beyond their wildest imaginations. Still they had gone on, captured the dead body of the Persian king, subdued the shores of the Hyrcanian Lake — and they had gone on. Now they were being asked to go on, and ever on — was there to be no end of their bootless travail in this gaunt and desert land? Five long years had passed in hard marching and hard fighting, many were dead of battle, of wounds and disease, others were worn out with hardship; they wanted to return to a place, some place where they could enjoy the wealth they had won. Instead they were being asked to go, and go, on and on. Now, to add insult to injury, Alexander was showing, more and more strongly, predilections toward Oriental usages and customs that were not to their liking. Persian noblemen were beginning to be adopted into his entourage in increasing numbers. Persian satraps had been restored to control of their provinces, even the more minor officials were left in their posts. To the victors should have gone these spoils, of which they were getting nothing. Also, the court itself was rapidly becoming orientalized, and Alexander himself, though naturally a Macedonian despot, had recently begun to show tendencies toward becoming an Oriental despot.

This seems to have been the attitude of much, perhaps most, of the army. Philotas had been only one of many who had voiced, with increasing acerbity, their complete disapproval of the state and direction into which things were drifting. It was said that Alexander, after the reports he had received in Syria, had suborned Philotas' mistress into further reporting what Philotas said to her in private. If this is true, it is easy to envision the young Delilah's insinuations calculated to put words and phrases into his mouth for the sake of having opportunity of making sensational reports and disclosures to her king, a not uncommon practice of spies, informers, and *agents provocateurs* today. There is need of reason for the grim animus the king showed toward Philotas, and the explanation is at least tenable.

This, then, is the situation our histories tell us existed at Prophthasia in the late autumn of 330 B.C. A young man named Nicomachus had been asked by a friend, Dimnus, to join a small group in a conspiracy aimed at Alexander's life. The former immediately told his brother, and sent him to report the plot to Philotas, who in turn had access to the king. Two days went by, and the news was conveyed to Alexander by other means, together with the information that Philotas had been told of the plot before. This is, if true, very difficult to explain away. The king did nothing obvious that afternoon. That evening, he, as was frequently his wont, invited a number of his officers to supper with him, among them, Philotas. At midnight Alexander called apart several of his most trusted officers — Craterus, Hephaestion, Perdiccas, Erigyius, Coenus, and Leonnatus — and sent them, with guards, to arrest those against whom the information had been lodged, Philotas first of all. Dimnus committed suicide rather than submit to arrest, but the others were all taken. Next day Philotas was placed on trial, Alexander himself standing as his accuser. Arrian's account of this is brief to the point of sketchiness, no details being given;

that of Curtius, occupying five chapters (VI, 7, 8, 9, 10, 11), so full and complete in every way that it cannot be other than wholly imaginary, for no known authentic history from which he could have taken the story ever reported it so fully. At this distance and time we have no way of evaluating the evidence which was submitted to the tribunal; but we do know that this method, which really amounts to trial by mob, could hardly guarantee an unprejudiced or dispassionate appraisal of the evidence. Philotas had made many enemies by his domineering personality and his tendency toward ostentation; even his father had rebuked him once for his assiduous pursuit of honors and rank. But until now, neither his fidelity nor that of any of his family had come under suspicion. The conclusion must have been foregone, the army declared him guilty. It may be that the king honestly believed what he evidently desired to believe, that Philotas would not conspire against him without the knowledge and perhaps promise of assistance, at the showdown, of his father, at least, and perhaps other of his relatives. Or again, it may have been sheer sadism, and knowledge that it was necessary to wring from the prisoner, by absolutely certain means, a pain-forced confession of complicity with his father. According to Plutarch, Diodorus, Justin, and Curtius, Philotas still insisted upon his innocence, asserting he had not reported the alleged plot because he completely disbelieved the truth of the story. This gave Alexander the chance he wanted. Philotas was taken into the privacy of a pavilion and there brutally tortured by Hephaestion, Craterus, and Coenus (who was, remember, uncle to Philotas), the three most intimate of Alexander's friends, to force him to reveal his associates. Torture, skillfully applied, will make any person confess any action, however untrue, nefarious, or even downright impossible. It seems to have been skillfully applied, while Alexander listened from concealment from behind a screen. When the prisoner had been tortured beyond endurance, the idea was suggested to him — and he confessed, implicating Parmenio, giving out a long story of how, though they had not planned to compass the king's death, they were prepared to seize power if anything untoward happened to him. When Philotas finally broke down, it is alleged that Alexander stepped from behind the screen and taunted the agonized wreck of what had once been a brave man with cowardice. The confession was read to the army, and the broken Philotas was immediately speared to death. The other accused, and the Lyncestian Alexander, dragged around as a prisoner for over four years, were similarly executed. The king could not now permit Parmenio to remain alive, he was much too popular with the garrisons in the West; and not only had he a command of several thousand men, but the great treasures stored at Ecbatana were in his keeping; with these his possibilities as a vengeful trouble-maker were too great to overlook. He dispatched a messenger, one Polydamus, with urgent instructions as to the need of haste, bearing a letter to the other officers now at Ecbatana, Cleander, Sitalces, and Menidas, ordering the death of Parmenio. Polydamus covered nearly nine hundred miles in eleven days on relays of racing camels, and outran tidings of the trial. The orders were carried out, and the old general summarily murdered. Despite the precautions taken at Ecbatana to prevent repercussions, the army there nearly mutinied, and were prevented from doing so only with great difficulty. In Drangiana, four other officers were suspected of complicity in the plot on the strength of their intimacy with Philotas. Brought to trial they were acquitted, and Alexander seems to have continued them in their posts. The hetairoi, formerly a single command under Philotas, were divided into two regiments, and given to Clitus and Hephaestion.

Late in October or early November the Macedonians continued the advance, passing up the Etymander (Helmund) River valley among the tribe known as the Ariaspians, an independent and self-governing people whose caliber and organization impressed Alexander very strongly. They had long ago been so hospitable to the army of Cyrus, when that king was here and in difficulties, that they had received the name of Euergetai, or Benefactors. Their attitude and orderly civilization was such that Alexander gave them additional territory near-by which they had long felt need of but not to the extent of going to war with neighboring tribes. Here we find a kind of left-handed confirmation of Alexander's choice of the Helmund valley route, for he tells us that the Gedrosians sent submission to Alexander, as well as the Arachosians. The former were inhabitants of modern Baluchistan, a people exceedingly unlikely to submit voluntarily to the yoke of a foreigner traveling upon a route, that is, from Farrah to Girishk, far from their own country and obviously going to miss it entirely. However, it was but a short distance from the Etymander River route into the land of the Gedrosians, and it were better to submit at once, without which the conqueror might pay them a visit and force submission upon them. The Arachosians were people farther up the river, into whose country he was entering, therefore submission would simply save them a great deal of trouble. They accordingly submitted. Moving on up the Etymander, Alexander founded another city on or near the site of Kandahar, calling it Alexandria-Arachosia, the modern name obviously stemming from it. Menon was made satrap of the new city and province, and given a force of forty-six hundred cavalry to beat off and put an end to the frequent irruptions of raiders from India through the several mountain passes debouching into this area.

News was brought that the Arians had again revolted as a result of another armed incursion of Bactrians under Satibarzanes, whom Bessus had sent to create a diversion in Alexander's rear, in the hope of keeping him out of Bactria. The Persian Artabazus, who had now won Alexander's complete confidence, was dispatched with six thousand Greek mercenaries, accompanied by Caranus and Erigyius with some six hundred Greek cavalry, to put down the insurrection. Phrataphernes, who had been made viceroy of Parthia and Hyrcania, was ordered to assist them in all possible ways. They found the enemy, and defeated them in a bitterly contested battle in which Satibarzanes was killed, Curtius says, by Erigyius in hand-to-hand combat. Also about this time Alexander was reinforced by eleven thousand veterans from Ecbatana, the seven thousand disaffected men of Parmenio's command, and four thousand additional recruits. It had been deemed wise to remove them from their central location to prevent a possible uprising. The army moved on, northeastward through the high valleys of Afghanistan, though it was now the dead of winter and the snow lay deep in the high passes. The army suffered severely and lost men and horses by cold and exhaustion. Another Alexandria was founded upon the site of modern Ghazni, and the army pressed on to the valley of the Cophen River in the neighborhood of modern Kabul, which may or may not be the place passed on to us historically as Nicaea. This is possible, but after a careful study of our limited data, plus numerous theories and several probabilities, is deemed unlikely. We simply were told that a place called Nicaea existed in the Cophen River valley; it cannot be located otherwise than by the knowledge of the fact that it could not be far from Kabul. This latter town is handed down to us as Cabura and later Ortospana, and we know its Persian name was Vaekereta. That is all. The army marched on. Northward lay the classical Paropamisus (Hindu Kush) Mountains, which the Greeks believed to be, and called, the Caucasus, towering in snow-clad menace, arctic and impassable, thousands of feet higher than the sixty-three-hundred-foot elevation of the site of Kabul. There was no choice save to wait for spring.

During the winter halt in the plains of Kohistan, a new city was founded, Alexandria-ad-Caucasus, believed to be today the village of Charikar, near Bagram, to guard the junction of the three roads from three mountain passes. A Persian was, as usual, given the satrapy, and also as usual, a Macedonian was given command of the garrison left here. There are today, and probably were then also, three principal passes leading over the range (and a number of small ones) and down to the plains of Bactria. The northeastern road runs up the Panjshir River valley, over Kawak Pass (at 13,200 feet altitude), and down to Anderab. The west road runs up the Kushan or Kaoshan Valley, over Kaoshan Pass (at 14,300 feet), and on to Ghori. The third or southwest road, the best and easiest and lowest, runs up the Ghorband Valley and over the Hajiyak or Irak Pass, and on to Bamian. Bessus seems to have expected Alexander to follow the latter route, and arranged to dispute the way. Hence he chose instead to take the Kawak Pass route, to get into the plains of the Oxus before Bessus could withdraw his army from the Hajiyak Pass, and take measures for defending the country in another plan.

During the stay here Alexander seems to have reorganized his army to a very considerable extent. It was no longer the army which had marched so blithely out of Macedonia, to conquer the Great King's dominions, five epoch-making years before. Their casualties from battle deaths had been heavy, their wounded far greater; still larger numbers had succumbed to disease and hardship. Many of their most popular commanders were dead, or in garrison or other detached service. Replacements from home outnumbered the originals, and Greeks now outnumbered these. Many foreigners had been brigaded with the Hellenes. So greatly had the army changed that it was now hardly correct to refer to them as Macedonian any longer.

The king must have known, for we see time and time again that he had an excellent intelligence system operating, that the type of warfare he would soon find in store would require greater mobility and by much smaller forces than he had formerly employed. The enemy next to be subdued were horsemen, accustomed to operating in relatively small units. Large-scale opposition and pitched battles were a thing of the past. He now needed light, fast-moving units to pursue and combat similar enemy units. The massed phalanx of the heavy hoplites were no longer of any use to him.

He had already divided the hetairoi into two hipparchies, or regiments; now each squadron was divided into two companies and each hipparchy was divided into eight companies, thus creating cavalry organizations of superior mobility, which, under the conditions inherent in the type of guerilla warfare

Alexander anticipated was coming, would be easier to handle and more useful than the former heavy assault unit. However, from now on we hear no more of them as the distinctive hetairoi, only as auxiliary cavalry. In fact, from now on it is impossible to differentiate, save in occasional instances, between any of the familiar units we have been able to trace heretofore. Their units, and even commanders, change without our knowledge. The hetairoi, now the auxiliary, were, in fact, so greatly changed and enlarged by additions that we find, in the Indian campaign, mention of five regimental commanders or hipparchs, Demetrius, Clitus (*not* Alexander's boyhood friend), Hephaestion, Perdiccas, and Coenus, the latter two removed from command of their taxeis of hoplites, and Coenus in command of the mounted bodyguard agema. The mercenary Greek cavalry were also enlarged into a regiment by the addition of Persians. Many other changes were made from time to time; we note them frequently but our data are so meager as to make hopeless any attempt to record them with any degree of exactness. At some time or other, either before or after this, we find that Alexander had ordered thirty thousand young and selected Persians to be put under training to fight Macedonian fashion, but the circumstances are left untold, though the inference is made that they were to be retained as much for hostages as fighting men. Nor are the circumstances told of the formation of other types of arms we suddenly find in use, such as the already mentioned mounted archers (hippotoxatai) and the mounted javelin men (hippokontistai). Other and similar changes will be noted in the future, but for lack of data, left uncommented upon.

With the beginning of spring, 329 B.C., the army marched, much earlier than was wise. They moved up the Panjshir River valley to the snow line, twenty miles below the pass on the south side, and started upward. The long column entered the snow, and struggled on through the drifts, piled higher and ever higher across their path. Many of the soldiers froze to death; many others went snow-blind from the unbearable glare of the sun on the snow, lost their way and perished. The losses in horses were also very heavy. The long heavy baggage and siege trains, laden with supplies, weapons, women, children, loot, and all the impedimenta an army acquires in its travels, had to be hauled up and through the pass by sheer brute strength of soldiers, slaves, and captives laboring side by side. On the north side of the pass the snow line was forty miles below. Sixty miles of snow, with sub-zero weather at night, and it took fifteen days to pass! The numbers of men who died in battle were numbered (such as they are) for us. The numbers of men who died in passages such as this we are but aware of, but not told. At last they struggled out of the snow and down into the lower foothills to find only a burned and desolate land, for Bessus had fled ahead of them, laying waste everything that might be of use to the invader. Two days later the gaunt and famished army reached Drapsaca, probably modern Kunduz. Bessus was still ahead. They followed him westward to Aornus, identifiable with either Kulm or near-by Tashkurgan. Bessus abandoned the city-fortress and fled again, with an army of seven thousand Bactrians, Sogdians, and a few of his Dahae allies. He crossed the Oxus River, burned all the boats for a long distance in each direction, and turned toward one of the Sogdian hill fort-cities for refuge. Immediately his Bactrians, realizing he had no intention of fighting for their native homeland, and unable to see the logic of fighting for the homeland of someone else, began to fall away from him, deserting and returning to their own homes. In Sogdia Bessus was joined by two powerful chieftains of that satrapy, Spitamenes and Oxyartes, who provided him with all possible assistance and reinforcements.

Alexander moved from Aornus to the capital city of Bactria (Balkh, the ancient 'Mother of Cities,' dating back to the time when the Turanian races who then peopled the land supplied the beginning of the Acadian civilization to Mesopotamia). This city, deserted by its defenders, surrendered without resistance. He placed a garrison in the citadel of Aornus, and when the area had been pacified, appointed Artabazus, the Persian, to govern it. He then led the army to the Oxus River, passing through what was, if large numbers of ruined town mounds and the vast remains of an intricate irrigation system are to be believed, a densely populated and prosperous region. Now this area is a vast dead desert, the land surface raised by tectonic action above the level where water can be led off from the river. The Oxus was reached at modern Khilif, then a city founded and built by Ionian exiles known as the Branchidae of whom Strabo tells us:[1] ' . . . Alexander destroyed also the city of the Branchidae [2] whom Xerxes [over eightscore years before] had settled here — people who had voluntarily accompanied him from their homeland and [for fear of Greek reprisals] because they had betrayed to him the riches and treasures of the god at Didyme [near Miletus]. Alexander destroyed the city because he abominated the sacrilege and betrayal.' It is a matter of record that Xerxes, with an army of several hundred thousand men at his back, raided the little community, despoiled the oracle, and carried the inhabitants away to settle them on the Oxus in an inhospitable land. It would have been stupidly suicidal for them to have attempted resistance to the horde of Persian raiders. Yet we find Alexander, generations later, pitilessly massacring their descendants for a crime, if it was a crime, of which, in that day when lives were short, their fathers' fathers could have known only at second hand.

Alexander, probably on information obtained locally, realized that the campaign in the Sogdian mountains and deserts would be especially difficult and laborious, a task for only the physically fit. He therefore weeded out the army again, dismissing the old and disabled or failing veterans, with the usual bonus, and sent them home. News also arrived that Barzanes had been sent by Bessus back to Parthia to raise disaffection there and that Arsames, his last appointee to the satrapy of Aria, had been

---

[1] Strabo, *Geography*, II, 11, 4–5.

[2] Holdich, in *The Gates of India*, says the name still survives as 'Barang' and 'Farang' in the mountains of Badakshan in northern Afghanistan, and is borne by people there who even yet boast of their Greek origin.

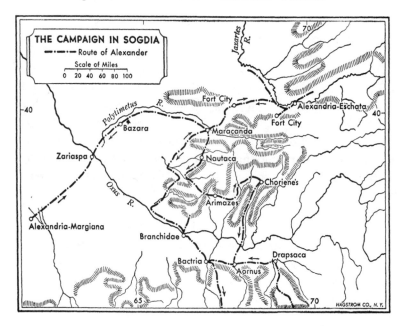

THE CAMPAIGN IN SOGDIA
—·—·— Route of Alexander
Scale of Miles
0 20 40 60 80 100

showing inclinations toward insurrection. Evidently the latter believed the terrible Macedonians would never emerge from the deserts and mountains of Afghanistan, and wanted to get back upon the side he believed would be uppermost. Strict injunctions were dispatched to Phrataphernes to apprehend Barzanes, and Stasanor, one of the king's companions, was sent to take charge of Aria, and arrest Arsames. These details and preparations for crossing the Oxus went ahead at the same time. The Oxus is here normally a half-mile wide, but now in the late spring was flowing bank-full with water from the melting snows of the far Pamirs around the headwaters of the river. As all boats had been destroyed, recourse was made to tent skins stuffed with straw to serve as floats; with these to aid the army, it was ferried over the river in another five days.

North of the Oxus, the satrapy of Sogdia was perfectly adapted to defense against an invader. The capital, Maracanda (Samarkand), was protected from invasion from the south by a high and rough mountain barrier and wide deserts, difficult of access and easy to defend. The people of the country were fiercely independent, brave and natural fighters, and had now gathered a very considerable army. The passes through the mountains were numerous and well adapted to passage through which mobile raiders could easily make incursions upon Alexander's rear. His first move was to send out a strong body of foragers for supplies. They quickly met the enemy in the foothills of the near-by mountain knot (probably the Kuh-i-Stan). A short sharp battle ensued, and the Macedonians retired with heavy losses. Alexander took to the field and contacted the enemy, who retired to a high hill. In the assault that followed, the attackers were victorious and the enemy fled. During the action Alexander was struck in the leg by an arrow which split the fibula, forcing him for a considerable time to what was, for him, the almost invalidism of chariot travel. Another forced march was begun, the army striking straight for the place where, according to information, Bessus was encamped. The latter had, by this time, lost the confidence and regard of the army by his constant retreats, and his officers and allies were in revolt. They secretly sent messengers who met Alexander on the way, with the proposal that they would deliver Bessus into his hands if he would send a suitably strong detachment to take charge of the prisoner. The most powerful officers in the Sogdian army were now Spitamenes, Oxyartes, Dataphernes, and Catanes, and it was they from whom the proposal emanated. Alexander instantly accepted the proposal, and detached Ptolemy, son of Lagus, with a command of mixed arms, six thousand strong, and dispatched him to take charge of the rebel, while Alexander followed more slowly. Ptolemy made, we are told, ten days' march in the space of four days, and arrived at the enemy camp to find it had been deserted the day before. The Sogdians must have been doubtful of the treatment they might expect at the hands of the Greeks, for they had fled ahead of them. The officers had, however, kept their promise, for they fettered Bessus in a near-by village, where Ptolemy found him.

The unfortunate prince, whose only crime, even including the murder of the pusillanimous Darius, viewed in the light of a national emergency, was his resistance to a foreign invader, was brought to a near-by road, and there, stripped naked, with a heavy wooden yoke and a halter about his neck, he was forced to stand on display as the army marched past. As Alexander rode up, he stopped his chariot, and asked Bessus why he had betrayed, made prisoner, and finally murdered Darius, who was both his king and his cousin. Bessus replied what was at least partially true: that he had not acted alone, but in conjunction with others, and that it was the general opinion of the clique that the action would be favorably received by Alexander. The conqueror then ordered the prisoner scourged and sent to Zariaspa (Charjui?), where, in a court of his peers (they were under the thumb of Alexander and could hardly do otherwise), he was condemned to a regicide's death. They cut off his nose and ears, and long afterward sent him to Ecbatana, where he was cruelly executed by crucifixion, his body being left unburied. The treatment meted out to Bessus has shocked even the panegyrists of Alexander, but many excuse the brutality on the grounds that the prisoner was tried and condemned by a Persian court according to Persian custom and usage, and the sentence was carried out by other Persians. The obvious answer seems not to have occurred to them: regardless of who composed the court, they acted as agents of the Macedonian king, and the conclusion is inescapable that, even if he did not specifically order it, he knew of and condoned the action. It may, of course, have been a measure of self-protection, a horrible example of the punishment a regicide might expect, for Alexander very clearly recalled that he occupied two thrones, both of which had been vacated to him through king murders. And it was always possible that he too might be singled out for a like fate. Howbeit, modern commentators are not the first to criticize Alexander for many of his actions, or the actions of his subordinates under his approval, active or implied, or instigation. Seneca, Lucan, and others condemn him unreservedly, and even our careful and complacent Arrian expresses his opinion of the affair in the following:

> This extreme severity to the person of Bessus, I deem in no way praiseworthy, and surely the mutilation of his nose and ears was an action not less than barbarous; though I cannot but think that Alexander was led into this by emulation of Median and Persian pomp and ostentation, as also by the cruel customs of the kings of these countries over those in their power. Neither was it in any way commendable in him to lay aside his Macedonian style of dress (seeing he was sprung from the race of Heraclidae) and assume that of his conquered races. And I cannot but wonder that he was not abashed, when he exchanged the decent covering of his head which he had worn in all his conquests, for the Persian turban, and weakly emulated, in habit, those whom he had over-come in the field.

The elimination of Bessus from his army by no means meant the end of Sogdian resistance. Spitamenes presently took the field as defender of his country, and proved himself a far more able and dangerous opponent. After destroying the whole of the center of Persian power in a huge and densely populated country, the setback that Alexander's meteoric career was now to receive was startling by contrast. This small corner of the Persian Empire, a segment barely three hundred and fifty miles square, was to test Alexander's generalship and the fighting qualities of his army for the next two years before it was com-pletely subdued and the freedom-loving inhabitants beaten into submission.

After the capture of Bessus, Alexander remained for some time in the rich plains along the Oxus, partly to replenish his sup-plies, but more to replace the heavy loss in horses sustained in the passage over the Hindu Kush. He then marched to Mara-canda on the Polytimetus (Zarafshan) River. Maracanda was quiet. He crossed the river, and marched on through the moun-tain pass to a city called the City of Cyrus, or Cyropolis. Al-though conflicting to some extent with the story of this area, it has been agreed that Cyropolis was, probably, on the site of

modern Khojend; though this identification is not wholly satisfactory, in some ways it is more logical than any other selection, although there are certain reasons why modern Jizak
might reasonably lay claim to the ancient title. This city, on
the Jaxartes (Syr, Darya) River, was at last the limit of the
former empire of Darius. Beyond the river lay the high mountains and boundless steppes of the nomad hordes of Asia, the
wandering and rootless peoples of Tartary, then a race of pure
Aryan descent, yet unmixed with the blood of the Mongol
hordes who were to overrun the land and leave their indelible
imprint upon it fifteen centuries later. Many commentators
laboriously build up the hypothesis that Alexander declared a
halt here at long last because he believed that here he had
reached a point a short distance beyond which lay the limits of
the 'inhabited world' (*oikumene*) and the deserts bordering the
earth girdling 'ocean stream.' This rhetorical speciousness is
disproved by the simple statement that even in that early day,
Cyropolis was a trade center, through which passed long caravans carrying the trade of eastern and western Asia, from Asia
Minor to far China, many months' journey distant. It is impossible to believe that now Alexander was wholly unfamiliar with
the silks, jades, and bronzes of China, and that his insatiable
curiosity did not force him to make searching inquiries into the
source of these beautiful objects and textiles, as well as the
destinations and beginnings of the long caravans. His reasons
for declaring a halt to further conquests in that direction were
the reasons which would stop any conqueror with his mental
attributes and acuity; namely, the aquisition would not be
worth the trouble; there was nothing in the nomad steppe
worth taking, while behind him lay the untouched cities and
riches of fabled India. Cyrus had halted the expansion of his
empire here for the same reasons, as well as the fact that the
combination of river, steppe, and mountains constituted a
natural and logical boundary. The location was an excellent
one from which to operate, if need be and they became a menace,
against the nomad tribesmen; it would also place control of the

important and lucrative caravan trade within his power. As a base for possible military operations, commercial control of the region, upon the site of the older settlement, Alexander founded a new guard-town, simply renaming Cyropolis to erase the name and city of the Persian conqueror to replace both with his own. While he was here, ambassadors arrived from the 'Scythians' of widely separated areas. Alexander accepted their overtures of friendship, and sent with them on their return home a group of his own companions with each embassy, ostensibly to carry friendly greetings to their rulers, but with specific instructions to act as spies. Upon their return, these must have confirmed Alexander's already formed opinion of the tribes. For they reported that the people were too poor and possessed too high ideals of justice to be an enemy worthy of consideration. We hear no more of this episode.

The riverine lands were well populated, and rich in the products of the country. At least seven additional small towns flourished in the vicinity. They must have been small, for the inhabitants were but farmers, and they must have been a people of peaceful disposition, for Arrian tells us the town walls were of mud only. Alexander placed small garrisons in each of them, partly as outguards for the newly founded Alexandria-Eschata or Alexandria-Ultima as it is sometimes referred to, partly because of his inherent distrust of the tribesmen across the river. The inhabitants of the lands south of the river were still unamalgamated into the body politic of the Persian Empire, and were still living under the primitive patriarchal rule as families, clans, and tribes. The Persians had wisely left them alone in their primitive organizations, acknowledging no central government and inimical to the idea of a master. Alexander planned a different form of government for them, and to that end notified the scattered unit-chieftains to meet him at a specified time in Zariaspa for a council. The people mistrusted the summons and the man who issued it. The word passed swiftly over the steppe that it was his intention to get the chiefs together in a single place under his own aegis, assassinate them all, and thus at one blow deprive the people of their leaders and reduce them to servitude. The rumor flashed through the land, carried by the steppe wind, and behind it swept the flame of revolt. In the guard towns the people rose *en masse* and destroyed their garrisons. Simultaneously, uprisings took place in Maracanda and the rest of Sogdia and Bactria, seemingly spontaneous, but obviously the result of careful preparation and community of thought and intent. Spitamenes and his friends probably thought, when they surrendered Bessus, that Alexander, satisfied at having eliminated the last of the murderers of Darius, would turn back and leave them to rule the outlying satrapies in their own right. Instead, the Macedonians had pressed on to the outposts of the empire, and were now engaged in consolidating it into their other conquests. It is possible that they, in accordance with the usages of the times and their own arrogance, were oppressive upon the people and earned their hatred by acts as well as the fact that they were foreign outlanders. This, combined with the equally intolerant attitude of the Sogdians, made friction and clashes unavoidable. Spitamenes was an intelligent leader, and undoubtedly aware of all factors. Alexander was far from his nearest base, the lines of communication stretching almost unprotected over hundreds of miles of deserts and mountains. His position was precarious, to an extent that it causes wonder he permitted himself to get into it. This was the Sogdian leader's opportunity; he saw it immediately, and swung into action.

So did Alexander. The nearest offenders could be reached easily and quickly. Like a whirlwind out of the desert, the Greek army struck at the little river towns. In two days five were captured by assault and most of the inhabitants butchered with cold-blooded efficiency, only the younger women and children being spared and given to the soldiers. The largest city (the strategically located Jizak?) was surrounded by a stone wall. Siege engines were constructed and missile-throwing artillery brought up. Then it was discovered that a small river, now dry, ran through the town. After dark, a number of men entered by this means and opened the gates. The army swarmed in, and again massacred the inhabitants. The 'Scythians' fought desperately. Alexander was struck down by the blow of a stone upon the head and neck, and Craterus was severely wounded. That same evening the Greeks moved out, and in the morning they assaulted and captured the last of the towns, after surrounding it with cavalry to prevent any survivors from escaping the massacre which followed.

While this was going on in Sogdia, the unrest and resentment of the invaders spread even across the Jaxartes, and an army of 'Scythians' gathered on the north bank opposite Alexandria-Eschata. They had heard of the revolt, and, imagining that Alexander would immediately turn back to quell or escape it, were prepared to cross the river to loot and harass the rear of the retreating invaders. Alexander marched back to the river and encamped opposite them. Almost immediately a messenger galloped in with ill news from the south. Spitamenes had arrived with a strong force and was besieging Maracanda. Alexander now realized, if he had not before, that the uprising was the work of Spitamenes and the noted chiefs who had associated themselves with him to recover their lost freedom. It was, however, to develop into that most deadly type of conflict, a real 'people's war' of the whole population. The murderous brutality of the treatment of the river towns infuriated the whole country. Whether or not the savagery of the destruction of these places was necessary is beyond discussing. But it does show a very different attitude on the part of Alexander from that which he displayed in the West, where his forgiveness and forbearance were outstanding in a day when mercy was quite unusual. From now on we unfortunately find this pitiless ferocity the rule rather than the exception.

Matters had taken a very serious turn, indeed, revolt in full strength behind him and an army of wild horsemen under his eyes only awaiting his departure, or any movement to the rear, to start an invasion. He detached a force of eight hundred auxiliary cavalry, in two squadrons under Caranus and Andromachus, fifteen hundred mercenary footmen under Menedamus, a guard of sixty picked cavalry, and placed the whole under direction of Pharnuces, a Lycian linguist and diplomat, and sent them to the relief of Maracanda. These he considered would be adequate to create a diversion sufficient to keep the enemy busy until he could arrive with the rest of the army. He then turned his attention toward finishing the fortifications of the new city, and pressed the work so hard that the construction of the walls was completed in twenty days. In it were settled some of the Macedonians who had become disabled or were too failing to be very useful in the field, and a number of unwilling Greek mercenaries. Also such of the natives of the country as desired were invited to make their homes within the protecting walls. Then, to christen the city and assure the protection of the gods upon it, he made the usual sacrifices and held the most brilliant games and festival that were possible under the circumstances.

During the construction of the walls, the 'Scythians' on the other side of the river rapidly made a nuisance of themselves. They were getting exasperated and restless at the inactivity forced upon them by Alexander's obstinacy in remaining to face them, while by all the rules of war he should have vanished from the area long ago. They assembled in groups, shouted taunts of cowardice upon the Hellenes, made insulting gestures, invited them across to test their mettle, and from time to time launched a desultory long-range high-trajectory arrow fire, which, though not deadly, nevertheless caused a few casualties. Presently this grew to be unbearable. Alexander moved his artillery to the riverbank, and opened a hail of arrows and stones, inflicting serious casualties upon the tribesmen. When one of their war chiefs was slain by an arrow which passed through his shield and breastplate, they withdrew from the riverbank and out of range of the projectiles. Alexander realized the necessity of making a swift punitive raid across the river, as he had done years before on the Danube, which would force the tribesmen to respect his arms thereafter and prevent them crossing upon a similar foray.

As usual before setting out upon an offensive, Alexander offered sacrifices, and called for a reading of the omens. Aristander, the soothsayer, pronounced them unfavorable. Alexander waited a day or so, then, the continued scoffing of the 'Scythians' becoming unbearable, made new sacrifices. Again Aristander pronounced the forecast unfavorable. The king impatiently answered that he proposed to move over the river and attack anyway; that he himself would rather run the most extreme hazard than continue to bear their insults and be a laughing-stock of a mob of barbarians. There were no boats to be had, so floats that had been previously prepared were brought to the river, and, under protection of a barrage of stones and arrows from the artillery, the army was ferried over. The first attack was launched by a squadron of the auxiliary cavalry and four syntagmata of the phalanx; these struck at the enemy's right wing. They were promptly surrounded by the tribesmen, who started cutting them down with arrow fire. A second attack, of the Agrianians, running alongside holding onto the stirrups of additional cavalry, was sent to their assistance, while Alexander, with the rest of the cavalry and the footmen, struck at the enemy's left flank. The 'Scythians' were decisively defeated with heavy losses, but inflicted upon the Hellenes a loss of one hundred and sixty dead and nearly one thousand wounded. The great heat prevented pursuit, and Alexander, after drinking of water that proved contaminated, was seized by a severe dysentery, which for a day or two nearly proved fatal.

The victory was, for Alexander, to produce splendid results. The king of the 'Scythians' sent him an embassy, with the explanation and apology that the men involved were not his subjects, but marauding freebooters, and placing himself at Alexander's services. The latter had neither the time nor the inclination to engage in bootless raids across the steppe beyond the Jaxartes, for Spitamenes was now a pressing and very serious danger in the center of the country. He therefore professed to believe the protestations of the ambassadors, deeming it wiser to do so for the sake of peace along the frontier. The 'Scythians,' if so disposed, could make his even now precarious tenure completely untenable. Alexander was never in so desperate a position before, and, with one possible exception, never permitted himself to get into such a compromising situation again.

While these events were taking shape along the frontier of the Jaxartes, matters elsewhere had progressed far less favorably. The Hellenes besieged in the citadel at Maracanda made one strong sortie upon the besieging forces of Spitamenes, and put them to flight with no difficulty. They probably hoped to draw the Greeks away from the city and into the open where the Greek discipline and style of fighting would be a disadvantage to them. The Greeks probably realized something untoward was planned for them, for they gave up the pursuit and returned to the citadel. The Asiatics halted their flight, promptly returned and resumed the siege. Shortly, Spitamenes was informed of the impending arrival of the relief forces Alexander had dispatched against him. He lifted the siege and retired toward what was now the capital city of the Sogdians, believed to be somewhere in the vicinity of, if not actually, modern Bokhara. Curtius, at one point in his wholly incoherent account of the campaign, refers to a river city of the Sogdians, which he transcribes as Bazara, if that can be taken at its phonetic value. No other historian mentions the place.

The relief party reached Maracanda to find their quarry gone. Anxious to distinguish themselves, they started in pursuit. A few days later they fell in with what must have been a band of migrating tribesmen peacefully moving from one grazing ground to another, a condition prevailing even today among these nomadic stock-raisers. Without stopping to make inquiries as to the exact status of the natives, but accepting as enemies everyone not a Greek, the Hellenes fell upon the nomads, killed many, and drove the rest into the steppe. The peaceful tribesmen, infuriated at the unjustified attack, sent six hundred mounted men to Spitamenes' assistance. The Hellenes pressed on along the river.

Spitamenes, by virtue of a constant stream of intelligence from his scouts, surmised that the Hellenes were illy led. He halted, in a plain between the desert and the river, to await the arrival of his pursuers. He knew the superior discipline and training of the Greeks rendered them more than a match for his own forces in pitched battle, and resolved to use other tactics against them. The Greeks came up, and formed into syntagmata. Pharnuces opened the action with a cavalry attack, led by himself. The light tribesmen retired before it, until his horses wearied. He halted, suddenly realizing something was very wrong, indeed. He began to fall back upon the main body. The tribesmen halted their flight, strung their bows — and the massacre began. They dashed up behind and on both sides of the compact Greek squadron. From all directions arrows drove in upon them, and men and horses began to fall. Detached ilae were ordered to make short attacks. They accomplished nothing. They could not reach the circling and swooping tribesmen who simply fled ahead of them until the pursuit stopped, then encircled them to prevent their return, resuming their deadly shooting. The decimated squadron finally reached the main body, only to find the same murderous drama being enacted there. Andromachus' cavalry had received the same treatment in an attempted charge, and had retired under fire also. The phalanx, covering with their long shields, were not suffering much, but were helpless, unable to hit back. The embattled expeditionary force drew up into a solid square and marched toward the river where they could see a grove of trees which would afford a desperately needed partial shelter. On the way, Pharnuces, who was much more of a diplomat than a general, tried to resign command in favor of one of the other leaders. None would accept it. They realized that the damage was done, and only fortune itself could extricate them. Yet, if any escaped, the onus of the disaster was certain to fall upon him. They marched on, losing men at every step, their leader demoralized, the other officers bitterly inimical to him. Caranus, leader of part of the cavalry, reached the wide, shallow, island-studded river first, and, imagining he could do better on the other side, led on. The infantry, now without any leader at all, for Menedamus seems to have been killed, followed, breaking their shield roof as they plunged down the bank. The enemy, seeing their broken disorder, spurred up and flanked them, the deadly hail of arrows flying thicker than ever. Caranus, though under heavy fire himself, courageously turned back to assist the broken mob, and the enemy promptly occupied the opposite shore. A small number, about three hundred of the phalanx, were rallied by some unnamed hero, turned back under a tortoise of shields, and grimly made their way back to the woods. The rest of the force, now attacked from all sides, resorted to an island in the river. The enemy surrounded it, and those who were engaged in the fruitless task of bouncing arrows off the escaping tortoise, left it and turned to the more exciting fighting on the river. These last were beaten down to a very small number, who were captured, but later slain. Three hundred of the footmen and sixty mounted men only escaped. Spitamenes returned swiftly to Maracanda and resumed the siege of the citadel.

When the news of the disaster reached Alexander, he had just finished setting things to rights in the Jaxartes area. Chagrined at the defeat of his column, and realizing the need of instant and decisive action to offset its propaganda value to the cause of Spitamenes, he called together the light footmen and half of the auxiliary cavalry. Bidding Craterus follow with the rest of the army, he moved post-haste to the south, traveling with such speed that he reached Maracanda, one hundred and seventy-three miles away, on the morning of the fourth day. Spitamenes fled into the desert at his approach, with Alexander in hot pursuit. The enemy crossed the river and disappeared into the steppe, where he could not be pursued. Reaching the scene of the river battle, Alexander gave burial to the bodies of his annihilated force. Then he laid waste the country, and mercilessly slaughtered the entire population of the farms, villages, and towns. As Arrian says, 'And thus he overran and depopulated the whole country through which the Polytimetus passes, for all beyond the place where the river loses itself in the sand is desert,' proving beyond question that the section referred to is the neighborhood of Bokhara. Other accounts say that more than one hundred thousand people were slain in this merciless devastation. Later, Hephaestion was sent out to bring in people by force to rehabilitate the area. It is believed that Alexander must have returned to Maracanda, for we read that he left the citadel there in command of Peucolaus with three thousand men.

The next few weeks were busy indeed for Alexander. He went south to Zariaspa, where he spent some time putting his soldiers into quarters for the winter of 329–328. The Bactrians, after the terrible punishment of the Sogdians, took heed to the lesson and remained quiet. The men were distributed among the several towns along the river, partly because here subsistence was easily come by, partly to garrison the long frontier. Phrataphernes reported in to his king with several captives, including the rebellious Barzanes, all of whom had been with Bessus at the death of Darius. Stasanor, who had replaced Arsames as satrap of Aria, brought the latter in for disposal. We have no record as to the disposal of the cases of any of them. Thither came also a very considerable body of newly recruited Greek mercenaries, convoyed by several officers, Asander, Nearchus, and Asclepidorus, all of whom had been recalled from posts in the West to more active service. Epocillus, Ptolemy, the captain of the Thracian cavalry, and Melamnidas, having completed their commission of escorting home the discharged Thessalians and others from Ecbatana, reported back for duty.

The old king of the western 'Scythians' died, and his successor sent a deputation to Alexander asking a continuation of the treaty of friendship, proposing marriage alliances with several of the Macedonian officers. Alexander sent them home again with assurances of continued amity. Then Pharaimenes, king of the Chorasmians, from southern Khiva (around latitude 40 north), arrived with fifteen hundred horsemen. He had a standing feud with his 'Scythian' neighbors to the west, and proposed to Alexander that they two join forces and subdue the land as far as the Euxine Sea. He, upon being questioned, was the first to tell Alexander that the Hyrcanian Lake was not, as the Greeks supposed, a gulf of the world-girdling ocean stream, but an inland sea with a vast expanse of inhabited land north of it. Alexander assured the bellicose tribesman that his mind was now occupied with plans for the conquest of India, but that after that was attended to, he would return to Greece and thence, with the help of the fleet, attack the 'Scythians' in the lands north of the Euxine Sea. Pharaimanes assured him that whenever he came, the promise of alliance and assistance would be remembered and fulfilled.

Alexander returned to Maracanda, apparently remaining there during the worst of the bitter winter weather typical of this region. And here, during the long periods of inaction forced by the fierce cold, the Macedonian habit of heavy drinking, to which Alexander was addicted in his leisure, was to produce shocking results. The murder of his boyhood friend Clitus and the germination of another assassination plot are directly attributable to it. Alexander's intense vanity and abounding egotism, never far under the surface, and now inflamed to the highest pitch by his incredible successes, measureless power, and the fawning sycophancy to which he was continually subjected, bore terrible fruit this winter. It is also proof incontrovertible of the degeneration of the conqueror, and of the feeling of the Macedonians that they were now in the hands of a power-mad leader whose insatiable demands took cognizance of nothing beyond the furthering of his own aims and ambitions. There can be no doubt that the canker of discontent and distrust of their leader had permeated most, if not all, of the remaining Macedonians, and that they looked upon the actions of their king with intense disapproval. The occasion and tale of the outburst appears, after careful evaluation of the several accounts, to have been according to the following account.

Upon the day generally dedicated to the Macedonian feast of Bacchus, Alexander, who officiated at the sacrifice, offered it instead to Castor and Pollux. At the feast that followed that evening, the heady wine of Turkestan was freely imbibed, and the conversations became directed toward Greek mythology, one phase of which was the alleged paternity of Zeus to the immortal twins. Some puling sycophant arose, and brought the question to earth by a long panegyric comparing Alexander to the twin demigods, to their detriment, commenting upon the fact that too many are prone to cast their eyes backward, seeing nothing good or great save those of ancient days, and ignoring that which occurs under their own eyes. Other guests (here Arrian inserts the parenthesized remark, 'such sycophants have always been destructive to the affairs of princes, and ever will') affirmed Alexander's deeds to have surpassed those of Castor and Pollux, and even those of Heracles. Clitus, and a few of the older Macedonians, had long known Alexander's weak susceptibility to flattery, and grew angry at his complacent vanity under it. Drunk enough at last to speak his mind truthfully, Clitus leaped to his feet, declaring forcefully that he could no longer tolerate the indignity of the remarks impugning the ancient gods, nor longer bear the untruthful flatteries designed only to please Alexander's ear. His actions were in nothing godlike, declared Clitus, nor was there anything surprising in them, seeing that his victories and acquisitions were bought for him by the labors and blood of the Macedonians of the army raised and trained by his father Philip. Alexander was furious at the public pricking of his bubble of self-esteem, an action on Clitus' part, considering the circumstances, singularly imprudent. Even Arrian says, regarding the statements of Clitus, though not questioning their truth, ' ... indeed, however just the reflections might be, I can by no means think they were seasonable at a time of such general drunkenness, but that silence had been much better.'

Someone with good sense managed to inject a new theme into the brawl, but soon conversation turned toward comparisons between Philip and Alexander, to the disparagement of the former by the new school of thought, of the latter by the old school. Presently some would-be comic started reciting stinging verses about several of the officers who had suffered defeats at the hands of the Sogdians. Clitus, still angry, wrathfully protested against ridiculing the veterans as cowards, when Alexander, now outwardly calm, but inwardly in a cold fury, remarked, 'Clitus seems to be pleading his own cause.' This baseless accusation further outraged the drunken captain. He leaned over the table, thrusting his right arm at the king, shouting in concentrated fury: 'You should be the last to name me coward — you who were fleeing the sword of Spithradates at Granicus when this right hand of mine saved your life. The valor and blood of Macedonians, and no other, raised you to the pinnacle you now occupy.'

Alexander seized the first thing his hand lighted upon, an apple, and hurled it straight at Clitus' face, and leaped to his feet reaching for his dagger. It had already been deftly removed by a prudent bodyguard. He sprang at Clitus, but was seized and restrained by his friends. He broke loose, shouting aloud in the Macedonian idiom — indication, in Alexander, of a return to stark savagery — for the trumpeter to summon the bodyguard, and struck the man with his fist when he hesitated. He shouted louder, crying that he was reduced to the same condition as Darius, when the latter was carried about a prisoner, with only his empty title. Clitus' friends hastily dragged him from the room, and Ptolemy led the drunken officer out of the citadel and beyond the moat, hoping the cold night air would sober him. But Clitus' rage was beyond control. He rushed back to the hall, entering by another door, raising and standing under the portière. Then in a loud challenging voice he began recklessly chanting the immortal Euripides' verses of rebellious discontent from *Andromache*:

> 'Alas, in Greece how ill things ordered are!
> When trophies rise for victories in war,
> Men count the praise not theirs who did the deed,
> But give alone to him who led the meed.'

Clitus stepped back and dropped the curtain.

Alexander instantly grasped the insulting implication. He

snatched a pike from the hands of a guard and hurled it straight at the still-moving curtain, and behind it Clitus went down, mortally wounded. Instant as was the king's rage, his repentance was equally fast. In a burst of tears he threw himself upon the dead body of his friend until friends drew him off and led him to his chamber. Here he remained three days, taking neither food nor water, in an excess of remorse — a remorse, however, which by no means excuses the deed. It is necessary to report, unfortunately, that the man who eventually talked him into his normal self again was one of whom we have the worst report as a flatterer. It is also on record that he continued to elevate and harbor other flatterers, some of whom bear scurvy reputations.

Early in the spring Alexander marched back to Zariaspa, with the intention of using the city as a base from which to erect a series of frontier forts against the horsemen of the steppes and desert. Soon afterward a series of occurrences arose testifying to the discontent rife among his forces. Also here too were the first definite manifestations of Alexander's belief in the prophecy of the Oracle of Ammon, and his intention to be worshiped as a god. To show the extent of his moral degradation it is permissible to quote direct from Arrian: [1]

> Callisthenes, the historian, pupil and nephew of Aristotle, one of disposition rough and inflexible, entirely disapproved of these methods of proceeding, for which he is worthy due praise; but what he wrote of this affair (if he really wrote it) is no great argument for his humility, viz., that Alexander and his exploits were in no way comparable to him and his writings; that he did not accompany him for any glory he himself might acquire, but that he was to build Alexander's glory sheerly upon the king's own virtues and actions. Some also say that when he [Callisthenes] was asked whom he deemed the mortal most honored by the Athenians; he answered, Harmodius and Aristogon, because they had slain one of the tyrants of their state, and put an end to tyranny. He was again asked: If anyone was now to put a tyrant to death,

[1] Arrian, IV, 10-11.

in which of the states of Hellas would he find protection? He replied that if in no other, surely he would in Athens. As to the adoration, it was agreed between him and the sophists (of whom Anaxarchus was chief) and those of the Persians and Medians of the highest rank, that as they were drinking, they should purposely enter into discourse, to be begun by Anaxarchus, asserting that Alexander was more worthy to be esteemed a god than either Bacchus or Heracles, for Bacchus was but a Theban, a people incomparable in any respect to the Macedonians; as for Heracles, he was indeed a Hellene, but his chief glory was, that Alexander was descended from him, and therefore the Macedonians might, with more reason and justice, attribute divine honors to their king than either the Thebans to Bacchus, or the Hellenes to Heracles. And there could be no doubt but that he would be worshiped as a god by his people after his death; it would be better to pay him the same adoration in his lifetime, for after his death no honors bestowed upon him by mortals could reach him.

These and many other things to the same purpose were said by Anaxarchus, and when he had finished, those who were of his party began to applaud the oration, and many declared themselves ready to begin their adoration immediately. The Macedonians, who disliked Anaxarchus' speech, held their peace, but Callisthenes, breaking the general silence, replied to Anaxarchus:

I cannot, Anaxarchus, deem Alexander unworthy of any honor which becomes a mortal man to accept: but divine honors and human honors are widely different, as well in other things as in rearing of temples and erection of statues. To the gods we consecrate temples, offer sacrifices, and pour libations; hymns we sing to the gods, but to men, praises, unaccompanied by adoration. We usually kiss men by way of salutation, but the gods are elevated above us and it is unlawful to touch them. But one sort of honors is the attribute of gods, another to heroes, and the honor paid to heroes is vastly different from divine adoration. It is therefore a matter of the utmost importance for us to avoid confounding these things with one another, and neither by extravagant accumulation of honors to pretend to exalt men above mortality, nor to debase the gods by robbing them of the worship that is their due. Even Alexander himself would become enraged if any private man were to usurp a royal title in an unlawful manner; with how much more justice may the gods become enraged if a mortal dares claim divine honors, or accept them if offered.

Callisthenes courageously continued, at length addressing his speech of warning straight at Alexander. Finally he ceased speaking, and those present remained silent. The Macedonians were pleased, but Alexander was furious. Restraining himself for the moment, he studiously ignored the historian, and spoke to the Macedonians, reminding them of the adoration they *owed* him. There was a profound silence. It had been previously arranged that Alexander should pledge each person present in a cup of wine, the recipient of the pledge was to drain the draft, receive a kiss of friendship and immediately prostrate himself before the king, then arise and back from the presence. Beginning with the oldest Persian present, each in turn performed the degrading act of self-abasement. When Callisthenes' turn came he strode forward. Alexander deliberately turned to Hephaestion and began a conversation. Callisthenes halted and turned on his heel. Leonnatus thrust out a restraining hand, 'Haven't you forgotten something?' he reminded. 'I only leave the poorer for a kiss,' returned the rigid and unbending writer. He brushed the hand aside and went out, imprudent perhaps, but courageous. There can be no doubt that Alexander's refusal of the kiss of friendship was the equivalent of a declaration of his hatred. Callisthenes was a marked man, and there can also be little doubt that this action was the reason for his death a short time later.

A few days later, Callisthenes was charged with complicity in a plot on the king's life. It appears that one of the pages, a boy named Hermolaus, was a student of philosophy, who had been tutored by Callisthenes, whom he greatly admired. On a hunting trip, the lad, being in the way of a charging boar, which Alexander had designed for himself, slew the animal. The king, enraged, ordered the boy publicly scourged and deprived of his horse. Hermolaus, deeply resentful of the disgrace, brooded over the matter and finally concluded that nothing but

Alexander's death could wipe out the injury. He communicated to five of his companion boy pages, and found them strangely amenable to the suggested attempt. Verily Alexander can hardly have been a demigod if all six of the youths hated him to the extent of planning regicide. Unfortunately for the boys, the plot was discovered. They were seized, and each, privately and separately, subjected to torture. Aristobulus and Ptolemy both (they were the main sources of Arrian's history) affirm that Hermolaus confessed he was instigated to the act by Callisthenes; others that the boy publicly disclaimed any instigation, but 'openly confessed that the plot was contrived by himself, for that it was beneath the honor of a free man to bear the injuries he had received from the king, and that he then related all the cruelties committed by Alexander: the unjust murder of Philotas, and the even more inhuman one of his father Parmenio; the rash and barbarous assassination of Clitus; his assuming the odious Persian dress; his edict, not yet rescinded, for having divine honors bestowed upon himself; and also his sloth, drunkenness, and luxury; all of which he could no longer bear, and he was willing at once to set himself and the rest of the Macedonians free from such intolerable slavery.' The pages were immediately stoned to death. Callisthenes was thrown into chains, and, according to Aristobulus, was carried around with the army, but soon died. Ptolemy, however, gives quite a different account, saying the philosopher was first tortured, then crucified. A terrible commentary this, for the occurrences of a single winter. It has been truly said that Alexander's friends were safer in the activity of the field than in idleness with him at the feast; the true test of a tyrant.

In the early spring, Alexander began to prepare for the long-postponed conquest of India, but again the flame of revolt swept the land. The Sogdians rose first against Peucolaus in Maracanda. The iron-handed suppression to which they had been subjected and the senseless slaughter of whole populations had, instead of cowing them, rendered them desperate and murderously vindictive. They had largely wintered in the mountains, and, with the melting of the snows, swarmed down into the garrisoned plains below. It was, however, luckily a popular uprising, without capable leadership under a single command. Spitamenes was still in the northern steppes.

The city of Zariaspa was garrisoned by a few convalescent 'companions,' eighty mercenary cavalry, and a few pages. The taxeis of Meleager, Gorgias, Polysperchon, and Attalus were dispatched, in units of varying sizes, through the whole of Bactria, to keep safe the quiet towns and subdue those in revolt. The rest of the army was divided into five flying columns, with Hephaestion in command of the first, Ptolemy the second, Perdiccas the third, Coenus and Artabazus the fourth, while Alexander himself took the last. The columns all took different routes through the country with instructions to rendezvous at Maracanda. From there Hephaestion was sent out to try to round up sufficient settlers for the depopulated Polytimetus country; Coenus and Artabazus were sent into the steppe on a swift raid because Spitamenes had been reported there. The rest of the forces made a tour of untouched areas and brought them into subjection. According to Curtius, Alexander moved along the Polytimetus, crossed the desert to the Oxus, and thence crossed the second desert to Margus or Margiane (the oasis of Merv), establishing a line of six guard posts en route, and establishing a town called Alexandria-Margiana.[1] It was destroyed by desert raiders a few years later, and still later was rebuilt and reconstituted by Antiochus I.

In the meantime Spitamenes, now prepared to resume the war, moved swiftly back into Bactria, fell upon one of the guard citadels, captured it and exterminated the garrison. Elated at his initial success the Bactrians moved swiftly on to Zariaspa. Probably unaware that the town was almost unguarded, they refrained from attacking it, but raided the river settlements, sacking and destroying the whole area. The little garrison sallied out and, in a swift surprise attack upon a considerable band of looting raiders, found them unprepared, scattered, and

[1] Pliny, *Natural History*, VI, 23. Also reported by Curtius, VII, 10, 15.

loading their trains, and routed them. On their way back to Zariaspa, proceeding in unguarded and careless disorder, they fell in with a body of the enemy, and in the fight that followed were all but annihilated. Craterus (we are not told where he was) arrived shortly, and drove the raiders back into the desert.

Artabazus, now a very old man, found the duties of the turbulent satrapy too great for his failing powers, and solicited Alexander's permission to retire. This was granted, and another Amyntas, the son of Nicolaus, appointed his successor, being given a command of newly formed Bactrian and Sogdian cavalry as a peace-preservation corps. It must have been known, or at least shrewdly suspected, that Spitamenes was planning large-scale raids upon Bactria, for Coenus was sent, with his own and Meleager's taxeis, to garrison the towns of the Oxus Valley. He was also provided a highly mobile force of mounted saris-saphors as an effective foil against the equally mobile raiders. It turned out that Spitamenes had, in reality, planned just such an attack as was being prepared for, and to that end he induced another body of four thousand 'Scythians' to join him. It was not difficult to persuade them, 'for they were extremely poor, having neither cities nor fixed habitations, nor possessing any-thing they were afraid to lose, were easily induced to join their forces to any nation.' Coenus, receiving intelligence of the approach of the enemy, met the raiders and decisively defeated them. Spitamenes fled again, but many of the survivors sur-rendered and made submission to the victors. The other tribes-men fled to a mountain retreat, but, a few days later, hearing that Alexander himself was marching against them, they re-volted against Spitamenes, cut off his head, and sent it as a present to conciliate the Macedonian king.

Winter (328–327) was now approaching, and the troops again went into winter quarters, Alexander spending the cold-weather months at Nautaca (Shahr-i-Sabz?), thus remaining with the flower of his army in a central location in preparation against contingencies. In the last few months the satrapies had begun to seethe with unrest. Autophradates, satrap of the

Mardians and Tapurians, had disobeyed several orders to report to the king, and Phrataphernes was ordered to bring him in in chains. From Drangiana came the report that the people there were meditating insurrection, and Stasanor was sent off to put an end to it. Atropates was sent to replace Oxydates in Media. Stamenes was ordered to Babylon to replace Mazaeus, who had recently died. Sopolis, Menedus, and Epocillus were dispatched back to Macedonia to fetch more reinforcements.

Alexander waited impatiently for the end of winter to eliminate the last strongholds of opposition. The plains regions were now quiet, but the mountains not yet wholly so, though there remained even there but two foci of serious resistance. One of these belonged to Oxyartes, one of the greatest and strongest of the Sogdian chieftains, who had taken refuge with his family and retainers in a hill fort called the Rock of Arimazes (Baisun), which he believed to be impregnable and had victualed for a long siege. Alexander found, after his arrival, that Oxyartes was not far wrong in his estimate of the strength of the place. It was located on top of a high hill, and was exceedingly difficult of access. The king summoned Oxyartes to surrender, and received the defiant answer that first he must get himself winged soldiers, for only such could get at him. Late in the evening the king caused proclamation to be issued to the army, promising twelve talents to the first man who should ascend the rock, with a reward for each of the next eleven in decreasing ratio, the twelfth man to receive one talent.

Three hundred men, skilled mountaineers and brave soldiers, volunteered to make the attempt. During the night they started up the cliff, making their way by means of iron tent pegs driven into the crevices between the frozen rocks, hauling each other up with ropes as they went. So dangerous was the ascent that thirty of the climbers fell and were killed, their bodies falling into snowdrifts and on ledges from whence they could not be recovered. When daylight came, the Sogdians on the cliff below them, imagining they were more numerous and better armed than they really were, were in consternation. Alexander sent forward his herald to proclaim that he had taken their advice literally and had procured winged soldiers for himself, and again summoned them to surrender. This time they agreed to submit. A number of prominent men and their families fell into the conqueror's hands, including Oxyartes himself, and his daughter Roxane, who had the reputation of being the most beautiful woman in all Persia, excepting the wife of Darius. Alexander was amazed and spellbound at the beauty of the girl. He treated her, as he had done all his other women captives, with the greatest of consideration, and soon married her, thus allying himself by one of the strongest of ties with the leaders of the country. Oxyartes became one of his most valuable assistants in the mediation and conciliation of many yet hostile elements of the country. This was met with grim disapproval of the Macedonians, and the historians of the period seem to have concurred with this same attitude. For four years we hear absolutely nothing more of Roxane, and she emerges again into sight only when, in 323, after Alexander's death, we are told she bore him a posthumous son.

But one more fortress and one small army, neither together, remained to be subdued. The fortress was the Rock of Chorienes (Hissar), and the army was being assembled in the valley of the Surkhab River, not far from modern Faizabad. The Rock of Chorienes, Alexander found, was another typical high-walled Afghan hill fort with but one narrow approach, built upon a shoulder of a mountain, and surrounded on all sides by deep ravines. The place, as it stood, was impregnable and unreachable. He resolved to take it, however, and by storm. A siege would require more time than he was willing to devote to the task, for now the conquest of India was compellingly uppermost in his mind. Frontal assault, or any kind of ordinary assault, was wholly out of question. But there was one other way. Fir trees were cut and converted into ladders to use for descent into the ravine. Once down there a careful survey revealed the whole bottom to be of solid rock, so it was planned to make the best of bad circumstances. The artillery was set up on the side of the ravine to sweep the fort's walls with missiles, and archers were posted to prevent the enemy from showing themselves to fight back. The first task was to construct sheds, covered with long poles and dried hides to protect the workers from missiles from above. These were moved into position on the bottom of the ravine, the army was divided into two shifts, and the labor began. A deep causeway of cut stone and earth was built across the ravine from wall to wall, and long piles driven into it. Upon the tops of the piles a floor was laid, and a cribwork of logs upon the floor; when these cribs reached the necessary height, stringers were laid from one crib to another and another floor built. Earth was laid upon this floor and smoothed into hardness, that the army might pass over as on a bridge. Chorienes viewed these proceedings with unalloyed surprise and dismay. He called a parley, and after a long conference with Oxyartes, surrendered. Alexander was so pleased with Chorienes that he required nothing of him save submission, and appointed him governor of the district. He then returned to Bactria to make final arrangements for leaving the desperately won provinces, but sent Craterus with the army against the assembling enemy army. In the battle that followed, the Greeks were victorious, the leading enemy chief, Catanes, being slain, and his second-in-command captured. Craterus followed Alexander back to Bactria, and immediate plans were made to depart on the conquest of India.

It is unfortunate that the minutiae of the details of the campaign in Sogdia and Bactria are fewer than in any of the preceding campaigns and more vague. This is probably because the area was less known by the early historians than the others, hence, their attempts to co-ordinate the histories *they* had, were not entirely happy. It is with difficulty that the narrative presented here, unsatisfactory though it is, is gathered into coherence. It is arranged into the sequences most logical, in the writer's opinion, in view of the vagueness and discrepancies in our sources. Other details and occurrences are indeed mentioned or referred to, but in such fashion as to be unidentifiable.

Some of them would be valuable if the slightest peg could be found upon which to hang them, or to permit them to be intelligibly woven into the narrative. Unfortunately this is impossible.

We have scattered through our sources many single sentences or statements, interesting *per se*, but maddening to a historian unable to find a single bit of confirmation elsewhere. Among these are many references to colonies founded in these two satrapies. Most, no doubt, were guard settlements, isolated military posts, perhaps merely temporary encampments, for our ancient biographers were often regrettably lacking in explicitness. Thus, though we have wholly acceptable accounts of the founding of but one Alexandria, at or near Khojend, there is another not improbable report, though only on the authority (as far as I can discover) of Stephen of Byzantium, of the founding of another, Alexandria κατὰ βάκτρα, on the northern slopes of the Hindu Kush, apparently designed to guard the pass-roads from the Kabul valley. Confirmation is lacking of this statement. Also in these two satrapies, according to Justin, *twelve* colonies were founded, according to Strabo, *eight;* according to Curtius and Pliny, *six;* while Arrian tells us explicitly of but *one*. In this and other remote regions many sites exist which the spade of the archeologist may some day prove of Hellenistic origin, and history will be rewritten. But determination of the correct number, if it is ever possible, will, unfortunately, be far in the future.

=XI=

THE CAMPAIGN IN
INDIA

PART ONE

Dᴜʀɪɴɢ the winter of 328–327 at Bactria, Alexander pushed to completion his plans for the maintenance of his hold and control upon the newly conquered satrapies, and the preparations for the continuance of his conquests into India. In order to do more than skim the surface of the surface of the history of the campaign and discuss the subject intelligibly, a digression is in order.

Before the advent of Alexander, the India we know did not exist, either ethnically, or, amazingly, even geographically. Thousands of years earlier, the Aryans (whose origin is still conjecturable) arrived in India and made the land their own. The Aryans were a tall, slender, blue-eyed people, restless, quarrelsome and warlike. They soon drove the nomadic aboriginal peoples southward into central India, to form a barrier between them and the smaller dark Dravidian tribes of the

310

south. Secure under the mighty barrier of the ice-topped Himalayan Mountains, they settled the land, and throve for thousands of years. At last the pressure of increasing populations and narrow tribe and clan 'nationalisms' forced migratory groups through the mountain passes of Afghanistan and Baluchistan into Iran and even farther. Indeed, there is reason to believe that all 'white' (that is, non-Mongolian) peoples west of India, both Asiatic and European, have descended from these migrants. Some moved farther, still retaining their tribal identities. Others (of whom one group will be referred to later), in the course of many centuries, now having forgotten their territorial descent, retraced their steps along the ancient routes over the mountains and back into their ancestral homeland. At last most of the wanderers came to rest in a region selected by themselves or forced upon them by circumstances; at first as clans or tribes. Later they amalgamated with other tribes to form small nations, and, still later, through political evolution and conquest, eventually empires, of which the gigantic Persian Empire was the ultimate development.

Cyrus the Great, the native of Persia (Iran; Fars; the Persis of the Greeks), had hammered that empire into shape; and we know that in doing so he had led his army to the Jaxartes River and into Drangia (Sistan), along the Helmund River and into Afghanistan. His successor, the first Darius, had further enlarged the empire by leading his army, in 512 B.C., through the passes of the Hindu Kush and down the Kabul River valley into the Indus. The campaign was easy and of short duration, and after Darius returned home, having obviously heard rumors or reports of the hitherto unknown latent possibilities of his latest imperial acquisition, he decided to verify them. Herodotus, writing more than a dozen decades before Alexander, reported (IV, 44) his action: One Scylax, a native of Caryanda in Caria, was commissioned, along with others upon whose veracity and probity Darius could rely, to make an expedition and tour of discovery into the new land. They went to India, and at Kaspatyros (Kacyapapura) built a fleet of small ships.

They sailed the length of the Indus, reached the ocean, and turned west along the coast of what is now Makran. Two and a half years later the time-worn voyagers passed up the Red Sea and reached Egypt.[1] Thereafter at least several trading voyages were made, not only between Egypt and India, but also between Persia and India; it is possible that a steady trade was built up, but this is unverifiable at the present date. But between Persia and India, as well as between Persia, Turkestan, and China, a well-organized and steady caravan trade had been carried on for centuries.

It must be admitted that Herodotus' works contained fabulous references to India, as did those of the physician Ctesias of Croton, whose very popular works were written after several years' residence in Persia. Both were based upon truth, but, exceptionally so in the case of the chronicles of Ctesias, with embellishments so monstrous as to give grounds, in case of the latter author, for well-founded charges of deliberate falsification for the sake of notoriety. He told of ants large as wolves delving gold in the deserts; of people whose ears were so huge that they were used as coverings against the inclemency of the weather; of others whose feet were so large their owners elevated them, during rainstorms, to serve as umbrellas; of giants and dwarfs and other invented and unpardonable monstrosities. The tales of Ctesias had wide circulation in Greece. It is understandable that a modicum of these mendacities should have gained credence in provincial Greece, but in their contacts with the peoples of Drangia, Arachosia, Bactria, and Sogdia, the army certainly

---

[1] That this report, from the official archives, the Magi, and other sources, was known to Alexander cannot, in the light of evidence and reason, be doubted. The works of Herodotus were widely disseminated even in that early day, and it is inconceivable that he, with his inquiring mind and insatiable desire to learn, surrounded by the best scientific minds and inquiring intellects of the day, remained in ignorance of the facts, despite the assertions of later historians. Herodotus also reported the circumnavigation, even earlier than 509 B.C., of Africa by an expedition of Phoenicians. These departed from the Red Sea, and returned, three years later, through the Gates of Heracles, the Straits of Gibraltar. They reported they had gone so far south that the sun lay upon their right hands. 'But this,' says Herodotus naïvely, 'I do not believe.' Yet there could be no better evidence to prove that they had indeed passed the equator and journeyed westward, thus laying the sun on their right hands.

learned enough to disprove these imaginative aberrations. Too, there were numbers of Indians, including the mahouts and attendants of the elephants among the allies of Darius at the battle of Arbela, and it is certain that some of them, from whom the truth could be learned, were numbered among the multitude of captives who fell into the hands of the victors. Certain of Alexander's chroniclers have discursively made capital of the conqueror's undeniable personal courage, in his invasion of India, as a headlong plunge into what he considered a land of terrifying monsters. Those who do so neglect consideration of historical facts, or deliberately ignore them. Arrian tells us, moreover, that while Alexander was in Sogdia he was joined by a renegade Indian chieftain named Sissicottus (Sasigupta) who had been an associate and ally of Bessus. When the star of that ill-fated pretender set, Sissicottus threw in his lot with the invaders. We hear from him twice again. Also the old king of Taxila,[1] from beyond the Indus, had sent him an embassy (evidence that news of Alexander's intentions had gone ahead of him) offering submission and alliance in exchange for military assistance against an offensive alliance of two of his enemies, Abisares (Sanscrit, Abhisāra, ruler of a territory which can be roughly designated as modern Kasmir and eastern Hazara) and Porus (ruler of the Paurava tribe, whose domain lay between the two rivers modernly called Jihlam and Cinab — vulg., Chenab). Thus, including the indefinite possibilities, captives, caravan followers, travelers, spies, and agents, together with

[1] This principality, of which Taxila is the Greek transliteration, is derived from either, of a happily fortuitous, combination of two Sanscrit words: that is, Takaç'ila, or 'Hewn Stone,' to differentiate the capital city, or the more probable Takkas'ila, the 'Rock of Takkas,' fortress city or citadel of the tribe of Takkas, these latter being a powerful people who anciently occupied the region between the Indus and Jihlam (vulg., Jhelam) Rivers. The ruins of their city, destroyed in the Arab-Muhammedan invasion (by Mahmud of Ghazni) in the early eighth century A.D., cover more than six square miles of land near Shakh-Dheri, not far from Rawal Pindi. References to the city appear again in the history of Appolonius of Tyana, who, in company with Damis of Assyria, visited it in 42 A.D., and again by the Chinese Buddhist Fa Hiuen, who arrived about 420 A.D., and who transcribes the name as Cha-shu-shi-lo; and lastly by the historians of the Muhammedan conquerors, a thousand years after Alexander.

the known sources of information, Sissicottus and the embassy from Taxilês, Alexander and his staff had a wide and accurate knowledge of the exact circumstances obtaining, in all particulars, to the region at least as far as several days' journey beyond the Indus; a knowledge far more accurate than that possessed by any modern European until a few decades ago.

There is further confirmation of the belief that Alexander was aware that it was possible to return from India by sea. In the autumn of 328 B.c., he dispatched messengers from Sogdia to the maritime cities of Phoenicia and Egypt, ordering the satraps there to send him a specified number of boat-builders, shipwrights, carpenters, workers in metals, and a large number of sailors. He also sent to Asia Minor, for his boyhood friend Nearchus, left there as a satrap, to relinquish his post and join him. Nearchus had made voyages on the island seas, and was later to be appointed admiral of the fleet for the immortal voyage from the Indus to the Euphrates.

Out of the welter of hypotheses born of imagination and lack of data on geographical, geological, and archeological conditions and changes in the tumbled mountains and plains of Afghanistan, India, and Baluchistan, previous chroniclers of this phase of Alexander's campaigns have strayed, often very far, from the actual facts. Only in the last decade or so have research and discovery reached the point of accuracy in many hitherto debatable points. In several, however, our data are still insufficient to permit definite identifications; these will be pointed out and discussed at their proper points in the narrative. In a few cases, our increased knowledge has served us but poorly, for we have learned enough only to disprove certain contentions, and insufficient to prove others to replace them. In order to determine the sites and locations of many of the places referred to, we must consult not only the Greek sources, but the geography of the regions, its rivers and valleys, its ancient routes and passes, the scores of ancient ruined sites, and even delve into the ancient classics of Asia. Thus we have the Sanscrit writings, the Prakrit versions of these, of various ages; the ancient Chinese works which are the records of the wanderings of two devout and scholarly Chinese Buddhist pilgrims of about 420 and 620 A.D., and the works of the Arabs' invasions and those of the Muhammedan Mughals of the eighth century and later. By careful study we can often trace, through the various tongues and scripts, a historical sequence enabling us to watch the changes due to age and the vicissitudes of war and conquest. These sources are many, far too many to give continual citations, but no single statement or identification has been made in this work without careful sifting of data, facts, possibilities and probabilities.

In the spring of 327, Alexander set out from Bactria on the long-projected conquest of India, dragging behind him a huge army, numbering, according to Plutarch, one hundred and thirty-five thousand, though it is possible that this might be the total, soldiers, slaves, women and children, camp followers, etc., of the whole expeditionary force and its trains. It is, however, possible that the army alone was this size. Though the conqueror's losses had been heavy, new accessions to the force in the form of new levies from Macedonia and large numbers of mercenaries hired from the soldier marts of Greece were continually pouring in. Added to these were large numbers of Asiatics, notably mounted bowmen, mounted and foot javelin men, and other light cavalry of various armament which were constantly being formed and incorporated into the army. We know that the western satrapies were forced to levy annual contingents for service with Alexander, but we are uninformed as to whether they were kept as local garrisons, for military police duty, or sent to the conqueror for active service in the field. It was, however, no longer a Macedonian, hardly even a Greek army; the former could hardly have been more than a leaven to the whole; the latter were more numerous, but still greatly outnumbered by the accessions of the Asiatics. That Alexander was able to weld these diverse and often inimical and hostile elements and factions into a cohesive force, working without friction to achieve their commander's will, speaks volumes in praise of the personality and caliber of the king and of his lieutenants. It must not be forgotten that many of the latter, after Alexander's death, proved themselves brilliant and resourceful rulers and military leaders in their own right and stature, but they were now overshadowed by the superior rank, the dazzling personality, and the military genius of their king.

A ten days' march, hardly possible by any other route than the Hajiyak Pass, brought the army to Alexandria-ad-Caucasus.[1] Here he found evidence of maladministration and incompetency on the part of those he had left in charge of the region. They were summarily removed from office, and probably from existence, for history knows them no more. Tyriaspes was appointed satrap, and another Nicanor as military governor in the area between the mountains and the Cophen[2] (Kabul) River valley. Settlement and development of the site had failed of fulfilling Alexander's expectations in the two years since its founding, for he drew into it people of the district, and again created military colonists of the failing and incapacitated of his soldiers, condemning them to perpetual exile in this far land. He then marched on to Nicaea,[3] where he sacrificed to Athene, then proceeded to the Cophen River.

Along the river somewhere, probably in the beautiful and fruitful Langam Valley near the junction of the Panjshir and Kabul Rivers, a halt was made. A herald was dispatched ahead toward the Indus, with orders to rulers of the principalities of the Indus Valley, and to Taxilês on the other side, that they

---

[1] Pliny (*Natural History*, VI, xvii, 21) states that the founding was north of Ortospana, which we know to have been Kabul. He calls it Alexandria Opiane. Opiane was a very ancient name, which still persists here. In the Sanscrit *Mahavanso* (Harding's translation) it is called 'Alisada' and 'Alisanda,' a city of the Iones, or Greeks, and is recorded as the birthplace of Menander (Sanscrit, Milinda) one of the Greco-Bactrian kings. It shared the fate of many other ancient towns, and was destroyed in the Arab-Muhammedan conquests.

[2] Kophês, according to some chroniclers; Koa, in Ptolemy's *Geography*; the Sanscrit Kubha. All designations seem to be merely a variation, according to the ears which first heard and recorded it, of the dialectic *cho*, *eu*, or *su*, meaning simply river.

[3] See earlier note regarding this place.

should meet him on their borders as he approached their territories. He seems to have tarried at least a few weeks, for Arrian says the kings came to him bearing as gifts those things deemed most worthy of royalty, and promising him twenty-five elephants if and when he should want them. He told his new subject kings to return home for the time, that he expected to subdue the country north of the Indus before winter, spend that season in the Indus Valley, and cross over the following spring, in company with them, to subdue the land to the eastward.

Here the army was divided into two parts. Hephaestion and Perdiccas were given one division, consisting of the brigades (in view of the enlargement of those units we can hardly call them taxeis any longer) of Gorgias, Clitus (the second), and Meleager, and half of the auxiliary and all the mercenary cavalry. By inference, it can be assumed that the greater part of the enormous trains and most of the newly raised levies of Asiatics were also turned over to them. It was expected they would have to do little fighting, as all the princelets on the line of march had already surrendered. They were ordered to proceed along the world-old route along the Cophen River, through the forty-mile defile today known as the Khyber Pass and down to the plain of Peshawar, then the kingdom of Gandhāra. They were to bring the region into subjection, then proceed to the Indus and prepare a bridge of boats over the river, against the coming of Alexander and the rest of the army. This column was to prepare a safe land, a wide swath through which their enemies could not pass, while Alexander was subduing the warlike peoples of the long river valleys and mountain valleys north of the Cophen. The people to the south of that line, in the grim Sefid-Kuh Ranges were few, and, he undoubtedly knew, unlike to prove a menace. Persons who thoughtlessly call Alexander harebrained in this campaign were never more mistaken. Every action shows, if analyzed, that he was acting upon the basis of careful reasoning and a most exact knowledge of the positions and characteristics of the towns, strongholds, and tribes of the country. From time immemorial the fertile and peopled valleys of the north have ever menaced the Kabul River valley, the people of the south never.

Hephaestion and his column marched away down the river valley, having no trouble until they reached the plains. Here Astes, king of Peucelaotis (Sanscrit, Pushkalavati, capital of ancient Gandhāra; its ruins lie about seventeen miles northeast of Peshawar), suddenly revolted and fled to his capital city. Hephaestion took the city after a thirty days' siege, after Astes was slain in battle. One Sangaeus (can this be the Greek form of the Sanscrit Sanjaya, *the victor*? There is today a Shinwari tribe called the Sangu, living in the Nangnihar district west of Khyber Pass), who had fled Astes sometime before, was appointed to control the district, as his insurrection seemed a guarantee of his good will toward the conquerors.

In the meantime Alexander, with the rest of the forces, had turned to his self-imposed task of subduing the northern tribes. The route was rugged and mountainous along the Choaspes (Kunar) River terrain. The people were the Aspasians,[1] beyond them the Gouriaeans, and still farther, the Assacenians.[2] After the army, with considerable difficulty, crossed the river, Alexander took the cavalry, and, mounting eight hundred of the hoplites, ordered the main body to follow more slowly, and marched swiftly up the fertile and now widening river valley. He rode through a land rich and teeming with crops of early summer, but totally devoid of human life. The inhabitants had

[1] The Aspasians, called also, by Strabo, the Hippasoi, are easily recognized as the As'vaki of the Sanscrit, the name deriving from the word *as'va*, or horse; the area being famous then as today for the quality of the horses bred there. The people themselves are even today readily identifiable under their own (Pukhto) dialectic variation as Asip or Isip, or by their more widely known Muhammedan variant as the Yusufzai.

[2] The Assacenians or Assekenoi are a branch of the Aspasians, but seem to be differentiated in the Sanscrit by varying the name dialectically into Assake; this last, with the additional Persian plural suffix, becomes Assakan, Arrian's transcription being only the addition of the Greek plural. Today they are the Aspins of Chitral, and the Yashkins of Gilgit. The proposition has been advanced that the name As'vakan still exists, by modifications, following philological laws, into the word Afghan. One difficulty in the way of accepting the proposition is that no tribe is known who call themselves Afghans. The Gouriaeans will be referred to later.

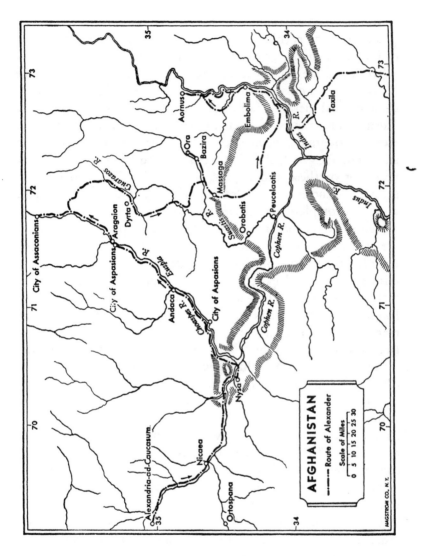

fled in terrified amazement at the sudden and unexpected influx of armored and ruthless invaders, taking refuge in the fastnesses of the bleak mountains or fortified strongholds and towns.

To determine the location and position of the places to be referred to, we must, taking due cognizance of the utter paucity of historical details, fall back upon elements of deduction. Taking for granted the changeless geographical features of eternal mountains, we must consider the scores of ancient ruined sites and, above all, their locations in regard to the ever-present necessity of these peoples for, above all things, defense and security. Another consideration is the fact that, despite half a dozen complete and sweeping conquests of the land, the ancient place names and languages, modified though they were, are still recognizable in many instances, through study of the philological factors inherent in those languages. Where these fail us, we can fall back upon a combination of both, plus the fact that Alexander had one invariable custom, that of never leaving any considerable number of free peoples on his flank or rear. Lastly, we must consider the time involved in the execution of his plan of subjection of this land. Thus we have the statement, by Arrian, that Alexander passed 'near the river Choes [or Choaspes] through a rough and mountainous country,' certainly an accurate description of the narrow Kunar River valley for some distance above its junction with the Kabul River. Farther upstream the valley, rich and fertile, widens to an average of five to seven miles, and has always supported a considerable population.

As he approached the first of the towns, the inhabitants withdrew to its vicinity, leaving a line of battle outside its walls. This unnamed place must have been Kunar, or some other of the ruined sites in that immediate neighborhood, though Kunar, from the extreme antiquity of its site, occupying as it does a most important position on the eastern bank in the bend of the river, is the most logical. The first assault was successful and the enemy driven back into the town, which was protected by a double wall. The invaders attacked the wall, and after a short but fierce conflict were driven back. Alexander himself was slightly wounded by a javelin which penetrated his breastplate. Leonnatus and Ptolemy also received injuries. The following day another assault was successful in carrying the outer wall, and the inner wall gave way before the scaling ladders. The people precipitately abandoned the town and fled to the mountains. Arrian says: ' ... but the Macedonians, pursuing hard after them, slew many in pursuit, and took many alive, who, because of the exceeding rage they had conceived against them, for the wound given their king, were all put to death.' The city was destroyed.

Alexander advanced to another place, called by Arrian Andaca, by Curtius, according to the imprint, Acadera and Adaca. About thirty miles up the river from Kunar is a modern village upon an ancient site, called Anda-raj, which was probably Andaca. The people, terrified at the fate of the lower town, surrendered. Other confirmation of the accuracy of the selection of this place as Andaca is the added information that here Alexander divided his forces, giving part to Craterus for the purpose of subduing the other chiefs of the country thereabouts. Obviously these 'other chiefs' could not have inhabited the Kunar (or Choaspes) Valley, nor could they have lived in the grim mountains to the east or west, for the simple reason that people in sufficient numbers to justify a military attack could not live and support themselves there. However, the Kunar River bifurcates at Anda-raj, one arm, the Kattar River, coming down from the northwest, the Kunar from the northeast. It is quite possible that the king (or his historians) may have considered the Kattar the main stream, and that Craterus was sent off up its valley. We are told that Alexander then took his forces and directed his steps toward the Euspla River, where, according to information, the general of the Aspasians (Arrian calls them the Aspii) lay. We find the name in no other text or account, but it is easy to read it philologically as the *eu* (a local term for river) and couple it with a variant of Aspii, thus obtaining a name obviously meaning the river of the Aspasians.

We are further told that Alexander made a long day's march and upon the second day came to the city of the enemy. When these perceived the approach of the attackers, they set their city on fire and fled to the mountains. The name of the place is not given, but the most likely site is Bir-Kot (a recurring name here), meaning 'the fort of heroes.' The Greeks pursued the fugitives and slew many, and Ptolemy, son of Lagus, engaged and slew their chief in Homeric gladiatorial combat. Alexander moved on, 'passing around a mountain and came upon a city called Arigaion,' [1] which he found burned and deserted. It is now called Har-nai. Some ten or twelve miles above Harnai the valley narrows to a bottle-neck about fifteen miles wide, and Alexander concluded Arigaion would be an advantageous and obvious place to garrison for the purpose of checking possible incursions from the north. Craterus marched in and rejoined his king after having fulfilled his appointed task of pacifying the Kattar Valley. He was ordered to rebuild and refortify the town, and people it with such of the natives of the country as could be brought into it; also such soldiers as were unfit for further campaigning were left as colonists.

'He then directed his march toward the place where the enemy had fled, and, coming to the base of a certain mountain, encamped there.' From here he sent Ptolemy to look into the possibility of obtaining supplies. Alexander must have made his temporary encampment in the narrow neck of the Chitral Valley, where the mountains rise in awesome peaks seventeen thousand feet high on both sides. Perhaps doubting the integrity of his informants who told him the enemy were just ahead,

---

[1] Ritter identifies the site with Bajaur in the province of the same name; McCrindle, in his book *The Invasion of India by Alexander the Great*, with the village of Naoghi. Many have accepted either identifications. But it seems both ignored or were unaware of the military and philological factors, consideration of which nullify both premises. Alexander was definitely subduing the populous Kunar Valley, which, farther north, was even wider and more populous, militarily a far more potent place than the sparsely populated mountains of Bajaur. Another reason: above Bir-Kot, and about ten miles north, is the very ancient sited village of Har-nai, quite definitely a modern form of Aragaion (the Tazik termination spelled variously -nai, -nih, or -ni, is the equivalent of the Sanscrit *gâ*, on), both meaning 'Snake-town.'

or perhaps for the purpose of reconnoitering, the main force was held here until Ptolemy reported back with his information. Ptolemy had gone 'a considerable distance' in advance up the valley, and now returned to report that the campfires of the enemy outnumbered those of the army. Eighteen miles from where Alexander's camp was pitched, today there stands the town of Chitral,[1] important in that region from time before history. We are told that the people of this area, who were flocking to the standards of their chiefs, were the stoutest warriors and best fighters in that part of the country. Alexander immediately marched toward the enemy. The battle was long and severe, for the enemy had posted themselves upon a hill from which they had to be driven. No town is mentioned, but it is reported that enormous numbers of livestock were taken, additional confirmation that this battle occurred near Chitral, where the valley is upward of fifty miles in width, the only place where livestock could be raised in numbers. Some of the cattle were so greatly superior to any the Greeks had ever seen that Alexander ordered a great herd of them to be driven to Macedonia to improve the breed there.

There must be assumed a passage of some time here, for we are told that Craterus finished his task of rebuilding Arigaion, and rejoined the army before it moved on. Then, having been informed that the Assacenians, with an army of twenty thousand cavalry and thirty thousand foot with thirty war elephants, were preparing to take the field against him, Alexander turned toward them. He crossed the high passes, and went on without resistance through the country of the Gouriaeans,[2] and crossed, but with much difficulty, the swift Gouriaios River, entering the lands of the Assacenians. These dared not stay to face him. Their army fell apart and the units dispersed and fled for their homes without fighting.

[1] The name Chitral derives from the Sanscrit Kshatralaya, meaning 'the abode, or city, of soldiers'; then apparently the most important city of the Aspasians.

[2] The Gouriaeans, in Sanscrit Gauri, both people and river, were named from the widespread Ghori, or Gawri, a tribe still to be found above Dyrta. The river is the modern Panjkora. It joins the Swat (Sanscrit, Suvastu; Greek, Suastus) River to form the Landai River, which is a confluent of the Kabul River.

Alexander now found himself in a land of giant mountains with a scattered but incipiently hostile people on all sides. On his right flank, in the Swat River valley to the south, was a populous and fertile land, full of inimical fighting men. If he attempted to sweep the mountains free of hostile elements, he would be exposed to flank attacks of the valley dwellers. Neither Arrian nor any other of our sources say as much, but careful study of the region permits no other conclusion. If he could defeat the valley dwellers, their subjugation would render unnecessary a hill campaign; his new subjects would be imposed as a barrier between the scattered hill tribes and his line of communications along the Cophen Valley. Alexander turned south through modern Bajaur, following the route that was probably the same as it is today, leading from Panjkora through Talash, over the easy Katgala Pass, and down to the ancient crossing of the Swat River, where the strategically located fort of Chakdara now stands.

Arrian simply tells us that 'Alexander first led his army against Massaga, the capital city of the country, and, drawing near to it, the inhabitants, led by a party of about seven thousand mercenaries "from the inner parts of India," advanced against the Macedonians, with design to assault their camp.' Except mention of a hill seven stadia (something less than a mile) distant, we are given not the slightest hint of any details by which the place can be identified. Therefore we are again forced to hunt for a clue. The wreckage of time and the whirlwinds of conquests which have swept through the Swat Valley in the last two thousand years have filled the valley and the neighboring lower hills with ruined sites. Many of them are plainly of vast antiquity, but we cannot say specifically of any of the ruined sites below Chakdara (as it certainly was) — 'This is Massaga.' It must, however, have been near, if not on the site of, Malakand. We have several reasons for reaching this conclusion. First it was the capital city, and it was defended by seven thousand mercenaries. The chief of the place is referred to as Assakenos, whom Sanscrit historians mention as having been a lord of the tribe, but a feudatory of King Abisares, on the other side of the Indus. It would seem, therefore, that Massaga was an opulent place, if independent, to be rich enough to hire seven thousand mercenaries. That number of men, regardless of how little the individual soldier may have received, were nevertheless expensive for a hill town to support, unless, of course, Abisares deemed the place of sufficient importance to defend with his own men. In either case, a city of that size, wealth, and economic importance could have come into existence only in the rich lower valley of the Swat, with easy access to the outside world of trade through the easy passes into the Gandhāra Valley.

In order to draw the attackers away from their town, Alexander ordered a simulated retreat. The Indians pressed hotly after the Greeks until they brought them under heavy arrow fire. The trumpet blared. Instantly the Greeks turned about and fell upon their disorganized pursuers, killing two hundred and routing the rest. They fled back to the city, with the Greeks close upon their heels. Alexander threw his army about the walls. The next day siege engines were brought into action under heavy fire from the walls, and Alexander himself was wounded in the calf by an arrow. A breach was made, and the attackers stormed in, only to be driven out again. A tower was built outside the wall, and archers and engines placed in its upper stories to bring the besieged under a barrage of arrows and stones. Next day a movable bridge was laid from the tower to the wall, but the hypaspists crowded upon it in such numbers that it broke beneath their weight, hurling the attackers to their deaths below. The Indians counter-attacked with such fury that Alexander sounded the retreat and drew off.

The following day another tower was constructed and another bridge brought up. As long as their chief was alive, the mercenary Indians behaved with the greatest gallantry, but on this day he was slain by an arrow. Unwilling to continue the bootless battle, the Indians sent a messenger to Alexander, with peace proposals. Recognizing their sterling qualities as fighting

men, and aware that it would cost him heavily in time and
casualties to capture the town against their continued resistance,
he granted amnesty on the basis that they join his army. The
Indians agreed, left the city and went into camp on a near-by
hill. Out of this incident come two stories; one, that the
Indians, having no intention of fighting other Indians on behalf
of the invader, planned to slip away at night. The other story
is that Alexander, enraged at their resistance to his godlike will
and at his own wound, decided to destroy them as a fearful
object lesson to others. Whichever story is true, the results were
the same. The Greeks surrounded the hill by surprise and
annihilated the whole contingent. Plutarch, usually so lauda-
tory of Alexander, admits this blemish upon his character.
Curtius adds that when the Greeks returned to the practically
undefended city, the young queen, widow of the dead king,
came forth to the conqueror and 'she brought her young son to
Alexander, and obtained not only a pardon but a continuance of
her former dignity: though it is believed her beauty pleaded
more than her eloquence, or the king's inclination to forgive.
However, she bore a son soon afterward, and whoever got it,
it was named Alexander.' [1]

Coenus was immediately dispatched up the valley to Bazira
(Bir-Kot, on the Swat) under the impression that the people
there, hearing and fearing the fate of those who resisted, might
capitulate. At the same time Alcetas, Attalus, and Demetrius
were sent farther up the valley to Ora (Udegram, about ten
miles above Bir-Kot). Coenus reached Bazira, but the citizens,
trusting to the strength of their hill fortress, today over six
hundred feet above the river, retired behind its walls. The
second expedition reached Ora, beat off one severe attack, and
started building a rampart around the outside of the place to
keep the citizens inside. Alexander planned to go to Coenus'
assistance, but a spy informed him that Abisares had dispatched
another expedition, this time to help Ora. He instantly changed
his plans and hastened to Ora, after sending orders to Coenus to

[1] Curtius, V, 1; also Justin, XII, 7.

raise a rampart against the defenders of Bazira, leave there a garrison large enough to beleaguer the place, and join him with the rest of the command. Coenus immediately did so and marched to rejoin his king. Hardly had he disappeared from sight when the Bazarians, disdaining the small number of Greeks in the little fort (half a mile from the foot of Bir-Kot Hill at the junction of the Karākar and Kandag valleys), sallied forth to annihilate them. They must have had the surprise of their lives, the survivors at any rate, for the Greeks slew five hundred of them and drove the rest headlong back to their hill. In the meantime Ora presented no difficulty. Alexander took it at the first assault, seizing much booty, including a number of war elephants. This news reached the pinnacled Bazirians. They became distrustful of the strength of the walls on their lofty hill, abandoned it and fled westward in the night to a mountain ridge, called a 'rock' in our histories, named Aornus; an example quickly followed by most of the remaining villagers in the country.

A short distance higher up, the valley of the Swat River narrows virtually to a gorge in the high Pamirs. Obviously no enemy was there in strength, for there was nothing on which one might subsist there. Also it was now late autumn, and the snow line on the giant peaks crept daily lower and the wind grew bleak with the cold of high altitudes. Alexander turned back south. It was unnecessary to pursue his way farther northward.

Only one peaceful incident is recorded for us out of this nine months' long report of slaughter and rapine. Arrian indeed does not insert it here, and Curtius gives it to us as having occurred in the obviously improbable location of the upper Kunar Valley. Arrian himself treats the tale as if he considered it apocryphal, as have almost all other careful transcribers of the tale. Indeed, upon analysis, without knowledge that has become ours in the recent past, it could hardly be considered credible, but now it can be said that the very parts which previously were considered false can today be accepted as guarantors of its authenticity.

Quoting Arrian: [1]

> Alexander then entered that part of the country which lies between the two rivers, Cophen and Indus, wherein Nysa is said to be situated. The city was built by Dionysus or Bacchus, when he conquered the Indians... only this I venture to say: That those things which the ancients have published in their fables, concerning the gods, ought not to be too carefully searched into, for, whenever the truth of any story became liable to be called into question, some god or other was immediately summoned to their aid, then all was made plain and easily accepted.

Arrian and many others have regarded the story as apocryphal, even those of much later ages, insufficiently informed, have adhered to the cynic view that it was a post-Alexander fable designed to bolster the flagging will-to-proceed of the army. This last is a rationalistic viewpoint, and is a case where theory must give way to fact. It was fortuitous circumstances only which gave the conqueror this thankfully received opportunity. The Nysaoi, or Nysaeans, can be definitely traced as one of those groups of Aryans (Arians) who had left India in the dawn of time, to retrace their steps back again an unknown period later, but believed to be around the eighth century B.C. They were the tribe called Licchavi by the Pali chroniclers, Nicchivi in the Sanscrit, and in post-Alexander histories as the Nishadas. They had migrated from the Elburz mountain region near Meshed, driven by the tribe later known as the Parthians. Their town was known to the Greeks as Nissa or Nicaea (modern Nishapur near Meshed), which was later to become the capital of the Parthian Empire. This being true, it was obvious that they were of the same basic stock as the Greeks themselves, and just as the Greek Hermes is simply a dialectic variation of the Hindu god Brahma, so is it true that the Greeks and the Nysaeans both recognized the parallelism of their theology, the god Dionysus. Historically the Nysaeans were the same generic stock as the Sakya or Sacae who were then the inhabitants of modern Badakshan and contiguous areas. Later they were

[1] Arrian, V, 1.

absorbed into the aristocratic Kshattriyas, the warrior caste of India. In Ptolemy's *Geography* the place is referred to as Nagara and Dionyspolis, this paralleling the Sanscrit Nagarahara or Nangenhar, whose ruins lie some five miles west of Jalalabad. Near-by is the mountain called Mar-Koh or Koh-i-Mor. Anciently the area governed by the Nysaeans seems to have been bounded on the west by Jagdalak Pass, the Kabul River on the north, Khyber Pass on the east, and the grim Sefid-Kuh on the south, a rectangle some forty by one hundred miles.

When Alexander reached the town he was met by a delegation of some thirty citizens under their chief, Akouphis, who entreated him to spare the place. They informed him that their town had been founded by Dionysus, according to their calculations, 6042 years before, on his invasion of India. The god, they said, had erected it as a memorial to mark the spot from which he had turned back. They reported that they maintained the Bacchic religion and the people were ruled justly as a free republic by a body of three hundred citizen legislators. Alexander was greatly gratified to be told this; it was his wish that the tale of Dionysus should be believed by the army, for it was his intention to exceed by his own the deeds of his legendary predecessor, that his own accomplishments might thereby transcend those of the god. Accordingly he confirmed the government in power, but ordered them to provide him a detachment of three hundred horsemen to serve as cavalry, and send as hostages one hundred members of the governing body. When the demand was made, Akouphis laughed: 'O King, how can a city be well governed if it be deprived of a hundred of its best citizens? Take the three hundred horsemen, or more if you wish. But if you wish to have Nysa continue to be well administered, take, instead of one hundred of its best men, two hundred of its worst. Then, upon your return, you will find an even better city.' Alexander dropped the demand for the hundred hostages, but took instead Akouphis' son and nephew. The Nysaeans told them that the near-by Mount Moeris held a certain memorial of Nysa's fabled god. So, it is said, they went there, and, finding the mountain abounded in ivy, laurel, and the vine, went into camp at its base. Here, desirous of impressing the army with his greatness in surpassing Dionysus himself, the king freely provided all the necessaries for a ten-day bacchanalian revel.

After ten days, the army moved on, and marched down into the Gandhāra Valley to receive the surrender of Peucelaotis. This done, orders were given for the reconstruction and resettlement of Orobatis (Arabutt, on the east bank of the Landai). A garrison was left in Peucelaotis under command of Philip, and Alexander moved on toward the Indus. Reaching the river, he again turned his attention to the matter of the Rock of Aornus, where the people (of modern Swat and Buner) had fled for safety, and yet remained.

We have been told that the Greeks believed Dionysus and Heracles had invaded India centuries before. Alexander had already passed beyond the region ascribed as the limits of the former's journey, but he wished to go farther. He was filled with a 'longing,' not to emulate the deeds of the gods, but to surpass them. It is interesting, not only to the historian, but to the psychologist also, to note this fact in connection with the actions of the Macedonian conqueror, especially as they can be linked to Heracles. Arrian, this time quoting from the history of Eratosthenes, says: 'All these references to that deity were circulated by the Macedonians in connection with the deeds of Alexander to gratify his pride by grossly exaggerating their importance.' [1] He adds that in the Paropamisus Mountains they found a cave wherein, they said, the legendary Prometheus lay chained until his rescue by Heracles — a far cry indeed from the former site, attributed to the Pontus, of the mythical prison. Thus we are told that Heracles himself had assaulted the Rock of Aornus,[2] but had found it impregnable, being forced by an

[1] Arrian, V, 3.

[2] Aornus is referred to by some careless narrators by the Greek translation as the 'Birdless' because, forsooth, it was so high that birds could not fly over it — obvious puerility. Thousands of refugee Indians were living upon it — a manifest impossibility in atmosphere so rarefied it would not support birds. Arrian gives the height as

earthquake to call off the siege. It is easy to rationalize that the failure of his demigod half-brother was the motivation of Alexander's attack upon the famous stronghold, but it is also clear that the military necessity of dispersing the large body of armed Indians on his flank was, if not as great, still a powerful incentive also. For many years the identity and location of this mountain stronghold was the cause of much conjecture and many solutions were proposed, but it has at last been identified beyond doubt as one of the seven-thousand-foot spurs of the mountain Pir-Sar,[1] some forty miles up the Indus from the ruins of Amb.

Alexander marched upriver to Embolima (called Amb today; anciently, in Sanscrit, Ambulima). Here he left Craterus, with orders to gather all the supplies to be found, against the possible need of them in a long-drawn-out siege of Aornus. The army then moved up to the mountain and tried to storm its precipitous slopes, but failed in several attempts. Finally Alexander ordered construction of a mound or causeway across a deep ravine, where, his military sagacity told him, was the most logical point for the attack to be launched. After several days' hard work the fill,[2] of logs, stones, and earth, was pushed far enough that archers and engines operating from it were able to bring the Indian defenders under a hail of stones and arrows. They were driven from their posts, and under the protection of their primitive barrage, the attackers swarmed up the steep face of the slope and stormed the ridge-top. The defenders were driven from it and across the flat mountain-top. Large numbers were slain, and many more, fleeing the wrath of the terrible armored

---

eleven stadia, or about sixty-seven hundred feet, a remarkably accurate report and an excellent showing for Alexander's bematistae, being only a few hundred feet out of the way. There are two possible derivations of the term, one the Hindi word *aranai*, still used in this locality to designate a ridge or mountain spur; the other, more probable, the Sanscrit word *avarana*, or the Refuge. This last is rendered more acceptable by the fact that we find Strabo referring to the place as Avernus, a better transliteration than any of the other ancient writers employed.

[1] Sir Mark Aurel Stein, who identified Aornus, has written the account in a book called *On Alexander's Track to the Indus*.

[2] Sir Mark Aurel Stein identifies this artificial work with a certain projecting mountain shoulder thrusting far into a deep ravine and facing against the ridge of Pir-Sar.

Greeks, fell over cliffs and were killed. The survivors escaped over the Indus, which washes the base of the mountain, and fled to the protection of King Abisares. Alexander thus became the master of the famous stronghold refuge, which the Macedonians probably now firmly believed (so easily do the lies of the propagandists gain credence, even in these days) had defied the efforts and god-will of Heracles himself. Alexander offered sacrifices to the gods, then placed the renegade Sissicottus and a garrison in charge of the area, with orders to construct a stone fort upon the mountain-top, where there is enough arable land to support a small village. The whole of the newly surrendered or subdued region west of the Indus was added to the viceroyalty of Nicanor in Alexandria-ad-Caucasus.

While the army was still here, intelligence was brought that Asikes or Erix (according to different transcribers), brother of the dead Assacenian king, had gathered an army of twenty thousand men and a number of war elephants and had assembled them in Dyrta (the district of Dyr?) and was prepared to resist further extension of Alexander's conquests into the mountains. Alexander at once marched out to find them. As the Greeks advanced, the Indians grew panicky. They revolted against Asikes, slew him, cut off his head and sent it to Alexander, then disbanded and fled to their homes and, many of them, back to Abisares. The war elephants were hunted down, and Indian mahouts rode them south to Gandhāra. The army, finding the route to the south very difficult, solved the problem by marching to the Indus, where they cut down trees and built rafts and boats to carry them down the river to where Hephaestion and Perdiccas had already completed a bridge (of boats?) across the river, against their coming.

The last phase of the campaign against the Assacenians had been trying to all forces, and they were given a thirty-day rest in which to recover. During the last part of the period, games were held, and, when they were partly finished, with music and merrymaking, the army crossed the Indus (at Ohind, about sixteen miles above Attock) in April, 326 B.C. Here the king found, awaiting his acceptance, two hundred talents of silver, three thousand fattened cattle, ten thousand sheep, and thirty elephants; also seven hundred Indian cavalry sent as hostage reinforcements by Taxilês. After the whole of the army were over the river, Alexander offered the sacrifices of thanksgiving he invariably made after the passing of a crisis, and finished the games begun on the west bank. They then proceeded toward Taxila, thirty-six miles eastward. The old King Taxilês had but recently died and was succeeded by his son, whom the Greeks called Omphis (correctly Amphi, of the warrior Kshattriya caste). The Greeks marched light-heartedly onward until they neared the city. While yet forty stadia distant, they saw Omphis coming toward them, attended by a large retinue and his army, the latter drawn up in battle array with the elephants ranged ahead of the line. Alexander, seeing the host of men advancing, immediately concluded the young ruler had withdrawn his fealty and decided to fight for his kingdom. The battle trumpets blared, and the invading force, working with machine-like precision, halted and began to break into closely knit blocks and lines as they swung smoothly into battle formation. Omphis, seeing from afar the commotion in the Greek column, at once grasped its meaning. He hastily rode forward with a few friends, to assure Alexander of his continued good will, and tell him that the army was only drawn up to receive him with honors. Alexander was so pleased with the appearance, speech, and actions of the young Indian ally that he gave him back his kingdom, and, say the historians, bestowed upon him the title of Taxilês.[1]

Upon the army's arrival at the city, Taxilês provided provisions and entertainment for the invading horde for three days. He also showed Alexander an account of the supplies he had already furnished Hephaestion on the Indus, besides the vast

---

[1] This is but a way of stating that Omphis had not formally assumed sovereignty at his father's death, but awaited Alexander's will in the matter. When the latter granted him the right of accession, he automatically assumed the tribal and dynastic title. The historians usually designated the Indians by their tribal titles, giving them as personal names.

provision he had sent the conqueror himself at the river. Alexander was so gratified that he returned the presents Taxilês had given him, and added many rich gifts from the captured Persian spoil and a thousand talents of gold. This liberality, while assuring adherence of the Indian to the cause of the invaders, deeply offended his own cup companions. One night at supper, Meleager, the phalanx commander, having drunk enough wine to make him truthful and careless of consequences, caustically congratulated Alexander upon his having found in India, if nowhere else, someone worthy of so munificent a gift as a thousand talents of gold. Alexander started up in rage, but recalling the terrible murder of Clitus under similar circumstances, controlled his temper, but made the grimly threatening statement that most men had as their worst enemy their own tongues. The remark had the effect of causing the dangerous subject to be hastily dropped.

The Indian had made alliance with Alexander in exchange for a promise of assistance in crushing the armies of two neighboring kingdoms. Taxilês' own kingdom lay between the Indus and Hydaspes (Sanscrit, Vitasta, and even today in Kas'mir called the Bedasta; English, Jihlam or Jhelum) Rivers. Northward, in the mountains, lay the kingdom of the hostile Abisares; westward beyond the Hydaspes, the kingdom of Porus. Abisares seems to have learned much from the fugitives from beyond the Indus, and, no doubt, heard much of Alexander's murderous maltreatment of those who resisted and his leniency with those who submitted and accepted his yoke without resistance, for he sent the conqueror an embassy headed by his own brother. Alexander accepted the proffer of submission and allowed Abisares to retain his kingdom. No offer was received from Porus. A messenger, one Cleochares, was dispatched to Porus, with the demand that he make submission, pay tribute, and meet him on the borders of his country when he came. Porus returned the grim reply that he would pay nothing, but would indeed meet the invader on his frontier, at the head of his army with weapons in their hands.

It is worth while wondering what Alexander would have done had Porus meekly submitted to his outrageous demands. He seems to have originally planned extension of his empire only to the Indus, the farthest bounds of the former Persian Empire, but not farther; and it is possible to consider wholly fortuitous the circumstances of Taxilês' invitation, which under the existing circumstances was hardly other than an invitation to pursuance of the conquests. Once across the Indus, his overpowering lust for conquest and his psychopathic refusal to brook the possibility of the continued existence of a free equal who would refuse to bow his neck before him drove him on anew to continued conquests in farther lands. Preparations for a new advance were begun immediately.

A curious interlude is noted here. During his travels in India, Alexander exhibited a great deal of interest and curiosity in the native wise men and philosophers. Those of this area, around Taxila and other northern places, are recorded for us as the gymnosophists, because they, being propertyless and homeless, were wanderers. They were a peaceful sect, owning nothing, and protagonists of self-abnegation, unlike the stiff-necked and intolerant Brahmans of the south. Outside Taxila dwelt a number of them. Onescritos was sent to tell their leader that Alexander, son of Zeus, wished to converse with him. Onescritos found them some distance from the city, and approached the first and nearest. This man, however, indifferently refused to talk to him at all unless he too would strip naked and lie down with them upon the hot stones in the burning sunshine. The one recognized by them as their leader and superior was somewhat more polite, but nevertheless unimpressed by the glittering and warlike Macedonian, and firm in his refusal to have anything to do with Alexander. His answer was that Alexander was no more the son of Zeus than he was, or, conversely, that both were the sons of Zeus, as were all men. He was wholly uninterested in anything so ephemerally transient as the conqueror of his country. Alexander had nothing he wanted, nor had he anything he feared to lose; in his ancient

wisdom his exaltation transcended anything earthly, and the conqueror could do no worse than slay him, a blessing which would
but release his soul from an undesired body. One of the lesser
ascetics, a man of little advancement, left his group aud joined
Alexander's train. His name is recorded to us as Sphines, but
the Greeks called him Calanus. We hear of him again.

Before the army was ready to move, Barsaentes, the satrap
who had instigated the resistance of the Drangians and Arachosians, was brought in as a captive, in company with an unidenti-
fied chief of some mountain tribe, named Samaxus, arrested for
espousing, abetting, and aiding his cause. Both were put to
death.

It is difficult, and sometimes impossible, to trace with absolute
certainty the routes followed by Alexander from the time he
left Taxila until he left India. Since that day such great changes
have occurred in the very topography of India that it will not
be incorrect to make the bald statement that the land of Alexander's conquests has ceased to exist. The very face of the
country has changed, tectonic action and stupendous earth-
quakes have caused great rivers to change their courses, not
once but many times. One river, then far greater than the Indus,
the Hakra or Wahinda, has *wholly ceased to exist*, its flow drying
up as late as a mere two hundred years ago. Two other great
rivers have combined in a single bed, creating an even greater
river. The entire center of India was covered, two thousand
years ago, by hundreds of cities and towns, a fruitful and fertile
country giving subsistence to millions of people; a land watered
by many streams, where today are but hundreds of blank ruin
mounds in the dreary and desolate Great Tar Desert. It will be
necessary, in view of the enormous mass of data collected and
studied, to follow, in general, a narrative style rather than
attempt to compress within reasonable limits, the numbers of
reasons, both actual and possible, for many of the statements
to be made.

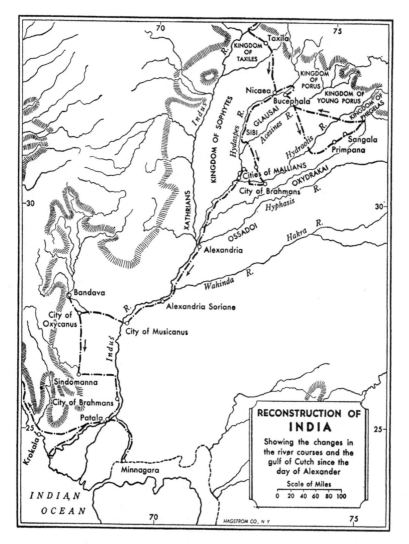

RECONSTRUCTION OF
INDIA
Showing the changes in
the river courses and the
gulf of Cutch since the
day of Alexander

Scale of Miles
0 20 40 60 80 100

From Taxila to the Hydaspes, Alexander had the choice of
two main routes and one of lesser importance. The first is the
ancient way, following the line of the great trunk road from
Shakh-Dheri to Jhelum; the second, more southerly, through
Chauntra and Dhudial through the Nandana Pass in the Salt

Range and down to the riverine plain below. The third route, still more southerly, leaves the vicinity of Shakh-Dheri, passes through Chakwal, then turns northerly and joins the second route to pass the mountains. At its debouchure into the plain, Jalalpur lies several miles to the left, to the right it runs down to the village of Haranpur,[1] situated upon a very ancient site at the equally ancient crossing of the Hydaspes (Jihlam) River. Alexander followed the second route, and camped at or near the site of Haranpur. There is a hint, in the histories, but nothing definite, of trouble with Spitakes, the chief of this area, who fled across the river to Porus, ahead of the invading army. They camped on the Hydaspes River, now swelling with the rains of the just begun wet season, and the melting snows of the gigantic mountains to the north. On the other side of the river, Porus, true to his unyielding determination to resist the invasions of his dominions, waited with his army drawn up in battle array to dispute the crossing. According to Arrian (and Curtius is in substantial agreement) the Indian army consisted of thirty thousand footmen, four thousand cavalry, three hundred war chariots, and two hundred elephants. Small though the Indian army was, outnumbered not less than four to one by the invader and his allies, it is indicative of their courage and warlike determination that they remained, holding their position firmly in the face of the overwhelming numbers of the never defeated Greeks. The latter were going to have to fight their way.

Alexander rode down to the rising river and made a long and careful survey of the situation as his army was going into camp. Porus remained where he was with the bulk of his army, but

[1] General Abbott, Sir Alexander Burnes, and several others have advanced the proposition that Alexander followed the first-named route. Mr. Vincent Smith, in his *Early History of India*, concurs with the thesis, and names the point of crossing at Bhuna, which he considers the site of Bucephala, and is ten miles above the town of Jhelum. General Alexander Cunningham (*Geography of Ancient India*, p. 157 ff.) considers Jalalpur, some thirty miles below Jhelum, as the site of the camp, and considers Dilawar, eight miles upriver, as the place at which the invaders crossed the river. A number of factors, too long to cite here, prove the impossibility of justifying this premise. In the light of a careful survey of the riverine terrain, reported by Sir Mark Aurel Stein in the *Geographical Journal* for July, 1932, both theories fail of convincingness. We accept his as the most tenable.

sent several detachments up and down the river to guard likely crossing-places and known fords to prevent or block the invader's anticipated attempt to cross. Alexander realized that Porus was fully prepared to fight, and was, moreover, sagacious enough to be difficult to outwit. This last was, however, absolutely necessary if the projected crossing was to be carried out, as he definitely intended that it should be. His first act was, therefore, to break the army into a number of strong detachments. Some were sent out to scour and lay waste the country, several of the forays being led by the king himself; some of the latter being upriver, to spy out the land, and find, if any existed, fords in the rising river. Other detachments were dispatched in other directions. Convoys of supplies were brought in in huge amounts, to impress the watchful enemy (who undoubtedly had spies also) that the Greeks intended to remain there until the end of the flood season, when the subsiding waters would give them a choice of several easily passed fords. The boats were brought overland from the Indus and assembled in numbers. They immediately became active, plying up and down river with numbers of men. Skins and tents were stuffed with straw to make floats. Large detachments lined the banks at several places, and were constantly shifted up or down river. All this was done with the intent to keep the Indians ever watchful and alert, to prevent them from resting or concentrating their forces at any one point selected as the best place at which to attempt a passage. Porus remained on the alert, meeting every visible move of the Greeks with a counter-move.

Alexander next made a public declaration, for the benefit of possible spies and informers, of his intention of remaining there the rest of the year if necessary, and his passage remained blocked. He continued, however, to keep up the movements of large units, and to attempt to steal an unseen passage, but for several days without hope of success. It was plainly impossible even to consider a crossing in the face of the watchful Indians; the horses of his main reliance, the cavalry, would never face the guarding elephants. They would bolt at the sight and trumpeting of the great beasts, and grow frantic with fear even at a distance. Also the Indians were well armed, well disciplined, and courageous, tall bearded blond men of the ancient Aryan stock from which the Greeks themselves derived. After a few days of constant maneuvering which was continually countered by Porus, Alexander realized the futility of maintaining a planless course of action. Then an idea presented itself and was shortly developed into a perfectly planned stratagem whereby he hoped to steal the much-desired passage. That night the greatest part of the cavalry were brought out and led along the river, and presently they set up their war shout, filling the night with their clamor. Porus, on the other bank, hastily mustered part of his army and followed them. The cavalry returned to camp. Day after day and night after night the detachments marched out, accompanied by a swarm of boats. Porus invariably followed every move for several days, but, after this had been done repeatedly, he at last wearied of the fruitless following and counter-marching and disregarded the increasing uproar. At last he heavily reinforced the river-bank guards and ceased from following the noisy detachments entirely, keeping the bulk of his forces in camp. As the days passed, he became accustomed to the din, and Alexander prepared to put into operation the scheme whereby he hoped to make the passage without encountering mass resistance by the defending army. They presented a very different obstacle to his further conquests from any enemy he had yet encountered. Small, even tiny in comparison to the gigantic yet inchoate horde from which he had won the Persian Empire at the battle of Arbela, it was nevertheless a superior fighting force, a close-knit, disciplined, well-officered army of courageous fighting men, intelligent and resolute. The crossing then must necessarily be made by stratagem, and this was at last perfected.

Arrian·tells us:[1]

> There was a headland [or promontory, the Greek ἄκρα] seated
> on the bank of the river, where the channel makes a great sweep-

[1] Arrian, V, 11.

ing bend, which was wooded. Opposite it was an island, unin-
habited, and also heavily wooded, consequently suited to his
[Alexander's] purpose and intent. Therefore, considering that
the place could be used for the concealment of both cavalry and
footmen, he determined to ferry them over to it. The headland
and island were one hundred and fifty stadia distant from the main
camp.

The main road from the camp to the site of Jalalpur ran
parallel to the river, but at a distance precluding movement
along it from being seen from the east bank. By this time
Alexander had, of course, received numerous reports from scouts
and spies, and his possession of an accurate knowledge of the
opposite terrain must be inferred. Guards were placed along
the river bank, at such distance that each could easily see his
neighbor, to prevent any person crossing the river and to receive
and pass along all commands or information. Then, for several
nights in succession, the army lighted additional fires, and
bustled noisily around, visibly busying themselves in apparent
preparations to begin the crossing; no doubt the subtle Greeks
chuckled to themselves in cynical pleasure when they saw the
Indians form their battle line and spent a sleepless night watching the beginning of a movement which would not take place.
Meanwhile, scores of dismantled boats were conveyed secretly
up the road to the place selected for crossing (Jalalpur is seventeen
miles, Arrian's one hundred and fifty stadia) upriver, and
assembled again behind the screen of the wooded headland.
Suddenly news arrived which electrified army and command
alike. Abisares had reconsidered his capitulation to the Macedonian; he had reassembled his army and was marching to
Porus' assistance, and was now but four hundred stadia distant.
Speed of action was imperative.

Craterus was given his own command, most of the heavy
hoplite phalanx, the Asiatic mountaineers, and the five thousand
men of Taxilês, and told to remain in camp, keep the fires burning, maintain the same guard and the usual semblance of activity.
He was given the strict order: 'If Porus [so Ptolemy, through

Arrian, quotes Alexander] advances against me with one part of the army, but leaves the other part with the elephants in his camp to oppose your crossing, then remain where you are. But if Porus takes with him a portion of the army and the elephants, then do you cross with all possible speed, for it is only the presence of the elephants that will make impossible the landing of the horses. The rest of the army can get over with little difficulty.' Such were the instructions given Craterus.

Another strong command was detached and placed under Attalus, Meleager, and Gorgias; these, the mercenary infantry and cavalry, were ordered to march out at nightfall to a point halfway to the crossing-place. Attalus was given Alexander's cloak and one of his suits of armor, to confuse possible hostile observers into believing it was the king himself. They were ordered to cross the river as soon as they became aware of the beginning of the engagement, if it was possible to do so. Alexander selected as his own force the heavy 'companion' cavalry, the cavalry regiments of Hephaestion, Perdiccas, and Demetrius; the newly brigaded light Sogdian, Bactrian, and Scythian cavalry; the whole of the hypaspists; the phalanx brigades of Coenus and Clitus, the thousand Dahae mounted archers; the foot archers and the Agrianians, a total estimated at from twenty to twenty-one thousand men. With these he marched out of camp at nightfall. That night the rainy season vindicated its name. The southwest monsoon was blowing, and a heavy storm of rain, with thunder and lightning, raged all night. The detachment trudged through the rage of the elements and reached the place where the boats, supplemented with hundreds of skin floats stuffed with straw, were waiting. These were dragged or carried down to the river bank, while the roar of the storm drowned out the unavoidable noises of the men, the clashing of weapons and armor, and the shouted commands. By daybreak the preparations were complete, and, now that it had served the Greeks well, the storm abated and ceased.

With the thirty-oared galley of Alexander, in company with Perdiccas, Lysimachus, Seleucus, and Ptolemy leading, the first of the heavy infantry moved out from the shore. They raced around the end of the island and landed, then immediately formed ranks, and moved out to guard against a possible assault upon the landing units. The whole of the cavalry, the men swimming with floats alongside their horses, were next brought over. These were seen, in the early light of morning, by Porus' river guards, who immediately galloped away to notify their king that the army was crossing and the long-threatened invasion begun. The cavalry were swiftly mustered into ranks and moved off, followed by the rest of the soldiers. Then it was found that they had landed on another and very large island, separated from the mainland by another arm of the river, ordinarily shallow and narrow, but now running a torrent, dangerously fast and full as an aftermath of the night's storm. At last, after much time had been lost, searchers found a place which could be forded. It is reported by Onescritos (later one of the chroniclers of Nearchus' historic voyage) that Alexander gave voice to his abounding vanity and hunger for praise and flattery, and also a hitherto unrevealed sense of humor. In the midst of the torrent, as the old Bucephalus hooves slipped and stumbled threateningly over the rounded stones on the bottom, he exclaimed: 'O Athenians, would you believe the toils and risks I run to gain your applause!' The water rose to the horses' heads, the infantry were shoulder-deep in the flood. Once across, the cavalry, five thousand heavy 'companions,' three thousand heavy auxiliaries, and three thousand light, were detached and taken by Alexander. Tauron, captain of the archers, was ordered to hasten forward as fast as possible to support them. The rest of the forces were to follow as expeditiously as was practical. Alexander led away to the southwest. He knew that Porus, faced with the double threat of the crossing of Craterus and Attalus, would be forced to divide his army into at least two parts, possibly three, to face the menace of their crossing on his flanks, and that he could use but a portion of his forces to confront the attack. It was always possible that the invader might have the opportunity of using the smashing attack of the cavalry alone, but if such seemed not feasible, he could always be guided by circumstances. If, on the other hand, the Indians should, faltering in the face of the necessity of unduly weakening their army by a double or triple division of their forces, break and flee, the cavalry were the perfect offensive instrument with which to pursue and smash the fugitives into utter panic-stricken rout. That last contingency, it transpired, was farthest from the minds of the Indians. Porus, brave and intelligent leader that he was, had no intention of supinely surrendering his kingdom without a fight to the finish.

Had Porus but correctly estimated the military guile of his enemy and instantly launched a smashing offensive, it is possible that he could have broken and driven the invaders back into the river, perhaps even saved his country from a repetition of the attempt at invasion. A defeat would, it is believed, in view of the attitude of the soldiers, have resulted now in the mutiny of the army that was but a month or so ahead anyhow. Unfortunately for Porus, he, like the Persian aristocrats, looked upon war somewhat as a chivalrous though highly exciting and dangerous sport, whereas to the deadly Greeks war was a murderous business of which the ultimate aim was utterly to smash and destroy and annihilate resistance. The difference between the two viewpoints was fatal to the defenders of their country. Now Porus had been outwitted and outmaneuvered, and he was quick to realize it, but he was still unaware of what he was facing. He was in a state of perturbed doubt. It was possible that the oncoming army were his allies, sent by Abisares, yet, if they were, why had they been on the wrong side of the river? If they were enemies, who was their leader and what was their strength? Across the river within easy eyesight was what seemed to be most of the invader's army, under Craterus, and it had already been reported that Alexander, with another force, was a few miles upriver, and seemingly preparing to cross. He promptly dispatched a reconnaissance column to investigate the approaching force. This column, under command of his own son, consisted of two thousand men and one hundred and twenty war chariots. By the time they appeared, Alexander had advanced some twenty stadia from the crossing-place, and was in the vicinity of the modern site of the village of Nurpur. When his scouts galloped back with intelligence of the approaching column, he sent forward the swift Dahae mounted bowmen, and led the cavalry onward more slowly, under the impression that he was faced with the vanguard of Porus' army. Presently the real strength of the forlorn hope was discovered by the Dahae, and swift messengers carried the news back. The heavy cavalry swung into their attack formation, a tight echelon, the light cavalry were thrown out on both flanks as a screen, and the whole, yelling like demons, hurled forward in a thunderbolt attack. Before their irresistible impact the outnumbered Indians were broken and shattered. Four hundred of their number fell in the first onslaught, including the son of Porus. The clumsy chariots were useless, literally stuck in the heavy clay, sodden and sticky from the night's downpour, and were captured intact, horses and all. The survivors fled back to their camp and reported that it was indeed Alexander who had crossed, and apparently with the bulk of his army. Porus then realized his sin of omission. His enemy had crossed the river without hindrance when a little more vigilance would have permitted him to make the attempt impossible or unbearably expensive. Now he would have to fight a pitched battle upon the open plain, instead of making a comparatively simple defense of a river crossing. And the battle would have to be fought while Craterus and Attalus menaced his flank, or a force sufficient to forestall them be detached, with the resultant weakening of his defense, for it was obvious now that they intended to cross at the first opportunity, to the assistance of their king. Though our sources are silent on this phase of the battle, we can give a résumé from piecing together bits of information from several other ancient writers. Figures have already been given of the strength of Porus' army. It is obvious, however, that not all were engaged in the coming struggle. The detachment of two thousand men and one hundred and twenty chariots had already been destroyed. Arrian says that elephants were among the guard left facing Craterus, and, as the latter did not attempt to cross until the battle was nearly over, we must assume that the big beasts were fairly numerous along his front. We can, therefore, assume that at least fifty of the elephants and hardly less than a minimum of five thousand men were so posted. Alexander had crossed by the use of boats. These were certainly then ordered downriver, no doubt to Attalus, Meleager, and Gorgias. Their failure to take part in the battle, considering their possession of transport facilities, can be read in no other light than that they too were prevented from crossing by the presence of a discouraging number of Indians and elephants on the opposite bank. Porus then can have had scarcely more than twenty thousand infantry, four thousand cavalry, if that many, and one hundred elephants, plus one hundred and eighty chariots to pit against the advancing Greeks. He assembled his army and his long battle line wheeled slowly and moved forward until it reached a place satisfactory to him. Here, in the vicinity of the modern villages of Badshahpur and Haria, he found the ground sandy and firm and free of clay, well suited to the maneuvers of his chariots and cavalry. He halted, dressed up his line of battle and waited the attack. It could hardly have been less happily formed for effective use against the solid and destructive impact of the Macedonian shock. The elephants, with their drivers on their necks, and with howdahs — towers, as the Greeks called them — full of soldiers on their backs, were posted in the front line, at intervals of a plethron (one hundred and and one feet) apart. It was expected that they would create panic among the horses of Alexander's cavalry and fear in the phalanx. In the intervals between the elephants archers were posted. Behind the elephants the Indian footmen were drawn up in a double line. There were no reserves. Additional infantry units were ranged on the wings parallel to the elephants, while the cavalry was equally divided between the extreme wings. Before the cavalry were ranged the chariots. Strangely, we have not a word of the activities of these vehicles in any of the accounts passed down to us. In view of their reported numbers, their obvious ineffectiveness can be only the result of swift and effective action against them, probably by the archers and mounted archers and the fast-moving javelin men who rendered such yeoman service against those other chariots at Arbela. At any rate, they accomplished nothing.

Alexander reached the battlefield, halted, and quietly watched the final touches and completion of Porus' battle line. Presently the hypaspists and other footmen hurried up by a forced march to join their king. Knowing that the time of his offensive was his to choose, he ordered them to rest to recover from the fast pace. Then he marshaled them into the solid block of taxeis he was accustomed to use, and ordered them into echelon. While this was being done he rode slowly along the front of his enemy's army, and as he did so, his brain, the brain of the best offensive strategist of that day, was working busily with the plans and details of the conflict that was to come.

The Indian line of battle was long, two to three miles, far too long and too thin to withstand even a semblance of a mass attack, and they had no reserves. Once that line was broken, or — his men got behind it — ! His blue eyes blazed as he visioned the possibilities of the thing that just occurred to him. The Indian right wing was far away, his left wing, due to the sharp westward bend of the river there, was 'up in the air' and not resting on the river bank, where Porus, by the most elementary rules of strategy, should have placed it. The elephants were the Indians' most effective weapon, not in lethal deadliness, but simply because the cavalry horses could not be forced into reasonable proximity with the great beasts. The Indian cavalry numbered but four thousand, and were divided into two divisions so widely separated as to preclude the possibility of joining each other. The Greeks, with eleven thousand cavalry and an additional thousand mounted bowmen, possessed overwhelming superiority in this hard-hitting arm. The Greek infantry, represented by the five thousand hypaspists, two thousand heavy hoplites, and the swift light troops, were a solid striking force, instinct with menace to the long thin Indian line. *This gave the attackers the inestimable advantage of overwhelming superiority at the point where the decisive action was to occur.* The plan of battle was simple. Alexander proposed to strike the enemy's left wing at the junction of the infantry and the elephants, turn right, and roll up the flank. Coenus and Demetrius were sent for, and ordered to hold back until the heavy 'companions' were engaged, then ride around the end of the enemy line and advance a short distance along his unprotected rear to attack the rest of the Indian cavalry when Porus, as was obvious he would, should order them from their useless position on the right wing and dispatch them to help their left. The footmen were placed under command of Seleucus, Antigones, and Tauron, with orders to attack when they saw the enemy's left wing breaking. The mounted bowmen were sent first, to throw the enemy into confusion with feinted charges and a storm of arrows. Following them, Alexander and the heavy cavalry hurtled in to the assault.

Porus had, in the meantime, divined Alexander's intention to attack, and sent for the rest of the cavalry. They came swiftly to the rescue, but with equal swiftness, Coenus, who had the shorter distance to travel, galloped at full speed in an arc around the left wing and fell upon the rear of the reinforcements. With perfect ease they turned both front and rear to meet the attack, but the massed weight of the Greeks was too great. They broke and, their horses, being accustomed to the big pachyderms, sought refuge between the elephants. Here (it would seem) they passed through the infantry's ranks and re-formed behind them. The elephants moved forward, only to be met by the solid massed phalangists and the light troops. These swarmed about them, discharging arrows and javelins at the men in the howdahs and into the animals themselves. Several crushed their way into the phalanx and did great damage, but the swordsmen ran in and began hacking at the elephants' legs. By this time the Indian cavalry had re-formed and came storming back into the battle. Alexander's cavalry, now massed into a single command, met and drove them back among the elephants and cooped them up among them. They could not force their own horses to follow, so they turned and fell upon the Indian infantry. The elephants, now being cooped up in a confused space, did no less damage to their friends than to their foes, trampling them underfoot as they pushed and wheeled about. Many of the elephant drivers were shot down by the Greek and Dahae bowmen. The elephants, without the accustomed and guiding hands, all suffering more or less from arrow and javelin wounds, and confused by the uproar of battle, began to grow unstable; then, as the push of the raging mobs became greater, they became frantic and attacked friend and foe alike in their mad attempt to escape. Alexander, seeing panic spread among the Indians, gave the signal. The phalanx closed up, locked their shields, and advanced behind a forest of projecting spear points. The Indian cavalry was cut to pieces and numbers of the elephants killed. The Indians broke and took to flight wherever they could find an opening in the Greek cavalry.

Meanwhile, Craterus, on the other side of the river, seeing the tide of battle setting against the enemy, hastily ordered the men into the boats and crossed over. They arrived at the beginning of the rout, and being fresh, immediately took up the pursuit of the broken defenders, killing in their retreat no fewer than had fallen in the engagement.

Porus, during the battle, behaved not only with the gallantry of a leader, but with the courage of a soldier, even when he saw the army melting before the massed spears of the phalanx and the elephants dead, riderless or in panic. He fought on as long as he could see any considerable body of his own men maintaining the contest. At last an Agrianian got within throwing distance and hurled a javelin at him. The projectile struck him in the right shoulder, the only portion of his body left uncovered by his fine armor, wounding him severely. He turned his elephant at last and began to retire. Alexander had been watching the Indian for some time, admiring his bravery and manliness. When he began to retreat at last, Alexander, knowing that presently the remorseless pursuit and slaughter of the fugitives would begin, and the pursuers would naturally concentrate their efforts on the king, was anxious to save his life. He therefore dispatched Taxilês, mounted upon a swift horse, upon that errand. Taxilês rode as close as he dared to Porus, and entreated him, now that the battle was lost, to stop his elephant and listen to the message he brought from Alexander. Porus turned around, and, seeing the speaker was his old enemy, poised his javelin. Taxilês instantly put his horse to the gallop and the projectile passed harmlessly by. Alexander sent another messenger, an Indian named Moeris, and an old friend of Porus'. As soon as Moeris delivered his message, Porus, faint with loss of blood from his wound, halted his elephant, dismounted, and was conducted to the victor. Alexander saw him coming and rode forward in front of his associates to meet him. Porus was a giant of a man, Arrian says, about seven feet tall. Alexander reined in his horse, struck with admiration at his appearance. He strode proudly on, defeated, perhaps, but unbroken and unabased, a brave man who had gallantly fought for and gallantly lost that which was his own. Alexander was the first to speak, asking Porus how he wished to be treated. It is reported that Porus answered, 'Treat me, Alexander, as a king,' and when Alexander, pleased at the reply, returned, 'For my own sake, Porus, that shall be done, but do you, in your own behalf, ask any boon you please.' The uncringing Indian replied that everything had been included in his first reply. Alexander, still more delighted with the second reply, restored his kingdom to Porus, without inflicting upon him the indignity of the customary monitorial Macedonian military commander. Porus became a staunch and valuable ally. Later his kingdom was extended greatly as the Greek conquests moved farther eastward, and still later, as Alexander withdrew from the country.

At this battle Alexander's famous and beloved horse, Bucephalus, died. Conflicting accounts are given us, some based on the report that the animal was fatally wounded during the fight, others that he died of old age, or it may have been both, a combination of old age and wounds. Bucephalus, in the summer of the year 326 B.C., had been Alexander's favorite mount for seventeen years, and Plutarch says he was now thirty-one years old, and was worn down by the hardships of long and arduous campaigning. Two cities were founded upon the river, of which one, upon the site of Jalalpur, was named Bucephala in honor of the horse; the other, Nicaea, the City of Victory, was built on the other side of the river, to commemorate the battle. Since the battlefield itself cannot surely be definitely located within a possible error of as much as five miles, so we cannot definitely locate the site of Nicaea. However, on the alluvial plain which holds the battlefield are three large modern villages built high on extremely ancient mounds, sites which have been in continuous use. These are Majhi, Haria, and Badshahpur. One of the three must be the site of Nicaea, with the probability resting on the latter place.

Diodorus places the losses of the Indian army at twelve thousand slain (wounded were usually slain in those days), nine thousand prisoners, and eighty elephants which were captured. The Greek dead he numbers at two hundred and eighty cavalry and over seven hundred infantry. The casualty percentage, on the basis of seven wounded to one dead, was shockingly high, nearly forty per cent of the forces engaged, grim attestation to the fury of the battle and the dauntless courage of the fighters. The heavy losses were very discouraging to the rank and file, and their morale, already low, fell even further, and seems to have contributed very largely to the famous mutiny that was soon to occur. The battle was fought either in late June or early July.

Those who fell in the battle were honored with a splendid military funeral and display, after which Alexander held a great celebration, offering sacrifices and holding the customary games and contests for the delectation of his god-guests, and a thirty-day rest was given the army. Craterus was then detached, given a heavy guard and the artisans and left to complete the building and fortifications of the new towns, and also to construct many additional boats of cedars (really deodars) which grew in plenty in the near-by mountains. Alexander moved southeastward against the Indians of the adjoining territory, a people transcribed by Aristobulus as the Glaucanicoi,[1] by Ptolemy as the Glausai. Their thirty-seven towns, several of which numbered over ten thousand inhabitants, peacefully surrendered to superior force, and the region was placed under domination of Porus. Abisares of Kas'mir, as an aftermath of the defeat of Porus, hastily returned home with his army, and sent the conqueror another embassy, including his brother, to make another submission, concretely expressing his abjection and subjection with a gift of money and forty war elephants. Several envoys also arrived from other independent Indians, and from another Porus.[2] Alexander, not unmindful of Abisares' attempted treachery, returned a cold and peremptory order to come in person and make submission, adding ominously that if he failed to come, Alexander would come to him. Phrataphernes, satrap of Parthia, arrived, apparently upon orders, bringing with him the Thracians to reunite them with the army. He soon returned to his satrapy. There was also news of outbreaks in the rear. Sissicottus, who had been left in the stone fort on Aornus, reported that the Assacenians had revolted, slain their governor, and were actively engaged in throwing off the Greek yoke. Philip of Gandhāra and Tyriaspes of the Cophen Valley were ordered to crush the rebellion and restore quiet and order.

The army marched on through a country of great forests where there were rhinoceroses, and where many of the men fell victims to snake-bites. The reptiles are described so clearly

[1] In the Prakrit Sanscrit this tribe appears as the Kalaka and Kalaja; in the Rajput chronicles as the Kalacha, of which the Greek Glausai is an excellent phonetic transcription. Aristobulus was also correct, for the second part of his transcription, the -anica, which he may or may not have employed in ignorance, means, in Sanscrit, a military unit or army, and, of course, the invaders were moving with the expectation of meeting the army of the Kalacha, or Glausai.

[2] Strabo (XV, 1) says this Porus was a nephew of the first. It would seem that his people were a part of the widespread Pauravas, occupying an undefined section of the Punjab to the eastward of the kingdom of the first Porus. That they were inimical to each other is not surprising; relatives who are also rulers are not infrequently enemies, even to this day.

that we can even recognize one species from the description alone, the extremely poisonous Indian whip-snake, whose victims die in agony. The rains continued very heavy, and the snakes, searching at night for a dry place, frequently crawled into the beds. Many men made themselves cord hammocks and suspended these from trees in the endeavor to escape the unwelcome bed companions. Arriving at the Acesines (today the Chenab or Cinab; Sanscrit, Asikni) River — it was running in full flood, fast and deep — the crossing was accomplished with great difficulty. Porus was sent back to his kingdom with orders to return with a contingent of the best fighting men he could muster and all the elephants he could gather, and rejoin Alexander. Coenus was left on the river with his brigade with orders to keep the passage open and assist the several detachments of foragers who had been left behind. Alexander moved northward toward the kingdom of the second Porus. He had, we are now told, sent an embassy to Alexander even before the battle at the Hydaspes, offering complete surrender, this more from hatred of his uncle than any love for the invader. Later he heard that Alexander had not only restored Porus' kingdom, but increased it. Now, fearing both kings, the younger Porus got together a small body of retainers and fled toward the mountains.

Alexander marched on and reached the Hydraotis, establishing many small temporary garrisons along the route so the heavily laden forage trains might traverse it in safety when they came along. Hephaestion was dispatched into the kingdom of the fugitive Porus with a strong command, to secure the country. He was then to head for the Hydraotis, and return down it reducing the free Indians along its banks, then add the entire territory to the domains of the first Porus. Beyond the river the people were small tribal units, living as independent primitive units, and the Greeks, considering their status equivalent to the autonomous cities of their own faraway homeland, call them the 'free Indians.' These groups can, by their very nature, have never been large, but they preferred freedom to servitude, and many tribes fought desperately to retain their freedom, though always heavily outnumbered. Some did surrender without fighting, others attempted to escape, but few got away from the remorseless cavalry pursuit.

Here it was learned that the Kathaians,[1] Oxydrakai, and the Mallians, independent tribes, had formed a confederation and were preparing to band together to preserve their ancient freedom. The Kathaians had fortified their capital city of Sangala, and were there awaiting both the onslaught of the invaders and the reinforcements of their allies. These people had already established their reputations as warriors, for some time before that Porus and Abisares had combined their armies and invaded the country. This unjustified invasion had so angered the tribesmen that their ferocious resistance had compelled the invaders to retreat without having accomplished anything commensurate with their vast preparations and intentions.

As soon as Alexander received the news of the coalition, he marched, and on the second day reached a place called Primpana, a town of the tribe of the Adraistai.[2] They surrendered upon demand. Alexander spent a day here, and was rejoined by both Taxilês and Coenus, who had marched hastily to rejoin the army. On the third day they left, and marched toward Sangala.[3] The city was defended by the Kathaians from behind a double

[1] Sanscrit literature gives us no help at all in localizing these peoples, and it is only by careful study of many factors that an acceptable conclusion can be reached. The best and most detailed study ever fully reported, will be found in the careful and scholarly work of Major G. H. Raverty, of the Indian Army, and reported in the *Journal of the Asiatic Society of Bengal* for July, 1892. No other work ever published has taken into cognizance the truly phenomenal changes, geographical, geological, ethnical, and climatic, in the Punjab of India since the day of Alexander. Major Raverty's paper is intensely difficult reading, and requires much careful study before it becomes intelligible, but it will greatly repay the patience of a serious student interested in the subject.

[2] Possibly Bheraneh, about twenty-five miles southeast of Lahore; the Adraistai seem to be the Sanscrit Airavati.

[3] There can be no objection to a well-founded belief that Alexander's line of march was now trending to the northward; our histories do not say this, indeed; they are so ambiguously worded that it is impossible to tell from them the line of travel at all. However, we must look for Sangala to the northward, and we find reason to conclude, though without conviction, and based only upon a number of possibilities and probabilities, that Sangala may be considered to have been at or near the site of modern Amritsar.

barricade of wagons, and severe fighting was necessary to drive them from their barricade. They then fled into the city and the battle was renewed there. The battle was deadly, and afterward the inhabitants were murderously treated, thousands being slain and more thousands made captives. Arrian, for the first time, gives us a complete casualty list of the attackers, stating that one hundred were killed and twelve hundred wounded. Two other towns near-by were summoned to surrender, but the inhabitants fled in terror instead. Alexander himself pursued them, but the greatest number escaped. Arrian says that about five hundred of them, those who, by reason of age or other infirmities, were slower than the rest, were overtaken and slain.

Porus and his troops were placed in garrison in the three towns and the army proceeded toward the Hyphasis (Beas. Sanscrit, Vipasa) River, Alexander intending to cross it and conquer the peoples on the other side also. He had no intention of leaving off the endless wars as long as a single man could be found whose neck was free of the Macedonian yoke. On the way he was met by the king of the area, whose domain lay between the Hydraotis and the Hyphasis. His name was Phegelas (Sanscrit, Bhagala, an offshoot of the aristocratic Kshattriyas of the warrior caste), who surrendered and accompanied the army. He told Alexander that the country which lay beyond the river was exceedingly fertile, the inhabitants good husbandmen, brave in war, and the country was well and justly governed. The report said that they had elephants greater in number than all other Indians. The people were the Gangaridae, whose king was Xandrames (Sanscrit, Chandramas, the 'Moon-god'), and the Prasii (this is an error — the Sanscrit word Prâchyâs means merely eastern, and is descriptive rather than generic), together possessing an allied army of twenty thousand cavalry, two hundred thousand foot, two thousand four-horse chariots, and over three thousand war elephants. The king considered the account, and asked Porus, who was present, if it were true. Porus replied that the account of the military strength was correct, but that the present king was sincerely despised by his subjects, and they desired so greatly to be rid of him that the invasion by Alexander would be the signal for them to revolt against him. The king was the son of a barber, of the despised lower classes, who, being physically handsome, had gained the love of the queen, and, through her connivance and influence, was advanced to a position as confidential adviser to the king. He then treacherously murdered the king and seized power, ostensibly as regent to the royal children. These were also murdered, and he reigned supreme. The story fanned afresh Alexander's insatiable desire for glory and power; though he feared to think of the fast and flooded rivers, harsh sands, and reptile-haunted forests that lay ahead. It seemed the fates themselves were forcing him onward, his abounding egotism forbidding him even to consider a halt in the ceaseless urge for conquest, though it was now carrying him into lands previously even beyond the dreams or imaginings of the Greeks. It is related that Anaxarchus one time was telling him of other worlds, the stars, which even in those days were known to be far larger than the earth. Tears came into Alexander's eyes as he envisioned larger worlds, when he was having so much trouble and difficulty conquering this small one. But now the army decided against it. They were immensely wearied of the continuous fighting and their unending labors, and they felt they must at last stop their senseless and unending warring. It may be that there was leadership in their attitude, but it seems it was absolutely spontaneous. Diodorus says that Alexander had already seen that the soldiers were worn by the interminable campaigning. The toils and dangers of the last eight years had reduced them to a state of misery, and he deduced that it would be necessary to inspire them again to further efforts. For death had made terrible ravages in their ranks, and the survivors had hopelessly concluded that his wars would never come to an end. Their Greek costumes had long been worn out, their armor battered and thin, and their weapons worn and blunted. They were dressed in rags and tatters and such as had clothing had made them from the cloth of Asiatic looms and cut in Asiatic styles. For seventy days they had labored on through a terrain infested with wild and dangerous beasts and deadly reptiles, and even these had taken heavy toll. The natives, too, were just as dangerous; though they were but small in number they often fought with berserk courage against the overwhelming numbers of the invaders and refused to stop until they were dead. And through it all the skies of the Indian rainy season had opened several times daily and rained upon them, until everything was wet and cold, their metal objects rusted or dulled with verdigris, their clothing and sleeping-cloaks wet and mildewing almost as they watched. The food was spoiling, and they could hardly get enough dry wood to build and maintain their fires for cooking and protection against prowling beasts and the night chill. Alexander was aware of all this, but he had so often used his flashing personality to gain his ends that he believed he could still continue to do so. It would be much harder this time, of course, but with a little thought he believed he could be assured of success. He had, consciously or unconsciously, reached a conclusion that every tyrant before and since has had at last to learn, that no man ever ruled any body of people without their consent; that the instant they ceased to give that consent, whether passive or active, that instant they were his masters, and continued to be the masters as long as they could act in unison. It was necessary to gain their consent; they, the almost slaves who had won for him his great empire, but against whom he was really powerless, unless they desired that he should be. If they could but be persuaded ——! Accordingly he gave them leave to take a stated time off and freely plunder the country — the country of the friendly King Phegelas. While they were gone upon their robbers' raids, he called the women and children together, and promised them, if they would persuade their husbands and fathers to continue, he would give them a stated food allowance and a subsistence allowance based upon a percentage of the men's pay. At last the raiders, carrying a 'rich and satisfactory' booty, returned to camp. He gathered them all together, and in a carefully weighed speech,[1] talked long to them in the endeavor to hearten them into continuance of the insane odyssey. But the men were utterly disheartened, and the shallow brilliance and the resounding phrases of their king's oratory fell upon unresponsive ears. After he had finished there was deep silence. None dared to speak in opposition to the king, but they were stubborn in their intent to refuse to go on. Alexander several times requested anyone who wished to speak his mind, though his views might be at variance with his own. At last Coenus, knowing the desires of all, and being an intimate friend of the king, spoke, Arrian says, to this effect: [2]

> ... I feel bound by my age, and the dignity of my rank, which requires that I should conceal nothing of our feelings. The toils I have undergone and the dangers I have faced embolden me to declare my sentiments freely. Much though I have done, greater exploits were done by you, and by many others who accompanied you from their homeland, so much and so great were they, it seems necessary and expedient to place bounds and measures upon our toils and hazards. For you must yourself see how great were the numbers of the Greeks and Macedonians who were with you at the beginning of this expedition, and how few are now left. As soon as you saw the Thessalians had no longer stomach for more war, and their courage began to fail, you permitted them to go home from Bactria [an error, which should read instead 'Ecbatana']; but of the rest of the Greeks, many of them were left in the cities you have built, some of them against their will. Others who accompanied the army either fell in battle, were incapacitated by wounds, or left behind in the cities of Asia; but by far the greatest number died of disease. Those few who remain are neither so sound in body nor so strong of mind as before. Those who remain have a great yearning to see their parents again, their

[1] Both Arrian and Curtius quote at great length what purports to be the speech he made here. Both vary little in substance, both obviously taken from the same source, but, read in the light of careful research, that source was plainly the writings of some rhetorician of a much later date. Hence, as it would serve no purpose to continue the perpetuation of a falsehood without historical basis, there is no point in quoting it.

[2] Arrian, V, 27. The quotation is given at length, not because of its purported authenticity, to which it can lay no claim, but because it describes so well what must have been the feelings of the army as a whole, and is a good exposition of their attitude.

wives and children, their native land itself; a desire understandable and pardonable in men who would return home in splendor derived from your munificence, raised from humble to high rank, and from poverty to wealth. Seek not then to lead them against their inclinations, for you will find them different men in the face of danger, and they will enter into contests with the enemy without heart. Do you also, if you wish, go home with us, see your mother again, set in order the affairs of Greece, and carry to the house of your fathers your numerous victories. Then, if it be your will, form and lead a new expedition against these tribes of eastern Indians, or against those on the shores of the Euxine Sea, or against Karchedon [Carthage] and those parts of Libya beyond Karchedon. Then but enfold your intentions and purpose, and other Macedonians and Greeks will follow you — young and vigorous men replacing those who have grown old and worn with hardship — men for whom war, through their inexperience with it, has no immediate terrors, and who will be eager to set out in hope of future rewards. They will follow you with all the greater alacrity from knowing and seeing the companions of your other toils and dangers who have returned home rich instead of poor, with great and merited distinction instead of their former poverty and obscurity....[1]

When Coenus finished his courageous reply to the king, those within hearing signified their approval with applause, while others showed by their tears their aversion to continue facing the ever-renewed dangers of battle and conquest, and how great was their desire to return. Alexander was stunned, despite the fact that he had anticipated something like this. For a moment he was silent, then a furious resentment against Coenus, for his

[1] This famous mutiny on the Hyphasis (Beas) must have been along the upper edge of the territory of the Oxydrakai (Kshudraka) tribe. These people occupied the river to a point downstream to the edge of the territory of the people called the Mallians by the Greeks. These were, correctly, the Malavas. In the Sanscrit writings the hyphenated name Kshudraka-Malava is universally employed, denoting the combination of the two tribes into a single political unit, however loose the unity may have been. Their union, running far into the future, was obviously at first a military alliance, later perhaps strengthened by a feeling of mutual regard and friendship. Certainly their attitude must have transcended mere convenience to last as long as it did. Curtius gives us a better transcription of the Kshudraka, calling them the Sudracae; Pliny, less accurately, the Sydraci.

freedom in accepting the invitation to express himself, seized him. Abruptly he broke up the conference and retired to his tent. The next day, his anger still high, he called still another assembly, harangued them a long time and accused them of abandoning him, closing with a declaration that he would go forward alone if necessary. Stony silence greeted the announcement. In blind rage and frustration he again retired to his tent and refused to admit or see anyone for three days. He was waiting and hoping for a change in the army's mood, a reaction not infrequent among bodies of troops, the hope they would change their minds, and yield to his persuasions and magnetic personality. On the third day silent gloom still reigned in the camp. The soldiers were offended at his wrath, but their minds remained unchanged. Cross that river they would not. The army was in passive revolt, and even an Alexander must give way to them. On the third day he emerged from his tent, and the customary sacrifices and reading of omens were held. Aristander may have been instructed as to his findings by Alexander, or he may have been instructed in private by a war-weary officer suggestively fingering a sword. The results were the same. The omens were found unfavorable for a continued advance. The gods had endorsed the attitude of the men, as the gods usually endorse the strongest side, and vetoed further conquest. Alexander could permit the gods to give him orders. That day a council of the officers was called, and he announced that, as the gods had decreed against the crossing, he was ready to turn back.[1]

Before this was done, however, he determined to leave behind him monuments that would be a lasting commentary, and mark for all time the boundaries of the empire now grown so great

[1] J. A. French (in his book *Himalayan Art*, page 65) reports there is a legend in Kashmir to the effect that Alexander visited the city now known as Kangra, and there set up a statue of his wife (obviously a Nikê, or Victory). Although none of our historians record a single fact that can give a base for this story, it is not impossible that Hephaestion, in his raid to the northward of the main line of advance, may have gone that far. It is also possible, of course, in a land where Alexander is still a great and heroic figure of legend, that the legend has no base whatever.

from such a small beginning. The memorial must be such as to match his accomplishments, if that were possible. Twelve great altars,[1] each as high as a fortified tower, were projected, and the army divided into twelve divisions to do the work. Upon the altars were engraved these words, the dedication of a monomaniac whose headlong career of international rapine was at last brought within boundaries: 'To my father Ammon; to my brother Heracles; to Athene the wise; to Olympian Zeus; to the Cabiri of Samothrace; to the Indian Helios; and to my brother Apollo.' In the center of the altars a column of bronze was erected, and upon it engraved the simple yet arrogant legend: 'Here Alexander halted.' In this last brief inscription was expressed all the grieved frustration of the man whom nothing before had ever been able to thwart; whose dominions now surpassed anything the world had ever known before. He had been raised to ineffable power by the unspeakable sacrifices of his army, at a cost in human misery and death too great to count, and was now forced to halt by the sheer inability of the mortal men of that army to drive themselves further. An ironical note enters here, and is worth recording. Sandrocottus (Chandragupta Maurya), who in later years was to break the Greek power in India and weld all the northern part of the country into an empire, was in Alexander's camp at the time. He later told Megasthenes that so great was the hatred of the eastern Indians for their king, if Alexander had crossed the Hyphasis, the people themselves would have assisted the invaders against their own rulers.

After the altars were completed, another great festival was held and sacrifices offered the gods. The whole of newly conquered country was committed to the suzerainty of Porus, and

[1] These twelve towering altars or traces of them have been sought in vain in recent years. Megasthenes, when he was ambassador a dozen years later to the court of Chandragupta Maurya (Sandrocottus in our story) from Seleucus Nicator, reported the Indian king made yearly pilgrimages to them, there to offer sacrifices in the Greek fashion. His son, the famous Asoka, is reported to have followed the custom also. Appolonius of Tyana, in 42–45 A.D., visited them and found the inscriptions still legible. There is good reason to believe the site was along the chain of heights paralleling the Beas River, some twelve or fifteen miles below modern Gaurdaspur.

at last the order was given to turn back. Joyfully the soldiers broke camp and turned their faces westward toward their long-lost homeland thousands of miles away. They crossed the Hydraotis River and marched on to the Acesines, reaching the guard town [1] (unidentifiable) which Hephaestion had been sent to build. The task was completed and here were left another unwilling contingent of men too broken by wounds, disease and hardship to continue the hard journey. Here too came Arsaces [2] whose domain adjoined that of Abisares, to make submission. Also the brother of Abisares, with a large embassy, came to Alexander, bringing a quantity of valuable presents and thirty additional elephants. They reported that Abisares was too ill to come personally, and begged Alexander's indulgence for his failure to do so. His own men corroborated the statement, and he, convinced at last, confirmed Abisares in his rule, and set the amount of the annual tribute he must pay. Additional sacrifices were made to the gods; the army crossed the Acesines and marched on to the Hyphasis River.

They reached the river, and immediately found themselves faced with the necessity of rebuilding Nicaea and Bucephala, whose mud walls had been much damaged by the rainy season. This done, attention was turned toward the fleet which had been built, Arrian says eight hundred boats. Of these eighty were thirty-oared galleys, and two hundred were flat-bottomed scows for use as horse transports. We are told elsewhere that native dyers had been brought in and made to dye brilliant cloths for awnings and streamers and other decorations for the fleet. While these preparations were going on, Coenus was taken

---

[1] These guard towns probably consisted of little more than a mud-walled fort with quarters for their garrisons. As successful uprisings against the Greeks occurred in the next few years, the forts and their garrisons were destroyed, the forts fell into ruin, and the sites returned to the jungle. In places where the sites continued in use, the brief occupancy of the Greeks made so little impression upon the people that the Sanscrit writers do not even mention legends of the occupation. These places are irrevocably lost to history.

[2] Uras'a, ruler of what approximates the modern district of Rash, the hill country between Kas'mir and the Indus. His territory would thus lie northward of Taxila and south of Hazara.

ill and soon died. Alexander had never forgiven him for his outspokenness on the Hyphasis, but now he gave him a military funeral with the pomp and military ceremony befitting his rank. He then called together his high ranking officers and all the ambassadors present from Indian potentates, and ceremoniously and solemnly invested Porus with authority as king absolute of all the conquered lands east of the river.

Curtius reports that at this time reinforcements arrived from Thrace, seven thousand infantry and five thousand cavalry. They were escorting a shipment, sent by Harpalus, of twenty-five thousand complete suits of armor,[1] and a large quantity of medicines and other supplies. Taxilês and Porus, in the meantime, had been raking up old feuds and fanning the smoldering coals of hostility. These Alexander forced to become reconciled, and strengthened the reconciliation with a marriage alliance. Both helped to the extent of their abilities in forwarding completion of his arrangements to get under way, and, one is tempted to believe, not wholly through devotion to their conqueror. Once he was gone, they would be rid, not only of him, but freed of the necessarily enormous exactions and requisitions of the army and its horde of followers. And in that early day, as in this, foreign conquerors were not wholly loved by conquered.

PART TWO, SINDH

The fleet moved slowly in order that the faster boats should not run away from the slower, and to maintain contact with the two divisions of the army ashore whose more circuitous route

---

[1] This brings up interesting conjectures. A complete suit of armor weighed in the neighborhood of sixty pounds. If the pack animals employed were the small mules or asses of central Asia, two of those suits would constitute for each animal a reasonable load for such a long journey. The medicines and other supplies must have been in considerable quantity to gain historical recognition. Taking the weights and quantities into consideration, together with the carriage requirements of the reinforcements and the cavalry remounts, the incoming train must have numbered at least twenty-five thousand animals with several thousand attendants and slaves; a staggering number to pass from the Hellespont across Persia and into India.

necessarily obliged them to travel farther daily. On the third day they halted at a point where Craterus and Hephaestion had been ordered to encamp on opposite sides of the river. Philip had also been given a considerable detachment, and he was following three days behind Hephaestion as a rear-guard for the enormous trains. This fact seems to indicate, not only that the natives of the area were undependable in their allegiance to the conqueror, but possibly even engaging in hostilities, although we are forced to read in between the lines to get an inkling of the conditions prevailing. It was hereabouts (though Curtius and Diodorus place the event elsewhere) that Sophytes (Arrian calls him Sopeithes, Curtius Sophitis; coins have been found bearing his name in Greek letters as Sophytes), king of the country covered by the Salt Mountains, came with a great and gorgeous retinue, and surrendered to Alexander.[1] Philip marched in two days later, and was immediately sent across to the Acesines River with orders to follow it downstream, sweeping its banks free of unsubdued peoples. The other divisions were sent ahead on their own lines of march. A number of river settlements surrendered at the approach of the invaders or upon demand; others, which resisted, were ruthlessly devastated by fire and sword. From this point on it seems Alexander's fury at his enforced return from the Hyphasis was taken out on the

---

[1] Arrian makes no mention of the following story; it probably seemed hardly credible to him, though Curtius, Diodorus, Plutarch, Pliny, and Aelian all pass it on to us. Curtius (IX, 1, 31), after describing the many good qualities of the people and their high mental standard and physical beauty, tells us of a type of hunting dog whose prowess was exhibited in an arena before Alexander: '... four of which, being let loose upon a lion, an officer took one which had fastened upon the beast, and cut off one of his legs, then another, and continued to hack and mangle him till he had killed him, yet was the dog so obstinate and savage that he would not let go, but left his teeth sticking in the lion.' A number of these dogs were presented to Alexander, many of which eventually found their way back to Macedonia to survive even to this day as the breed now known as the Molossian mastiff. That they were identical to the ferocious-looking hunting dogs depicted in the bas-reliefs of the palace at Nimrud (circa 640 B.C.) and the palace of Assurbanipal at Nineveh (668–628 B.C.; these bas-reliefs can be seen in the British Museum) there can be no doubt. They were also probably the terrible war-dogs of the Mongols (Mughals) at the time of their conquests, and probably the ancestors of the modern Bunjara and Polygar dogs, fierce and intractable brutes standing about thirty-two inches high at the shoulder, used today in India for hunting tigers and panthers.

Indians, for, savage as were his actions in Bactria and Sogdia, his ruthless murderousness along the rivers of India was greater. He had absolutely no regard for human life or suffering, but it must also be admitted that he had as little for his own. Unfortunately, however, those he ruthlessly destroyed had not his own paranoiac obsession of kinship with the gods and the intense conviction that he would at last sit with them on high. He is described,[1] now, as a man of dark and gloomy thoughts, having no regard for human life, and facing death with a complete unconcern, mystically and sublimely confident that only by the omnipotent will of his father Ammon could aught happen to him.

He moved rapidly down the river to the land of the Mallians, and, as he fancied, their allies, the Oxydrakai, for he had received information that they were the most warlike of all the Indians. He was now told that they had sent their women and children to their strongest towns for safety and plainly intended to give him a hostile reception. Hoping to reach and attack them before they were thoroughly prepared for defense, he pushed ahead with all possible speed.

In five days' traveling time from the army rendezvous, he reached the confluence of the Hydaspes and the Acesines, where several boats were sunk and many damaged by the violence of the currents and eddies created by the junction of the two streams. Two of the larger galleys crashed together and were sunk with most of their crews. Alexander's own craft was in such danger that he removed his clothes and prepared to swim for safety. When the fleet got through, Alexander, who had feared a disaster of greater magnitude, drew up in a bay behind a headland and landed. His first act was to give a fervent thank-offering to the gods for his passage, then start repairs on the damaged boats. Nearchus was ordered to take command of the fleet, complete the repairs, then proceed on down to the territories of the Mallians. Alexander took his men and 'made inroads into the territories of the barbarians [Arrian gives them no name, but

[1] Athenaeus, XII, 53.

365

it is clear that here is meant the people called the Siboi by Curtius, the Sibi by Diodorus] who had refused their submission, to prevent them sending succor to the Mallians. He then rejoined the fleet.' The Siboi probably suffered relatively little, for Arrian says the tribesmen were a pastoral people, who dressed in the skins of wild beasts and fought with clubs. They also, he says, branded their cattle with what the Greeks called a club, which they concluded to be in commemoration of their tribal founder and colonizer, mythically Heracles.[1] People of this type, nomads, or at most dwellers in small family or clan groups, could have been punished only with expenditure of much time and energy spent in their pursuit; the raid was therefore probably hardly more than a threatening demonstration.

It is impossible to say with absolute certainty just where the next incidents occurred, for although there has been little change in the beds of the Five Rivers in their upper courses due to the hilly character of the country, in their lower courses they have changed often and widely. It is safe to say that all of them flow at present far to the westward and northward of the courses they followed in that day. There is reason to believe that the junction of the Hydaspes (Jihlam) and the Acesines (Cinab) was at that time some thirty-odd miles northeast of Jhang, in the district of the same name. If such was the case, the Siboi must have been a small tribe to the east of the Hydaspes (and were probably the ancestors of the half-wild pastoral Jats who are the primitive settlers of the district), for Alexander never permitted unsubdued peoples who might be a grave source of danger to remain in his rear. Had they been west of the river, Craterus would have had the task of attending to them. After the junction of the two rivers into a single stream, the single one continued to bear the name of Acesines.

[1] This is intelligible only when it is understood that even today most Indians of the west claim to have been founded by Rama, son of Krishna. As the Greek Heracles was equated with Krishna, it was easy to alter Rama into Krishna into Heracles, thus satisfying their need to recognize their own pantheon in the doings of all, even foreign, gods.

Alexander found Hephaestion, Craterus, and Philip had already reunited their forces. Craterus was given the elephants and Philip's troops and ordered to scour the west bank of the river and proceed downstream. Hephaestion was given a large detachment and sent across country to the banks of the Hydraotis River. He was told to be there and move downstream in five days' time. Ptolemy, son of Lagus, was given a division and told to wait three days after Alexander had left, then turn and follow the Acesines downward. Alexander with his chosen forces marched two days after Hephaestion left, following upon his tracks to a point halfway between the two rivers. He was then to turn southwest and parallel the routes of the three other columns, sweeping both rivers and the country between free of unsubdued tribesmen. Any Indians fleeing from one column would thus fall into the hands of another, regardless of the direction they chose to fly. Nearchus was ordered to take the fleet and go ahead of the armies ashore.

Alexander had selected for his division his usual and favorite hypaspists, archers, and Agrianians, the mounted Dahae bowmen, and half the heavy 'companion' cavalry; that is to say, probably seven thousand footmen and thirty-five hundred mounted men. He marched late in the afternoon, from a point probably some twenty miles above Jhang, and halted late in the evening at a small stream (possibly the little Ayek River). The men ate their frugal rations and rested awhile. Then he issued orders that every man should fill whatever water vessel he had, for there was no more water between the bivouac and their objective. They marched all night across an arid waste (the Sandar Bar) fifty miles wide, toward a city to which the Mallians had fled for security. We are not told in what direction he traveled, but, judging from the conditions prevailing in this terrain, and from the context, it must have been east by south, or even east, which would have brought him northward of the site of modern Kot-Kamaliah, and probably to the site now known as Samandar, which is possibly where the city stood. In the morning, the Mallians, never dreaming of the grim tenacity of purpose of the Macedonian, that he would cross such a desolate country, went out as usual to their fields, unarmed and unprepared. The Greeks suddenly arrived and fell upon them. Many were slain, terrified and unresisting, before a defense could be made ready. The rest fled to the city and barred the gates. The first of the army to arrive was the cavalry. They now surrounded the city and awaited the arrival of the footmen. When these came up, Perdiccas, with two of the cavalry brigades and the fleet-footed Agrianians, was dispatched posthaste to another near-by town with orders to bottle up the inhabitants of the place to prevent any escaping to carry the news of the sudden invasion to the rest of the near-by Indians, but to refrain from attacking the town until Alexander himself should arrive. An immediate assault was then made upon the walls, whereupon the Indians abandoned the town proper and fled to the citadel. Here they held out for a time, but soon the raging attackers, under the eyes of their imperious young king, carried the walls and broke in. The entire population, some two thousand men, women, and children, were brutally massacred. Perdiccas, in the meantime, reached the place he had been ordered to besiege, only to find it abandoned. The inhabitants had already received the terrifying news. Hearing that they had but recently fled, he dispatched the cavalry hastily after them. Many were overtaken and slain, but the majority, urged by fear of death, managed to reach and hide in the marshes along the river, where the heavy horses could not follow.

Alexander permitted his division to pause from their murderous labors, to loot, eat, and rest, then marched again shortly after dark. At daybreak, after marching all night, they reached the Hydraotis River. Here at a ford he found that parties of the Mallians, fleeing from the invasion, were crossing the river. Like a madman, demoniacal with blood lust, he remounted and rushed after them. Many were slain at the ford. He led the cavalry through the river, shallow now at the height of the dry season, and mercilessly pursued the panic-stricken fugitives across the plain. Many more fell victim to the pursuers, but many others escaped, taking refuge in a near-by small town. Alexander waited until the hypaspists came up, then dispatched Python, with his taxis and two chiliarchies of cavalry, to the refuge. It fell at the first assault, and again large numbers fell to the ferocity of the Greeks, though they also took a number of prisoners. They then returned to the camp near the river, where Alexander and his men were resting after a night of marching and a half-day of fighting. After giving them a short rest he marched to a near-by city of the Brahmans where other of the wretched Mallians had fled for refuge. At his approach they shut themselves up in the citadel. Alexander, his berserk murderousness unabated by the slaughter of the morning, himself led the van up the scaling ladders. The Brahmans, their fighting men outnumbered by the far better-armed attackers, set fire to their refuge rather than surrender, and while the smoke billowed up in clouds, the invaders ran about the keep, slaughtering every person within reach of their weapons. Those in the citadel perished in the flames, and Arrian reports five thousand died here, for so great was their courage that few of the Indians would ask or accept quarter.

The following morning Python and Demetrius were detached, given a command of light cavalry, and dispatched to scour the forested river banks for escaped fugitives. Alexander with the rest of the forces moved back toward the river, on the other side of which, he was informed, lay the capital city of the Mallians. Their fighting men, instead of waiting for him to come to them, had decided to carry the war to him instead. They were awaiting his approach on the other side of the river. Alexander trotted off with the cavalry to see, after ordering the hypaspists to follow with all possible speed. When he reached the river, he saw his enemies posted on the opposite bank, which was steep and difficult of ascent. Nothing daunted, he plunged ahead. The Indians, seeing the daredevil attackers in the middle of the stream, withdrew from the bank and started to retire, yet keeping their ranks in good order. The Greeks reached the other side, swarmed up the bank, and took up the pursuit. When the Indians saw how few the attackers were, they halted, faced about, and prepared to offer battle.

Alexander rode near to the enemy, and decided their close-packed ranks too well disciplined and warlike for his limited force. He therefore rode around on their flank and began charging them, though never to the point of actual contact. Meanwhile, the Agrianians and other light footmen hurried up ahead of the heavier hypaspists. The Indians, seeing the reinforcements arriving, wheeled around, and, suddenly becoming panicky, broke and fled headlong to 'the strongest of all the cities that lay near.' This may, as some have interpreted it, mean their capital. But it seems to me that if the capital had been meant, the statement would have mentioned it, especially as we had the previous reference. Many were caught and killed on the way, but those who escaped entered the city and barred the gates. Alexander threw a cavalry cordon about the walls and awaited the arrival of the hurrying and breathless infantry. When they came up they were distributed in several bivouacs about the city [1] investing it closely. Heavy guards were posted, and, it being late in the afternoon, the men off duty were permitted to refresh themselves and rest after their day of hard fighting and forced marching.

The following morning Alexander divided his command into two parts, himself taking one, Perdiccas the other, and assaulted the town from two different points. The low mud walls were a

[1] This city is confidently identified by General Cunningham as Multan, a conclusion which, though demonstrably erroneous, has been widely and blindly accepted by many. Cunningham's survey of the area involved must have been of the most sketchy and elementary sort, for it is impossible otherwise to understand why the scholarly general could have made so many errors in his identification. The place cannot be identified — any assertion to the contrary notwithstanding. In the time of the Arab conquests, a thousand years after Alexander, the junction of the Acesines and the Hydraotis (Cenab and Ravi) Rivers occurred some twenty miles *above* Multan. The Ravi was *then* at the *southern limit* of its *then* meandering valley. Since that time it has, due to tectonic and other earth movements, moved northward again. It is safe to say, judging from ancient channels and a careful study of the Arabic chronicles, at around Alexander's time the Hydraotis and the Acesines met at a point between Shorkot and Sidhuki Sarai, probably nearer the former place, which is some seventy-eight miles north of Multan. The ancient channel so confidently traced by General Cunningham would seem to be far more ancient than Alexander's day.

slight barrier to the impetuous attack, and the defenders soon abandoned it, fleeing to the greater security of the citadel. Alexander's men found a small gate in the town wall and soon battered it down and entered unopposed. But Perdiccas, on the other side, had no gate to enter, and, being in possession of only a few scaling ladders, found it more difficult to scale the wall and took longer to get in. The first force reached the citadel and tried to force an entrance, some immediately beginning sapping the wall; others brought timbers to use as scaling ladders. Alexander, thinking the men who brought the first scaling ladder were much too slow, impatiently snatched it from their hands, placed it against the wall, raised his shield over his head, and began to climb. Hard upon his heels came the bodyguard Peucestes, carrying the ancient sacred Trojan shield from the temple of Athene at Ilium. Third to mount the wall was Leonnatus, and by a different ladder, Abreas, one of the soldiers whose bravery and services had been rewarded by making him a *dimoirites*, one who received double pay and allowances. Alexander reached the coping of the wall, rested his shield against it, and brought his long sword into swift and deadly action. He soon cleared a place on the parapet and leaped upon it. The Indians retreated along the wall, and, not daring to come within reach of the berserk Macedonian, began to hurl missiles at him. The intruder was a magnificent sight as he stood there limned against the sky, his polished armor gleaming, and the long white plume of his helmet swaying in the breeze. Several Indians, on the ground below, ran up and began hurling javelins and stones at him. Within a few seconds he was the target of a score of projectiles. Realizing that if he stood there momentarily longer, he would risk death without having accomplished anything, but if he leaped to the ground inside the citadel he might, by the unexpectedness of the action, astonish the Indians into momentary paralysis, in which time, though he might be soon slain, he would die as became a son of Ammon and brother of Heracles after godlike feats and deeds which would be long remembered by mankind. At this instant the hypaspists, in terror for the safety of their king, mobbed the ladders and began to ascend in such numbers the ladders broke under their weight just as Leonnatus and Peucestes swarmed over the top of the wall. An instant later Abreas leaped to the wall, just avoiding a fall as that ladder too broke under the weight of the clawing mass of armored men, struggling upward. As Alexander touched the ground, he slipped off balance from the force of his landing and nearly fell to the ground. With cat-like quickness he recovered his equilibrium, sprang back against the wall, and the long sword licked out like a silver flame. Several Indians rushed him, including the commander of the citadel. The long blade cut him down. The rest retreated. All this took but an instant. With a shout Abreas flung himself from the wall, to be followed a second later by Leonnatus and Peucestes. Several Indians leaped forward again. Alexander stooped swiftly, snatched up a stone in either hand, felled an Indian with one stone and drove the others back. Abreas, Peucestes, and Leonnatus sprang to the assistance of their king, and together the four faced their foes, their swords dealing death and wounds. Abreas was struck in the forehead by an arrow and fell dead. A stone hurtled through the air and struck Alexander on the helmet with stunning force. Dazed for an instant, his muscles relaxed and lowered the protecting shield. Instantly an arrow flashed over the top of the shield, and struck with such force it penetrated the breastplate, so that, Arrian reports, air from the punctured lung bubbled out with the well-ing blood. Still he stood upright and fought back for several minutes, until at last dizziness and faintness overcame him. The conqueror's arm sagged and he collapsed with a crash of armor upon his shield. Leonnatus leaped toward his king, and Peucestes bestrode his body, raised the ancient Trojan shield and fought. Soon he and Leonnatus were both seriously wounded. Meanwhile the hypaspists, still outside the wall, were becoming frantic. They had seen Alexander leap into the stronghold, and they had broken the ladders in their eagerness to follow him to the top of the wall. Several drove wooden pegs into the mud wall, and, not without difficulty, managed to climb up. Others formed a pyramid of their own bodies and boosted others up. Still others rushed to the gate and began to batter it down with a great beam. The first men to reach the top of the wall immediately flung themselves down. There they saw Alexander on the ground and raised a howl of grief and rage. A deadly struggle ensued over the prostrate body. Presently those who were desperately smashing at the gate beat it down, and the hypaspists, frantic with fear for their king and rage at the defenders, burst in. They immediately began killing the Indians, sparing not a single soul in the citadel, man, woman, or child.

Others hastily improvised a stretcher and carried Alexander back to camp. Arrian had before him, as he wrote, two different accounts, the most credible of which follows. The physician Critodemus,[1] after sawing the arrow shaft in twain, lifted off the gorget, and found the arrowhead was so firmly embedded in the bone that it had to be cut out. This he told Alexander, and several of his friends gathered about asked for permission to hold him during the operation. 'A man who can hold himself needs no one else to hold him,' returned the king. He nevertheless fainted under the operation, which made it easier to do the work. The wound was so dangerous that for several days his life hung by a thread, and he was necessarily kept quiet, with a refusal of visitors.

Downriver, at the main camp, rumor was bruited abroad at last that the king was dead, and uneasiness quickly spread through the host, doubt and unease over the appointment of a new commander. This would be the first necessary move, and unfortunately there were a number of officers who could

---

[1] Curtius says the name of the physician was Critobulus. Pliny (*Natural History*, VII, 37) gives this statement a certain possible of authenticity, for he says that a physician of that name attained great celebrity when he extracted the arrow which put out Philip's eye, and it is quite possible that Alexander would have his father's physician along. Still another account has it that Perdiccas cut out the arrowhead with his sword as there was no physician present. The account I have followed seems the most credible.

reasonably assert their right to lay claim to the title. All were friends and followers of the king, and it began to look as if, regardless of who was chosen to wear the mantle of command, internecine strife could be predicted almost with certainty. And if this took place, the army, thousands of miles from home, was surrounded by hostile peoples longing for some such opportunity to get revenge for the unspeakable and unjustified brutalities that had been inflicted upon them. And if they should escape civil war, how, without the guiding hand and personality of Alexander, could they return home through the Asiatic deserts and mountains, through tribes yet unsubdued and likely to fight bitterly to prevent their passage and retain their own ancient liberties? The whole army was permeated with fear of what the future might hold. Then came the welcome news that Alexander still lived. Suspecting a trick by the officers, the soldiers refused to believe it. Even when a letter came from Alexander, predicting his early return, they distrusted it, fearing that the clique surrounding the king had concocted a forgery to keep the men quiet while they agreed on a plan of action. This news was carried back to Alexander. In order to prevent the men from getting out of hand and starting an insurrection out of pure fear, as soon as he was able to move he had himself carried to the Hydraotis River, and thence sailed down to the camp at the junction of the Hydraotis and Acesines, where Hephaestion was in command of the camp and Nearchus with the fleet was waiting. When the boat drew near to the camp, the king ordered the awning removed from the poop where he lay and raised his arm in salutation to the dense throng of anxious soldiers lining the river banks. At last they were convinced that he still lived, and a roaring cheer rent the air. At the landing-place he disdained the stretcher that was brought for him and called for a horse, mounted and rode to the door of his tent, then dismounted that he might be seen walking. The army was satisfied at last. So was Alexander. The army, which for months had been verging upon open mutiny, which had refused to cross the Hyphasis River and die to further his egotistic and murderous glory, was his once more, heart and soul. Later, when Craterus and Ptolemy ventured to remonstrate with him for risking his life for the sake of the capture of an obscure village, he answered that he would willingly act the same way again. Then, warming to his subject, he expatiated long upon the subject of his divine origin, and even aired his intention of having his mother Olympias deified and worshiped as a goddess.

While recuperating from his wound, Alexander received envoys from the Mallians who had escaped or survived the captures of the towns, begging amnesty and offering submission. The Oxydrakai from the northeast, horrified at the catastrophic descent of the conqueror upon their neighbors, and fearing their turn was coming next, likewise sent emissaries, the leading men of all their towns, bearing gifts and supplications for peace. Evidently someone had been coaching them as to the correct approach, for they told him that they loved the freedom which they had preserved intact from the time Dionysus came to India until Alexander's arrival. Since it was reported to them that Alexander was of the same race of the gods (a nicely calculated statement, designed to please him, and yet not commit themselves to perjury) they were willing to accept him as their king, and as satrap anyone he might care to appoint over them; they would pay the tribute he demanded, and give hostages to suit his desires. His answer was an order to send him immediately one thousand hostages, the flower of their nation, to be kept as hostages if he wished, or be used as auxiliaries in his conflicts with other Indians. They accordingly selected and sent him a thousand of their best men, gratuitously adding five hundred fully equipped war chariots. He kept the chariots, but returned the hostages, perhaps using the vehicles as they were, perhaps rebuilding them into wagons for the supply and baggage trains. He then, as his last act in these territories, made Philip satrap over the Oxydrakai and Mallians, giving him the Thracians and a number of other troops as garrisons and peace-preservation corps, and left them in the town whose widespread ruins are today known as Shorkot.

While Alexander's wound was healing, the woodworkers and shipwrights were kept busy building a considerable number of new boats. He accordingly took on board about a third of the 'companion' cavalry, ten thousand infantry, and a number of light footmen, and sailed down to the junction of the Acesines and Indus Rivers. Here Perdiccas, who had been sent to subdue a small independent tribe called the Abastanai (Sanscrit, Ambastha, historically a people of the lower Cinab) along the lower reaches of the Acesines, having finished his task, marched in and joined him. Presently the two other divisions also marched in. Here he founded another city also named Alexandria.[1] During the stay at this place, Oxyartes, who had been reported for malfeasance or misfeasance and was summoned, marched in from Bactria, and reported to his son-in-law king. What was done we have no way of knowing, but Alexander appointed him as satrap of the Paropamasadae, vice Tyriaspes, who, according to what must have been well-authenticated reports, had also wrongfully used his authority. He was ordered hanged. The grim old Bactrian warrior was ordered to keep peaceful the turbulent mountaineers, with special stress upon the rebellious Aspasians. Soon afterward, in anticipation of the conquest of the territories that lay between his newest city and the sea, the conqueror gave these lands into care of Oxyartes, proof at least of the regard in which he held the father of his beautiful wife.

[1] From this area, the probable site of Alexandria, to the delta of the Indus is over four hundred miles. Our narrators have dwelt very briefly on this line of the campaign, giving us little more than the bare details of shocking massacres of tribes inhabiting unnamed towns, and mentioning no single outstanding feature of the country by which our search and identification of routes and places can be guided. Our Sanscrit sources are almost equally useless, so we turn to the Arabic. Thus we find, adequately described and located, a place called Askaland-Ussa, an easy corruption of Alexandros-Uchcha, the latter word meaning 'high.' At the period of the Muhammedan conquests, the Indus still followed its ancient route, and Askaland-Ussa (modernly called Uchch) was a place of great importance. Later, the river shifted its bed to another farther west, leaving the town waterless and forty miles from the new line of flow of the river. The place, now without a dependable water supply, was then deserted. The area was first explored by Masson, who reports it to be 'chiefly distinguished by the ruins of former towns, which are very extensive, and attest to its former pristine glory.'

While this was going on in India, the Greek soldiers who had been ordered into perpetual exile as garrisons in Bactria, had begun, as Greeks generally did, to quarrel among themselves, and revolted. The strange land, new people, new ways, and the overbearing harshness of their superiors, as well as the home-sickness which afflicts all persons, especially those of a narrowly nationalistic outlook, were intolerable. Careful plans were laid by their leader, Athenodorus, and, taking to arms, they had little difficulty making themselves masters of the citadel. Athenodorus planned to make himself king, not from imperial ambitions, but in order to obtain the necessary authority to control the turbulent soldiery while he led them on the long and weary journey back to their homeland. Unfortunately for him, however, another prominent Greek, Biton, hating him from envy, laid a plot, and invited him to a feast where he was assassinated by a native of Margiana hired as a killer. The following day Biton convoked an assembly of the garrison and proclaimed that he had acted in self-defense to forestall a similar attempt by Athenodorus against his own life. A few of his listeners believed, but many remained suspicious, and after these had thought the matter over thoroughly, their suspicion of foul play quickly received credence by the entire garrison. They took up arms to put Biton to death. Several of the leading officers, realizing the extent of the men's dissatisfaction and the explosive discontent it was engendering, managed to talk the angry but leaderless mob into a calmer attitude, and they agreed to leave the murderer unmolested. Some days passed, and Biton, now prey to many fears and anxieties, began to plot against the man who was largely responsible for calming the soldiers, probably fearing that if the men listened to him once, they would possibly look to him for leadership. The plot became known, and Biton and his hired killer were both seized. The latter was put to death at once, but, in order to obtain a confes-sion and the disclosure of his complete plans, Biton was put to torture. This was just begun when, for some unknown reason, the soldiers ran madly for their arms. Biton, in the excitement, jerked himself free from his tormentors, and ran, naked as he was, to throw himself upon the mercies of the soldiers. The sight of the miserable wretch caused such a revulsion of feeling that they forced his jailers to free him. Nothing more was done about him, but when, after Alexander's death, three thousand Greeks in one body tried to return home from Bactria, Biton was among their number. After suffering many hardships on the way, they were finally (Diodorus, XVII, 99) set upon and exterminated by the Macedonians, as deserters from their posts.

In India, Alexander was once more playing the part, for the nonce, of the luxurious Oriental despot, now that his elemental and bloodthirsty savagery was temporarily slaked. He ordered a great banquet given and sent word that all local chiefs and kings should attend. At the banquet was an Athenian, a famous boxer named Dioxippus (Pliny, *Natural History*, XXXV, 11, states that he was painted by Aleimachus as a victor in the Olympic pancratium), outstanding for his great physical strength, and one of the king's temporary favorites. Among the hangers-on and courtiers were several who, in ill-concealed dislike of the man, used to jest at him, more than half in earnest, remarking that they had a good-for-nothing full-fed beast in their company, who, while others went forth to fight in deadly battle, did nothing but rub himself with oil and take exercises in order to raise an appetite. As the banquet proceeded, a Macedonian named Horratus became somewhat drunken, and began sneeringly to taunt the boxer, finally challenging him to prove his manhood by combat the next day. Dioxippus calmly accepted the insolent challenge. The following day the soldiers gathered in a dense mob about the field selected as the arena, and betting and tempers ran high, largely along nationalistic lines, Greek against Macedonian, each country betting on and backing its own.

The Macedonian came armed to the teeth, with shield, sword, javelin, and sarissa. Dioxippus entered the other side of the arena, his oiled body naked except for a skull cap ornamented with a garland of flowers, carrying no weapon but a stout knotty club. The spectators gasped at his temerity in thus preparing to face, in mortal combat, the Mars-like and heavily armored soldier. Dioxippus, his body thrown slightly forward, raised on the balls of his feet and danced warily forward. The Macedonian, never doubting the outcome and wholeheartedly confident of victory, hurled his javelin straight at the advancing Greek. Dioxippus swayed lightly sideways and the lethal weapon flashed past to stick quivering in the ground yards behind him. Before his enemy could shift the long sarissa to the charge, the Greek leaped forward and struck it a mighty blow with his club, shattering the shaft. Horratus dropped the broken weapon and reached for his sword, but Dioxippus sprang in against him, suddenly tripped him up and hurled him violently to the earth. He then jerked his sword away, planted his foot on the neck of the prostrate soldier, and raised his club to brain him, when Alexander himself prevented it. The result of the duel was mortifying to the Macedonians, even Alexander himself, whose nationalism saw, not a trial of skill or strength, but only that the boasted fighting qualities of the Macedonians had been lowered in the estimation of the barbarians who were his guests. He was then only too ready to listen to those who disliked the Athenian. A few days later another attempt was made upon the boxer. At a feast which he attended, a golden bowl was taken secretly and hidden beneath his pillow. Dioxippus was then charged with the theft, on pretense that it had been found in his possession. He now saw clearly the trap they had laid for him and that the whole of the Macedonians were against him. He arose, retired to his own tent, and wrote a letter to Alexander, exposing the machinations against him, then committed suicide; an act of even greater folly than his acceptance of the challenge which a wiser man, under the circumstances, would have refused. Alexander read the letter aloud to the assembled guests and knew the charges were true, convinced by the immoderate joy expressed by the calumniating Macedonians.

Alexander was wounded probably early in January, 325, and it seems it was April or May before he moved again from the site of his newest Alexandria. Now that the king had completed the construction of his new city, he was again ready to move on. The Xathrians (Xathroi; the Kshattriya of the Sanscrit, a mixed blood tribe of outcastes), along the Indus above the city, had sent submission, and were ordered to build a number of additional boats which they delivered at Alexandria. From the south came additional emissaries from another tribe, the Ossadoi (the Yaudheya or Ajudhiyas, now the Johiyas, still living in the same area they then occupied, the lower reaches of the Sutlej River, which the Greeks called the Hesidrus), also bending before the invaders. They were probably fearful at the reported series of Alexander's successes and horrified at his excesses, and hurrying to forestall the certainty of the latter when his army should reach their country.

Craterus was again placed in command of a division of the army, this time the larger part, including the elephants, and ferried over to the west bank of the Indus, as that side was better adapted to the passage of the heavy infantry and the great trains. Hephaestion was to continue down the east bank. Alexander again embarked and sailed downriver to the tribe briefly referred to as the Sogdi, in modern Sindh, leaving the Punjab behind forever. Here he founded another city, Alexandria Soriane.[1] The country was left under the control of

---

[1] There are two obvious possibilities as to the location of this site, but both with too many ramifications to discuss at length. One, the more probable, is today called Sirwahi, ninety-six miles below Uchch. The other is, that it may have been the strong fort called Bhatia by Ferishta, the Arab chronicler, this being one of the few strong sites in this flat country. The matter is not greatly material, anyway.

One of the inexplicable circumstances about the chroniclers of Alexander's Indian campaigns is their absolute failure even to mention the existence of the Sutlej River, though later Greek sources do so under the name of Hesidrus. The other, even more inexplicable, is their failure at any time to refer to the greatest of all eastern Indian rivers, variously called the Ghaggar, Hakra, and Wahinda. This mighty stream, entering the Indus from the northeast, was larger than the Indus, and flowing as it did through a region then densely settled (as we know from the hundreds of ruined city sites) gave sustenance to millions of people in what is now largely blank and blistered desert. This river ceased to flow into the Indus only late in the eighteenth century. The countries along its shores were not only populous, but, as we learn from

Oxyartes and Peithon, the latter being given a sizable detachment of troops to keep the tribesmen pacified. Then the expedition got under way again, moving downriver to the land of King Musicanus (the tribe, perhaps, now represented by the Moksis, and bespoken, in the Sanscrit, as the Mushikas), which, Alexander was informed, was the richest and most populous in India. The whole river valley impressed the Greeks very favorably as the vast armada moved southward. The river banks were then, as now (even though the river has moved miles from the path it then followed), thickly populated by a hard-working and thrifty peasantry. These were now dark, and small, mostly of Dravidian stock, far different from the tall warlike men of the north. And the Greeks seem to have held them in utter contempt. Musicanus especially had aroused Alexander's ire. In the long stay of the army at various places along the river, Musicanus had neither made his submission nor sought his friendship by ambassadors, nor had he sent him the valuable presents he was accustomed to receive; and, what was probably worst of all, Musicanus had never even asked him for anything. He was therefore unbearably contumacious, guilty of ignoring the approaching conqueror, a thing the continuance of which could not be permitted. So swiftly did he descend the river that he was opposite Musicanus' city before the Indian even knew he was on the way. Musicanus was taken aback by the sudden visitation, but decided to make the best of it. He therefore gathered together a number of elephants, loaded them with presents and made his appearance before Alexander with abject apologies for his crimes of omission. Alexander could always gracefully pardon anyone who sufficiently abased himself before his godhead. He therefore forgave the king, admired his rich

the Sanscrit, Prakrit, and Arabic chronicles, both politically and militarily powerful. In view of this fact, it is astonishing that Alexander did not take steps against the peoples of the area. It may be, of course, that his conquest of Musicanus, as will presently be told, placed a barrier against their incursions to the Indus and prevented them being a threat to it. But this question, too, has many ramifications and implications to the militarist, and the circumstance must remain one of the greatest puzzles to the careful and conscientious student of Alexander's history.

kingdom, the beauty of his capital city,[1] and restored his kingdom to him. He did not wholly trust the king, however, for, to prevent and guard against insurrection, he had Craterus build a citadel fortress in the city, and stayed personally to see it done. A strong garrison was placed in the citadel, because the town, with its favorable site upon the Indus, and just south of a low pass in a range of limestone hills, was a centrally located point from which to threaten neighboring peoples and keep them in subjection.

After securing, as he thought, Musicanus' kingdom, Alexander took the cavalry, archers, and Agrianians, and marched against a near-by tribal king called Oxycanus, or, as Curtius calls him, Porticanus. (His capital was at the huge ruin mound now called Mahorta, or, more correctly, Mahorddha, 'the great lofty city' on the little Ghar River, some ten miles from Larkhana. It is not far today from the Indus River, *as it now flows*, but was then some forty-five miles distant from it as it flowed in its old bed.) Curtius calls the tribe the Praesti, having misread his text, unaware that what he thought a name was instead but a Sanscrit word designating a low flat country. Oxycanus had also been guilty of the same action, or rather lack of action, Alexander had considered contumacious in Musicanus, that of ignoring him. He stormed the first city he reached, then moved swiftly on and stormed and captured Mahorta, where Oxycanus himself was made prisoner. The loot was given to the soldiers, but several elephants taken were considered among the king's portion. Several other small towns hastily surrendered. Alexander then moved south toward Sindomanna [2] whose king,

---

[1] Alor, though now in ruins for a thousand years, was formerly a rich and powerful city until the Indus changed its course sometime after the early eighth century. It was then abandoned, because its water supply had become undependable.

[2] Sindomanna, the present Sehwan, is easily traceable through history by the fact that it is the Sewistan of the Arab chronicles, the capital city of the Sewis or Sabis. The great mound it occupies today is composed of the detritus of thousands of years of occupation of the site upon the jutting shoulder of the Lakka hills. Today the Indus washes its base, but in the third century B.C. the Indus was at least fifty miles or more to the eastward, and the water supply for the town was drawn from the great Manchur Lake, itself of vast antiquity. It is conjectured that the name was derived from the

Sambus, fled ahead of him, for he feared that since Alexander had made friends with Musicanus, who was Sambus' enemy, he was also his ally for offense and military aggression. Outside the city a delegation met him with presents of elephants and other valuables, assuring him that Sambus had fled, not because of fear or hatred of the Macedonians or sinister designs upon Alexander, but for fear of what Musicanus might do, with his increased power, after Alexander's departure. Alexander accepted the presents and homage, and moved swiftly against another town, unnamed in our histories, but apparently quite near-by. Ptolemy mentions a place in this territory called Bandava which is obviously Gandava (the Kandabil of the Arabic) the *B* and *G* being interchangeable. The town contained a number of Brahmans, irreconcilably inimical to the invaders. They had successfully exhorted the populace to resistance. The town fell at the first assault, and the Brahmans were taken and put to death.

While Alexander was attending to this area, news was brought that Musicanus had revolted, captured the fort, and put the garrison to the sword. Orders were sent to Peithon to end the rebellion. He swept swiftly back to Alor, capturing it and several other rebellious towns. Garrisons were placed in them, and Musicanus and a number of Brahmans crucified along the main roads and left there to serve as object lessons and warnings to the survivors. The people, overawed by the swift and drastic action, philosophically resigned themselves to servitude of the foreigners.

At some place a group of ascetics were seized and brought to the king. Alexander had a deep and genuine interest in these people; the mystical side of his nature was deeply stirred by their total obliviousness to things mundane. It is possible that he may have even passingly envied them their disdain of property; he whose restless avidity of glory, power, and the possessions of others would be assuaged, if at all, by nothing less than the

---

Sanscrit compound *Saindhava-vanam*, or *Saindhuwan*, 'the abode (or city) of the Saindhavas' tribe.

possession of the whole world and all that was in it. One of
the ascetics stamped his feet upon the ground, and when the
king inquired, through an interpreter, the meaning of the action,
he was told: 'Every man, Alexander, possesses only as much of
the earth as he stands upon. You, as a man, are not different in
any way from anyone else, save that you make a greater stir, in
being more restless and creating more trouble, both to yourself
and others. But in a short time you too will die, and of all your
vast empire you will possess then no more land than will serve
your body for burial.'

In the lower parts of India he had many Brahmans hanged or
brutally crucified. They were a proud and haughty sect, whom
he seems to have disliked, in contradistinction to the humble
gymnosophists. Once several of them, captured after having
incited a tribal town to resistance, were brought before him.
Plutarch tells us that he told them that he intended asking
questions, to which answers would be required, and upon the
wisdom of the answers would depend their lives and freedom.
The questions are interesting, if correctly reported, in the almost
childish naïveté of the attempt at profundity. The first: Why
had they incited the people to resistance? Why did they not
bury their dead? Had they any possessions? Why had they no
ruler? What is a king? How long should a man live? What is
the most wicked thing on earth? What is the most intelligent
animal? How can a man make himself a god? The answers
reported to us are not particularly brilliant, and none outstanding except that Alexander himself, they said, was the wickedest
thing on earth for having killed so many people and having
wrought such widespread misery and desolation. And that a
man çan become a god only by superhuman acts. The answers
must have appealed to some phase of the conqueror's nature,
however, for he set the men free later.

He then returned to the river where the fleet was waiting
him, probably about where Marija Dand now lies, on the banks
of the ancient Indus bed, some sixty-five miles east of its present
one. Here he found the prince of the Patalans, whose domain

lay in the delta of the Indus, who had come upriver with a gorgeous retinue, to surrender both himself and his kingdom. Alexander restored both his lands and his rank, requiring nothing of him save that he should supply the army with whatever they should need when they reached his country.

He seems, by this time, to have laid his plans and decided upon his future course of action, for he here divided his army into two parts. Craterus was given the phalanx, much of the auxiliary cavalry, apparently most of the Asiatics, the men who were failing or in poor condition, and the elephants, also probably most of the trains. They were ordered to proceed, by way of Arachosia and Drangia, to Carmania, there to rejoin Alexander when he should arrive. Craterus was told to look into the administration of the regions through which he was to pass — for the king had received several reports of abuse of authority and corruption upon the part of the satraps and commanders of these areas — and put an end to the reason for the complaints. This was, no doubt, done with cold-blooded efficiency. For we gather that Craterus was an honest, honorable, and upright soldier; further, that he was also somewhat dour and irascible and prone to be overbearing and abrupt. He marched away through the Mulla (not the Bolan Pass, as many have believed) via Kalat and Quetta, for both these sites are very ancient, to Alexandria Arachosia (Kandahar), thence down the Etymander (Helmund) River into Drangia, passing south of the Lake of Aria (Sistan), and crossed the desert by the ancient caravan route into Carmania.

The remainder of the army was again divided into three parts, of which one was to accompany Alexander with the fleet. The second and largest division, under Hephaestion, was to move down the east bank; the third division, smaller and more mobile, was given to Peithon to comb the west bank. These units were intended more to impress the populace of the riverine terrain than for actual utility. It was expected that, as Musicanus' rebellion was ended and the prince of Patala had surrendered, there would be no more resistance. On the fourth day, however, the fleet reached a city at the southern extremity of the kingdom of Musicanus, a place inhabited only by Brahmans, and called by Arrian 'The city of the Brahmans.' [1] Here too they had effectively roused to will to resist Alexander; and when he arrived, they closed their gates against him and refused to acknowledge his demand that they capitulate. They were a courageous, even foolhardy people, for the town was small, poorly fortified, and the inhabitants could hardly have mustered more than a few thousand fighting men, braver than wise for all the vaunted intellectual and spiritual attainments of the Brahman caste. Alexander, contemptuous of their few numbers, sent the Agrianian javelin men to make a feint attack against the walls, then retire, in order that the inhabitants would think they were retreating and cause them to pursue. That was precisely what happened. The Agrianians, after a brief skirmish under the wall, suddenly began to withdraw. The Indians hurried out in pursuit until the rest of the army, led by the king in person, rushed up and fell upon them. The fighting was short but sharp, then the Indians broke in the face of superior numbers and armament and fled back to the town. Out of three thousand men they lost six hundred killed and a thousand captured. The invaders also lost heavily, many of the wounded later dying of infection of their injuries. Ptolemy was also wounded and infection set in. For a while he was in grave danger, but ultimately recovered. The following day the Indians of the city, despairing of success where all the rest of India had failed, surrendered.

Alexander moved on down the river to Patala,[2] where he

[1] Curtius calls the place 'Harmatelia,' which means the same. Of the same basic stock back in the dawn of time, the Greeks and Indians had also the same gods. The phallic Greek god Hermes was but a softer pronunciation of the name of the phallic Indian god Brahma, as the Greek god Heracles was but the Indian god Krishna transplanted into an alien land. The city was Brahmanabad, and it was destroyed in a terrible earthquake sometime after about 950 A.D. and before about 1021 A.D., according to the Arabic chronicles.

[2] That this place really existed is certain, for we have references to it in the Sanscrit under the name of 'Potala,' meaning 'a station for ships.' Few, if any, of the places mentioned in Alexander's itinerary have been a more fertile source of controversy than

found that the prince (Curtius calls him Moeris), despite the assurances he had been given, had gathered all his people and fled in terror to the jungles with all they could carry, leaving the country completely deserted.[1] A squadron of light cavalry was dispatched after them, and returned with a number of captives. These were talked to and released to tell the fugitives they were free to return to their homes and farms without fear of molestation or reprisals. Most of them took advantage of the amnesty and returned. We are not told if the prince accepted the offer, but in view of the fact that the Greeks were the object of a considerable amount of hostilities, some of which are re-

has this site. General Cunningham (in his *Ancient Geography of India*, p. 279 ff.) commits the enormity of identifying Patala with the huge and ancient mound upon which the city of Hyderabad now rests. It is impossible to understand why the scholarly general was guilty of such a palpable error. He must have considered the military aspects of the mound, upon a location upon the Indus at the head of the delta, without taking into consideration the fact that, when the Arabs reached the delta a thousand years after Alexander's time, the Indus still flowed miles to the east of the site. At the time of our history it flowed still farther east. It is utterly impossible, as many indifferently informed persons have done, to base arguments for identifications of ancient places in India upon modern hydrographical conditions, for those conditions obtained for only a limited period. Of several other suggestions as to the site of Patala, the best is Thata, a hypothesis which, however, can be easily refuted. Since that day, according to Major-General Hague in his *The Indus Delta Country*, the delta has advanced several miles seaward, a distance which he computes, due to several very extraordinary circumstances, at only eight miles. At Thata, even today, when the coast line has advanced, and the river channel consequently lengthened, the tide is very noticeable, and it is clear that twenty-two centuries ago the site was nearer the sea, and the tide would have been stronger. According to all our sources, the tide was unnoticeable at Patala, for it was only after Alexander and his party had traveled a considerable distance downriver that they met what was to them a new and frightening phenomenon, the tide. That reason alone, even if uncombined with others, is sufficient to preclude the accuracy of the identification of Thata with Patala. I am taking the liberty, after a long and careful study of the multitudinous factors involved, as well as a personal investigation of the region, of locating Patala, out of a number of nameless and ruined ancient sites, at what I believe was the head of the delta *in that period*, a place about thirty-five miles southeast of Hyderabad and about sixty-five northeast by north of Thata.

[1] According to Strabo (XV, 1, 17), who says his account was taken from Aristobulus, the voyage from Nicaea to Patala took ten months to complete, from about early in November to early in September. This statement was accepted by most writers as accurate, and subsequent time checks based upon it. Plutarch, however, says the elapsed time was seven months, which would imply that Alexander reached Patala sometime late in May or early in June. This is much more plausible than Strabo's time period, in view of my analysis of the time of the starting of the voyage of Nearchus, which see.

ported and more hinted at, it is reasonable to assume he did not.

Hephaestion was immediately put to work to build a citadel and fort within the town, and another detachment was sent out into the delta to dig wells at a number of places. They were attacked by the natives, and a number slain. Other detachments were then sent out to guard them and the task was soon completed. At Patala, the Indus divided into two arms or branches, one of which ran southwest, the other and larger to the southeast, both retaining the name of Indus. Alexander planned to descend the southwest arm on an exploration trip by boat. To this end Leonnatus, with a thousand cavalry and eight thousand infantry, was ordered to proceed by land down the river bank. It is doubtful, if conditions of the delta were then as now, and there is no reason to believe they were any better, that they got very far. The delta is a desperately bad country, with dense forests and great swamps, badly cut up by deep lagoons and muddy creeks. It is infested with snakes, crocodiles, and man-killing tigers and panthers and hordes of noxious and disease-carrying insects. It was also the season when the river was in flood, carrying an enormous volume of water from the heavy rains of Sindh and the lower Punjab, and flooding many of the low-lying parts of the more southerly portions of the delta.

Alexander selected several of his best ships, those of two and three banks of oars, together with a few galleys, and set out. They had no pilots, for all river dwellers fled precipitately to the jungle as soon as they saw the fleet approaching. Soon they were in difficulties. The southeast monsoon was blowing with great strength, driving up waves from the ocean which, meeting the strong current of the river, kicked up a sea, dangerously damaging several of the craft. After much difficulty they found a quiet backwater, beached the boats, and began extensive repairs. A detachment of light troops was dispatched inland and soon found and captured a number of natives. These were brought back and impressed into service as pilots. The voyage was resumed, and on the third day the taste of the water became salt. They continued, until, near the river's mouth, it was several miles wide. Here the full force of the monsoon struck them, raising a sea so threatening they were glad to find an island in whose lee they could shelter. The men landed and scattered in search of provisions. The tide, which was running out, presently grounded the boats, much to the astonishment of those remaining on board, to all of whom, accustomed as they were to the tideless Mediterranean, this was a new and undreamed-of phenomenon. Their discomfiture was increased by a considerable number of great Indus delta crocodiles which crawled up on the sandy beach, dangerous man-eating brutes, as they had learned by this time. To increase their astonishment and terror, the tide soon turned and came back. It began to raise the ships, gently at first, then with increasing power and velocity. Suddenly it swept fiercely up in a high compact wave,[1] hurling the boats violently about. Some were crashed into each other, and driven ashore and damaged. These were repaired as well as the limitations of place and time would permit. While the work was going on, two galleys were sent to check the veracity of the statements of the pilots that a large island, called Cillutas, lay some twenty-five miles (two hundred stadia) ahead. They reported back that they had seen it, and the whole fleet proceeded there. Off the point of the island Alexander offered sacrifices to those gods to whom, he said, his father Ammon had instructed him to sacrifice. He then sailed on, passing clear of the land and out on the high seas, chiefly (says Arrian) that he might later boast of having navigated the outer ocean beyond India. Here he sacrificed several bulls to the gods of the sea and poured a libation to them, afterward flinging the gold sacrificial vessels into the water as a thank-offering. He

[1] Several Asiatic rivers, including the Indus, at their mouths are afflicted by a tidal phenomenon known as bores, a high and violent wall of tidewater rushing upstream against the current, when the force of the tide finally overcomes the weight of the downward rush of the river's flood. In the Hoogly River, the bore rushes upstream at a speed as great as seventeen to eighteen miles per hour, and the roar of the raging waters can be heard for miles. At new moon periods and the spring tides their effect and power are devastating to anything in their path, even to large ocean-going steamers. It was this, then, the Indus bore, which took the Greeks unawares; and they were fortunate to have got off so lightly.

then prayed earnestly to the gods to conduct safely over their domain the naval expedition he proposed to send, under command of Nearchus, from India to the Persian Gulf and the mouths of the Tigris and Euphrates Rivers.

On his return to Patala, Alexander found the citadel completed, and immediately put Hephaestion to building a naval yard and base. He himself sailed down the other arm of the Indus to what is reported as a great lake.[1] Foraging expeditions were sent out far and wide to obtain supplies, and preparations were begun to leave. For leave they must. Though our sources do not even hint at it, the army's sufferings and losses in the swamp and jungle-strewn delta, intensely hot and unhealthy, infested by poisonous snakes, tigers, panthers, and, above all, by unbearable hordes of disease-carrying mosquitoes and other insects, must have been exceptionally high. These conditions must have been unbearable to the armored Greeks, wholly unaccustomed to them as they were. We have also the statement (by Strabo) that the Indians, unreconciled to their Greek conquerors, who considered them as scarcely better than beasts, were getting out of hand and gathering a storm-cloud of revolt. The Macedonians, too, anxious for the beginning of the long-delayed homeward march, were beginning to get rebellious and sullen. It was time to go.

[1] The arm of the Indus followed southeast by Alexander is now dry except in time of exceptionally high floods. The lake mentioned is called today the Rann of Kachch, a vast swamp area, but which is still inundated from July to October by the floods from many rivers. In 1819, a terrible earthquake caused profound modifications of the whole Rann, a thing which is known to have happened several times since Alexander's day. It is reported that he landed and traveled with the cavalry three days along its shores, and sank several wells. He returned to Patala and sent down a large detachment to dig more wells, construct a harbor, and build a town, placing the builders in it as a garrison. We do not know what the area was like in that day, but now none of the activities reported would be possible at all in that pestilential swamp. The harbor and town were referred to as Minnagara, and are wholly unlocatable.

═XII═

THE RETREAT
FROM INDIA

ALEXANDER's project, when he left Bactria, of conquering India was, as we have seen, a difficult task, but by no means one reckless or impractical. Adequate preparations and provision were made beforehand. But the exploit that was to be his next project was to be both. Westward from the mouths of the Indus and its tropical delta stretch the bleak and deadly deserts of Baluchistan, which area the Greeks called Gedrosia, whose southern coasts are called Makran. It is today full of strange and unaccountable relics of antiquity; this ancient land in whose defiles and deserts Alexander not only was to lose his way but half his army as well. It is, strangely, an old country, replete with the ruins of hundreds of ancient villages and towns which have risen, flourished, and died without leaving behind a word of written history. Today gaunt desert jackals roam the broken and eroded walls that once sheltered mankind, in places where no man now does or can live. Ridges of hills, striking roughly east to west, divide the country into a cosmic corduroy. Between them run lateral valleys, often as much as ten miles wide, flat and rich of soil but waterless and desolate. In those few places where a dependable water supply runs from the hills are gathered a few people who cultivate the soil intensively, and the excellence of their dates was once celebrated. Along the dry watercourses that run through the dead valleys are hundreds of ruined village mounds, and, still faintly traceable, the irrigation ditches that gave them life. Back in the mountains are still to be seen huge water storage reservoirs with dams to impound the water that no longer runs down their naked stone kloofs and their once terraced slopes. The water has failed here, as it has failed in Syria, Assyria, and Anatolia. The country has been little explored by Europeans and no archeological work or studies have ever been carried on there; but it is safe to say that the scientist of the future who can read aright these ancient ruins will add enormously to the fund of knowledge of man.

In the infinitely distant past, ethnologists fancy, the Dravidian aboriginal peoples swarmed out of the highlands of Baluchistan and into the Indus Valley, and remained there, long protected by the aridifying lands behind them from assault along the same route. A thousand years after Alexander, the fanatic Arabs, yearning for a death which would automatically elevate them into the Muhammedan paradise in the conquest or conversion of infidels, halted their inspired crusade on the edge of the Makran, gazed with burning eyes on its bleak desolation and turned back, saying that it had been placed as a barrier by Allah himself to the passage to India. Thousands of years before him, the mythical Assyrian queen Semiramis had lost all but a bare score of her army in an attempt to pass eastward along this same route. A couple of hundred years earlier the Persian king Cyrus, son of Cambyses, met with equal disaster there, and lost his army also in the burning sands. Alexander cannot have failed to have known what was confronting him in this passage, but this, instead of daunting him, but served to raise his perverse and egotistic pride and drive him on to do something new and astonishing, and which prevailed over both common sense and the knowledge that where those others had failed, the price exacted of any other army to attempt the passage would be ghastly. Yet do so he must. He was constrained to show the world that where the armies of Semiramis and Cyrus failed, his army, led by such a general as himself, the inspired son of Ammon, could get through.

He moved out of Patala in the scorching heat of August, in the year 325 B.C. Lack of accurate knowledge of the geography of the Makran has hitherto prevented the accurate determination of the route the army followed on its terrible journey. Indeed, it is only in the last few decades that modern discovery has permitted the route to be determined, or that authentic knowledge has been had at all of it. Alexander led his army through Gedrosia in 325 B.C. and not until over two thousand years had passed, to be exact until 1819 A.D., was another European recorded as having passed that way.

He reached Krokala (a town situated on an island near the shore of what is now at or near Karachi) in nine days, then swung northwest toward the foothills. A large detachment was sent along the shore to dig wells in order that Nearchus, when he arrived with the fleet, would find an adequate water supply. From Krokala he marched five days through the land of the Arabitii, who surrendered peacefully, to the Arabius (Purali) River. In those days the sea extended in a wide deep bay inland at least as far as the modern village of Liari. He crossed 'where the river was neither wide nor deep' some distance below the site of Lus Bela (the Armabil of the Arab chronicles). The natives to the westward, the Oritae, were, at this point, widely scattered, not strong enough to fight with any hope of success, but were unwilling to surrender their ancient freedom. At his approach they abandoned their homes and their small arid farms and fled into the desert. Alexander pressed after them all night, and in the morning reached an inhabited district. He halted and called up all the cavalry, divided them into several detachments and ordered them out to the right and left in a long line. Then, telling the infantry to follow more slowly, he moved ahead in a wide front, sweeping the country as he advanced. Most of the inhabitants fled ahead of them, but many were ridden down and either slain or captured. They soon reached a small stream, halted and went into bivouac until Hephaestion arrived with the rest of the forces. They then moved on to the village, named Rhambakia,[1] which was the seat of the tribal government. Alexander was pleased with its location, and envisioning a populous military colony there, if a population were drawn into it, ordered Hephaestion to attend to the matter.

Then, with several thousands of his most mobile forces, the conqueror struck swiftly for a point where, according to information received, the Oritae and Gedrosians[2] had posted themselves in a narrow pass[3] which they hoped to hold against him.

[1] The position of this place has long been a matter of considerable conjecture, and, unfortunately, is still so today. To locate it we need to find a site that fulfills at least three major requirements: it must be really ancient; it must be some thirty to forty miles (the estimated distance of a night and morning's march) from the presumed place of the crossing of the Purali River; and lastly, it must be considered that a tribal capital must necessarily, in a land where continual warfare was waged, be a point of military and strategic value. Of sites of this type we have two, one now known as Khair-kot (the Kambali of Edrisi, the Arab chronicler) northwest of Liari and obviously placed to command the Hala Pass. Another is called Kotawari, and lies to the southwest, but so near the sea as to preclude the possibility of the essential antiquity. The name Rhambakia seems to have been derived from the aboriginal (but then ousted) Rhamnai tribe of Dravidians. The Oritae seem to have been comparative newcomers to the locality. They were not an Indian people. Earlier we have references to a tribe called the Utoi. If this was also the Oritae, we may be justified in considering them the ancestors of the modern Hot tribe of central Makran, but this is by no means more than a guess. The present inhabitants of the Bela region are the Lumri Rajputs.

[2] Gedrosians. There are two possibilities as to whom this name was applied. The obvious one, the Gadurs, are seemingly a people of recent origin in the Makran. They claim, and there is no reason to believe falsely, to be of Arabic origin and descent. The other group are the Gadaras, now largely Sidi half-castes, but the slight amount of investigation that has been done about them seems to point to the fact that they are of undoubted ancient origin. Bellew has advanced the possibility that they were the people of whom Herodotus wrote (from hearsay) calling them Asiatic Ethiopians, and who were mentioned in the Sanscrit as the Garudas. They must have been a numerous and strong people in that day, to have impressed their name upon the whole territory.

[3] This pass might have been either of two; the turning pass at the northern end of

Apparently, however, they considered discretion the better part of valor, for when he came up, the unarmored and ill-armed natives took a good look at the armored and disciplined Greeks, and fled. Their chiefs came in and surrendered both themselves and their country into his hands. He ordered them to pass the word to all the people, now fugitives hiding in fear of the invaders, to return to their homes and that no harm should befall them. He wanted them to settle his new military town. One Apollophanes was appointed governor of the territory, and Leonnatus was left there, partly to overawe the tribesmen, partly to gather and convey to the seaside a large store of supplies for Nearchus, whom he was to assist in any way possible. Hephaestion quickly finished building the citadel in Rhambakia, and rejoined the army.

The march continued into 'the territories of the Gedrosians, the greater part of the way being through a desert.' They crossed the pass, and, paralleling the Phur River, turned southeast toward the coast. Arrian describes, not the terrain whereby we could gain a clue to the route, but the trees of the country. We can easily recognize the stark and thorny euphorbia and its acrid juices, which today, as then, dots the plain in clumps 'which produces shoots, or stems, with thorns so strong and so thickset that if a horseman should be entangled thereby, he would sooner be pulled from the horse than freed from the stem'; the tamarisk trees from which exuded the precious gum myrrh, eagerly gathered by the commercially minded Phoenicians with the army. They reached the coast and were astonished to find mangroves growing out of the bitter sea water. They turned west, reached the mouth of the Tomerus (Hingol) River, and there, among the few and scattered Oritae, they sent our foraging groups to wring supplies out of the people. Little was obtained, but this was assembled at the seashore for delivery to Nearchus when he should arrive. Alexander, true to his

the Hala; or the water parting of the Phur River, and was probably the former. Had it been the latter, we would doubtless have a reference of some kind, by at least one of our sources, to the river. We have none, however, and other circumstances, too, point to the Hala.

tactical principles, prepared to advance along the coast and maintain contact with the fleet, which had not yet arrived.

An unexpected obstacle arose to the continuance of the line of march. On the other side of the river loomed the utterly impassable barrier of the Malan (modern name) mountain range, its seaward end dropping abruptly and precipitately into the water, and barring passage. Alexander was forced to turn inland and search for a route through the range. They marched north over the stony and difficult terrain, past the ancient and sacred shrine of Hinglaz,[1] vainly seeking a way to turn the magnificent but terrible and impassable range. Forty miles beyond Hinglaz they reached the point where the Parkan River, no longer flowing now that the rainy season was over, joins the Hingol. They went by this route. There is no other way they could have gone. They turned westward along the bed and valley of the Parkan, skirting the northern base of the Taloi Hills. They wanted to get back to the coasts as soon as possible. Yet it was a ghastly error that Alexander chose this low valley. On his left as he went were the bleak stony Taloi Hills, on his right the bleaker and rougher mountains of Baluchistan. In the hot stony and sandy valley there were no springs, and the only waterholes they found were a few left with a little scummy and lukewarm fluid from the rainy season and fouled with the visits of desert animals. There was even little of that. The wilderness of sandy hillocks and sandier wastes with their tough and scanty grasses reflected the fierce late summer sun like a bake-oven. The men began to fall from exhaustion in the

---

[1] This ancient shrine even today draws crowds of pilgrims yearly. Known now as the shrine of Siva, it was originally the shrine of the Persian goddess Nana. And Nana is of such extreme antiquity that she permits us to conceive of a chronology even older than that of Egypt. In the famous cylinder of Assurbanipal, the king of Assyria, we read that in the year 645 B.C., he captured and destroyed the city of Susa, and carried the statue of Nana, by her own express command, to Urukh (now Warka), from whence she had been carried away 1635 years before by a conquering Elamite king who invaded Akkad. Thus we have historical proof that Nana was an established deity as early as 2280 B.C., with grounds for a reasonable assumption that she greatly pre-dated that period. Nothing has changed around the shrine of Hinglaz in thousands of years. It was a venerated place in that day when Alexander passed, and even then ran back into the mists of the past.

terrible heat. As they advanced farther to the westward, the water, scarce before, ceased entirely. It was here, in the bare two hundred miles from the Hingol River to the coast, that the appalling miseries the army was to face were found. Twenty-four days were spent in this journey, a journey so awful that words fail to be of use in describing it, and the imagination fails in its conception. Arrian gives us this bleak description: [1]

> The heat was so great, and their lack of water so unbearable that many men, and most of the beasts of burden, died: some being suffocated in the broiling sands, but the greatest part of thirst. There were many tumuli, or small hillocks of sand over which they had to pass, where no firm footing could be had, but they sank deep into it as in new-fallen snow. The animals suffered no less than the men from heat and exhaustion. The great distance between stops [probably meaning water stops, for they averaged less than ten miles a day] was one of the causes of hardship, for lack of water often caused them to continue the march farther than they otherwise should. If they happened to find a little water after an all-night journey, their sufferings were a little relieved, but if not, and the march continued through the excessive heat, many died of thirst and exhaustion.
>
> The men began to slaughter the beasts of burden for their own use when provisions failed, afterward offering the excuse that they had died of heat or thirst, and none inquired into the facts. Even Alexander knew what was being done, but their necessities pleaded in their behalf, and he deemed it more prudent to conceal his knowledge of the truth, than seem to authorize it by admission, and permitted the acts to go unpunished. Soon they were reduced to such straits that neither the sick nor the exhausted and broken could be drawn any farther, partly through lack of draft animals, and partly because the soldiers were themselves unable to drag them any farther through the sands, and broke them as an excuse for abandoning them. As Alexander and his suite rode past, the abandoned and doomed, freed at last of their fear of what he could do to them, cursed him with bitter and terrible imprecations for bringing them to this plight. On this account many were left behind, some by reason of sickness, others from exhaustion and

[1] Arrian, VI, 24, 25, 26.

thirst, and none took care either to help them or to restore them, for the army moved blindly ahead and the whole was in such danger that they were obliged to neglect the individual. If any chanced to fall from fatigue, when they awakened, if they had strength, they followed upon the track of the army, though few ever came up with it, the greater part sinking in the sands like sailors in the ocean, and so perishing. Another accident also happened. The country of Gedrosia, like India, is subject to rains when the Etesian winds blow, but the rain falls, not on the plains, but in the mountains. 'When the army was camped one night by a small brook for the sake of the water, about the second watch of the night a sudden dreadful inundation swept down the stream with such force that many women and children who followed the camp, together with many pack animals and the royal furniture, were swept away. So furious was the deluge that many of the soldiers were also swept away, and many others lost their weapons in the flood; also many others, nearly crazed by thirst, upon reaching the brook, drank to excess, and died.'

At one time on this *via dolorosa*, it is reported 'the army was pursuing its march through the sand under a sun already high because a halt could not be made until they reached the water, said by the guides to be farther ahead. Alexander himself, distressed by thirst and heat, was marching on foot at the head of the army that the soldiers might, as they usually do in a case of this kind, bear up more cheerfully under hardship when they saw their misery shared. In the meantime, some lightarmed scouts, ranging ahead, found a little muddy water in a dry stream bed, collected it in a helmet, and brought it to Alexander. He took it, thanked them graciously, and poured it on the ground within sight of all. Ancient authors, and modern ones too, have made much of this incident, and it would be interesting to know if it were a grand gesture or a libation and prayer to the gods for assistance.

At last even the guides were lost, the track they knew had become obliterated in the windblown sand. Amid the deep sands, wavering in the heat haze, everything was the same, the endless soft dunes, and the endless gravel valleys from which rose no single known landmark, no clump of trees to mark the course, no hilltop peeping above the hot and uncertain horizon. The army was now nearly frantic with fear of death and disaster. Nearly half the men were dead, more were dying at the rate of hundreds each day, most of the pack and riding animals were worn out or dead and eaten, the women and children of the train must have been nearly decimated. For two hundred miles the wake of what was now little better than a mob of hunger- and thirst-stricken scarecrows was littered by the bodies of thousands of once stalwart warriors, the wreckage of wagons and chariots loaded with sick and wounded, now dead, and the fabulous loot of half a conquered world. All these had been left behind, valueless now, and mere impediments the possession and retention of which would only deter them from reaching the water which alone would keep them alive. Hardened though Alexander was, he could no longer bear to witness the plight into which his blind egotism and colossal vanity had led this once proud and picked division of his army. With his bodyguard pounding along behind, he rode away in company with several friends. At last the horses of the escort gave out, and the king went on with only five boon companions. At last these reached the seacoast. They scraped away the shingle on the beach and found fresh pure water. The hell of thirst was over. Gleeful messengers raced back to guide the army to the spot. It must, in the very nature of the terrain, have been very close to Pasni that they reached the coast. From there, along the ancient routes, the guides knew the way.

Henceforth, though the march was not easy, it was by no means extraordinarily difficult. They followed the shore for seven days, then reached the ancient and much-used road (better known in that day than in this) from the coast to Carmania. This follows up and across the Dasht River and into the Bahu Valley, via Banu Kalat and Sarbaz, through a region subsequently great in Arabic history, and on to Pura or Poura.[1] They

---

[1] Poura, the ancient capital of Gedrosia, has been variously identified. Some conceive it to have been Bampur or Bunpoor. Others have made the even more erroneous

arrived there after sixty days in the desert, probably in early October. One report says that only a quarter of the men arrived who had left India; others say about half the army died on the way.

Upon his arrival at Poura, the king found bad news. During his long absence in Bactria, Sogdia, and India, the affairs and conduct of the empire had suffered greatly. Corruption and oppression were reported from every side. Astaspes (Arrian erroneously says Apollophanes), satrap of the district, was immediately deposed for incompetence, for we are told that he had been sent messages from some point along the route to dispatch supplies hurriedly to the starving army and had failed to do so. Thoas was appointed in his place. But Thoas died almost immediately, and Alexander sent for Siburtius, satrap of Carmania, replaced him with Tlepolemos, and made Siburtius satrap of both Gedrosia and Arachosia. A swift messenger, mounted on a racing dromedary, sped in from India, bearing a letter reporting that Philip, in central Sindh, had been plotted against by the mercenaries of his command and murdered. The Macedonians had exterminated the mutineers and sent for instructions. A reply was dispatched with orders for Taxilês to take temporary charge of the dead satrap's government until a new administrator could be selected and sent.

After giving the army thirty days' rest, Alexander marched, in the middle of November, into Carmania, where Craterus, their routes intersecting, rejoined him. This province had submitted in 330 while he was in Persepolis, but he had not yet set foot within its boundaries. Craterus brought with him, in

identification of Fahraj, this place being about halfway between Bampur and Kirman. It would seem, however, in view of the ancient caravan route which, even in Alexander's day, ran through here to skirt the northern edge of the Makran on the way to India, that Poura was at the site of a great and ancient ruin to the east of Bampur, today called Fardan. In view of the then existing caravan route, of which Alexander could have not remained ignorant, he can be accused only of willful disregard for his army or an incredible disbelief in the difficulties of the seashore route he chose. Of course he desired to maintain contact with the fleet; there were other and more logical plans which, if followed, the disastrous march would have been rendered unnecessary.

chains, two minor chieftains of the former Persian government who had been in rebellion. They were promptly executed for treason.

Almost on the heels of Craterus, others came racing across country to rejoin Alexander. Stasanor, his heroic friend who was satrap of Aria and Drangia, arrived from his country. Pharimanes, son of the old reliable Phrataphernes, satrap of Parthia and Hyrcania, marched in with reinforcements for the army. Cleander, Sitalces, and Heracon, murderers of Parmenio, came in from Ecbatana. These last were immediately accused before the king, not only by the people but by their soldiers as well, of looting the ancient treasures of the temples and many other sins of omission and commission. A swift trial followed, and Cleander and Sitalces were found guilty and condemned to death. Heracon escaped the penalty for the nonce, but was soon afterward seized by the Susians and put to death for looting one of their temples. Harsh and swift judgments and punishments were the order of the day, with the intent to discourage similar actions by others in the high places, and to impress upon the populace that acts of oppression by those in authority would not be tolerated. Stasanor and Phrataphernes seem to be the only ones who showed genuine loyalty and a really intelligent grasp of the situation, for both, when they heard that Alexander had passed through Gedrosia, realized a modicum of the hardships of the journey and the losses it would entail. They therefore arrived with huge columns of camels, donkeys, and horses, laden with every possible variety of useful supplies. Both supplies and beasts were very welcome, and were immediately parceled out to the surviving soldiers, who were given several days' rest.

Before they moved on again Alexander, with his realization that something must be done to help the men forget or at least dull the memories of the horror of the desert march, and the memories of those thousands of their comrades, friends, relatives, wives and children, whose bones had long since been picked clean by the ravens and vultures and fought over by the desert jackals, made arrangements in accordance. They moved out. Alexander as usual rode at the head of the army, but now upon a canopied platform built upon two wagons lashed together. The satraps and rulers had lined the way with frequent caches of supplies, and great jars of wine, free and open to all, lined the route. Seven days were required to cover the two hundred miles through Carmania to the next stop. Alexander sat with his friends upon the wheeled platform drinking heavily from golden vessels to the music of flutes and pan-pipes, coming back from India with feasting and reveling and rejoicing, even as had his mythical progenitor and example, Dionysus. The army decked themselves with garlands, and danced or staggered along behind. Any man — or woman — who desired wine had enough to be inebriated all day, and dead drunk all night. Alexander drank and shouted with the rest, perhaps, as has been said, to drown the memories of the ghastly route that lay behind, perhaps in emulation of the god Dionysus, whose exploits he honestly believed he had emulated and surpassed. The picture thus presented in the stories of Plutarch, Justin, and Diodorus is also reported but without credence, by Arrian. But it seems Plutarch, student of human nature as he was, and writing from sources long since lost to us, is correct. Alexander cannot be judged as a dignified general and emperor, for at no time was he quite normal, and it is easy to read in his reported actions definite signs of deterioration, both mental and moral. It is also capable of determination that the borderline between what is generally accepted as normal and the edge of lunacy was passed, in the record of his actions, about the time he crossed the Hindu Kush into India. He had inherited, as a child, not a little of his mother's wild and mystically orgiastic nature, and from now on, it becomes more and more apparent. Thus the army advanced for seven days until the amazing supply of wine was exhausted, and shortly they reached a town called both Salmous and Alexandria,[1] and here, in what was then a land of

[1] Either Gulashkird, or more probably that great ancient town, lying wholly unexplored and in ruins, some twenty-five miles north-northwest of Gulashkird.

plenty, another long halt was made. A great and rich thank-offering was made to the gods for the victories in India and for preservation and rescue from the jaws of death in the deserts of Gedrosia; games, a music festival, and another orgiastic Diony-sian bacchanalia — the customary Greek celebration, in which they thanked the gods for their help and their own joy in living.

No word had come from Nearchus and the fleet, and Alex-ander, his mercurial spirit rebounding from the callousness that had led the army into the desert, began to feel grave anxiety for their safety. His admiral should have sailed soon after his own departure, and that was now over four months ago. Today we know that it is but a little over seven hundred and fifty miles from Alexander's Haven (Karachi?), where Nearchus was to start, to the harbor (at Gumrun, Bandar-Abbas), some seventy or one hundred miles south of Alexander's camp.

In the meantime, the fleet had reached the mouth of the Anamis (Minab) River, a pleasant country where an abundance of supplies were procurable. They scattered about the country, glad of a holiday and a respite from the sea. Some of the men went farther than ordinary, and met a man whose dress was that of a Greek. They accosted him in Greek and were told that he was indeed of Alexander's army, which lay in camp not far distant. The sailors were delighted at the news, and conducted him to Nearchus, where, being questioned, he replied that it was five days' journey to the camp. The stranger also brought the chief of the district to Nearchus, who obtained from him instructions and directions how to reach the camp. Next morn-ing Nearchus ordered the ships drawn up on shore, partly for making needed repairs and partly for their safety. A double rampart was thrown up about the camp, and another precaution-ary rampart and a ditch were run from the seashore to the river across the landward side. This required a few days, and then Nearchus, having assured the safety of the camp and fleet, was ready to report to his king.

While this was being done, the district chief, knowing Alex-ander's anxiety for the safety of the fleet, envisioned himself as the recipient of a great reward for being the first to bring news of its arrival. He hastily set out for the army's camp. When he made his report, the king was torn between skepticism of the story — and its source — and the will to believe. A few days passed without confirmation while several messengers were dispatched to bring Nearchus. Some went but a short distance and returned; others failed to come back at all, possibly falling victims of the desert raiders which our history says were active between the camp and the sea — even as they are today. Finally the exasperated king ordered the chief placed under rigorous arrest as the author of false reports. One group of messengers, however, with horses and chariots, on the way to find Nearchus, met him and Archias, the second in command, on their way with only five attendants. The messengers failed to recognize the travelers, whose faces were weatherbeaten and sunburned from exposure, and who were ragged and emaciated from hardship. When Nearchus asked them the way to the camp, the charioteers gave the directions readily, but prepared to continue their journey. Archias, however, guessed their errand, and advised Nearchus to ask them about it. The answer was, of course, that they were going for Nearchus; and upon his identifying himself and his companions, they were immediately taken up and conveyed to camp. Alexander received them with joy, and swore by Zeus and Ammon that the safety of the naval expedition meant more to him than the whole of his conquests in Asia. The unfortunate district chief was released from unjust durance. Alexander again offered sacrifices to Zeus the savior, Heracles, Apollo Alexicacus the preventer of misfortune, to Neptune and the other sea gods for the preservation of the fleet, and held yet another festival to thank them. Nearchus was given the place of honor at the celebration, in honor of his voyage.

This amazing voyage from the Indus to its end at the Tigris River is one of the greatest of all ancient historical chronicles; amazing not only for its display of fortitude and the unquestioning bravery of the personnel of the fleet, but for the studious accuracy and lack of rhetorical and imaginative embellishments of the account. But it must be borne in mind that Nearchus was making no voyage of discovery. He was merely checking on the accuracy of the reports of previous voyages, and preparing data for the resumption of sea-borne commerce along these coasts.

When Alexander left the Indus Delta, Nearchus hastily pushed his plans for departure to completion. Almost as soon as the conqueror disappeared in the east, the Indians, now no longer overawed by his presence, flared into revolt and began seriously harassing the sailors. Presently the fleet got under way, sailed down the Indus and coasted along to the eastward against the heavy prevailing winds and sea. After several days of difficult traveling, they reached a harbor (now silted up, but probably at or within a few miles of Karachi) which they called Alexander's Haven.[1] Here the strong winds and seas forced them to lay up twenty-four days. Finally the winds ended and they set forth again, if the meteorological conditions prevailing today with the southeast monsoon are the same as then, about the middle of September. They coasted eastward, hugging the shoreline closely, and reached a large commodious harbor which they called Morontobara, the 'Women's Haven,' now represented by the great depression of the Sirondha swamp-lake, left there and went on to the mouth of the Arabius (Purali) River, where they found another lake some distance upstream. They moved on, making several halts, and reached Cocala, along the coast, where they found Leonnatus awaiting them with a great store of supplies. The natives had revolted and slain Apollophanes, but Leonnatus defeated them in a decisive battle and crushed the insurrection. Here Nearchus remained ten days, taking on

[1] It is impossible to cite here the wealth of detail of the geological and hydrographical changes in the Indus Delta and the coasts to the westward, along which Nearchus passed and where he made halts; nor to attempt here to give more than a bare sketch of the voyage. Those who care to investigate deeply into the subject are referred to General Haig's little volume, *The Indus Delta Country*, and Sir Thomas H. Holdich's exhaustive work in the April, 1901, issue of the *Journal of the Royal Society of Arts*.

stores, and repairing the ships which had been damaged in a gale. A number of the crews and guards were found unsuited to the uses of the fleet. They were given to Leonnatus, and replaced with an equal number of his men. From Cocala they went on to the mouth of the Tomerus (Hingol) River, reaching the point at which Alexander had been forced to turn inland along the mountains. From here on all contact with the army was lost. The river emptied into a lagoon, upon whose shores stood the huts of the inhabitants. The natives, numbering about six hundred, immediately gathered to prevent the landing, though they were utterly without protection and armed only with spears with fire-hardened wooden points. The lightarmed men leaped overboard from the ships, swam ashore, and formed ranks in the water. Then they raised their war-shout and charged. Simultaneously the missile weapons on the ships opened fire with a hail of arrows and stones, and the ill-armed natives, unable to strike back, fled to the mountains for refuge. Arrian adds that they were hairy all over their bodies, living on fish only, possessing no iron, and using only stone implements. The fleet halted six days to make needed repairs in the shelter of the lagoon.

Several days after leaving the Tomerus they reached Malana, a name yet surviving almost unchanged in the bold rocky headland of Ras Malan. This they report as marking the boundary between the lands of the Oritae and the Gedrosians. Beyond here they passed an estimated six hundred stadia along the shores where dwelt a degraded people called the Icthyophagi, fish-eating savages. They then reached the harbor of Bagisara (today Damizar, the eastern bay of the headland of Urmara), where they reported going to a village called Pasira, and located sixty stadia, or about seven miles, inland. Next day they sailed again, around the great promontory, night finding them still out to sea, not daring to approach the rocky shore on which the surges pounded heavily. A day or two later they reached Calama (Khor Khalmat) and were fortunate to find a few supplies. These were eagerly seized upon. There has been a considerable extension of the land seaward here, and their next stop, the island of Carnine or Carabine, is now part of the mainland, the projecting headland of Giaban, connected with the shore by a low sandspit. From Calama they sailed along the coast called Carbis (now Gazban), rounded the high jutting promontory (of Djebel Zarain) and put into the commodious harbor of Mosarna (modern Pasni, now almost silted up). Here they at last obtained a pilot, a Gedrosian named Hydraces, who promised to guide them to Carmania. From that time on the history is little more than a repetition of landings for supplies, though these were usually obtainable in limited quantities only, and they were often on the verge of starvation. One day a number of whales, disporting themselves near-by, almost threw them into a panic, until, under instructions from the pilot, the men beat upon the water with their oars, shouted and blew trumpets until the disturbing animals withdrew from the vicinity of the noise. At another time they came to an island called Nosala or Nuhsala (Hashtala; vulg., Astola) around which hovered an atmosphere of mystery; according to legend it was once the home of a Nereid whose lure to men was beset with much evil. Nearchus sailed around it to disprove the legend that all who approached it were drawn ashore to vanish forever from the ken of man. Farther into the Persian Gulf, there loomed up on their left the high black promontory which was, they were told, called Maceta (Ras Masandam), belonging to Arabia. Still keeping to the right shore, however, they reached the mouth of the Animas River, and pulled ashore, with results already recounted.

Alexander wished to appoint another commander of the fleet, to save Nearchus a continuance of the hardships, but the admiral begged so earnestly for the privilege of completing the voyage that consent was finally given. Nearchus returned to the coast under protection of a small armed guard, and arrived safely only after beating off attacks by three small bands of desert raiders who were hovering like vultures around the army.

The army was again divided into two, Hephaestion being

given the greater part, together with the elephants and the baggage trains, and sent to continue the march along the sea-coast to Persia. This route, now that winter had come, was mild; water and adequate supplies obtainable, and the land and naval units could easily maintain contact with and co-operate with each other. Alexander, with the heavy cavalry, and the light footmen and the archers, set out for Pasargadae, the city of Cyrus, arriving there probably in January, 324. Here he found the tomb of the Great King had been broken into and rifled of the mortuary treasures in the six years that had elapsed since his first visit, and he ordered Aristobulus to restore it to its original condition. Aristobulus did a good job of the restoration, and gives us, through Arrian, a careful description of it. Even today, over twenty-four centuries after the death of Cyrus, it is still there, cut deep into the walls of a cliff hard-by the ruins of Pasargadae, but despoiled again of its costly ornaments and golden coffin; but there is still to be seen, though now worn into illegibility by the malice of time, the beseeching and almost tearful last prayer of the once all-powerful monarch: 'O Man, whoever thou art or whencesoever thou comest (for I know thou wilt come), I am Cyrus, founder of the Persian Monarchy; envy me not, therefore, the small portion of earth wherein my body lies enclosed.'

This seems to mark another and significant change in Alexander's conception of himself. We cannot, of course, know when any change really took place; we can only try to read into his actions, as they are disclosed to us, the reasons of which they were the result. First he was merely the king of Macedonia, then hegemon of Greece; next king of Egypt; still later he was king of Persia, and lastly he had made himself also king of much of India. Then he arrogated unto himself the title of the 'Lord of All Asia.' Now, as he stood in front of the tomb of the founder of the Achaemenid royal line, he was wholly the successor of the Great King. The refusal of the army to cross the Hyphasis River had embittered him toward them, and it is not improbable that their rebellion may have been one of the guiding factors underlying his choice of the ghastly route he chose through the deserts of Gedrosia; a resolve to break the army to his absolute will even though they all perished in consequence. That this might easily be so can be read into his actions but a short time in the future when it will be seen that he had long nurtured plans either to oust or wholly subordinate the Macedonians to Asiatic troops within his army. It is also not wholly unlikely for a king with his psychological make-up deliberately to bring the army into the condition they now found themselves. Certainly his callous cruelty cannot be denied, nor, by the thinking, glossed over. It is even not wholly impossible that the Macedonians who survived that desert trip held a deep and abiding rancor against him as the cause of it — a thing often known among the fighting men of an army. Yet it is but human nature of a curiously distorted but not unusual type to hate those persons whom one has greatly wronged, and we have seen that in the last three or four years he had grown far away from the old Macedonians. Soon we see additional manifestations of it. As this attitude grows, so does his cold bitterness, and the less does he try to hold in check his tyrannical temper.

While he was here at Pasargadae, the Median satrap, Atropates, marched in with a number of prisoners, the Mede Baryaxes, who had assumed the upright tiara, with the title of king of the Medes and Persians, and his following. The whole group were executed in a mass. Phrasaortes, satrap of Persepolis, had died some time before, and his place usurped by one Orsines. The latter was accused of many crimes, robbing temples, despoiling tombs, and the unjust executions of many men. He was brought to trial; the charges were proved, and Orsines was crucified over the gates of Persepolis. Peucestes, he who had so bravely defended the wounded Alexander in the Mallian citadel, was appointed satrap in his stead. Later history tells us that this was one of the few such appointments Alexander made that he had no cause to regret, for Peucestes ruled wisely and honestly long years after Alexander's death. Atropates was told to return to his post, and Alexander, having received reports from several sections that many things were seriously out of joint in the kingdom, resolved to return to the capital from whence it was most easy to start a clean-up of the situation. He marched rapidly toward Susa. Hephaestion and the army met him at the Pasitigris (Karun) River, where the former had built a bridge against his coming. Nearchus too had arrived, pressing the journey in order to reach the crossing-place in time to greet and rejoin his king. They went on together to Susa.

=XIII=

RETURN AND END

ALEXANDER had been absent from Persia, Babylonia, and the other central satrapies for six years, longer and shorter periods for the western and eastern satrapies. It was, indeed, time for him to return from his far conquests. Several times reports of his death had received credence through the land, and symptoms of restlessness and revolt had become manifest. In Bactria several garrisons had begun determined insurrections. In Media the exactions of the now executed commanders and their arbitrary disregard for the rights and religions of the conquered peoples had aroused them to dangerous discontent and seething hatred for their oppressors. In Ecbatana and Babylon, Harpalus the treasurer, almost as soon as Alexander had vanished into the eastern deserts, began to use the royal treasury's funds as if they were his own. His reckless extravagances, his palaces, harlots, and regal and overbearing independence had become scandals in a land not easily given to being scandalized. The power of corruption given him by his control of unlimited wealth had enabled him to defy all attempts to bring him to justice. He feared no man except Alexander, and he doubtless believed there was no possibility that the king would ever survive the campaigns afar and return to bring him to justice. When he heard at last that the king was approaching, he fled westward, taking with him a small army of servants and fifty thousand talents in gold. His first stop was in Cilicia, where he lived with an Athenian courtesan in grand style, even forcing the inhabitants to prostrate themselves before her. Some years before [1] he had, during a shortage of grain at Athens, sent that city several shiploads free, and for this act had been granted citizenship of Attica. He therefore went there, arriving with thirty ships of war and six thousand hired mercenaries, and attempted to foment rebellion against Alexander. At this time he also bribed Demosthenes,[2] the act resulting in the famous trial of classical history. Harpalus was but one of the offenders in high places. Other satraps, notably those of the West, had emulated him in varying degrees, their peculations had been often very great. Several had gathered armies, native and mercenary, and established themselves almost as kings in complete independence. In Greece the pot of unrest was beginning to boil again, and in Macedonia affairs were in turmoil. Ever since Alexander's departure, Olympias had made things difficult, and frequently virtually intolerable, for the faithful old regent, Antipater. About this time the king's widowed sister Cleopatra, whose husband, the king of Epirus, had been slain in a petty war in southern Italy, returned to Macedonia, upset the power of the aged regent, and herself assumed control. Olympias went to Epirus and assumed power there. Alexander was duly notified of the circumstances, and wryly remarked that of the two, Olympias had made the best choice, for the Macedonians required a strong man's hand at the helm and would never be quiet under a woman's rule. Perhaps that knowledge dictated the queen mother's choice, but we will never know.

---

[1] Athenaeus, XIII, 586.
[2] Athenaeus (XIII, 341, 342) says the bribe was fifty talents in gold.

One of his first acts upon arriving at Susa was to hear charges of many crimes preferred against the satrap Abulites and his son Oaxathres. They had been numbered among the many who believed Alexander would be slain in his conquests or would never return from India. It would be interesting to know just what the charges were, or the comportment of the accused, for either or both must have enraged the king to an extraordinary degree. During the trial his temper (Arrian says this was now less curbed than formerly) got the best of him; he seized a spear from a near-by bodyguard, ran it through the body of Oaxathres, and ordered Abulites to be bound and thrown beneath the feet of the horses, there to be kicked or trampled to death. Again he was the raging killer who had murdered Clitus, dragged the resolute defender of Gaza to death behind the chariot, and ordered the brutal killing of Bessus, Musicanus, and the Brahmans and the seven thousand defenders of Massaga.

Sometime here at Susa there occurred an incident so strange that the story is told us by several writers. Calanus, the Indian sage, now an aged man of seventy-three, had begun to suffer some kind of illness (judging from Plutarch's account, possibly dysentery), so acutely that he decided to put an end to his existence, for he despaired of recovery and deemed his life now useless. The king vainly endeavored to dissuade him, but Calanus was inflexible, saying if he could not have the end he desired he would choose another. Alexander at last acquiesced, and directed Ptolemy to build the funeral pyre of the Indian's choice. When all was arranged, Calanus, carried in a litter, for he was unable to mount his horse, was conveyed forth, crowned with a garland of flowers and singing Indian hymns, followed by the army in solemn procession of infantry, cavalry, and even the elephants. Calanus reached the pyre and halted. He gave his horse, a fine animal from the Cophen Valley, to Lysimachus. The cups and vessels and rare cloths which, by Alexander's order, adorned the huge pile of wood, he removed and presented to near-by friends. The king was not present, as he deemed it improper for him to be present at the immolation. Calanus had not bade him farewell, and, when reminded of it, returned ominously, 'I shall see him soon in Babylon,' where, as a matter of fact, Alexander was soon to die. The sage cut off his hair and burned a little of it, then mounted the pyre, wrapped himself in his cloak, and lay perfectly still while the enveloping flames crackled high in the hot air. As he mounted the pyre, the war trumpets (for so Alexander had ordered) blared, and the elephants trumpeted forth a last wild farewell. And Arrian concludes the chapter by a statement, as ominously correct today as it was two thousand years ago, 'These things have grave authors asserted concerning this sage, and this is an example of no mean import to those who study mankind, to show how firm and unalterable the mind of man is, when custom or education has taken full possession thereof.'

Calanus had begged Alexander and his other friends to make merry that evening, to celebrate, not his death, but the release and departure of his spirit into a better world, and the request was taken in the spirit with which it was made. At the banquet everyone soon became intoxicated,[1] and Alexander proposed a drinking bout. The proposal was hilariously accepted, and several prizes were offered to those who could drink the most. The first prize was won by one Promarchus, who is reported to have drank twelve quarts of wine (a kadoi full), but who also, it is said, died in delirium tremens four days afterward. Another account says that the party was so wildly unrestrained and the drinking so heavy that forty additional celebrants died also as a result of it. Plutarch does, indeed, as has been frequently uncritically cited, say that Alexander drank much less than reports usually credited him with; that he often sat far into the night with his wine untasted in front of him, talking with his friends and adorers. But though this statement was made, yet Plutarch himself, who had, as he wrote, data now long lost, records several of his prodigious drinking bouts; certainly enough to make very suspect any single statement to the con-

[1] Athenaeus, X, 436–437.

trary. Moreover, Eumenes in his *Journal* [1] records that Alexander drank a great deal, so that after a spree he would on occasion sleep for two consecutive days and nights, while fuming and impatient commanders and other officials waited vainly at his tent door for instructions and orders. Several times we are told of his drinking himself into a coma. Again, Athenaeus makes reference to a man who performed the remarkable feat of drinking more than Alexander himself. Certainly Alexander may have, in general, drank only enough to become moderately intoxicated, but he also most certainly did, as had done Philip and his forefathers before him, on not infrequent occasions drank as rapidly as possible until he was wholly stupefied and dead drunk.

Ever since the mutiny on the Hyphasis, it seems, a new set of plans had been slowly perfected in Alexander's mind, and at last the fruition of it became known. When, just ten years earlier, he had crossed the Hellespont, it was indeed to conquer at least part of Asia, but to do so as a Macedonian revenging the indignities and conquests of the Persians in Macedonia and Greece. The ease of the conquests, the adulation of the conquered, and the gullibility with which everybody swallowed his Ammon-sanctified claim to divinity, and several other factors changed and enlarged his plans beyond recognition of the original. Instead of being barbarians, the people of his newly conquered lands had many characteristics whose value he recognized and respected. The hard-fighting warriors of the northeast cherished their freedom; in the Nile Delta men of different races lived side by side in peaceful co-operation; in Mesopotamia there was much of quiet strength and endurance among the mixed populace. The empire was conquered, but now he was faced by another task almost as great as the original conquest. He must hold it together, not by force, but at least by the consent, active or passive, of the people themselves. Passive consent must be

---

[1] Müller, *Fragmenta Historicorum Graecorum*, ed. C., p. 125. Carystus of Pergamum, also cited here (IV, p. 357), says Alexander carried his revelry abroad in the dawn, in his ass-drawn chariots.

changed to active consent. And there was but one way of accomplishing this, conquered and conquerors both must be
brought to realize that there was no essential difference between
each other, first to learn toleration, second the liking and mutual
respect that usually follows familiarity. The idea had been
growing a long time, and the plan to be put into operation soon
would be such a radical departure from the attitude of the older
Macedonians that their serious objections to it were a foregone
conclusion. That was to be expected. They were a hard and
narrow people, *en masse* hating the more social, tolerant, and
broad-minded Asiatics, and they had entered upon the terrible
campaigns for what they could realize in worldly wealth. Few
of those who had so blithely crossed the Hellespont with
Alexander remained alive. Those who did had undergone unbelievable dangers and superhuman labors. Now they wanted
their rewards for their pains and sufferings, in consonance with
the universal psychology of the soldier: to the victor belong
the spoils. The glory and power of their king was his alone,
and they wanted a few of the things that make life tolerable,
their own wives and children, a house and farm to call their
own, and an end to the rigors and dangers of the soldier's life.
To them the expansion of Macedonian interests meant (and such
is the case, universally, even today) only exploitation of others
by Macedonians. That had originally been Alexander's understanding also; but now his new understanding and conceptions
relegated Macedonia to its proper sphere, a rather unimportant
and small segment of his empire, and very far away. However,
he intended to do his best, as he saw it, by the Macedonian
soldiers. He would also insure the adherence of his Asiatic
empire when, as he planned, he would shortly leave on his conquest of the remaining part of the reachable world, Arabia, the
rest of Africa, and Europe. This, he concluded, could best be
done by an act the report of which would be swiftly noised
throughout the length and the breadth of the empire, as proof
of the sympathy and love and acceptance of equality of the conquered by the conquerors. To this end he began to circulate the

story that he had found Darius dying, and that that monarch, with his last breath, had handed him his kingdom as his successor. For a long time he had considered the wisdom of the policy of marrying one of the daughters of Darius, thus, in the eyes of the Persians, legitimizing his claim to the succession, and the propaganda he set afloat was to prepare his subjects for the act.

It was now but a short time until the spring festival of the greater Dionysia and the remaining time was spent in the preliminaries of matchmaking on a gigantic scale. Thousands of the men and officers were living with native women, by whom they had already produced thousands of half-breed children. Additional thousands of children, whether by consent or rape is immaterial, were now growing up throughout the line of march of the army. A woman rarely thinks wholly evil of the father of her child, and, in that day as in this, the attitude of the women was a factor worthy of much consideration. They were the mothers of children, and they were the ones whose first teachings and viewpoints were large factors in the promulgation and maintenance of the attitude the children would carry into adult life. In the meantime, why not also bring up among the influential nobility a legitimate group of children, recognized as Greco-Persians, thus substituting a new ruling class of affinities balanced by the blood of both peoples?

Alexander celebrated the ending of his Asiatic conquests with a grand five days' festival, at the end of which, to symbolize the joining of Europe and Asia into a single unit and bond, an event unique in the annals of the world was held. He and his friends and high ranking officers, ninety-two of them, took Persian brides from the noblest families of the whole country. Alexander took for himself Statira,[1] the eldest daughter of Darius, and, as it was possible there were still persons who yet refused to recognize Darius as other than an interloper and regicide of the real king, he took also to wife Parysatis, daughter

[1] Plutarch and Diodorus call her Statira; Arrian, confusing her strangely with the widow of Memnon, calls her Barsine.

of Artaxerxes III (whom the Greeks called Ochus), who had died in 338, fifteen years before. Statira is said, now that she had grown to the full bloom of womanhood, to have equaled her mother's widely extolled beauty. We are told she was of marriageable age during the siege of Tyre in the winter of 332, or perhaps fourteen or fifteen years old; she was now probably twenty-three or twenty-four. It is conjecturable that Alexander had been considering marrying her for several years, for otherwise it seems she would have been married, as a political move, if for no other reason, to some prince or nobleman in Alexander's service. What the reaction of Sisygambis, the old queen mother, may have been to the ramifications of the whole affair we are not told. It was probably favorable, however, for at Alexander's death, she mourned him like a son. One complicating factor must have been the presence, of which we later have a hint, of Roxane here, but this seems to have bothered him not at all. At any rate, Statira seems to have been reckoned henceforth as the first of Alexander's three wives, and had she borne him a male child, the boy would have been the prince apparent.

Hephaestion, his bosom friend, was given Drypetis, a younger daughter of Darius, for the king wished their children to be cousins, as closely bound by the ties of relationship as the fathers were by friendship. It is worthy of note that the friendship of these two boyhood playmates had survived the vicissitudes of the years and was now as strong as it ever was, since he wished to share with his friend the creation of the new Persian royalty he was founding. Alexander also had a deep affection for Craterus, who reciprocated, though it was said that Craterus loved the king, while Hephaestion loved Alexander. The elderly marshal was given Amastrine, a niece of Darius; Artakama and Artonis (sisters of Barsine, who had already borne Alexander a bastard son) were given to Ptolemy and Eumenes; Perdiccas received the daughter of the satrap of Media; and Seleucus, commander of the new corps of Persian youths, the daughter of the Bactrian chief Spitamenes, whom the Greeks had pursued to his death in the steppes of Sogdia. Alexander wished to placate the family and tribe, and this was an easy and cheap way of doing so. The other officers and companions received other noble brides. The soldiers who had taken Asiatic wives were given gifts and their names recorded. These, says Arrian, numbered about ten thousand, and Plutarch, nine thousand.

The nuptials of the ninety-two officers have been preserved to us through Arrian; and mostly through Athenaeus (XII, 538 ff.), who cites the works of Chares of Mytilene, who in turn was master of ceremonies at the feast. The latter tells us:

> It was a hall of a hundred couches (each large enough for two to recline at table) and in it each couch was decorated with twenty minae worth of silver, and decorated as for a wedding. Alexander's had feet of gold. And he had bidden all his Persian friends, who were given places on the opposite side of the hall from himself and the other bridegrooms. The hall was decorated in sumptuous style, with expensive rugs, and hangings of fine linen, and tapestries of many colors wrought with threads of gold. And for the support of the vast tent which formed the hall there were pillars thirty feet high, plated with silver and gold, and set with precious stones. Around the sides were costly portières and hangings, embroidered with figures and shot through with golden threads, hung on silvered or gilded rods.

He goes on to say that everything was done to trumpet signal, whether the beginning of the feast or the pouring of libations. Famous jugglers, showmen, actors, poets, and singers of the Grecian world were there as entertainers. The ceremony itself was that of Persia, Arrian saying simply that the brides were brought to the grooms, greeted with a kiss, and seated upon the couches.

After the wholesale marriages, further to enhance his popularity with the army — the Macedonians were again growing outspokenly critical of many of his actions — he issued a statement that anyone in debt could have, as a gift, a sum sufficient to pay it off merely by giving in his name and the amount owed. This sounded unbelievable, too good to be true, and the suspicious Greeks immediately suspected the reason for the order was an attempt to find out those who had been living beyond their pay and means. They no longer trusted Alexander, they distinctly distrusted his motives, and they were suspicious and wary. Very few registered, a fact he soon knew. He merely reproved them for their distrust of him, saying that a king should always be sincere to his subjects, and they should not presume to question his veracity or intent. That probably threw them into a hysteria of cynical rage; they knew Alexander too well. Seeing their attitude and unshakable distrust, he had to have some way to overcome it, and at last, as complete evidence of his good faith, he set out tables with money upon them and ordered his paymasters to accept the mere statement any soldier should make regarding his indebtedness, and immediately to pay the sum without question or registering the man's name. Curtius, Diodorus, and Plutarch say that ten thousand talents were laid upon the tables to be distributed, and that Alexander got back only one hundred and thirty of them. Under the circumstances, it must be regarded as surprising, indicative of the moderation of the men, that any at all was turned back. It was later told him that some men reported non-existent debts and received money to pay them, but, be it said to his credit, he shut his eyes to the fact and refused to go back on his pledge not to investigate the authenticity of any of the claims. In addition to this, he took further steps, partly to reward services already rendered, and partly to assure a continuance of them. To a number of his friends who had rendered signal services he presented golden chaplets of honor. Peucestes received one for his gallantry at the city of the Mallians; Leonnatus for his share in the same action and his later services in the land of the Oritae; Nearchus for his voyage with the fleet; to Onescritos, the commander of Alexander's galley; to Hephaestion and several members of the bodyguard for other services.

Some years earlier, Alexander had given orders for the formation of a guard of some thirty thousand young Asiatics of the nobles and richer classes, to be regimented and trained in the Macedonian style. For the first time we are told they were trained by Seleucus, and since that officer was with Alexander in India, obviously the 'Epigoni' or 'The Successors,' as they were called, were there too, though our historians mention neither them nor any other Asiatic troops, save the Dahae bowmen, in any reported action. After the mutiny on the Hyphasis, Alexander seems to have realized that Coenus was right when he insisted upon the necessity of continuance of the world-conquest, if it were continued, with fresh young troops, rather than the hardship-worn veterans whose fighting power was greatly diminished by a too personal knowledge and acquaintanceship with death and wounds. As any experienced commander knows, troops which have fought a little, just enough to be tried, are far more dashing and spirited than so-called hardened veterans; these last know only too well, through suffering and pain, what war is, to be classified as *good* soldiers. After the mutiny, therefore, Alexander ordered the Epigoni greatly enlarged and their training intensified. Now, here at Susa, realizing that at last his Macedonians had become wholly estranged from him, Alexander gave up the impossible task of trying to retain their old enthusiasm for him. Very well, he would show them they were no longer necessary in his scheme of things, nor even important.

Once more, as in Bactria, he was definitely the Oriental potentate, under the spell of the grandeur and immensity of his position as supreme head of a gigantic empire, with kings acknowledging fealty and ready to jump at his beck and call. In Bactria and Sogdia he had thoroughly alienated his Macedonians and even the docile Greek mercenaries by his lavish pretensions, an impression he had tried to live down in India where he acted almost wholly as a plain Macedonian warrior king. He had failed; the memories of his men were too long. Now, at last, he realized that from here, the heart of his empire, he could call to him countless hordes of Asiatics, possessed, with equal training, of just as good as, if not better, fighting qualities than his original army. The man supply was almost unlimited; at his disposal the wealth of the Orient, and he knew he could win the loyalty of his subjects here as he had done in faraway Macedonia. He need no longer heed the likes or dislikes of the Macedonians. There was no longer any need to conceal from them the fact that he was an Asiatic potentate, and that the Asiatics were his people, far more valuable to him than the Macedonians.

Accordingly, at Susa, he held a carefully staged review of the Epigoni, and demonstrated that they had graduated from the cadet stage into well-trained, thoroughly disciplined, and dependable soldiery. It is not recorded that the other troops were reviewed. Indeed, it is possible that the Macedonians at least were calculatingly encouraged to attend as spectators, while the king, deliberately emphasizing his new status, dressed in the costume of Persian royalty, and watched both spectators and paraders with a grim smile of triumph. The anger and surprise of the Macedonians can be surmised when they saw the hated Asiatics moving with perfect precision through the movements and evolutions of their own drill; the object lesson of the king struck home, and they were furious. They now knew — for there were many princes and nobles enrolled even in the 'companion' cavalry, and many squadrons of Bactrian, Sogdian, Median, and Scythian cavalry had been formed and more were being formed — that Alexander, the kingling they themselves had raised to his immensity of power, was deliberately flaunting their uselessness in their faces. Surrounded by his docile new army, he was free to do as he wished, and he cared not at all whether they liked it or not.

He was secure in his position. Surrounded by vast forces of Asiatics as well as his European soldiers, commanding the wealth of Asia, firmly seated on the Persian throne and married to the heiresses of the power and prestige of two former monarchs, he was now perfectly assured of the safety of his enormous empire when he had completed his plans for the subjugation of the rest of the world and should move on to attempt it. In his exalted frame of mind he understood at last the real insignificance of the tumultuous little peninsula called Greece, and

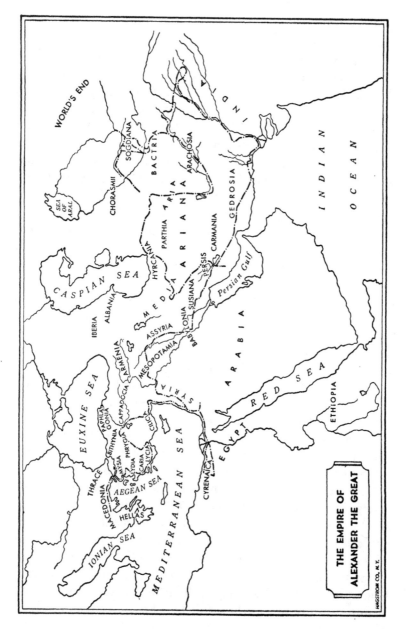

WORLD'S END

SOGDIANA

BACTRIA

ARACHOSIA

I N D I A

CHORASMII

SEA OF ARAL

ARIA

ARIANA

GEDROSIA

INDIAN OCEAN

PARTHIA

HYRCANIA

CARMANIA

PERSIS

MEDIA

PERSIS

Persian Gulf

CASPIAN SEA

SUSIANA

IBERIA

ALBANIA

ASSYRIA

BABYLONIA

ARABIA

ARMENIA

MESOPOTAMIA

EUXINE SEA

CAPPADOCIA

SYRIA

RED SEA

PAPHLAGONIA

BITHYNIA

CILICIA

ETHIOPIA

THRACE

PHRYGIA

LYDIA

LYCIA

CARIA

MYSIA

EGYPT

CYRENAICA

MEDITERRANEAN SEA

MACEDONIA

AEGEAN SEA

HELLAS

IONIAN SEA

THE EMPIRE OF
ALEXANDER THE GREAT

HAGSTROM CO., N.Y.

423

almost with contempt he dispatched orders throughout Hellas that he intended to be unquestioningly obeyed — one that certainly had far-reaching repercussions, and is still often misunderstood even today. He ordered the Greek states, but not Macedonia, for that was outside the Corinthian League, to recognize and worship him as a son of Zeus-Ammon and hence an incarnate god. This did not apply to Persia; there the cult of the king-god had been developed in the third millennium B.C., but had disappeared about the time of Hammurabi, around 2000 B.C. The idea, therefore, was definitely not Oriental, and must be considered wholly Greek. With these people the dividing line between gods, demigods, heroes, and men was very fluid; it was hard to tell where one began and another ended. Several of the Greek city-states complied with his demand. Megalopolis hastened immediate recognition of his godhead and even erected an altar to it. Sparta acceded unwillingly and with bad grace. Athens was furious at the order. Demosthenes still blindly hated Alexander's equally blind militarism, and blindly failed to recognize that the order emanated, not from Alexander the hegemon of Greece, but from Alexander the king of Macedonia, pharaoh of Egypt, king of Persia and Babylonia, and lord of all Asia, who was also prospective lord of the world. Demosthenes inveighed sarcastically upon the order, but accepted it: 'Let him be the son of Zeus if he wishes, or the son of Poseidon for all I care.' Lycurgus the orator exclaimed bitterly: 'What kind of god is this Alexander, at whose temple one must purify himself on going out instead of before entering?' Demades seems to have been the only realist. Instead of kicking against the pricks, he proposed that Alexander be worshiped as the thirteenth of the Olympian gods, as an aspect of Dionysus, whose legendary exploits he had surpassed. When the matter was hotly debated in the assembly, he, mindful of the unwisdom of opposition to the conqueror's expressed demands, warned them 'to take care lest in guarding heaven they lose earth.' Even the aged Diogenes the Cynic heard the order and cried, 'If they make Alexander Dionysus, they should equally make me

Serapis.' Yet it cannot be said that historical precedent was lacking for his case, of whom Heracles was an outstanding example. Lysander the Spartan was another: at the height of his power, some seventy years before Alexander's day, he had been worshiped as a god with altar and paean by the Samian oligarchs. Clearchus, the tyrant of Heracleia, had also been worshiped by his subjects, at his express command, as a son of Zeus. And even Philip, Alexander's father, had had his statue placed among the gods in the temple of the Ephesian Diana (Artemis) by his enthusiastic allies in that city. Further, he had caused his own image to be included as the thirteenth in the procession of the twelve gods of Macedonia on that fatal morning at Aegae when the assassin's knife demonstrated upon his own person the futility of claims of immortality by mortals.

Two additional occurrences this year served to keep the Athenians in a furor. First Harpalus, absconding with the imperial treasury, appeared in Greece. Twice in the previous six years, when there had been a severe shortage of food grain in Attica, he had made enormous contributions to the city to tide the populace over until the next crop season. For this public benefaction he had been rewarded with citizenship. Now he left his fleet and army at Tenares in Laconia, and repaired to Athens with the intention of raising the citizens to revolt. By advice of Demosthenes he was denied admittance to the city, for already messengers sent by Philoxenus, Alexander's treasurer in Asia Minor, had arrived with the demand for the surrender of the embezzler. Harpalus departed, but returned with only two triremes to Piraeus and begged admission as a suppliant. Philocles, strategos for that year, finally permitted him to enter. No direct order for his arrest had been received from Alexander, so Demosthenes suggested he be arrested and the stolen moneys impounded in the Acropolis. This was done, and soon letters arrived from Antipater and Olympias, both demanding his surrender. He escaped to Crete, where he was murdered soon afterward.

The other occurrence was the appearance, in July, of a herald with an edict from Alexander, ordering the recall of all political exiles of all cities, on pain of summary punishment. Most states obeyed at once, but the Athenians, subtle and obdurate as usual, at once dispatched an embassy to argue the matter with the king. They had no desire to lose the island of Samos, where, a generation before, the Samians had been evicted from their lands and holdings and replaced with Athenian cleruchs. They were thrown into a fever of excitement that almost became open revolt, which boiled furiously for several months, until a new occurrence caused a new wave of indignation to supplant the old. That is the kind of place Athens was. But at the moment they had no intention of surrendering Samos. Soon the air was full of rumors that revolt and war were impending. That the rumors gained prominence even in Alexander's camp is inferred by the record that at a great feast at Ecbatana in the late summer of 324, one of Alexander's friends, a man named Gorgus, caused a herald to proclaim publicly, on the behalf of the people of Samos, that if Alexander would besiege Athens, he would personally donate to the army ten thousand equipments and as many catapults and other artillery as would be needed for the task.

In early spring, in obedience to the necessity of personal knowledge of the river delta and the coast, Alexander marched to the Tigris, and, taking the hypaspists and a squadron of the heavy cavalry, boarded the fleet. Hephaestion, with most of the army, was dispatched by land to the Persian Gulf, while Alexander sailed down to it. He reached the coast and sailed along it to the mouth of the Euphrates (in that day the Tigris and Euphrates had separate mouths), made a careful tour of inspection, and returned to where Hephaestion had gone into camp on the Tigris. Then after sending Hephaestion overland to Opis (not far from modern Baghdad), he turned upstream again. On the way, the fleet encountered several weirs and dams erected in the river to prevent the passage of a hostile fleet. These he ordered removed, as a device of cowards who feared to face an enemy.

At Opis he proceeded with the reorganization of the army. This had been going on apace for the last three months. He had already opened the ranks of the 'companions' to Asiatics of high birth and personal qualifications, enrolling, we are told, besides others, no fewer than eight young princes of the realm, and the sons of many satraps and chieftains even in the aristocratic agema. And it was common knowledge that details were being worked out to break up the newly formed Asiatic foot forces (except the Epigoni) and incorporate them into the sadly decimated ranks of the Macedonians. This was the final insult; an unbelievable and inexcusable breach of the Macedonian sense of the fitness of things. The name of the Epigoni, the Successors, was read aright; the old soldiers revived their old fears of the king's Persian leanings, and discontent broke into open sedition. They buzzed through the camp like angry hornets. Nearly two years had passed since the Hyphasis mutiny. Since then they had fought dozens of murderous engagements, and their ranks were appallingly thinned; death by battle, disease, and the nightmare crossing of Gedrosia had taken terrible toll. And they were hardly any nearer home than they were two years ago. Alexander's Persophilia, always distasteful to the rank and file, had recently become so oppressive that it goaded them beyond endurance. Their attitude was equally irritating to Alexander, but at last, in the hope of conciliating them, he called them together and announced his decision to discharge and return to Macedonia 'all of them who, by age, infirmity, or loss of limbs, found themselves unable to undergo the fatigues and hardships of war'; but, he added, 'that whoever were inclined to stay with him should taste so largely of his royal bounty as to become the envy of those who remained at home, and excite other Macedonians to share their toils and dangers with them.' This declaration — instead of pleasing the Macedonians as he had hoped — showed such complete lack of understanding or regard for their situation and circumstance that it infuriated them again.

Plutarch is the only narrator whose writings give us a hint

of the reason for their attitude. He says: 'The Macedonian soldiers, who were old and infirm, finding they were to be sent away, cried out that they were unjustly and infamously treated, to be thus cast aside after they had been worn out in his service, and sent home in worse condition than they were when they went abroad.' Economic necessity — the requirements of the day, food and drink — governs the world. Macedonia and Greece were small countries, relatively dry or stony and infertile, capable of supporting but a limited population. Huge numbers of slaves were employed by the few men who owned most of the country, numbers so great that for many decades, despite their fratricidal wars and what amounted to almost migrations by untold numbers of young and propertyless men into foreign lands and seas, the population had exceeded the ability of the region to support them. Despite the removal of these numbers, Greece had long been afflicted by a large number of homeless and rootless wanderers, for whom, unless they took to predatory lawlessness and pillage, as many had, the land could not provide a living. Landless free men were in an intolerable position. They could not work for others: the others had unpaid slaves to do it for them. The professions were occupied by slaves in every field, working for the benefit of a master, to whom went the results, increments, or rewards of their labors and accomplishments. The free man was disinherited in his own homeland, free, but hardly free to do more than starve quietly or sell himself as a mercenary soldier or turn robber or pirate. The broken Macedonians knew only too well that, when they returned to their poverty-stricken homeland, nothing awaited them there but the blank face of poverty. Their pay — whatever it was — was such that they had none of it saved; the vast loot they had captured lay abandoned in the deep hot sands of Gedrosia; and their physical incapacity was a terrible handicap in a barren and harsh land. Economic laws ruled ancient lands also, and poverty, hunger, and hardship were just as real then as today.

A storm of wrath burst from the assembled Macedonians, and thousands of voices took up their grievances: 'You have used us up and now cast us aside! You are no longer a Macedonian but a Persian! You have lost your love for your countrymen, and want to replace us with Asiatics! Very well, take them, and you will see if you can conquer the rest of the world with these Persian dancing boys! Let all the Macedonians go! Keep all or keep none! Why don't you join forces with your father Ammon and let him fight your wars for you?' Challenging and mocking voices, freighted with the pent bitterness and rancor of years of hardship and suffering, shouted at him, calling him a renegade and sneering at his pretensions to divinity. To Alex-. ander's astonishment and indignation (the astonishment and indignation of all tyrants who have no thought or regard for the comfort or lives of their subjects, when at last they meet an unexpected expression of popular opinion), he was facing an angry and outraged mob. The situation was fraught with terrible possibilities, and the more thoughtful of Alexander's officers on the platform must have realized it. A vociferous and angry mob is liable to do almost anything. But Alexander, never really thoughtful and mentally shallow, was in a towering rage, too great to permit him to think of possibilities. He leaped like a maniac from the platform, and, at the head of his strong bodyguard, plunged into the throng. In a few moments he had seized or pointed out thirteen of the most outstanding of the mutineers, and ordered the bodyguard to lead them out to immediate execution. Curtius says they were bound and thrown into the river to drown. Had they but had a leader —— ! But conjecture is useless, the uproar was an automatic outburst of popular rage, and there was no leader. In the terrified silence that followed the unexpected swiftness of his act, Alexander remounted the platform, and, facing their sullen silence, addressed them, his anger giving passionate eloquence to his words — a typical tyrant's spellbinding speech, a curious tissue of bombast, half-truths, and boasting: [1]

[1] Arrian, IX. This speech, put into Alexander's mouth by Arrian, reports him as calling Philip his father. Despite Alexander's personal convictions that Ammon was his father, the common soldiers would have nothing to do with this assertion, and con-

What I am going to say to you, Macedonians, will not be said with intent to divert you from going back to Macedonia, for you may go, all of you, immediately, so far as I am concerned. But I want to remind you of what you were, and what were your conditions, before you entered into our services. And I shall begin first, as I ought, with my father Philip. When he found you, you were a poor, miserable, and wandering people, many of you dressed only in skins, feeding a few small flocks upon the mountainsides, which you could not hold without continual fighting for their protection against neighboring mountain tribes, frequently without much success. Instead of skins he gave you clothes to wear, and took you from the barren mountains into the fruitful plains below, and taught you to fight the tribesmen so you were no longer compelled to resort for safety to inaccessible strongholds to preserve your lives, but to your own valor. He brought you into cities, gave you equitable laws and statutes, and civilized customs. He gained for you sovereignty over those barbarians, they who had before continually harassed and oppressed and enslaved you, and from being subject peoples he made you free.

He annexed the greater part of Thrace to Macedonia, and, by seizing the towns upon the seacoast, brought an abundance of good things by commerce, and made the working of the mines a steady source of employment to you. He made you master of the Thessalians before whom you used to cower in fear. He humbled the Phocians, and gave you a broad highway into Greece, instead of a narrow and difficult path. The Athenians and Thebans are paying us tribute and obeying us, and they look to us now as their masters, for which I claim part of the credit. He penetrated into the Peloponnesus, settled its affairs, and was publicly proclaimed commander-in-chief, captain-general of all the Greeks in the coming war against the Persians, bringing thereby to himself not more glory than to you and your state of Macedonia. `These are the things which my father did for you, great things if considered alone, but small if compared with what I have done.

From my father I inherited a few goblets of gold and silver, a treasury containing hardly sixty talents and five hundred talents in debts. I borrowed eight hundred more talents, and set forth

tinually stoutly rejected and ridiculed it. As Alexander was speaking to the soldiers, it is likely he did use the term they understood and approved.

from a land which could support not even you, and opened for you an unmolested passage of the Hellespont, though the Persians were the masters of the seas. At Granicus I overran the satraps of Darius with my cavalry. I added to your empire the lands of the Aeolians and Ionians, of Phrygia and Lydia, and I took Miletus by storm. I gained other places by surrender, and to you I gave the wealth that was in them. The wealth of Egypt and Cyrene, which became mine without fighting, are yours; Syria, Palestine, and Mesopotamia are yours. Babylon, Bactria, and Susa, the riches of the Lydians, the wealth of the Persians, the treasures of the Indians, all are yours, and the Outer Ocean is yours. From among you come the satraps, and the generals and the taxiarchs! And what have I from all these vast spoils except this purple robe and this diadem? I have kept nothing for myself, nor can anyone point to any treasure-troves of my own apart from these possessions of yours and those kept in store for you. I have no need to keep anything, for I eat as you eat, sleep as you sleep. Indeed, the fare I eat is often far simpler than those among you who live well; and I know I often sit up at night to watch that you may sleep in quiet and safety. Some of you claim you have endured toils and hardship; will any of you say you endured any privation I did not share? Who of you can say he endured more for me than I did for him? Come, now, let anyone of you who has wounds bare himself and show them, and I will show mine. No part of my body, in front anyhow, is free from scars; nor is there any kind of weapon that has not left its marks upon my body. I have been wounded by the sword in hand-to-hand fighting, I have been pierced by arrows, and by bolts from catapults. I have been pelted with stones and pounded with clubs, while leading you to victory and glory and for your own enrichment, through many lands, and the seas, across great rivers and mountains and plains. I have celebrated your weddings at the same time as my own, and the children of many of you will be kin to my own.

Those of you who had debts I freely paid, without inquiring how, despite your good pay and rich booty, you contracted them. Many of you have chaplets of honor as awards for your bravery and my esteem. Whoever has been killed met a glorious death and received a splendid funeral. Statues of many in noble bronze have arisen in their native cities. Their wives and children have been freed of all taxes and imposts and exempted from all required public service. Not one has ever died in retreat under my leadership. And now I propose to send home such of you as are no longer fit for service, and to make you the envy of your neighbors.

But you *all* wish to leave me. Very well. Go, all of you. Go home and tell them how you have treated your king, Alexander, the conqueror of the Medes, Persians, Bactrians, and Scythians, who brought under his rule the Uxiians, Arachosians, and Drangians; who subjugated the Parthians, Sogdians, and Hyrcanians, and carried his arms to the shores of the Hyrcanian Lake [Caspian Sea]; who has marched over the Caucasus, crossed the Oxus, the Tanais, and the Indus, which had been crossed before only by Dionysus, and who crossed the Hydaspes, the Acesines, and the Hydraotis, and would have crossed the Hyphasis save that your hearts turned to water with fear; who penetrated even to the Great Sea by both mouths of the Indus; who marched through the deserts of Gedrosia with his army where no army ever passed before; and took the lands of the Oritae and Carmania — go home, and tell them that when you returned to Susa you deserted him and went away, leaving him to the protection of the conquered foreigners. That report may appear glorious in the eyes of men, and righteous in the eyes of the gods. Get you gone!

Alexander turned abruptly, descended from the platform, and walked quickly into the palace, alone. The rest of the day, and the next, he refused to see any of his friends, except perhaps Hephaestion; sulking like a spoiled child he even refused to wash or change his clothes. The soldiery, without leadership or guidance, were dazed by the unexpectedness of his abrupt dismissal of them. When two days had passed without word from, or of, Alexander, grave forebodings took the place of their anger. Soldiers today, and even more so then, are creatures of soldier-psychology, accustomed to look to their leaders for guidance and actions, and when this is withdrawn, their unaccustomedness to thinking for themselves leaves them wholly at loose ends. They had spoken as men are prone to do, without thought or plan as to result, and the result was profoundly shocking to them; they had been dismissed, masterless and

alone, in a far country. On the third day they received a new
and even greater shock. Alexander sent for the leading Persian
officers, and began forming a new and Persian army, with organizations in the Macedonian fashion, creating the Persian hypaspists, Persian agema, and Persian pezetairoi, placing Persians
in command of them and selecting Persians to be his 'kinsmen'
members of his bodyguard, court, and other groups closest to
the throne. He then sent orders to the Macedonians to leave
the camp, or, if they wished, to take up arms against him. The
surprise action took them aback, and they suddenly went into
a frenzy of grief. They rushed to the gates of the palace, flung
their weapons upon the ground, and began to cry out for Alexander, promising to deliver up the instigators of the mutiny,
and vowing they would not leave the gates, but stay there day
and night until he forgave them.

At last Alexander came out to them, and the older Macedonians rushed forward and threw themselves before him, crying
and pleading. When he saw his old friends and followers re-
pentant before him, his emotion choked him, and he too burst
into tears.

Then one Callines, 'an old and worthy hipparch' of the
'companion' cavalry, stepped forward and addressed the king.
'What grieves us so greatly,' he said, 'is that you have made
some of the Persians your kinsmen, privileged to greet you with
a kiss, whereas none of the Macedonians, save a few of your
friends, may have that honor.'

Alexander interrupted him swiftly, reverting back to his
impulsive youth, 'But I regard you all as my kinsmen,' he cried.
'And from this moment on I shall so call you.'

Delightedly, Callines stepped forward and kissed him, and the
others flung themselves forward to kiss his hands, his garments,
his feet, anything they could reach of him. Then, in wild
hysteria, they snatched up their weapons and began a mad
dance about him, shouting and laughing, until, in the end, they
marched back to camp singing a hymn of thanksgiving to
Apollo.

Thus the last effort of the old Macedonian spirit to assert itself ended in failure, and that ancient independence which was theirs when Philip mounted the throne was crushed at last. Alexander's sheer will power had won. The Macedonians were subdued, but they were still a vague factor, and must publicly avow a oneness with the Persians. A great love-feast (*agapē*) was prepared, at which nine thousand Macedonian, Greek, and Persian officers and men of all ranks were invited. The Macedonians were seated nearest the king, then came the Greeks, then the Persians, and lastly the other Asiatics — for once, and probably this once only, relegated to seats 'below the salt.'

As the banquet opened, Persian and Greek and Macedonian sat at last in peace. The king and his guests both dipped wine from the same bowl to pour as libations to the gods, while both Greek and Persian Magian priests invoked the blessing together. Alexander then offered up the fervent 'Prayer at Opis,' [1] the exact meaning of which has been the subject of much speculation ever since that day upon which it was uttered. Unfortunately, we are not told the words used in this, the ultimate expression of his political development and considered intent. We are, however, told that he, with all the fervor of his mystical nature, besought the gods to grant to the Greeks and Persians, among other blessings, the greatly desired last and greatest blessing, unity and concord of hearts. It is easily comprehensible that he should earnestly desire to bring about, between the stiff-necked and insular Macedonians and Greeks and the much more tolerant Persians, a mutual acceptance and understanding of

---

[1] W. W. Tarn, in *Cambridge Ancient History* (VI, 437) and elsewhere, notably the *Journal of Hellenic Studies*, has brought forth the suggestion that in the famous 'Prayer at Opis,' Alexander offered confession of his sweeping belief in the brotherhood of all mankind, the philosophical conception later preached by Christ and Zeno. This theory is wholly untenable. Arrian and Curtius both specifically state the prayer was for concord between the Macedonians and Persians only. It is the author's belief, familiar by long association with a number of the more outstanding military minds, that Alexander's mentality, exemplifying both the perfect military mind and the elements of the equally purblind religious paranoiac fanatic, was wholly incapable of grasping such an elusive ideal.

each other, a common regard for the undeniable good qualities of each, for only in this way could grow a firmer feeling between the two, a bond of mutual liking and respect, very necessary if the hard-won empire were to continue to exist without force and compulsion. His political aim was that both conquerors and conquered should live in harmony, for only thus could his Asiatic empire be held together while and when he moved on, perhaps forever, to add the rest of the known world to it. He had no illusion as to the *vae victis* attitude of his own soldiery toward the Asiatics, and it is notorious that hatred, intolerance, or contempt by one of two groups will be shortly heartily reciprocated by the other. In his world, that meant friction and — war, both of which he must avoid by all means from now on. The harsh intolerance of the conquerors must at all costs be done away with; the Persians must remain loyal through a mutual regard for the Greek elements among their rulers, as well as through loyalty to the husband of the daughters of their native kings. Otherwise, when he had gone, it would not have been difficult for them to upset his already established kingdom and effectually destroy, by their unrest and the necessity of reconquering it, his dream of enlarging it still further. Other peoples and their possible addition to the empire could not have now been considered as existing in a sense applicable to his invocation; Alexander, we conceive, had no thought of them, nor of any union save that which he had found necessary between the soldiers of his European and Asiatic forces, their officers, and the native officials. And it was for this limited objective that he so earnestly prayed. To this extent, and this only, ran his desire, at least at the moment. He had built his empire by the sword, and by the sword it must needs be maintained, with Alexander at the top, the foci of the wide world's homage. No military conqueror can rise — by virtue of the limitations of his military mentality — above the political-social ideals of his day, and this was a day when the ethical ideals — and those of the military mind have advanced shockingly little since — were those of the wolf, when the eager and bloodthirsty gods urged

435

eager and conscienceless butchers — like Alexander — to further rapine and slaughter.

After the festival was over, Alexander adhered to his original program and intention of retiring the worn and unfit of the Macedonians, of whom ten thousand veterans were selected for dismissal. It seems this act was dictated by two reasons; one, the necessity of eliminating the men who were more or less incapacitated, but it seems also partly at least based upon the intent to reduce further the Macedonian contingent, with their ever-present threat of dissidence and hostility to his own ideas. Each man was given full pay for the period until he should reach home, and an additional talent for traveling expenses. Those who had Asiatic wives and children surrendered the latter to the king upon his promise to see them cared for and the boys reared as soldiers, and later to bring them himself to their fathers in Macedonia. Craterus,[1] who was very popular and much liked by the Macedonians, was placed in charge, with Polysperchon as second-in-command. Craterus was now elderly, worn with hardship and suffering from illness. He was also ordered, when he should arrive, to take charge of Macedonia in Antipater's stead, and send the latter back to Alexander with a levy of young soldiers to replace the old men. Antipater was an efficient and soldierly officer,[2] but too little the courtier to be successful at the well-nigh impossible task of maintaining internal peace among the royalty left at home. He had been at odds with Olympias ever since the king's departure, often to such an extent that Alexander feared for the peace of the kingdom. Olympias had written several times charging Antipater with insolence and the abuse of his delegated authority, and accused him of acting as if he were king instead of regent. The general's letters, on the

[1] Plutarch (*Eumenes*) says Craterus had earned the love and admiration of the Macedonians and incurred Alexander's displeasure on a number of occasions by upbraiding the king for his Persian profligacy.

[2] Athenaeus (XII, 548–549) says Antipater, despite the power he held and the wealth at his disposal, still lived according to the customs of the old Macedonia, in Spartan simplicity and frugality. It is further recorded that he was a stern and strict disciplinarian.

other hand, charged Olympias with arrogance, cruelty, and un-justified and malicious meddling with the affairs of state. The wordy warfare continued wearyingly until Alexander is reported to have complained that he was paying dearly for his nine months' lodging (ten months according to the Greek calcula-tions), referring to the period of Olympias' pregnancy while car-rying him. At any rate, it was felt that Antipater would be better freed of her proximity and called for service in Persia. It is also possible that the general's leaning and preference toward oligarchy was displeasing to Alexander, who by now realized the way to keep the Greek city-states futile was to maintain them in democracy.

Alexander then proceeded, since summer was drawing on, through the Zagros Mountains to the old summer capital of Ecbatana. Diodorus (XVIII) mentions that along this route was a small place called Celenae, peopled by the descendants of a Boeotian colony transplanted from Greece by Xerxes. On his march we are told that at one point quarters were set aside for Eumenes,[1] but were taken by Hephaestion as lodgings for one of his favorite musicians. Eumenes in rage came to Alexander with his complaint, angrily declaring that they who would remain in favor must throw away their arms and learn to be musicians or actors. Alexander at first agreed to the justice of the complaint and chided Hephaestion, but later grew angry with Eumenes for daring to find fault with his friend, accounting the freedom he had taken more as an affront to his majesty than a reflection upon Hephaestion. Sometime later the two quar-reled again, a great deal of bad language passing between them, and again Alexander put a stop to it. Hephaestion seems to have partaken of his master's temper and arrogance, for we are told elsewhere that he and Craterus also fell out with each other several times.

At Ecbatana another great festival [2] was held, and while it

[1] Plutarch, *Eumenes*.

[2] Probably the Oschophoria, 'Carrying of Grape Clusters,' Dionysiac festival about the end of October.

was going on, Hephaestion was taken violently ill. Alexander hastily left the sports and hurried to his friend, but arrived too late. Hephaestion was dead. Alexander made his frantic grief a display in which the psychologist can easily recognize the symptoms of childish emotional development. With a shriek he threw himself upon the body of his friend, clasped it in his arms and sobbed and moaned all day and night. At dawn they forcibly pulled him away. But even then he would not leave the room, either to change his clothing or even wash, eat, or sleep, but lay on a couch alternately silent or weeping. Once he roused himself sufficiently to hack off his long golden hair with a knife, but for two days longer he lay there. Then once more he roused himself, this time to order Hephaestion's physician, Glaucus, crucified. On the third day, still unshaved and unwashed, his face covered with tear-streaked grime, he personally placed Hephaestion's body in his chariot, and himself drove it to the palace for the final preparations. The whole land was ordered into mourning, even the horses having their manes and tails clipped. He ordered that no chiliarch should ever be put over Hephaestion's cavalry regiment, but the unit was to bear forever the name of its last commander. Then he held another game and music festival, more sumptuous than any other he had yet shown, in honor of the dead. In the meantime, he employed a certain Stasicrates to design and build Hephaestion a funeral monument in Babylon at an expense of ten thousand talents. Stasicrates was the visionary who had proposed to cut Mount Athos into a statue of Alexander, which in its left hand should hold a city of ten thousand inhabitants, its right hand pour a river into the sea — a monument which had never reached more than the speech stage. Luckily Alexander, when the project was broached to him, had been realistic, replying in the negative, saying that Mount Athos was already the monument to the folly of one king, referring to the time when, during the invasion of Greece, the Persian king Xerxes had tried to cut a canal through it. He also sent orders to Egypt that two great *heroons* (hero shrines) should be erected to Hephaestion there, one on the island of Pharos, the other in the city of Alexandria proper, the city which was to be the capital of his western dominions after their conquest. To this end he sent a letter to Cleomenes in Egypt, promising forgiveness for the crimes of which many reports had accused him, and even for such crimes as he might commit in the future, giving him, as it were, *carte blanche* in thuggery, in return for satisfactory services in the design and building of the extravagant memorials. Messengers were also dispatched post-haste to the Oasis of Siwa to consult with his father Ammon as to whether Hephaestion might be given divine honors as a god, or as only a hero.

It had now been some time since his friend's death and the first frantic outpouring of Alexander's grief had worn off, but the mad-melancholy remained, and to him that meant the call to murder again. Early winter arrived, and the snows lay deep on the high Zagros Mountains. In them, north of the Uxiians, lived another tribe, the Cossaeans, a predatory and unsettled people. The Persians had sent several expeditions against them into their mountains in the endeavor to subject them, attempts which the tribesmen easily evaded. They merely abandoned their small villages and valley farms at the approach of the soldiers, and fled to the mountain heights where they were safe from pursuit. Alexander needed someone upon whom to slake his mad thirst for blood, and the Cossaeans were the most convenient objects upon which to do so. In the winter they could not escape into the icy peaks. He gathered his army and went storming in upon them. In a forty days' campaign he swept the region clean, slaughtering every person, regardless of age or sex, upon whom he could lay hands; they were, he declared darkly, a blood sacrifice made to the spirit of Hephaestion.

He turned back to Babylon, perhaps in February, 323, which, in preference to Susa, he had planned to make his eastern capital, on account of its central location and the already existing network of roads binding it to the rest of the empire. As he drew near the city he received embassies from most of the nations of the known world, come to offer homage and establish friendly

relations with the new lord of all Asia. From the Italian peninsula came Bruttians, Tyrrhenians (Etruscans), and Lucanians,
and, it is said, Romans; [1] from North Africa came Libyans,
Carthaginians, and men from the Sahara and Ethiopia; from
Europe came Gauls and Iberians, of whom, we are told here, the
Macedonians thus heard for the first time. From Europe also
came representatives of the warlike Scythians. All of these
peoples had heard of the fame and deeds of the conqueror, and
were rushing to forestall his possible designs upon themselves.

As he crossed the Tigris he was met by messengers of the
'Chaldean' priests, who well knew his superstitious nature,
with a warning against entering Babylon, for they said the god
Bel or Marduk had issued an oracle that it would be unlucky for
him to do so. Alexander refused to accept the warning, shrewdly
guessing the priests didn't want him to find they had disobeyed
his instructions — tantamount to orders — in 331 to rebuild
the temple of the god. He quoted them a line from Euripides to
the effect that a prophet was a man who made a good guess as
to what was most likely to happen, and prepared to go ahead.
He may have had, in his rôle of Achilles, now that his Patroclus
(Hephaestion) was dead, a fear that he too was to follow in the
footsteps of those two friends of the heroic age, for Patroclus
died first and Achilles did not long survive him. Therefore, when
the priests of Bel begged him, if he insisted on disobeying the
godly injunction, to enter by the west gate rather than the east,
he consented. The army marched around the city, but finding
the way was barred by extensive marshes, they turned back, and
entered the city by the east gate.

Immediately upon entrance, he plunged with fiery zeal into
work, the preparations for continuance of the wars. With
Hephaestion dead, however, the labor was of a different type
from before. His superstitious nature was more manifest, and
his nerves were going back on him. He was in a highly strung

[1] Livy (IX, 18) makes the incredible statement that Romans had never heard of
Alexander. To accept this statement, however, would be to admit that they had
never heard of the Greeks either, a thesis impossible and absurd.

condition that drove him at top speed both day and night. He worked hard, he played harder, and, as the combination of the two broke down his physical stamina, he (Plutarch says) gave way wholly to the fears of his ingrown superstitions, his mind grew disturbed, and he grew so timorous that when the least thing unusual happened he deemed it a prodigy. His court became thronged with diviners, soothsayers, and priests of all sorts, whom he kept constantly busy making sacrifices and reading omens. Now, too, an ominous story reached him. Upon his return from India, so the story goes, Apollodorus, military commander of the garrison of Babylon, hearing of his severity with other officials and fearing the same treatment to himself, wrote his brother Pythagorus, a soothsayer and diviner, asking for assurance of his own safety. Pythagorus, in an answering letter, promised to make the prediction, but, in order to do so, he must have the names of the persons he feared. Apollodorus replied that he chiefly dreaded the king and Hephaestion. The first sacrifice Pythagorus offered was inspected for Hephaestion; the omens were threatening, and the soothsayer wrote his brother, then at Ecbatana, to have no fear of Hephaestion, for the latter would surely die soon. He next divined for Alexander, and here, too, to his surprise, the same ominous predictions were made. Apollodorus, as a mark of the sincere good will he bore his king, communicated the matter to Alexander and warned him of a threatening danger. Alexander commended his honesty and integrity, and upon reaching Babylon, called for Pythagorus. He interrogated the frightened soothsayer, but received a simple and straightforward reply, and permitted him to go with a commendation also.

Orders were sent to Phoenicia to build a number of ships, then disassemble them, transport them to the Euphrates and raft them piecemeal down to Babylon, where they were to be reassembled. Several thousand men were put to work digging a naval harbor at the city, whereon to assemble the fleet, with the necessary complements of warehouses for storing materials and quarters for the men. Others were sent out to bring back cypress logs for timbers. An officer with a great sum of money was dispatched to the coasts of Phoenicia and Syria to procure a vast quantity of naval stores and hire seamen for the fleet, for the king projected an expedition to plant a series of military and naval bases and colonies along the shores of the Persian Gulf. It was his opinion that this coast might in time become as rich and populous as the Mediterranean coasts. Arrian [1] says: 'He made these extraordinary preparations for fitting out a fleet on the pretense of making war against the Arabians, a populous nation, because they had neither sent ambassadors to him requesting his friendship as all others had done, nor made him any presents, nor paid him homage; but my opinion is that it was only his ungovernable ambition which urged him to that attempt, an ambition which no acquisitions, howsoever extensive, were capable of satisfying.' He adds later that Alexander planned to conquer the Arabians and force them to worship him as a god.

He had already dispatched, while at Ecbatana, an expedition of exploration and discovery to the shores of the Caspian Sea. The Greeks believed this body of water to be a bay of the earth-girdling ocean and, despite the assurances he had received from the 'Scythian' king in Sogdia that it was an inland sea, Alexander had doubts regarding it. The leader of this expedition was one Heraclides, of whom we are told only this one fact. He was given a number of shipwrights and instructions to build a fleet to use on the exploration. The task was no doubt halted at Alexander's death and left uncompleted. Another commander, Archias of Pella, who had been second-in-command with Nearchus, was dispatched about the same time from Babylon (for his account of his voyage is such that it has been calculated to have occurred in the winter season) in a thirty-oared galley down the Persian Gulf. He went only as far as the island of Tylos (Bahrein), then grew fearful and turned back. Another ship, under Androsthenes of Thasos, was sent out. He seems to have gone scarcely farther than did Archias, and he too turned back. The third ship, under Hieron of Soli, was dispatched, this

[1] Arrian, VII, 20.

time with positive orders to follow the coasts of Arabia around to the Red Sea, and into the Egyptian port of Heroopolis. He sailed away down the Persian Gulf, reached and rounded the headland of Maceta, which Nearchus had sighted on his voyage. As he gazed on the interminable vista of the rocky coast stretching out of sight in the hot sunshine, his courage too failed, and he turned back, bearing to Alexander the news that Arabia was astonishingly large, not less in size than India. Equally barren of results was another expedition headed by Anaxicrates, who left Heroopolis in Egypt in an attempt to reach Persia from that direction. He managed to get as far as the strait of Bab-el-Mandeb, and was forced to halt by lack of water.

While this was being done, in Babylonia, Alexander's plans included new works elsewhere also. He issued orders for construction of a pyramid, rivaling in size any of those of Egypt, over Philip's grave at Aegae in Macedonia. Six great temples were projected for erection, two in honor of Zeus, two to Athene, and two others to Apollo. Of the first two, one was to be built in the Macedonian holy city of Dium, the second in the holy city of his mother's people, Dodona, which was the seat of the worship of Zeus-Naios, equated in his mind as the Egyptian Ammon, his father. The temples of Athene were to be erected on the site of heroic Troy, and apparently in the Cyrene (though Diodorus, XVIII, says Kyrnos, Corsica, in obvious error), where the goddess reputedly once dwelt. The temples of Apollo were to be built in the two places most sacred to him, Delphi in Greece, and upon the island of Delios in the Aegean.

During this time the construction of the great tomb for Hephaestion was being pushed. Just outside the city walls a great square, a stadium on each side, was cleared, leveled, and filled. Upon it a quadrangle was built consisting of thirty rooms roofed with the trunks of palm trees. On top of this rose the brick tomb, divided into five huge stories, each forty feet high, and each rising steplike, smaller in size, to the porticoed temple at the top, two hundred feet above the ground. The outside of the first story was to be ornamented with a row of projecting ship's gilded prows, sixty on each side, with gilded figures of archers and men-at-arms grouped about and on each prow. The second story was to be ornamented with huge projecting torch-holders twined with golden snakes, and between them, gilded eagles in flight. The third story was to be covered with a great frieze of lions and other wild animals; the fourth was to be encircled with a sculptured frieze depicting the battle of the centaurs; the fifth, by alternating golden bulls and lions. In the temple hollowed columns were designed to carry afar the voices of concealed singers and chanters. Work had begun upon this extraordinary monument when, in May, the messengers sent to the Oasis of Siwa to inquire about Hephaestion returned with refusal of deification of the latter, but with authorization to pay him honors as a hero.

Apropos of the story of the monument, we are told [1] that, when Nearchus was preparing the fleet at Babylon, Alexander found the treasury temporarily empty. He sent a number of his friends a request for a loan, assessing each a certain number of talents, in Eumenes' case, three hundred. The secretary sent one hundred only, with the declaration that he had had difficulty in raising that sum. Alexander accepted neither the money nor the story. Instead, he gave private orders that Eumenes' tent should be set on fire, intending to catch the latter in a manifest lie when the valuables and money were carried out. The conflagration spread much faster than was anticipated, and nothing was saved; even the archives and papers of state were destroyed. Yet Alexander was correct about the money, for the gold and silver, melted in the heat of the fire, was afterward gathered up and weighed, and found to have a value of a thousand talents. Eumenes saved himself, however, and was restored to favor by making a very large contribution toward the cost of Hephaestion's memorial.

Upon receipt of Ammon's authorization, Alexander held a gorgeous dedicatory ceremony of the unfinished tomb, and it is believed Hephaestion was laid to rest there against the comple-

[1] Plutarch, *Eumenes*.

tion of a permanent burial place in Egypt. It seems to have been Alexander's intention to have him gradually elevated and worshiped, if not as a deity, at least as a hero.

Thus time passed, while Alexander labored hard during the daytime at being the military conqueror and Persian emperor at the same time, and a profligate and drunken wastrel at night. Now that his best friend had died, his old abstemious self-control seems to have vanished entirely. His extravagances, and those of his friends, upon whom he lavished the loot of the empire, were the scandal and the admiration of that and later days. When he entertained his friends at dinner, as he often did, the cost was never less than a hundred minae of silver.[1] And when his friends entertained him, the expense was even greater.[2] It was the custom for them to encase whatever was to be served as dessert in a sheet of gold. This was carelessly torn from the tidbit and cast aside as waste, to the no little profit of the servants and slaves. There could be but one source of funds for this lavish and prodigal display, if it were not obtained from graft and misuse of power by the friends of the king, and that was the imperial treasury. Alexander obviously either closed his eyes to their piracies or perhaps even abetted them; in either case it boded ill for the empire. He himself had now blossomed out into the accepted magnificence of full Oriental despotism, with daily displays of his grandeur.

> In the park there was erected a golden throne and couches with silver legs, upon which he sat while transacting business in company with his boon companions. During dinner every sort of contestant and entertainer exerted their efforts to entertain and amuse the king, and it is said that during the course of that last dinner Alexander himself acted from memory a scene from Euripides, and, pledging in unmixed wine [that is, unmixed with water, hence strong], with zest compelled others to do likewise. Alexander also wore sacred vestments at his dinner parties, at one

[1] Müller, *Fragmenta Historicorum Graecorum*, ed. C., p. 125.

[2] Athenaeus (IV, 155) citing the works of Agatharchides of Cnidus, and his *Asiatic History*.

time putting on the purple robe and thin slippers and horns of Ammon just like the gods; at another time the costume of Artemis [Diana the huntress] which he even wore about in his chariot,[1] wearing the Persian garb and showing above the shoulders the bow and hunting spear of the goddess; while at still other times he went garbed as Hermes [the phallic Greek god, who was also the messenger of the gods; portrayed generally as a nude beardless youth at *this historical period*]; on other occasions as a rule and in everyday use he wore a purple riding-cloak, a purple tunic with white stripes, and a Macedonian hat with the royal fillet; but upon social occasions he wore the winged sandals and broad-brimmed hat [of Hermes] upon his head and carried the caduceus [the rod of Hermes] in his hand; yet upon other occasions he bore the lion skin and club of Heracles. What wonder then [this is an aside of Athenaeus' who seems to have been writing about 180 B.C.] that the Emperor Commodus [of Rome, died 192 B.C.] later also had the club of Heracles lying beside him in the chariot with the lion's skin spread out beneath, and desired to be called Heracles, when it be seen that even Alexander, Aristotle's pupil, got himself up like so many gods, to say nothing of the goddess Artemis? Alexander sprinkled the very floor with valuable perfume and scented wine. In his honor much myrrh and other kinds of incense went up in smoke; a religious stillness and silence born of fear held fast all those who were in his presence. For he was hot-tempered and murderous, reputed, in fact, to be melancholy-mad. . . .[2]

Polycleitus of Larissa, in his eighth book of *Histories*, says Alexander slept upon a golden couch, and that flute-players, male and female alike, always accompanied him to camp and drank with him until daybreak. Alexander's courtiers also indulged in extravagant luxury. One of them, Agnon, would permit only gold nails to be used in his boots. Cleitus, when he had business to transact, walked about on purple cloths while conversing with those who had audience with him. Perdiccas, who still retained his fondness for the old gymnastic sports, always

[1] Carystus of Pergamum (*vide Fragmenta Historicorum Graecorum*, 375) says Alexander carried his carousing to the extent of reveling in ass-drawn chariots.

[2] Athenaeus, XII, 125, 132, 157. Also *Scriptores Alexandri Magni*, 118. And Aelian, *Historia Varia*, VIII, 7.

had in his train loads of goatskins sufficient to cover the floor of a stadium; he was also followed by long trains of animals carrying sand imported from Egypt to be used on the floor of the wrestling arena. Leonnatus and Menelaus, who were fond of the chase, used to carry about with them game nets a hundred stadia (about twelve miles) long, to be used to surround the hunting ground wherein they pursued the quarry. Moreover, the famous plane tree of gold, and even the golden vine under which the Persian kings' often sat and held court, with its clusters of green crystals (emeralds?) and rubies from India, and gems of every description, exceedingly costly though they were, appeared of less worth than the expense lavished daily on all occasions at Alexander's court. For his pavilion alone contained a hundred couches and was supported by fifty golden uprights. The canopies stretched over the upper part to cover the whole were elaborately worked with gold into sumptuous embroideries. Inside and all around it stood, first of all, five hundred Persian 'apple-bearers' (the royal Persian guard) with gay uniforms of purple and quince-yellow; after them, a thousand bowmen, some dressed in flame color, others in crimson, others in dark blue. At the head of these stood five hundred silver shields (the hypaspist agema). The figure given permits us the deduction that, as the agema, nominally at least, numbered one thousand, they stood a watch-and-watch routine. It is interesting to note, too, that the apple-bearers take precedence over the Macedonian agema, relegating them to a secondary position. In the center of the pavilion was placed a golden chair, sitting on which Alexander held court with his bodyguard stationed close on all sides. Outside the tent the elephant division, with full equipment, were kept posted, as were also a thousand Macedonians in their national dress, next a thousand Persians, and a body of five hundred men wearing the purple garments of special privilege. And the number of his friends and servitors was so great that no one dared approach Alexander, such was the majesty associated with his person. On one occasion Alexander wrote the cities of Ionia, directing them to send him all their purple dye. When the

447

letter was read in Chios in the presence of the sophist Theocritos, he declared that now at last he understood the meaning of the verse in Homer:[1] 'Purple death seized him, and a fate overpowering.'

Along with the imperial luxuriousness we find, if Athenaeus[2] is truthful, the base of Plutarch's hints of moral irregularity and verification of Alexander's tendencies (not uncommon thing in that region in that day, or this either) toward homosexuality. Once at least, at the theater he is reported to have been caressing one Bagoas, a beautiful and favorite eunuch. When the audience saw this, they applauded vigorously. Nothing daunted, he leaned over and kissed the eunuch. If this be true, it is a strange thing when considered that he was in possession of three of the most beautiful women of Asia, for not only were his two latest wives with him, but also probably Roxane was here too, for we hear of her presence soon. It is also said that he had kept with him the Athenian girl Thais,[3] she who had set on fire the palace of Xerxes in Persepolis.

While the fleet and ships' basin were being made ready, Alexander sailed down the Euphrates personally to determine the military importance of the swampy and channeled delta country. Long before this the Persians had built a great canal, made practical by a long dam, to carry off the flood waters and for controlling their sweep into the delta. Alexander inspected the canal, and ordered changes in it, designed to increase its efficiency. He also founded the town of Alexandria-Charax (Muhammera?) and settled it with Greek mercenaries, then returned to Babylon. The tale is told that on the way back a high wind blew off his high erect tiara and the royal fillet. The tiara sank, but one of the sailors immediately dived overboard and swam after the fillet. Fearing the water might injure it if he held it in his hands, the man placed it on his head and swam back to the galley. Alexander promptly rewarded him with a silver talent

[1] *Iliad*, V, 83.
[2] Athenaeus, XIII, 602–603
[3] Athenaeus, XIII, 576.

for the courageous service, and ordered him executed for daring to place the symbol of royalty upon his head. Nearing Babylon, in deliberate defiance of the Chaldeans' prayers to enter the west gate, Alexander passed it by and entered the east gate.

During his absence, several armies had arrived as reinforcements; Peucestes brought twenty thousand men from his satrapy; Philoxenus others from Caria; Menander others from Lydia, and Menidas marched in with a large body of cavalry. These were to be used first in the conquest of the Arabs, and afterward, as was discovered later, in wider conquests.

A few days after his return to Babylon, Cassander, son of the old regent Antipater, arrived from Macedonia, sent to defend both his father and himself against accusations and charges brought by their enemies who had come to Babylon for that purpose. As an illustrious son of his illustrious father, he was naturally a guest at dinner that evening. Presently Persian nobles, also guests, began to arrive, and, as court usage dictated, they first prostrated themselves before the king. Cassander, unused to such a novelty and unaware of or disbelieving that Alexander was now lunatically and fanatically certain of his godship, burst out laughing. Alexander had been drinking, and in a drunken and passionate rage leaped from the throne, seized Cassander by the hair with both hands and pounded his head against the wall. The next day, when Alexander was sober, Cassander approached him on the subject of the accusations, when Alexander interrupted him with the demand: 'Do you think I believe these people would have come so far to accuse Antipater if they had received no injury from him?' And Cassander replied, 'The fact that they have come so far from the sources of evidence is verity of the falseness of their charges.' Alexander became furious, calling the speech a sophism of the type Aristotle always employed. He angrily declared that when the charges were heard, if he believed Antipater and Cassander guilty, both would be punished severely. The king's insensate rage frightened Cassander, making such an impression upon him that years later, when he himself was king of Macedonia, he was observed to tremble at the mere sight of a statue of Alexander.

In the official memoranda (*hypomnemata*) discovered in the archives immediately after his death, we are given a short résumé of the plans of the conqueror for a continuation of his wars.[1] Craterus also, now on his way back home, was bearing a sheaf of sealed instructions to the satraps of the Phoenician coast, ordering them to begin immediately construction of a thousand warships of many types, to be used in a forthcoming naval campaign against the Carthaginians and other peoples of the North African coast, prior to their use against others of the Mediterranean seaboard. Other orders were sent to Egypt for the beginning of construction of a road from the mouth of the Nile to the Pillars of Heracles (Gibraltar) so the army might advance that way. Naval docks were to be built at a number of designated spots to facilitate the simultaneous advance of both land and sea forces, and enable them to work together.

Alexander also began to remodel the army, all arms except the heavy cavalry being greatly changed from the older Macedonian formations. We have sufficient data to enable us to follow these changes easily, but, as the reorganization was never completed or used, there is no point in detailing them here. The fleet was finally reported ready, and was put through constant exercises and drills on the river. A few days later, after the customary sacrifices, he feasted his friends, and sat up late at the banquet. He drank very heavily, and at last called for the cup of Heracles (which held six quarts) in which to drink the health of his friend Proteas,[2] son of Lanice, his boyhood nurse. Proteas drained the cup; Alexander failed in an attempt to do likewise. After the party broke up and Alexander was preparing to leave, one of his friends, a Thessalian named Medius, begged him to

---

[1] W. W. Tarn, in *The Journal of Hellenic Studies* (1921), holds the belief that these were forgeries of a later date, not earlier than 200 B.C. But in this writer's opinion, this theory is untenable. The notes are reliably reported by too many sources and it is impossible to conceive that Alexander, a young man of thirty-two, should cease his attempts at world-conquest, when battle and acquisition were the breath of life to him, and when we know he had long projected additional conquests.

[2] Athenaeus, X, 434, and Müller, *Fragmenta Historicorum Graecorum*, pp. 121–157.

come as his guest awhile. Alexander went with him, still accompanied by Proteas. There were twenty persons present at Medius' party, and Alexander pledged the health of each one, receiving and accepting the same number of pledges in return. He then left the party and returned home about sunrise, feeling a little indisposed and feverish. He took a bath, ate a little food, and had himself carried out to officiate at the customary morning sacrifices. Afterward, he returned to the palace and slept all day long. We are told his fever began on the eighteenth day of the Macedonian month Daisios (June 3, 323). That evening he had a severe headache, and it has since been conjectured he was suffering from malignant malaria. He was carried down to the river and ferried over to the palace on the opposite bank, where in the royal gardens he proposed to remain until the effects of the drinking bout, for such he supposed it to be, had worn off. On the morning of the fourth he felt somewhat improved. He bathed, dressed, and officiated at the morning sacrifices, after which he spent the day with Medius, talking and playing at dice. During the day he felt still better, and issued instructions for his commanders to report for orders the following morning, and ate a good supper that evening. Later in the evening the fever returned and he was very ill during the night. Next morning, the fifth, he had to force himself to rise, bathe, and attend the sacrifices, after which he summoned Nearchus and told him to have the fleet ready with all equipment and supplies, and ready to sail on the twenty-third of Daisios, the eighth of June. The following day, though more ill, he insisted again upon arising to attend the sacrifices. Nearchus, later in the day, reported that the fleet was ready, prepared to sail, stocked with provisions and supplies, and the crews standing by awaiting orders. During the day the fever grew worse. On the morning of the seventh he bathed again, but his weakness was so great he had to be carried to the sacrifices. Later, though nearly delirious with fever, he talked with a number of his officers, postponing the date of the departure. He was then moved to another near-by pavilion which had a swimming pool hard-by the river, the water lending an illusion of coolness to the stifling heat of a June day in Babylon.

Here for a while he lay alone, then sent for Roxane. His first wife, still faithful, came to him. For several minutes he tried earnestly to persuade her to have him secretly carried out and cast into the Euphrates [1] in order that men might believe, when they became aware of his sudden departure and disappearance, he, as one of the race of the gods, had returned to the gods. Roxane rejected the proposal in horror, and Alexander furiously upbraided her, saying she envied him his divine origin.

The tenth and eleventh came and passed and the fever burned on. The next day the rumor spread through the army that he was dead and the fact was being hidden from them. A great many officers and 'companions' came to the palace, and as a body demanded they should be allowed to see with their own eyes whether the king yet lived. They were at last permitted to pass through his room single file, but, though Alexander was conscious and recognized them, he was too weak to speak, greeting them only with a slight movement of his hands or eyes. That evening several of his friends went to a near-by temple in which the god was famous for healing and inquired of the mouthpiece of the god if Alexander should be brought there. The reply, through the priest, was in the negative. He would be better left where he was.

The following day the ill king was worse, and hardly conscious. Late in the afternoon, however, the delirium lifted a little and his mind cleared. Perdiccas, standing close to the sick-bed, doubtless recognizing that death was very near, bent over and spoke to Alexander, and the latter weakly handed him the imperial seal ring. Perdiccas bent lower, and asked to whom he wished to leave the throne. No doubt in that one last lucid moment Alexander achieved a higher degree of understanding than he had ever known before, an understanding which is given to many only when it is too late. Around his dying bed were grouped his officers, hard, unrelenting, avari-

[1] Arrian, VII, 28.

cious, and power-mad men whom he himself had trained in their way, waiting only for his death to begin rending the empire. Perhaps, too, he could already see the glittering armies going forth to tear it apart; to hear the shouts and screams of men locked in deadly battle; and the snarl and howl of the jackal and hyena over the battlefield afterward. And he knew to whom the sovereignty would fall at last. His answering whisper, 'Kratisto,' 'To the strongest,' was hardly audible. At sunset on June 13, 323 B.C., the conqueror breathed his last.

THE END